THE I
NORM

Date Due

813.54

ROLLYSON CARL

THE LIVES OF NORMAN MAILER

AYR $32.95

**Donated to the
Ayr Library**

THE LIVES OF
NORMAN MAILER

A BIOGRAPHY

by CARL ROLLYSON

PARAGON HOUSE
New York

First American edition, 1991

Published in the United States by

Paragon House
90 Fifth Avenue
New York, NY 10011

The author is grateful to the Scott Meredith Literary Agency for permission to reprint excerpts from
Advertisements for Myself © 1959 Norman Mailer, *An American Dream* © 1964 Norman Mailer,
Cannibals and Christians © 1966 Norman Mailer, *The Executioner's Song* © 1979 Norman Mailer,
The Fight © 1975 Norman Mailer, and *Existential Errands* © 1972 Norman Mailer.

Norman Mailer's introduction to *Genius and Lust* © 1976 Norman Mailer used by permission of
Grove Weidenfeld, Inc.

Library of Congress Cataloging-in-Publication Data

Rollyson, Carl E. (Carl Edmund)
     The lives of Norman Mailer : a biography / by Carl Rollyson. —
1st American ed.
          p.   cm.
     Includes bibliographical references.
     ISBN 1-55778-193-1 : $22.95
     1. Mailer, Norman—Biography.   2. Authors, American—20th century—
Biography.   I. Title.
PS3525.A4152Z874   1991
813'.54—dc20
     [B]   91-8120
                                                                          CIP

Manufactured in the United States of America
Set in Times Roman
Interior Design by Virginia Norey

To Lisa

CONTENTS

ACKNOWLEDGMENTS

W HEN I BEGAN the research on this biography in the spring of 1988, I asked Diane DiMartino in the Baruch College Library to do a computer search of both published and unpublished items about Norman Mailer. Through that search I discovered the *Esquire* Collection in the Bentley Library of the University of Michigan, which provided me the opportunity to examine several Mailer manuscripts, including the typed installments of *An American Dream*. The Bentley Library is a handsome building within which to work, and its staff have always been prompt and helpful in processing my requests. Scholars using the library should be sure to see the cartoon in the men's room: It depicts a monk seated at a desk studying a manuscript. Behind him are two large filing cabinets, one marked "Sacred" and the other marked "Top Sacred."

On one of my frequent visits to Ann Arbor I had the opportunity to interview John Aldridge, a Mailer friend of many years and an astute critic of American literature. I thank him not only for patiently answering my questions but for responding to my interpretations of Mailer's life and work.

Closer to home I was fortunate to be able to interview Sandra Kraskin, director of the Baruch College Gallery, who does not know

Mailer well but who, for a time, lived in the ambiance of his world. Similarly, Elizabeth Reis, Professor of Education at Baruch, who knows of Mailer only by reputation and has had occasional sightings of the man in Provincetown, gave me a sense of him as a figure in local lore. I'm grateful to Howard Negrin, director of the grants office, for helping lead me to Jere Herzenberg, who proved most informative about her period of working with Mailer.

Richard Sisson and Richard Weinberg recounted for me their days at Harvard with Mailer. Similarly, Harry Levin, who did not know Mailer during those years but who taught at Harvard, supplied a valuable introduction to the milieu of Mailer's college years, as did David Saunders, class of 1943. Stanley Karnow and Kenneth Lynn, both Harvard graduates, got to know Mailer in Paris and generously supplied me with certain telling details.

When I called him up, Max Lerner had interesting things to say about Mailer and Robert Lindner and about the kind of joshing rivalry between himself and Mailer that went on the 1950s and early 1960s; the two men, for a time, bore some physical resemblance to each other.

Helen Meyer was helpful in providing background information on the period during which Mailer was preparing *An American Dream* for book publication, and I am pleased to acknowledge Carole Klein's aid in arranging the interview. Rust Hills, fiction editor at *Esquire*, remembered for me what it was like during the days Mailer was writing his serialized novel.

William Styron shared part of an afternoon with me carefully describing both his good and his bad experiences with Mailer, trying to present a fair and accurate picture of their times together. Similarly, Irving Howe was incisive and direct about the days he spent in Mailer's company and about his evaluation of Mailer's work. Larry Shaw, who introduced himself to me after a talk I had given at the National Arts Club, provided an entertaining and insightful picture of what it was like to meet Mailer and to size him up.

Norman Rosten is a good friend. His warm feelings and knowledge of his Brooklyn neighbor, the "other Norman," gave me a glimpse of the writer's everyday life as well as of the sources of his fiction. Also in Brooklyn, Larry List and Belle Huffman spoke fondly about their meetings with Fanny Mailer and shared with me their sense of just how clear she was about her son's importance as a writer.

Kevin Ray of the Washington University Archives, John M. Olin

Library, arranged for me to examine a few items of Mailer correspondence. Lynda Fuller-Clendenning of the University of Virginia Library, Special Collections, kindly sent me complimentary copies of the Mailer letters in the Henry Meacham Collection. Cathy Henderson of the Harry Ransom Humanities Research Center, University of Texas at Austin, arranged for me to examine the correspondence between James Jones and Mailer in the James Jones Collection. Eric Neubacher, the wizard of interlibrary loan at Baruch, saved me countless hours in obtaining dozens of articles and books.

It seems that with every biography I write, I change jobs or take on a new one. Indeed, every year I have been at Baruch I have had a new assignment. While I was writing this biography, I took on the position of acting dean of the school of Education and Educational Services while retaining the title of associate provost. I had superb staffs to rely upon and to help with the details that go into producing a biography. In the provost's office: Thank you Katherine Curtis, Debra Dorry, and Miriam Allen. In the dean's office, thank you Lee Fisher, May Rips, and Yat Wong, and the student assistants: Anita Anthony, Amy Chan, Boon K. Lim, Rudy Thebaud, Kok Yee Wong, Jaim-Liang Liou, Zhitao Lu. I do not offer them adequate compensation with these acknowledgments—except perhaps for May, who liked to read my mail.

Joel Segall, the president of Baruch College, and John McGarraghy, acting provost, provided me the support and good cheer that made it much easier to balance the demands of scholarship and administration.

At Paragon House, Lelia Ruckenstein, my editor, has been a constant prod and inspiration—what every editor should be. I could not have asked for a better one.

Writers are often asked about whom they write for. This book is dedicated to Lisa, my wife, and always my first reader.

FOREWORD

THIS IS NOT A GOOD TIME to be publishing a biography of Norman Mailer. He still provokes great distaste in women, and I find myself cringing in explanation of my reasons for writing about him. He has not published a truly successful book since *The Executioner's Song*, and perhaps at this late date he is past producing another triumph.

There is probably nothing I can say—no point I could make about the brilliance of his work or about his historical significance—that would sway readers disposed against him. My hope is that even those hostile to him will read this foreword out of the sheer curiosity he can probably still command.

Let me ask you to project beyond yourself and beyond this present moment to—say—thirty years hence, when Mailer the man almost surely will not be on the scene. What will be left? The books, the movies, scads of interviews, personality profiles, and documentaries of several kinds. Someone will write a biography for an audience that has not just seen Mailer on television or read some snide reference to him in a magazine piece. Mailer will not be so much with us. The biographer will have to write a book less concerned with Mailer as a contemporary figure. There will be no interjections—no flashes forward to what

Mailer is "now"—as is the case in the biographies of him by Hilary Mills and Peter Manso. There will be, in other words, a greater sense of Mailer's life as history, unfolding moment by moment as it had to unfold for Mailer himself.

As for me, I can't wait thirty years. I've tried to write that biography now—as a whole story, even though the story is not at an end. Sometimes one can, with a pen, get a purchase on the future.

THE SHITS ARE KILLING US

NEW YORK, 1954. John Maloney, an Irish drunk and a friend of Norman Mailer and William Styron, was an enormously gifted man but "hopelessly down the tubes," Styron recalls. A little older than these young writers, he had been an editor in a publishing house. His main profession was drinking. He talked with a wonderful literary sense; he cared deeply for books and wrote well, reviewing for the *New York Herald Tribune*. He had a sort of flaky mistress in the Village; it was a rocky relationship. One day he stabbed her and fled. At first it all seemed very Dostoyevskyan and serious enough to be considered an assault. Finally, Maloney turned up on Styron's doorstep. Phone calls were made, the cops came, and Styron, Styron's editor Hiram Haydn, and Mailer went down to jail to bail Maloney out. Eventually the charges would be dropped, but at the time it seemed a momentous event. After Maloney's release, they went to a bar. When Maloney and Haydn stepped out for a moment, Styron remembers Mailer saying to him, "God, I wish I had the courage to stab a woman like that. That was a real gutsy act."

Years later Styron would repeat Mailer's words in a whisper. Mailer had spoken in envy of Maloney, in wonder and excitement over such an act, a performance he admired, one he wished he could rival. What kind of man would need a knife to let loose his emotions and to show his bravery? A man who was not himself, a man who saw society as conspiring to take away his true self. This is the thwarted man who could not let the Maloney incident alone, who would have to perform his own version of it more than five years later when he stabbed his wife Adele at the party that was supposed to be the kickoff for his New York City mayoral campaign.

By the time Mailer took a knife to his second wife, he was approaching the end of the 1950s in an apocalyptic mood. This was the age of conformity, of mass man, the weakening of the ego, the extinction of individuality, the increase of psychopathy—so wrote his friend, the psychoanalyst Robert Lindner, and so wrote Mailer in his controversial essay "The White Negro." It had been a dismal decade. After the great success of *The Naked and the Dead* in 1948, his second novel had been mauled by the critics, and his third had received no better than a tepid reception. Now five years without a novel, with only the promise of one eating away at him, he experimented with literary and political essays, some of which broke new ground as journalism but did nothing to appease his literary ambitions.

In desperation Mailer engaged in various blood rites—fights and contests of strength with friends and strangers—indulging the psychopath Robert Lindner said every man carried within himself. It would have been easy for Mailer to conform, given his middle-class Jewish background and Harvard engineering degree; instead, he dug deep for the instinct of rebellion, an instinct Lindner believed held the spark of originality

> since it reveals itself as a drive or urge toward mastery over every obstacle, natural or man-made, that stands as a barrier between man and his distant, perhaps never-to-be-achieved but always-striven-after goals. It is this instinct that underwrites his survival, this instinct from which he derives his nature: a great and powerful dynamic that makes him what he is—restless, seeking, curious, forever unsatisfied, eternally struggling and eventually victorious. . . . Man is a rebel . . . man cannot submit, cannot surrender his birthright of protest, for rebellion is one of his essential dimensions. He cannot deny it and remain man.

Mailer felt he was fighting for his life, searching for his true identity. When he received an invitation to write a fifteenth-anniversary report to his Harvard class of 1943, he replied "with the desire to be destructive and therefore useful":

For the last few years I have continued to run in that overcrowded mob of unconscionable egotists who are all determined to become the next great American writer. But, given the brawl, the wasting of the will, and the sapping of one's creative rage by our most subtle and dear totalitarian time, politely called the time of conformity, I do not know that I would be so confident as to place the bet on myself any longer or indeed on any of my competitive peers.

Mailer had considered writing the usual sedate account expected of alumni, but then he decided to "fuck it, let's have something in this class report which is a little less predictable." Too many young men, in Mailer's view, had failed to nourish the instinct of rebellion—to say fuck it in their prose as well as in their lives; consequently, the America of the 1950s was a land of mediocrity and repression. People worried about whether their children would adjust; psychiatrists earned a good living helping everyone to regulate their behavior according to societal restraints. Lindner thought it tragic that so much individuality should be destroyed and attacked his colleagues for advocating therapies that turned people into conformists. He liked Mailer's rebelliousness. Human progress required rejecting the status quo. A human being should be a catalyst for change.

Yet Mailer had grown up a good liberal, reading columnists like Max Lerner and forming opinions that were not much different from those of his fellow progressives. For a time he even resembled the bushy-haired Lerner—a fact that seemed to amuse but also to bother him, for he thought liberals like Lerner had become a little too comfortable with their opinions. When the two men first met at a party in the mid-1950s, Mailer praised Lerner and admitted he had been influenced by the columnist, but then Mailer challenged him, saying he had become soft, he had not fought enough, and he had to give way to a new generation. Lerner realized that Mailer wanted to be that new generation.

A friend of Lindner's, Lerner wrote an introduction to Lindner's most popular book, *The Fifty Minute Hour*. They discussed Mailer and his penchant for violence and his restlessness. Lindner told Lerner that he had become Mailer's analyst. Edith Begner, a friend, remembers that Mailer "started going down to Baltimore to see Robert Lindner in '52, right around the time of his divorce from Bea [Mailer's first wife]. He was so depressed then. . . ." Adele Morales, Mailer's second wife, remembers Lindner's visits to their apartment:

> *He and Bob were crazy about each other. Norman loved him, and I liked him too, though they didn't seem to pay much attention to me. Norman went down to Baltimore regularly, and I went along a couple of times. It was mainly social, but also Lindner was writing something and Norman was working with him on it. But it had nothing to do with therapy. Norman in therapy? Anyone who thinks that has got to be kidding. Norman always hated the idea of therapy, and probably still does.*

By her own account, however, Morales knew little about what the two men shared; what mattered was how deeply they cared for each other. If Lerner wanted to understand Mailer, Lindner suggested Lerner should read his book *Prescription for Rebellion*, in which he delineated the character of the rebel in terms that explained much of Mailer's behavior.

When Lindner died of a heart ailment in 1956, Mailer reprinted excerpts from Lindner's work in his *Village Voice* column in lieu of talking about the man. "Lindner was almost alone among analysts in his sustained argument that the healthy man was a rebel, and that it was crippling for psychoanalysis to try to adjust a patient to the warpings of an unjust world." The passages Mailer selected are, of course, as revealing of Mailer as they are of Lindner:

> *And it is this sensitivity—in short the analyst's own person—which is the single instrument, the only tool, with which he performs. Only on himself, and on nothing else, does he depend.* [The Fifty Minute Hour]

> *I am of the opinion that the definitions of maturity which assail us in such profusion currently are uniformly founded on the tacit hypothesis that human development is linked to human passivity.* [Must You Conform?]

Mailer also quoted a long passage from *Must You Conform?* about the instinct for rebellion that suggested men had no choice but to rebel. Mailer's quirkiness, ambitiousness, and feistiness were *mandated* by his nature as a man. Every slip back into safe prose, every time he ducked a challenge, meant Mailer betrayed himself.

Lindner's death was an irreparable misfortune for Mailer who almost choked on the words that could adequately describe what amounted to the death of his alter ego:

> *his charm, his generosity, his intellectual curiosity, his foibles, his weaknesses, his kindness, his ambitions, his achievements, his failures, and his great warmth (he was truly one of the warmest people I have known), but to write immediately about a man so complex, so individual, and yet so much part of our generation would do him a disservice, for Bob Lindner was nothing if not alive, and he would have loathed a facile eulogy.*

Advertisements for Myself is full of attacks on jargon-ridden experts who type people and straitjacket them with societal norms. Mailer takes after these analysts with a personal animus born of his own loss of Lindner. Mailer may have been expressing only the temper of a moment when he confessed "Robert Lindner's death has left me in an ugly mood," yet his subsequent writing suggests how isolated he felt. Finding no other analyst who might be regarded as a kindred spirit, he engaged in a "self-analysis."

The italicized passages in *Advertisements for Myself* are the result of this self-analysis, which might be compacted into Mailer's declaration that "the shits are killing us." He knew he would not be understood:

> *Now, in the writing of our days, when no ache of evidence can ever be believed unless it is presented by a Doctor of Jargon, a remark like "the shits are killing us" is so declarative that fifty pages of closely reasoned argument should follow in support.*

Society did not want men to behave like men. Hemingway—Mailer's favorite example—was idolized but also despised because he made everything into a test of one's courage, and who can bear to have one's integrity always on the line? What has always fascinated Mailer about Hemingway is the way he made life a contest of strength. In his work with Lindner, Mailer had to consider whether he would have the stamina to stand up to every challenge. Every time he backed down or shied away from a risk he might be diminishing his instinct for rebellion, his very individuality.

To find his true identity, Mailer would have to murder that nice young man his mother had taken such pains to raise. She had indulged him, taken possession of him in such an absolute way that he would always be her boy. She had made him into a "tot of destiny" (to use Lindner's description of the psychopath's mother, who imbues her child with a grandiose self-image). Not finding a world co-extensive with his will, the child, as in Mailer's case, "acts out" in infantile ways, not having learned how to cope with society at large.

Mailer knew that stabbing Adele was morally indefensible, but he could not stop himself from acting out. Later he would dissociate himself from the deed, saying he could not identify with what he had done. Yet the element of excitement and of performance, of "Look at what I have just done," seems a part of his motivation. There comes a time in the lives of some men when they have to take the extreme course—if only to observe themselves doing it, to show that they are capable of achieving what they have only imagined themselves performing. And Mailer, more than most men, has pursued life as though it were literature, in which he could ceaselessly invent himself.

1.

THE EDUCATION
OF A NOVELIST
(1923–1943)

A PROFESSIONAL ALL HIS LIFE

Norman Mailer's maternal grandfather, Chaim Yehudah Schneider, was the unofficial rabbi of Long Branch, New Jersey, renowned for his religious devotion and scholarship. Ordained at the age of sixteen in a yeshiva in Russia, he conducted services at the *shul*, even though the small Jewish community of Long Branch could not afford to pay him. He had never wanted a congregation. "Rabbis were *schnorrers*," he would say, and he did not want to live "that way." He was a dreamer who had his religious doubts and a volatile man who paid little attention to the daily realities of life. Seated squarely in a chair, holding a cigarette in his dangling left hand and spreading the fingers of his right hand over the armrest, the goateed unofficial rabbi of Long Branch, New Jersey, looked the part of the principled Talmudic scholar accustomed to visits not only from neighbors but from other rabbis who respected his learning. Such a man had to have a well-developed sense of his audience. Barney Mailer, Norman's father, often thought his son's genius came from Rabbi Schneider. Marjorie ("Osie") Radin, one of Norman's cousins, identifies a different trait in Norman's grandfather passed on to him and to his cousin Charles ("Cy") Rembar: a tendency to be "excitable" and to "flare up."

The rabbi's family owned a grocery store in Long Branch. When they ran afoul of the law for opening on Sundays, the youngest daughter, Fanny, was delegated to defend them. She was only sixteen, yet in court she ably spoke for her father, whose English was poor. Scared but persuasive, she pointed out that they were a religious family that had to close their meat compartment on Saturdays. On Sundays they were open only in the morning when their customers expected to be served. The family did not mean to flout the law: With their shades drawn they went about their business in as quiet a manner as possible. Fanny's plea prevailed, and the Schneiders were allowed to stay open on Sundays.

Fanny and her sisters became the business brains of the family. Rose, Rebecca, Jennie, and Fanny formed a formidable team that managed a very tight budget. They had trouble collecting bills and had no help from their father. At a very early age, Fanny felt she had to be the practical one. Along with her older sister Rebecca, she worked ten and twelve hour days with gusto, needing only a ten-minute nap to revive her prodigious energy.

Fanny, who did not marry until her late twenties, was a particular woman who found good manners and style very appealing. Isaac ("Barney") Mailer was a prince of a man—elegant, handsome, always immaculately dressed, courteous, and a little exotic: a Lithuanian-Jewish immigrant from South Africa who spoke with a Cockney-Yiddish accent and wore spats. He had been in the South African army in England during World War I. Faced with the choice of taking free passage back to Johannesburg or to the United States, he decided to visit his brother-in-law, Dave Kessler, who had emigrated during the war and had become quite a prosperous man, having built a candy factory that specialized in chocolate-covered cherries. Barney lived with the Kesslers on President Street in Brooklyn and met Fanny one winter weekend in Lakewood, New Jersey, where her family was operating a resort.

Barney, a charmer, liked to play the English gentleman. Norman later thought of his father as

> *an impoverished figure out of Chekhov . . . a dapper gentleman in a bewildering world, a man of such sentimentality that phrases like "the passing parade" would always bring tears to his eyes. He was marvelously involved in himself. So involved that when he would write me a*

letter in college it would be fourteen pages long, but the first ten would be concerned with the curious sentiments he felt in himself starting to write a letter to his son. He was always analyzing his own emotions at all times. . . . What he talked about never had anything to do with what he was really feeling.

Barney's flamboyance and even a trace of his British accent would filter through to Norman, who would later remark: "That baroque element in my style, the sidewinder in me. That all comes from my father in some funny way."

Barney liked Fanny's family and turned down a good job in another part of the country when she made it clear she would not move. They were married in 1922. After a big wedding in a Manhattan hotel, they spent a one-week honeymoon in Atlantic City before settling in the Flatbush section of Brooklyn. Barney said little about his relatives in South Africa, who had not been able to attend the wedding. Norman's sister, Barbara, remembers being told that her father left South Africa and enlisted in the army as part of the bargain he made with his family when they agreed to pay off his gambling debts: "It was the army or jail."

The next year, on January 31, Fanny gave birth to their son, Norman Kingsley Mailer. Fanny remembered the hard labor that lasted some twelve hours. Motherhood shocked her. She knew nothing about how to care for this fragile-looking seven-pound baby, but "Norman was perfect, a really lovely baby," she recalled, and her sisters came in two-week shifts to help her with the initial nursing period. Given the Hebrew name Nachum Malech, Norman King, Fanny thought of him quite literally as the family's sovereign, but it sounded silly to call him king in English, so Fanny's niece Marjorie suggested Kingsley, the name of one of her favorite authors.

Barney had been an accountant in South Africa but never troubled to become licensed in his new country. Still, he managed to settle his family in a middle-class, English-speaking Jewish neighborhood in Brooklyn and commute to his job at a big firm in Manhattan. Even with a skimpy wardrobe, he always appeared neat and prosperous—perhaps a little too fastidious for Fanny, who suspected her husband's minute attention to detail prevented him from thinking in larger terms about his position in life.

By the age of six, Norman presented signs of greatness to his mother.

A first-grade teacher, impressed with his progress, told Fanny: "Mrs. Mailer, you have to realize your son's pleasures in life are going to be solemn ones." When he sat down, hunched over, folded his arms, and shot you a glance, he gave off an air of seriousness, of taking the measure of things—an impression encouraged by the way his mother dressed him, in crisp white shirts and ties. He was a handsome boy with prominent ears and a winning personality. On occasion Fanny would deck him out in a Spencer jacket, a pin-tucked shirt with a Peter Pan collar, pleated short pants with knee socks embroidered at the top, and Buster Brown shoes. Norman, smiling broadly, with his hands in his pockets, looked like quite a sport—the junior counterpart of his natty father.

When Norman was nine his family moved from Flatbush to Crown Heights, a Jewish, middle-class (with a few rich Jews) neighborhood and away from what Fanny called the "cheap *goyim*," mainly Irish. Apartments in the new neighborhood were larger and its proximity to Prospect Park made it a coveted location. In this tolerant, nurturing atmosphere, Norman flourished. Fanny believed in indulging him, in making him feel loved. She reveled in the way he attacked whole-heartedly anything that interested him. So what if he made a mess out of his room! The boy accomplished things, she told her husband, who disliked disorder. Barney might complain, but he did not discipline his son. (In later years Fanny could not remember Norman ever getting a spanking.) That was Barney with most people, however. He had a very welcoming, easy attitude. He was partial to gin and liked to have a good time, which included a rather expensive gambling habit.

Fanny ran things. Says Rhoda Lazare Wolf, a close friend of the family, Fanny took on the problems, and as a result Rhoda remembered her as having a perpetually "furrowed brow." With Barney you could talk sports and baseball statistics, but what Fanny thought really mattered. Rhoda could see that Fanny regarded herself as "special." No wonder, then, that she would have a son she would view as "*very* special." Norman and Barbara (born on April 6, 1927) would often tell amusing stories about their mother. They were obviously very fond of her, but to an outsider this "strong woman" seemed formidable and intimidating, and Rhoda confesses to having been "afraid" of her.

Fanny provided the fire in the family, but Barney held his own as the adoring father. He was absolutely "mad about Barbara" and more than willing to tolerate his son's antics, calling him (as Fanny so often did) a "genius." In later years, he thrived on parties and celebrities, and his son included him in big affairs.

Having absolute confidence in his parents' love for him, Norman was a respectful child. After all, he had a mother who went to school when he was in the third grade to complain about a low mark he had received. He had been penalized for absences that occurred during his family's out-of-town trips on business. Fanny argued that her son was a superior student and should get nothing less than an A. He should be skipped a grade, she maintained, and refused to sign his report card. Fanny claimed the teacher made Norman nervous. How was that? the teacher wanted to know. Well, her son respected authority and the woman's huge bulk intimidated him. Fanny hated the teacher ("a big fat Irishwoman") and suspected her of anti-Semitism.

Norman spent his summers in Long Branch, staying with his sister, Barbara, at his Aunt Jennie's hotel. Rose, another of Fanny's sisters, was a schoolteacher who made up plays for the children, who presented them to the guests. Fanny always put Norman in the picture, photographing him, for example, in a kilt and tam-o'-shanter when he played a Scottish shepherd. Like his older cousin Cy (born in 1915), Norman was the center of attention. Whenever Fanny and Barney had business matters to attend to, Osie (Cy's older sister) would take Norman into her care. This meant that Norman often spent enjoyable times with his bright and articulate cousins. Indeed, Norman had impressive support: In addition to his genial father, aggressive mother, his tender and extremely influential Aunt Rebecca, the avuncular Dave Kessler (a source of financial support), he could rely on his Aunt Rebecca's husband, Uncle Lou, a formidable male figure who silenced rowdy children with his piercing light-blue eyes and floored an employee who had gone berserk with one right-hand punch. Norman was so full of high spirits that adults had to be sure he was fully occupied. Usually this was no problem, given his powers of concentration, but one summer even Fanny grew testy when he appeared to be at a loss for something to do. She got him a pad and pencil and directed, "Here, write something."

He teased his sister, Barbara, but was very tender and protective toward her and at the Crown Heights apartment shared a room with her. They had the kind of close relationship "fostered" between Osie Radin and her brother Cy; it was something the family "insisted on." The two of them were watched over by a close-knit family.

The Depression took a terrible toll on the Mailers, although they did not like to talk about it. Barney was out of work for years, and the indefatigable Fanny supported the family with a small oil-delivery business. Barbara remembers how businesslike her mother was—arguing in the middle of the night with customers, attempting to persuade them that they could wait until morning for their oil deliveries or that perhaps they had a problem with their furnace. She wanted to "avoid the overtime of taking the truck out on a late delivery." Barney disliked this business, in part because his brother-in-law, Dave Kessler, had provided the start-up money and Barney and Dave had not been successful in attracting new customers. Then Fanny "stepped in," as she later put it. Barney retreated from the business, preferring to open an office with one of Fanny's cousins, a CPA. Fanny would work from early in the morning to five or six at night, relying on the family's black maid, Agnes, to take care of the children.

Norman remembers that his mother "had a way of driving my father. He'd go out looking for work and when he came home we'd throw our arms around him . . . and my mother would say, 'Ask Daddy if he got a job today.' He would shake his head sadly night after night." Her husband had disappointed her, but she loved him and cherished the wonderful illusion of style he had created for her. Together they put all of their hopes into the education of their son.

It snowed on the thirteen-year-old Norman's bar mitzvah day, and he worried that no one would come. Everyone would be there, Fanny assured him, and she was right. Putting together the resources had not been easy. Held at the Congregation Sharei Zedek, "hardly a number-one temple, even for Brooklyn," Fanny and Barney did their best to satisfy their "middle-class pretensions." Fanny cooked to save on expenses but managed to hire two waitresses to set the tables for the reception. "It was all pretty desperate stuff," their son recalled. All the way from Long Branch the family gathered to witness a traditional rite of passage; they were startled to hear the bar mitzvah boy talk about Spinoza, that excommunicant and atheist. Rabbi Schneider, who had died in 1926, would not have been so disturbed, for he was known to have been a great admirer of the philosopher. As Norman expressed his wish to emulate "great Jews like Moses Maimonides and Karl Marx," he noticed his "wealthy relatives in their fur boas" and was struck by "this sort of shift in the animals, and the rabbi looked very pale." Norman subsequently realized that his "marvelous old Hebrew schoolteacher" had been a Marxist and "probably a Communist." The speech meant little to this thirteen-year-old who had "heard of Moses" but thought the other two figures were "somewhat strange." Years later when he questioned Fanny about the incident, she proffered nothing more than one of her enigmatic smiles, but Norman knew how she felt about it: "She didn't care what the guy ended up doing—if he was famous and Jewish, that was good enough for her."

Norman did not take much interest in Judaism. He talked it over with one of his boyhood friends, Arnold Epstein, and confided that he regarded himself as an atheist. He found it a little disagreeable to be Jewish, an identity forced upon him and not something he had sought of his own accord. "I am not a typical Jew," Mailer told an interviewer, admitting that he had spent his childhood "rejecting Jewishness at a great rate."

Many years later, Norman remembered his childhood as quiet and uneventful: no gang violence, no fighting on the way to the candy store—just a lot of touch football and rollerskate hockey, in which a hard body check could send him sprawling across the sidewalk and up a banked small lawn. To Mailer, it seemed a compact world; even the ethnic elements were well contained.

Norman's friends saw him as someone special. Some were under the impression that he played fewer sports because his mother feared injuries. He was very self-involved, somewhat remote, and known more as a good student than as an athlete. None of the kids in the neighborhood seemed as considerate of their parents as Norman was of his.

By the sixth grade, Norman had a reputation for building the most elaborate and sophisticated model airplanes in the neighborhood. Already nearsighted, wearing glasses embarrassed him; it set him apart as a "premature expert."

The boys noticed Norman's manners and his father's formality when they visited. Fanny was pleasant but protective of everything her son did. This kind of civilized behavior puzzled the boys. None of them had a father as tidy and well-dressed, who walked the block with a hat and umbrella in hand. Their homes were rowdy and they behaved like little savages. No one put on quite the show the Mailers did: It was almost like visiting the gentry. The Mailers were not rich but could seem so to adolescents who watched them move to better apartments within the same building. Even Norman's middle name, which sported romantic and exotic connotations to at least one friend, appeared extraordinary. He got a genuine leather baseball glove before the other boys did and a brand-new clarinet when he exhibited interest in playing the instrument. Most of them had a little loose change, but Norman could always come up with a few bucks to spread around generously.

The clarinet-playing worried Fanny and Barney when they learned their son had worked out a scheme for a trio in the Catskills. Actually, he wanted to meet girls. With a clarinet he would get into the swing of things. Mostly, however, the music sessions were just plain fun. He and his buddies could barely carry a tune and usually collapsed on the floor in laughter—but never at his house.

At fourteen and fifteen there were lots of things—like drinking and smoking—that Norman had to try out away from home. Fanny opposed his idea of sleeping in the Bowery one night, and when he returned home from an evening with the derelicts she refused him entrance until he gave her every scrap of his clothing, which she tossed into the incinerator.

Norman's parents never spoke about sex, and he had to get his information from boys who talked ignorantly about girls who were good or bad lays. As he later put it, "Sex had enormous fascination for everyone, but it had no dignity, it had no place. It was not a value . . . it had to do with the bathroom—it was burning, it was feverish, it was dirty, cute, giggly." He could read about it in *Spicy Detective*, with its pictures of girls with "projectile-shaped" breasts and "tremendously pointed nipples." A woman would be tied up with one arm under a breast, making it protrude even more as the villain advanced to take his pleasure of the scantily clad beauty, who had only a torn panty covering her sexual treasure. Norman enjoyed the pictures, but they were not very educational.

A better bet was watching obliging girls undress in front of lighted windows. Norman learned a little more teasing girls on the street, one of whom would talk quite explicitly about sex. Others put on a good wiggle walking down the block. There were no whores around, but one girl allowed boys to put their hands in her pockets and get a good feel. The Star Burlesque was a weekly rendezvous point. Condoms were joked about, and Norman seemed to know a little more than his contemporaries because he hung out with older guys, but his girlfriend Phyllis, a pretty, well made-up, stylish girl, would not make it with him. It bothered Norman that nearing college age he was still a virgin.

Fanny sensed a deep trust between Barbara and Norman that in some matters even excluded her, a fact she seemed to accept and perhaps welcome, for she was proud of the way Norman behaved as a "big brother." Barbara's close friend Rhoda observed how Norman would boost his sister's confidence by calling her attractive—an important thing to a girl whose breasts were developing quickly and who felt awkward about it. Rhoda wished she had a brother like that to tell her such nice things. Barbara always cherished her big brother's reassurance: "He encouraged me when I was going around thinking I was dumb, fat and klutzy. He kept saying I was beautiful, just as he did when his daughter Kate was an adolescent and all hunched over and self-conscious." Never feeling the urge to rebel against his parents, he realized that Barbara did need to create a space for herself.

"Norman was always trying to start a process of change in a direction he thought was liberating or expanding," Rhoda remembers. So he would take them on the roof to show them how to blow smoke rings. He even organized "kissing lessons" for Barbara and Rhoda in front of his parents. Barbara was a willing subject, but Rhoda did not trust her feelings during such demonstrations, which included a session on ballroom dancing. Norman knew she was shy, but he contended that you should push your inclinations to the limit. He meant to be kind to her, and Rhoda came to see his attentions as rather noble.

Norman, an excellent student at Boys High in Brooklyn, where his interests were in math and science, was, according to one classmate, a "shy youngster—very quiet." Adventure novels like *Captain Blood* thrilled him, but he was indifferent to literature. He preferred Tom Sawyer, the romantic, over Huck Finn, the realist. Tom liked to invent heroic fantasies for himself based on his reading, which Huck thought were rather silly. Tom was compulsive and thorough, a planner and an exhibitionist, and this had enormous appeal for Norman. Tom exemplified the manly virtues and believed in bettering himself. He was competitive and speculated on the best way to get ahead. In Mailer's childhood reading—particularly in *Captain Blood* and *The Amateur Gentleman*—the hero was the superior individual, abandoning his inferior origins and earning through his "odyssey" a place in the "privileged class."

Norman wrote one piece of unpublished fiction, *The Martian Invasion*, a novel about Americans invading Mars. The villain, Dr. Huer, was modeled after a character in *Buck Rogers*. Norman managed to fill up over two hundred pages in three paper notebooks. His only appearance in a school magazine was a piece on model airplane building. School to him was homework. It was almost like a job. He did not date, and when he returned home his neighborhood pals, who were a year or two behind him in school, made him feel suspended between two worlds. Even worse, he was undersized for his age, skinny and short, and certainly no fighter. Indeed, he would later admit to being a "physical coward."

Yet by the age of sixteen, Norman seemed quite an accomplished young man. He spoke "glowingly" about his cousin Cy, a groundbreaker: The first in the family to go to Harvard, he epitomized the "level of worldliness" to which the family aspired. Barney's brother-in-law, Dave Kessler, always touted Cy and Norman together, saying "Those two boys will go far." On Fanny's part, there may have been some competitiveness. If Cy (her sister Rebecca's son) had gone to Harvard, then Norman must go there. Nothing was too good for Norman, who accepted the precedent his cousin set without evincing any resentment. Indeed, Cy's sister, Osie, and his mother, Rebecca, actively campaigned to send Norman to Harvard because another faction in the family, the Kesslers, favored MIT, thinking it more suitable to Norman's mathematical and scientific abilities. Osie argued that Norman needed a well-rounded education, and Rebecca probably sensed that aeronautical engineering would not be Norman's ultimate career choice.

One of Norman's high school classmates, Dr. Alfred Siegler, remembers the subway ride he took with Norman from Brooklyn to the site of the College Board Examinations: Norman seemed to have no doubts about his "ability to enter Harvard." After some thought, the neighborhood concurred: Who else but Norman Kingsley Mailer, "the brain," would go there? He was destined to be great. Everyone could see it in the way he had methodically built those model airplanes with intricate moving parts and sophisticated designs. In retrospect, Rhoda summed up the community feeling: "It's as if Norman's been a professional all his life."

THREE THOUSAND WORDS A DAY

At sixteen, Norman knew how to pose in elegant, sophisticated fashion for a photograph: in a dark suit and tie, a cigarette protruding out of his languid right hand, and with a look of calm, studied composure. With vigorous, thick, dark hair, wavy but carefully tamed with hair tonic and closely cropped, he presented a trim picture of himself, a serious adolescent with a jawline that tapered severely to a strong chin that made his ears more prominent.

Norman had little idea of what Harvard was all about. When Fanny took him shopping for his college clothes, he insisted on flashy things that seemed entirely inappropriate to her—"trousers with orange stripes," for instance. He had to admit later that his outfits were an embarrassment. On his first day at Harvard he had speedily shown up at the Phillips Brooks House, thinking its casual invitation to visit an important obligation, and introduced himself to a startled pipe-smoking senior at the desk. During Freshman Week, there was nothing much to say or to do in the empty house, since it was a charitable institution.

Norman blundered into situations that proved he did not know his way around—like the time he accompanied his friends to the Old Howard, a burlesque house. To get in he lied about his age, saying he was seventeen. Told he had to be eighteen, he shoved forward his identity card and said, "You've got to be eighteen to be a freshman at Harvard." His ploy worked, but his classmates used the episode against him during arguments, jumping up and waving their identity cards and yelling: "I'm eighteen! You've got to be eighteen to go to Harvard!"

Harvard had its quota of Jews, who tended to stick to themselves. They rarely encountered overt anti-Semitism, but Norman remembered one incident. Norman's adviser in engineering, a "crusty old man," could not have approved of his "gold and brown jacket" with "green and blue vertical striped pants and saddle shoes." Noticing his advisee's Brooklyn accent, he recommended a speech course. Norman wanted to take German. That seemed unnecessary to the adviser, who suggested he would "pick it up." "Well, sir, if I can pick up German in the course of a year or two, I don't see why I can't learn to speak English," the freshman rejoined.

This is one of the few unpleasant incidents Mailer can recall from his years at Harvard. Even though he and his fellow Jews were grouped together, by his own account it "never occurred to us that we were in an incredibly subtle ghetto." He was rather "innocent" about this manipulation of social classes and ethnic groups, he claims, and he now seems rather admiring of Harvard for having contrived such a benign regime of discrimination.

Until the 1920s Harvard had not had many Jewish students; roughly ten percent of students in Mailer's class were Jewish. Professor Harry Levin, on the faculty at the time Mailer was enrolled, was a Midwesterner from a Jewish family who had never experienced discrimination at Harvard, although he was surprised to hear the chairman of a meeting of the Modern Language Association congratulate Harvard on its "broad-minded breakthrough." It was assumed then that "you had to be of Anglo Saxon descent if you were to really understand English literature," Levin recalls.

If Levin did not experience discrimination, he realized that "day to day, one was made to be aware that one was a Jew. University files indicated certain categories, 'A & E' meant Andover and Exeter, but there were other notations, including that one was Jewish." Kingsley Ervin, Harvard class of 1945, observes: "I don't think people realize how rigid and elegant and scary the atmosphere of Cambridge was before the war. Very eighteenth-century, a mixture of Boston Brahmin and the literary faculty's elegance." Richard Weinberg, one of Mailer's Jewish roommates, from Memphis, Tennessee, remembers that people in his part of the country thought of Brooklyn "as a place where the tough and underprivileged lived. Also, we were repelled by the accent." Mailer would later tell Adele Morales that he had "suffered" at Harvard and "felt like a fish out of water." Her impression is that "it was probably a combination of his family and not having much money and being Jewish, but also his feeling that he was unattractive—physically unattractive—and so he was always worrying about being accepted."

Bea Silverman, Mailer's first wife, draws a picture of him, "a little Brooklyn boy," competing with Harvard's wealthy, upper-class Christians. "He felt he never fitted in," Bea recalls, although he was not ashamed of his heritage. He just did not want to make an issue of it or feel burdened by it. Also, he was "always the youngest and smallest in his class, and he did not develop physically until later. Even at Harvard he was young, short, and skinny. I believe that's why this business of boxing and being tough came out later on in life," Bea surmises.

In late-night bull sessions Norman and his classmates would discuss their backgrounds, their classes, teachers, plans for the future, and try to fathom the Harvard mystique. They had no fraternities; instead there were exclusive clubs—so exclusive that it hardly bothered him that he could not be a member. As a social system it was so foreign that one of his classmates doubts that Norman ever figured it out. As a public school boy he had neither the background nor the experience bred into the private school graduates of institutions like Phillips Exeter Academy and St. Paul's School, many of whom were rooming together at college and deeply familiar with the genteel code of behavior.

Yet Norman did not feel excluded. He was a very private person, close to his family, and not particularly concerned with the preppie types from Andover and Exeter. He was a nice boy from Brooklyn whose most devastating experience in his freshman year seems to have been his failure to make crew because his arms were not long enough for rowing in team formation.

There was nothing glamorous about a fast-talking boy whose ears stuck out and who kept his hair closely cropped, so that its tendency to curl was arrested in wiry waves. His major, aeronautical engineering, suited his studious nature. He kept to himself and did not join his roommates, Maxwell Kaufer and Richard Weinberg, for late-night snacks at the Eliot House grill. Most of the time he could be found at his desk studying. He rarely left campus and did not go out on dates. His parents had made a big sacrifice to send him to Harvard, and he was not going to let them down.

Kaufer recalls, however, that he and Weinberg had some difficulty getting along with Mailer and decided not to room with him after freshman year. Norman "lavishly decorated" his part of the dormitory room with "semi-nude pinups"—not exactly an outrageous thing to do, but certainly not what might be expected of a freshman if he wanted to emulate Harvard's traditional taste for "old prints and pewter mugs." In *The Naked and the Dead* Mailer would portray Robert Hearn's Harvard roommates as "gentlemen" who warn him not to do anything "excessive" that might ruin their chances of getting into a club. Kaufer and Weinberg did not dislike Mailer—they found him "pleasant" and "engaging"—but "There was a different kind of chic prevailing and perhaps we thought the Brooklyn image was not part of it," Kaufer suggests.

Fanny visited her son once a term. He would take her on a walk; she might make a few repairs to his clothing and meet a few of his friends, although she did not like to share him. She brought family news to Norman and would return home with details about her son's college life. As always, she had the utmost faith in him and presumed he knew how to tread carefully through this new world of rich boys and upper-class WASPs.

Rhoda began to notice changes in Norman whenever he was home from college. He was a bit more outgoing, opinionated, and paternal toward her. He advocated less inhibited behavior. "Fuck, shit, piss," he would shout at his annoyed but also amused mother, who found it hard to be censorious. In fact, she would giggle and leave the impression that his behavior tickled her. "Norman would delight in teasing her like a lover," his first wife has said. He would sit down to a meal of lamb chops and while the others were cutting their meat he would pretend to be carving away at his penis. It was outrageous, but he would grin like a "dirty-little-boy," Rhoda recalls. Barney seemed much more upset about this behavior than Fanny.

For much of his freshman year Norman concentrated on engineering. He had few outside interests, paid little, if any, attention to politics and did not participate in the active student union. F. O. Matthiesen, the faculty member who most attracted students because of his closeness to contemporary literature and to leftist politics, seems to have had no influence on Mailer. For students under Matthiessen's sway, "almost anyone else would seem hopelessly old-fashioned," Professor Levin suggests. Like many freshmen in the fall of 1939, Mailer was an isolationist, and the ferment on campus between leftists and liberals and conservatives hardly touched him. He had not come to college well-read and had faked a bibliography required of him by Harvard, claiming to have read *The Rise of Silas Lapham* and other classics.

Nevertheless, by late December Norman was avidly reading modern American literature, an outgrowth of a required course, English A. The decisive writer, as far as he was concerned, was James T. Farrell, whose Studs Lonigan novels opened up a gritty, lower-class world just "one notch" below Norman's own. Farrell represented a tough, proletarian writer, not some impractical literary aesthete. Norman had never realized that literature could gauge itself so closely to experience. It had never occurred to him that he could cultivate his identity by writing about where he had come from. Literature, quite literally, stimulated him for the first time to see that who he was and who he might become could be a matter of his own literary invention. Reading Farrell had, quite suddenly, changed his life.

In the figure of Studs Lonigan, Mailer found the first of his many Irish alter egos. Studs swaggers. He is a small guy who has the nerve to take on bigger men. He is afraid to get hit, yet he never backs down from a fight. He is a romantic who dreams of conquering the world and of mastering beautiful women, but he is also one of the boys, embarrassed by his mother's coddling of him and offended by his father's demands for obedience. Studs is a dreamer, a "hero in his own mind," and a fitting model for the young Mailer, who had heretofore found his champions in English adventure stories.

Literature as taught in English A had something in common with engineering: It had its own rules and techniques, which were critically analyzed in class. Norman thought that with enough practice he could become proficient, a professional at writing as he had been at model airplane building. Though writing touched him far more personally than engineering ever could, he approached it with the same methodical mentality that had made him an excellent science student. "This business of inspiration is shit," he remarked to one of his friends as he tried half a dozen different ways of developing the same theme.

Encouraged by an A+ in English A for a novella, Norman wrote fourteen more stories by the beginning of his sophomore year. Rhoda Lazare Wolf and other friends of the family already knew he wanted to be a writer, to follow the example of James T. Farrell. When Rhoda graduated from P.S. 161, Norman, home after his first year in college, wrote in her yearbook: "We both graduated from 161, but I went to Boys' High and you will not. I'm going to Harvard and I doubt if they'll let you in. That's still all right. You don't have to follow exactly in my footsteps to be famous, too. Until they burn 161, Norman Mailer, Babbie's brother." He drew "two small footprints" after the phrase "in my footsteps" and added another line, signing himself "Normie Mailer," although that was a name used only by the boys. He also put a question mark after "Norman Mailer," for Rhoda knew he was considering changing his name as a writer.

Should he sign himself "Norman Kingsley Mailer? N. Kingsley? Norman K. Mailer? Or Kingsley Mailer?" During the summer after his freshman year, his Aunt Rebecca gave him his own room in a big cottage in Long Branch, where he wrote in the afternoon and into the night, often getting up late. She sent up his meals so that he would not have to interrupt his work, and he showed her everything he wrote, for she had "a love for literature," a belief, in her daughter Osie's words, that "writing was the greatest art of all." Osie was "very well read and a writer herself," according to her brother, Cy, and got her share of Norman's manuscripts to comment on. Fanny thought of her father, the rabbi, and wondered if her son's dedication had been bred into him. The whole family respected his labor. They were highly literate and knew what it meant to be a writer.

In the fall of 1940, Norman took Robert Gorham Davis's writing class, English A1. Students were expected to turn in about six typewritten pages every two weeks, and Davis would often read their work in class, which he did with Mailer's first assignment, a story set in a Catskills resort concerning bellhops who bed the wives of husbands who are in the city during the week. A husband discovers his wife's infidelity and shoots her and her lover. In a takeoff of "The Short Happy Life of Francis Macomber," the narrator, a bellhop, notes that the bullet wound has entered the back of his friend's head and blown away his entire face. The story ends with the narrator terrorized and vomiting at the thought of the atomized face he is breathing in with the air or stepping on in the gobs on the carpet.

Davis criticized the overwrought ending. To show how it damaged the story's suggestiveness, he reread a portion, sending himself and the class into a fit of giggling. Norman wanted to murder him but was mollified later when his teacher apologized, confessing that he had not realized what would happen. Much later, Mailer compared this class to being a "novice in the Golden Gloves."

Nothing at this point could destroy Norman's ambition to become a professional writer. To one of his roommates, Seymour Breslow, he seemed more confident his sophomore year. He talked about writing, and he was showing his stories around as well as finding a place for himself on the *Harvard Advocate*—evidently with the aid of Bruce Barton, Jr., son of the famous advertising agency executive, who prevailed against the objections of one "stuffy" junior. The magazine's offices, an entire floor of five rooms, were to Norman "five mystical chambers full of broken-down furniture and the incomparable odor that rises from old beer stains in the carpet and syrup-crusted empty Coke bottles in the corners." This "sweet and alcoholic and faintly debauched" atmosphere held the portent of "little magazines and future lands of literature." Reading the old issues of magazines in which the early work of T. S. Eliot, e. e. cummings, Malcolm Cowley, and others appeared was like "extracting genealogical marrow from old print." Writing meant art, fame, money—every measure of success he could think of. He analyzed Hemingway's prose and commented on the way the writer used the "visual structure of a sentence to have impact."

Mailer's interest in writing brought him a new set of friends, in
cluding George Washington Goethals, the descendant of an old New
England family, who resembled, according to Harvard classmate
George Crockett, a "delicate . . . Meissen figurine, pinched features in
an elongated face like a Parmigianino shepherd, pale, alabasterlike,
cherry lips." Like Mailer, Goethals fancied himself a writer while also
trying to acquire a reputation as a boozer and athlete. Crockett suggests
Mailer was "very fond of George—as one would be of an angora rabbit.
He was blond and downy, and perhaps soft to touch." Goethals concedes
his friendship with Mailer (who described himself to Goethals as a
"third-generation Brooklyn Jew") was somewhat odd, but they had a
"mutual empathy" as opposites who perhaps wanted a bit of each
other's makeup and who were willing to trade New England reticence
for Brooklyn flamboyance. Norman's roommates were somewhat jealous
of Goethals, and Goethals's roommates could not understand what he
saw in a classmate who seemed "so un-American and wasn't interested
in things like beer, girls and baseball." But Mailer was changing,
affecting something of the Harvard accent, and adopting "the quiet
grays, the understated shirts, and the challis ties that Mt. Auburn Street
club men wore."

With Goethals, Mailer wrote an initiation play for the *Advocate*, a
parody of *For Whom the Bells Tolls*, entitled "For Whom Your Balls
Squall," which included a hilarious parody of Martha Gellhorn, dubbed
Martha Getshorned. In the play, Martha gets "horned"—a feat accomplished by Norman with a large baloney sausage. When he did not
fantasize a life as Rocky Graziano knocking everyone out, he came on
like his favorite actor, the pugnacious John Garfield, whom he liked to
refer to by his real name, Julie Garfinkel.

Treating himself like an athlete in training, Norman wrote three
thousand words a day, sometimes riding the subway in search of material for his fiction—watching, for example, a man grope a woman's
sexual parts and writing about it. "It was like an anthropologist going
after field data," Goethals recalls, when Norman discussed his discovery of the Boston Irish and his absorption in their clannishness. He
would start arguments about the need to include bowel movements in
literature and sit down with one of his classmates to read aloud the sex
passages in *Ulysses*. Still a neophyte himself at sex, he used literature to
acquire a worldliness he had not yet experienced on his own.

While there is some evidence that Mailer tried to ape Hemingway's swaggering maleness, much of it seems to have been merely adolescent enthusiasm. Still only seventeen and prone to throwing forward passes in his dorm, applying football blocks on anyone who crossed close to him in the halls, and tearing up the goalposts after home football games, he was in the trial-and-error stage, searching for what suited him. He even took up squash, a sport he had earlier associated with Harvard's more effete students. He was acquiring an encyclopedic range of knowledge. Normally he did not show off, but he had a low tolerance for liquor, and in front of large audiences he could become a "bully and a lout."

But Norman had no reputation as a campus bad boy. Goethals remembers his generosity, congratulating Goethals on his election to a prestigious eating club, the Signet society, and presenting him two books by Faulkner with a note saying he thought Goethals had it in him to be a great writer. Invited to Professor Davis's house, he impressed Mrs. Davis with his sweetness and fine manners. He was self-possessed without seeming the least bit arrogant or testy. She liked his openness and beautiful eyes, and his sensitivity charmed her. She could not know that in Brooklyn he had always been "a little ashamed of being smart." It was a relief to be at Harvard, where it was more of a disgrace if "you were maybe not smart enough." The Davises almost never invited students to their house, so Norman had to know his presence was a special compliment. In later years, Mrs. Davis often wondered about what had happened to this nice, modest boy and why Norman did not put this side of himself in his writing.

PROSPECTING

"The Greatest Thing in the World," written during Mailer's sophomore year, presents one side of his attraction to fiction. It is a fast-paced story about a down-and-out teenager, Al Groot, who bums rides around the country and just barely escapes with his winnings from a band of brutal pool sharks. It is the kind of story, Norman told himself, a professional should be able to write—with taut, quick character sketches and with a hint of a socially redeeming theme about the toughness, the ingenuity, and the desperation of the poor. Probably modeled after the Davey Cohen episode in *The Young Manhood of Studs Lonigan*, in which Davey anticipates that he will be beaten up and robbed of his dice-game winnings on the Toledo docks, Al knows better than to insinuate himself into the company of these men who only want to take his money. It is this playing with fate that gives the story tension. No larger claims can be made for it. This was a Depression-era narrative about a drifter, a quick, deft, naturalistic vignette, but it had no heart—as Mailer admitted to Goethals, with whom he exchanged opinions about his early writing: "He used to say that he could write scenes well and depict certain characters like Al Gort [Groot] but that he basically distrusted his ability to deal with emotional feeling," Goethals recalls. As Mailer confessed in *Advertisements for Myself*, the story "reads like the early work of a young man who is going to make a fortune writing first-rate action, western, gangster, and suspense pictures."

"Maybe Next Year," written in Mailer's junior year, brings to bear not only his reading of Faulkner but also feelings about his own childhood and family background. The narrator of the story is a child who speaks in literal, repetitive terms reminiscent of Benjy in *The Sound and the Fury*:

> *I'd go out in the field, across the road from my house and slide down the steep part of the grass where it was slippery like dogs had been dirty there, and then I used to climb up the other side, up the big hill on the other side, and walk and walk through the fat high grass until I would come to the railroad tracks where I'd just keep going and going and going.*

This account of a child getting his bearings in the adult world, constantly warned by his mother to stay away from the hoboes (the dirty old men) recalls Norman's sheltered world and his mother's injunctions to keep the dirt out of his talk and his clothing. While the boy of the story fears the adult world he also yearns for it, since it represents an opportunity to get beyond the smothering, antiseptic comforts of home.

Andrew Gordon points out how "Maybe Next Year" prefigures Mailer's lifelong obsession with dirt and with a "cluster of themes" that have dominated his unconscious. Like the boy in his story, Norman wanted to "dirty himself in freedom." The boy's father is weak and is constantly attacked by the mother, and the boy is obviously looking to identify with male figures. Not finding a satisfactory substitute for his father, he falls back upon the authority of his mother, rejecting the bums he has sought out and even injuring one badly with a rock. Sadism is the only form of control the boy has learned from his domineering mother.

Like "The Greatest Thing in the World," "Maybe Next Year" takes its complexion from the Depression. It is a savage story—certainly more savage than anything Mailer experienced at home—but it suggests the aspects of his childhood that made him feel vulnerable and angry and far less than a complete person. "Maybe Next Year," as Gordon suggests, is about a longing for power and control.

Mailer has been extremely reticent about his childhood, especially about those aspects that may have contributed to his fiction. Jack Maher, who courted Norman's sister in the summer of 1944, got the impression from Norman that Barney was a weak father. It was not anything Norman said; there was just the feeling Maher took away of Barney as a "gray, failed man."

Barbara was startled when Norman came home from college one day and announced, "Our father is an unusual man." It did not sound like her brother was describing their father. Then Norman revealed that Barney was a "gambler and had run up huge debts." Norman's cousin Osie remembers that he always defended his father, even though she thought the gambling was "crazy." Barney used to borrow money from her mother "on the qt" and make sure neither Norman nor Fanny knew. During his gambling bouts Barney would not show up and Fanny would have to cover for him. Rhoda Lazare Wolf speculates that Barney's gambling endeared him to Norman; certainly by the sound of the way Norman described it to Barbara, Barney had suddenly become more mysterious and interesting, with a "life of his own" that no one in the family could quite fathom. Barney "had found the road to freedom and independence," says Rhoda: "It was like he had developed his own selfhood, and Norman began to see him in a totally different way." In fact, he romanticized both of his parents, making "so much more out of these situations than really existed."

THE QUEST FOR EXPERIENCE

"The Greatest Thing in the World" won *Story* magazine's first prize in June 1941. This national recognition confirmed Mailer's decision to become a writer. He was still something of an anomaly—neither writing nor always dressing like the rest of the *Advocate* staffers. Bowden Broadwater, known himself as a stylish aesthete, recalls that Mailer's "very black, oiled, wavy hair" and his "shiny green gabardine jacket" made him seem like a "preppy Frank Sinatra." "The Greatest Thing in the World" might be a dreadful story in the estimation of some *Advocate* staffers, but they could not deny its author's vitality.

By the end of Norman's sophomore year, his work had already attracted the attention of Roy Larsen, executive editor of *Time*, and Ted Amussen, an editor at Rinehart and Company. A career as a novelist seemed well within his reach, and his literary prize had convinced his family that writing could be more than a hobby. That summer, back in Long Branch, he worked on what turned out to be an eighty-thousand or ninety-thousand-word novel entitled *No Percentage*. Years later Mailer remembered it as a work about a rich boy who hitchhikes around the country to "discover what the world's all about" but who fails himself, not having the guts to jump into a boxcar.

The author had set off on such a trip to gather material for the book and admits to a squeamishness that made it difficult for him to listen to a North Carolina redneck's graphic account of a two-night fucking spree. Nevertheless, in Virginia he lost his virginity to what he described (in a letter to a friend) as an old bag whore. He related the incident as a kind of joke on himself—a young man's comic determination to lose his innocence, washing himself down with Lysol afterward.

The very idea of such a trip horrified Fanny: her son bumming around, "sleeping out in the open grass," without a sweater or a change of clothes! She knew she could not stop Norman, and that as a writer he had to base his work on experience, on "real" life, so she held her tongue—just making sure that when he returned home he entered through the basement, took off his clothes, and was deloused.

Mailer couched his memory of *No Percentage* in terms of the main character's quest for experience, but at least one of his friends remembers that the novel focused on middle-class Jewish "parents who thought they had a child prodigy and were suffocating him with attention." While more than one editor expressed an interest in *No Percentage*, it was not published and Mailer came to regard it as a "very bad novel." He would never again attempt to publish anything so directly based on his family life, for in the act of trying to declare his independence in a novel he inescapably reminded himself of an identity he found "absolutely insupportable—the nice Jewish boy from Brooklyn." The best he could do was to acknowledge ruefully his roots in the fugitive sentences of later works, such as *The Armies of the Night*, where he refers to himself in the third person: "Something in his adenoids gave it away—he had the softness of a man early accustomed to mother-love."

FANTASY MAN

In his junior year at Harvard, Mailer sat in Theodore Morrison's English A3 class and apparently made no deep impression on his teacher. Yet Morrison recognized his pupil's great promise and often devoted classes to Mailer's stories. He was "easily the best writer in the class," of whom great things were expected. He had that "aura of a special talent," recalls Oliver Allen, one of Norman's classmates.

Stories poured out of Mailer—not only six stories set in the subway but another based on his summer travels in the South called "Four Pamphlets for Jesus," his effort to depict a redneck preacher. Then there were the imitations of Fitzgerald and Hemingway, a story about a "German anti-aircraft crew reacting with fear to a British bombardment," and many others. He spoke of writing "the shit out" of himself, meaning to strip himself of clichés. Goethals admired his friend's remarkable "degree of detachment" in not writing about himself but objectively sizing up others. To some of his readers—like George Crockett—Mailer seemed "cold" and without Faulkner's or Malraux's ability to express "compassion for their fellow man." Mailer's fictional heroes were sophisticated urban intellectuals, athletic and sexually accomplished, who were

> *nevertheless tortured by higher thoughts—the meaning or meaninglessness of life, money, love and power. His themes were always too big for his undergraduate abilities, and he was always his own hero. Writing for him was a kind of purgation, and was also his remaking, after doing away with the old Mailer.*

He was slinging four-letter words around, emulating Hemingway's gin habit, and beginning in earnest on his conquests of women:

> *In Brooklyn, we called kissing a girl "getting to first," touching her tits was "second," and putting your hand up her crotch was "a three-*

bagger." I remember one night I went back to my room after a date in Cambridge. My roommate, Marty Lubin, was at his desk studying, and I went by, putting my fingers under his nose. "Get a whiff of this!"

He had installed himself in more elegant surroundings at Dunster House, which had a fine library, dining room, and a reputation for being livelier and freer than the other residences. To some students he seemed a poser—always playing some role; for others he had a charming, comic sense of his own limitations, and they simply accepted him as a budding writer whose main mission was to cultivate Norman Mailer. Harvard, like everything else, turned into a Norman Mailer project, "something big and impressive against which to define himself," as one of his college friends expresses it.

Sometimes Norman put on an act as the poor Jewish boy from Brooklyn. A goy could not understand a Jew, he maintained with one gentile friend. He played the "slum child" and identified with the proletarian subjects of the fiction he admired. Several of his friends also thought he might be trying to save himself embarrassment. If he made a point of his Jewishness, then no one could humiliate him with it. He did not attack the WASP establishment and had no particular interest in its personalities and precepts, except for the son of novelist John P. Marquand, whose coming to Harvard had been headlined in the *Crimson*. As an *Advocate* recruiter, Mailer had "kind of hovered" over him, saying he supposed Marquand would "want to come out for the *Advocate.*" Mailer seemed to be putting down Marquand as a son of privilege who expected the royal treatment.

Norman's social and political attitudes may have been influenced by Beatrice Silverman, a Boston University student he met at a concert in the middle of his junior year and who was now his steady girl. She had strong convictions about her Jewishness and about America's obligation to enter the war. She sensed in Norman an incipient radicalism. The word for her was zaftig. She had an earthy and arousing quality that made Norman the envy of his friends. She was also very amusing and gay, sure of herself and not at all competitive with him—although some members of his family, including Fanny, thought otherwise. They saw Bea as the selfish, dominant type, but Norman defended her. At least one of his friends felt Bea had a motherly quality, and Norman apparently delighted in her spirited attacks on Harvard stuffiness. She was proud, outspoken, and sassy—a fine pianist who appreciated his utter devotion to writing. She could be stridently ideological—a welcome change for a boy bent on sharpening his own edges—but she had a sense of irony that prevented her from becoming a fanatic. Best of all, she had no compunctions about going to bed with him. Thanks to the generosity of Uncle Dave Kessler, he had an old De Soto hardtop coupe with an enormous trunk he had outfitted with a mattress. Norman, the eighteen-year-old junior, the "baby" of a class whose knowledge of women was slight, suddenly became a man of considerable experience, lecturing along with Bea about the freedom of their sex life. They were a consciously provocative couple: swearing loudly in public, drinking and arguing in what some friends regarded as a pretentious manner. Bea believed she and Norman "had an honest and good relationship." He did not put on an "act" for her, she is sure, because she would have called him on it.

Goethals remembers that his friend's "preoccupation with sexuality was always overt and always completely devoid of emotion." Norman talked of going to Hollywood, writing scripts for three hundred dollars a week, and screwing a "different girl every day." Yet at Harvard, his only girl was Bea. Norman was no swinger, but there were these "constant fantasies and verbal allusions to screwing this or that person." It was part of a persona he was already building up for himself. Or as Goethals concludes, "The degree of fantasy Mailer has about himself is extreme." On occasion it could be quite dramatic—like the night Norman stumbled in on Pete Barton and Fred Jacobi, two of his friends who lived in Lowell House. As the two roommates eyed each other trying to figure him out, he sprawled into an upholstered chair, affected a lethargic manner, rolled his eyes, and asked: "Have you ever been so tired you didn't even want to sleep with a girl?" Barton and Jacobi, rather perplexed, said yes as Jacobi thought about the rumor that Mailer liked to paste photographs of his friends' faces on the bodies of men and women in pornographic poses. Neither Jacobi nor Barton had much experience with women, and Jacobi feared Mailer suspected as much. He soon left, having created a mystique his friends did not think to question. To Eric Larrabee, another classmate, Norman seemed intimidating: "muscular and wiry . . . [in] T-shirts and blue jeans before they were as common as they later became. . . . [He] had worked in an all-night hash house and knew about *life.*"

At other times, the ridiculousness of Mailer's posturing was quickly exposed. "Nice to know a *percocious* writer," a clubman said by way of greeting Norman, who took the deliberate mispronunciation of the word as an insult. He was up on his toes, bouncing around like Rocky Graziano, rubbing his thumb against his lips like a professional boxer and putting up his fists. Norman had trouble getting in a real swing, and the two men scuffled, with the slightly heavier one holding Norman "at arm's length while he in turn churned the air harmlessly with his flailing arms." Recognizing the futility of the fight, Mailer quit, saying, "Christ, I'm a real asshole, aren't I?"

CLEANING BED PANS AND WASHING OLD BUTTS

Norman began the summer after his junior year working at Mattapan, Boston State Hospital. With a friend, another talented writer, he figured on acquiring yet another kind of experience for his novelist's résumé. On day four he had to join the other attendants in subduing a crazed black kid and to watch them bludgeon him into submission. When he complained, he was reassigned to a ward full of senile old people, "cleaning bed pans and washing old butts." He lasted seven days—the shock of the change from Harvard was too great. His companion had left even earlier. Fanny believed her son left the job because he could not stand the thought of her frenzied with worry over the vicious conditions in which he worked. His first attempt at making sense of his experience took the form of a play, *The Naked and the Dead*, which he hoped the Harvard Dramatic Society would produce. When they rejected it, he gave up any further thought of writing plays.

A WAR HAD BEGUN AND WOULD CHANGE MY LIFE

By Mailer's senior year the campus had been transformed: "Special military units trained at Harvard, and R.O.T.C. uniforms altered the tone of the Square." The attack on Pearl Harbor had made everyone, except the most diehard isolationists, supporters of the war, and he was excited, knowing that "a war had begun and would change my life." Some of his classmates took accelerated classes in order to join the armed services as soon as possible. Mailer continued in his four-year program, enrolling in more writing courses even as he completed a major in aeronautical engineering (not a taxing subject for him and acceptable to his parents, who wanted him to have a solid occupation to fall back on). His immediate concern was not enlistment but to incorporate this new vast subject—war—into his fiction.

In the fall of 1939, Archibald MacLeish addressed Harvard freshmen on the likelihood of war, calling it a fate this new generation was not likely to escape. In a series of articles in *The Nation*, MacLeish argued it may have been a mistake to have so much revisionist disillusion in the writing about the First World War because now people were held over by those views, which did not suit this new war. Sooner or later America would find itself in the war, defending its democratic principles. "He turned it into an attack on pacifist intellectuals," Harry Levin recalls. After MacLeish's speech, Mailer imagined this striking scene:

> *We were going through the barbed-wire when a machine gun started. I kept walking until I saw my head lying on the ground.*
> *"My God, I'm dead," my head said.*
> *And my body fell over.*

By his senior year, the writer had to take the subject more seriously, to consider what it might be like to be in a war facing death—although even in his short and perhaps facetious piece he was already speculating on the shock and the terrible immediacy of war when a man might very well become witness to the disintegration of his own body.

In "A Calculus at Heaven," a novella written for Robert Hillyer's English A5 class, Mailer confronted the war's implications for himself and for his country. Although he assumed the great novel of the war would be set in Europe, he felt he had no choice but to focus on the Pacific theater: Americans were already at war there, and his "progressive-liberal" bias led him to ferreting out the "reactionary overtone" of the Asian fighting. Besides, he had far too little experience to handle the "culture of Europe and the collision of America upon it."

Patterning his fiction after that of Dos Passos, Mailer devised a cast of characters who represented a cross section of the nation: Father Meary, an Irish priest; DaLucci, an Italian from Terre Haute; Sergeant Rice, an American Indian; Wexler, a New Jersey Jew and star football player at the University of Minnesota; Bowen Hilliard, a painter and literary man, WASP son of an army colonel, and a Yale graduate. As this company of soldiers bide their time, awaiting a Japanese attack of overwhelming strength that will surely kill them, they try to fasten on the meaning of their lives, struggling vainly to maintain a belief in the significance of their actions that much of their past history has denied or proved illusory. Meary has never been sure of his faith, DaLucci has never found a core of belief worth preserving, Rice has only had the stoical comfort of his own physical prowess, and Wexler dies in the very act of retelling a favorite football story.

Bowen Hilliard, the captain of this company, is an alter ego for the author, who has confessed to creating a romantic image for himself of "a hero who is tall, strong, and excruciatingly wounded." Unlike the other characters, Hilliard has the vocabulary to articulate the urgent search for meaning that the war has heightened. Hilliard is a painter who has failed to make a living during the Depression. He has sold out to his wife's family, become a draftsman, and then written a sour autobiography reflecting on the failure of America's promise and his own. A passage quoted from his book sums up his credo: "To die in terms of a subsequent humanity is a form of emotional sophistication that may be achieved only by a people of that nation which puts its philosophy in action." Americans, in Hilliard's view, do not act as though they believe in their ideas. They have no faith, so there is no truth to their actions, and no more than a "crude moral calculus" which is the equivalent of desperate betting on the odds at death, hoping that heaven will come through like a winning football team. He speaks from bitter experience, realizing he has given up his own convictions in order to make a living and support his wife. Not even the war sustains Hilliard, for when Rice asks about the reason for war and why Hilliard feels justified in thinking America will win, Hilliard has no answer. It is obvious that the war is merely a holding action, a reaction to Japanese aggression that does not have its own basis of belief.

These were Mailer's sentiments as well, and like Bowen Hilliard, he was a romantic hero manqué:

> *Certainly in my years at Harvard the question of my identity was paramount. The most interesting question to many of us in those days was, what do you really think of me. I remember once having a long talk with my roommate Marty Lubin, and I primed him—I wanted to come back with some fish. So I talked for about half an hour, analyzed his*

character in great detail. He listened, and when I got all done I said,
"Marty, what do you think of me?" He paused and then he said, "Ah,
gee, Norm, you're just a good guy." At which point I was ready to throw
him out the window from the fifth floor of Dunster.

Norman Mailer found in the subject of war the crucible of his conviction as a novelist. In order to know what he really believed, he had to
know what was worth dying for. Malraux, quoted in "A Calculus at
Heaven," provided the principal spring of Mailer's literary aspiration
and of his sense of himself as a man. Bowen Hilliard writes in his
autobiography: "Malraux says that all that men are willing to die for
tends to justify their fate by giving it a foundation in dignity." After
Edwin Seaver accepted "A Calculus at Heaven" for his anthology, *Cross-
Section*, Mailer confided to him that he wanted to be "another Malraux." Mailer realized that for his words to have any purchase on reality,
for his character to be something more than a nicety of manner, he would
have to test himself repeatedly in the conflicts arising out of war. He
could be neither a whole man nor a complete novelist if he did not
literally fight for what he wrote.

In June 1943, on the Harvard campus, Mailer and Goethals talked
about the war. Goethals cannot recall that his friend had any particular
position on the war, and both of them tried to take the "threatening
future lightly." Mailer saw the necessity for opposing Hitler, especially
for someone who was a Jew. "I'm going to enlist and get into the
goddam army and get it over with," he vowed.

2.

THE NAKED AND
THE DEAD
(1943–1948)

THE OUTSIDE WORLD

In the spring of his senior year at Harvard, Mailer began work on a novel, *A Transit to Narcissus*, based on his brief brush with the brutal life in a mental ward. His play on the subject had dramatized the crude, violent condition of patients penned up in a screened-in porch. The novel maintains the play's sense of vicious imprisonment but filters the scene through the consciousness of Paul Scarr, a college man in his junior year beset by a fear of physical violence and by a bad conscience as a result of his failure to join the forces in Spain fighting for the Republic. Like Bowen Hilliard in "A Calculus at Heaven," he yearns to "feel a certain magnitude in his action" and seeks an absolution for his absence in Spain, where he should have stood with the doomed Loyalists, making a "tragic good-bye." Scarr dreads the idea that the asylum will brutalize him, and that he will become just like the other attendants who beat the inmates to restore order and to express their need to dominate. Yet he does not respect his own pacifism, which seems born of fear, not conviction. *A Transit to Narcissus* is Mailer's "first coming to grips with a theme that would not so much haunt me as stalk me for the rest of my writing life: what is the relation between courage and brutality?"

Mailer had fled the mental hospital at Mattapan after a week rather than accommodate himself to the assaultive behavior of the other attendants; his alter ego in *No Percentage* had felt humiliated at his aversion to hopping on a boxcar. This "good son of the middle class"—as Mailer later called himself—craved yet shied away from action. Upon graduation from Harvard he continued to write *A Transit to Narcissus*, expecting to be drafted in the summer of 1943, watching his friends go off to war and feeling lonely.

Stanley Karnow, Harvard class of 1945, had encountered Mailer on a few occasions and remembers that he was viewed as "kind of a heroic figure on campus—even in those days" and assumed that Mailer had enlisted: "Given the atmosphere of the time, the idea of not being in the service was just horrendous. To be hanging around Cambridge or something when everybody else was in the army was pretty rough."

As the months stretched into March of 1944, Mailer's anxiety (he subsequently acknowledged) was reflected in the "lugubrious weight" of his novel's style. The work had grown to over 180,000 tortured words. The trouble, the author knew, was with himself. Like his main character, he was feeling inadequate. Mailer has admitted he was "a little frightened of going to war, and a great deal ashamed of not going to war." And he was not nearly mature enough to handle a novel that tries to analyze not only its main character's psychology but also the political structure of society. For the asylum is controlled by a syndicate that also controls local and state government. Knowing almost nothing at this point about politics and society, Mailer flounders in his presentation of such stereotypes as the small-town crusading newspaper editor and the cynical syndicate attorney. The institutions in this novel are largely abstractions and demonstrate just how crucial Mailer's service in the army would be for shaping his sense of society.

As Scarr becomes implicated in the corruption of the asylum and gives way to his impulse to beat the inmates, he searches for comfort and total acceptance from one of the asylum's female attendants, Marion Gannon, a buxom lover who consoles him by burying his head in her breasts but whom he increasingly resents because she is not content to mother him. Scarr's earlier sexual initiation has been effected with his father's housekeeper/mistress, thus beginning his quest for a maternal figure who will protect him from the outside world.

A Transit to Narcissus was written very close to the bone, the product of a young man cherished in the bosom of his family who was more than a little terrorized and fascinated by the big world that awaited him. How could any environment be as safe as Fanny Mailer's home? Yet how could he grow as a writer if he did not know this dangerous world? Mailer has speculated that other writers have become battle-hardened at an early age by growing up in "hostile families" where they had to establish an identity, a sense of importance that contradicted the wishes of their parents. For Mailer it was just the opposite: He would have to be "alert to the street": "My mother and my father treated my sister and myself as important people. At home, we were the center of the universe. It was the outside world that was difficult."

Norman and his sister did inhabit a rather enchanted world their friends envied. Barbara, then in Radcliffe, exuded the kind of idealized love for her brother one might find in a medieval romance. In the spring of 1944, Barbara and Adeline Lubell Naiman (who roomed with Bea's sister Phyllis) got to be good friends. To Naiman, Norman appeared to be "big brother and hero." Barbara wanted to please him, and Naiman saw her as under her brother's "shadow," which seemed more a matter of Barbara's doing than Norman's. It was almost as if she, like the rest of the family, had invented him.

In the eight months following his graduation from Harvard, Mailer worked furiously on *A Transit to Narcissus*—quite literally a voyage into himself. He was sure he would be killed in the war, if he ever got there after his long wait to be drafted—and *A Transit to Narcissus* is his desperate effort to plumb his sensibility before he got into combat. Indeed, the many savage scenes in the novel, and Scarr's gradual mastery of violence, are the equivalent of war. Not having ever to defend himself to his family, Mailer was writing to justify himself to the world.

Mailer suspected that his full emergence into the outside world would somehow have to be abrupt and violent, and he invested Paul Scarr with a similar presentiment:

> *His need was action of the most powerful and positive kind, conclusive and binding, and he found it in the certainty that beating the patients gave him, as he did not find it in making love to Marion Gannon.*

The woman represents only the security of home and the status quo, the very protectiveness and conservatism that prevented Mailer from finding out if he was really a man. Scarr savors his tensing to action, a physical sensation that he finds pleasant, and when he finally comes to blows, he feels the joy of release and excitement, conquering his "almost mystic fear of bodily contact." It is then that he realizes his dread of going to Spain has actually been a reflection of his "deep fear and attraction to brutality." Mass murder, in fact, quickens his imagination as he recognizes the attractiveness of fascism and the weakness of his former liberalism. His identification with the power of violence becomes as absolute as his previous abhorrence of it.

As Scarr allows his will to be expressed in the physical beating of inmates, his counterpart, newspaper publisher George Cowles, is beaten up by the syndicate for his attacks on it. Curiously, Cowles takes some satisfaction in the beating, feeling that his injuries redeem what has been his rather weak opposition to corruption. He has to feel personally vulnerable before his political ideas seem important to him. Both characters are extraordinarily self-centered, with Scarr's dream of war almost a verbatim repetition of the scene Mailer conceived during his first year at Harvard:

> The day was very gray, and the dark brown earth was hollowed by shell craters, he was completely isolated on the most enormous field he had ever seen. He kept walking and came to a barbed wire fence which he started to crawl over very carefully. But then from nowhere, a machine gun started firing at him. He continued to walk until his head lying on the ground saw his body moving forward.
> "My God, I'm dead," his head said.
> And his body fell over.

Scarr pictures the scene of his death "on the most enormous field he had ever seen," where the action focuses entirely on him with a magnitude his author had imagined for himself.

Both Cowles and Scarr find in violence and in fascism a seductiveness that makes liberalism, the gradual correction of societal wrongs, seem cowardly and ultimately ineffective. Liberalism, in their view, means compromise and obfuscation; it is soothing and comfortable but also flaccid. The fear that is stimulated by violence, on the other hand, makes Cowles "exist in nakedness," so that he relinquishes the protective barriers between himself and the world he has heretofore tried to evade. In short, he is finally willing to suffer for what he believes in.

Scarr, on the other hand, uses violence to vent his frustrations and to feel, if only momentarily, powerful. He and another attendant miscalculate in their beating of an inmate and after his death are charged with manslaughter. Scarr also comes within a moment of murdering Marion Gannon and is stopped only by her refusal to play the victim. When she does not allow him to place a knife against her naked chest, his urge to kill her dissipates, for she shatters his illusion of being in control. Unlike Cowles, Scarr still has not come to grips with his fears or with his urge to violence. His irresolute behavior and the novel's inconclusiveness are manifestations of Mailer's own confusion.

BURNED OUT AND MARRIED

In January 1944, still waiting for the draft, Mailer tinkered some more with his novel, making Scarr's fear of physical violence even greater, adding references to his timid childhood and to his early affairs with women, one of whom, Doris, is clearly modeled after Bea Silverman's poised and proud rejection of sentimentality and gentility:

> *People, even profoundly sincere people, look upon taking a crap as something not to be discussed, as if instead of being another part of life which contains man's joys and sorrows to some extent—it is instead part of the evil in man, part of his tragedy that even the pope leaves a stink in the can.*

Like Bea, Doris delights in shocking people. Bea's habit of challenging people's pieties spurred Norman to examine his own vulnerable convictions.

By Mailer's count, his desperately revised novel went to twenty publishers, most of whom found it depressing, confusing, and unpleasant. (It was not published until 1978, when Howard Fertig issued a special facsimile edition.) The scenes in the mental ward are vivid and have a documentary quality, but the work lacks pace. "Never is there a novel where as many people go out for walks to think things through, and do so for so long as the style requires," Mailer observes. What is lacking—even by comparison with his other college prose—is directness and fluency. Yet the mature writer notes that his basic themes are there: "the nearness of violence to creation, and the whiff of murder just beyond every embrace of love."

A Transit to Narcissus was a devastating novel to write, for Mailer deliberately turned in upon himself before he had the experience to develop the shields of the various personae who would appear in his later work. His identity as a writer seemed threatened by this disturbing work, as he implied many years later to an interviewer: "I was ready to think I was burned out before I even started *The Naked and the Dead.*" He lived at home, wrote in a small rented room, and courted Bea, who proved remarkably receptive to pleas for marriage. In spite of her independence and protofeminist stance, she behaved like Doris in *A Transit to Narcissus*, who "melted before [Scarr]" and "loved him unselfishly, wisely, womanly." Like Doris with Scarr, Bea had a very powerful sexual hold over Mailer.

When Norman and Bea decided to get married, he brought her for a visit to Ted Amussen, an editor at Rinehart considering *A Transit to Narcissus* for publication. Amussen can still envision a "very embarrassed" and "sweet" Mailer introducing Bea. Amussen kissed Bea "in glee. I thought she was marvelous." To Barbara Mailer, Bea confided that Norman wanted to write the Great American Novel. His plan was to send Bea long letters about combat so that a record would be left should he die in the war.

Norman and Bea went through a civil ceremony in Yonkers in February 1944 shortly after he received his draft notice, eloping so that Fanny could not prevent, in Bea's words, "her little genius" from getting married. Fanny wanted the marriage annulled but only succeeded in getting the couple to consent to a traditional Jewish ceremony under a *chuppah* at the Silverman home in Chelsea, Massachusetts. A few weeks later he was in the army and she enlisted in the Waves, with Private Mailer joking to an old roommate that he had to salute his wife before fucking her.

Mailer's marriage and his decision to seek combat marked an important stage in his declaration of independence. Fanny, of her own accord, would not have let him go. Given the opportunity, she would make sure that both Norman and Barbara adhered to her family line—as Barbara discovered to her great cost in the summer of 1944 while her brother went through basic training. Jack Maher, on furlough, visited Cambridge and fell in love with Barbara, who was rooming with Bea's sister Phyllis. Maher was Catholic, a Midwesterner, and everything that

Fanny Mailer did not want for her daughter. Rhoda Lazare Wolf remembers that Fanny was so upset that she feigned a heart attack, refusing to get off the floor until Barbara promised she would not see Maher again.

Barbara resented her mother's action for many years, and by her own admission only learned (about fifteen years later) to follow her brother's tack: present Fanny with a *fait accompli*. For, once Fanny realized that a child of hers could not be budged, she relented. Barbara had only to say: "If you love me, you'll accept it." Barbara Probst Solomon (who would meet Fanny and Barbara aboard a ship sailing to France in 1948) admired Fanny, "the Rock of the Ages," but she saw no mellowness in her. She was quite willing to break her daughter's heart in order to keep her sense of the family and of its values intact.

GOING TO WAR

After the long, anxious wait, going to war was something of a relief, even an anticlimax. At Fort Bragg, North Carolina, Mailer went around interviewing men about their sex lives. Taking notes already for his war novel, he acted so much like the professional that no one seemed to object to his questions or to find it odd that he did not talk about his own personal life. It was a nervy thing to do. He apparently played his Harvard background for all it was worth, though he did not announce his ambitions as a writer. He later described himself as "an arrogant nasty young man. I thought I knew everything."

The army took a terrible toll on Mailer. When Bea visited him in late March 1944 he "looked like a skeleton with his big ears sticking out." He had had diarrhea and was down to one hundred twenty-five pounds. In a group photograph of the 4th Platoon Battery taken at Fort Bragg on August 2, 1944, he still looks gaunt; all traces of adolescent plumpness are gone; his shirt is pressed smoothly against his hollow chest and flat stomach; his pants, obviously too big for him, are bunched up with a belt. He performed poorly in malaria-control training and on the infiltration course, handling the fire-control instruments clumsily and never really mastering the M1 carbine in firing practice. He had scored 147 on the Army IQ test, but he had to put up with the stupid sergeant who ruled his life. When Mailer's company was restricted to quarters because of dirty sheets (clean ones had not yet arrived), he discovered he could not reason with the sergeant about the matter. Mailer often misplaced some item such as a toothbrush at inspection and caused his outfit to be punished. They had to pick up after him—a grown man who was used to mothering and who felt "there wasn't anything I could do as well as anyone else." He kept to himself, reading voraciously and writing, and usually dragging his ass on various chores—though eventually he got the hang of it. If he could figure out a short cut (like finding a way to avoid most of the twenty-five mile hikes or sleeping in when he was supposed to be on the deck of his troop ship) he took it. One of his buddies, Clifford Maskovsky, observes that Mailer hated officers and always looked for ways to test "the system." He did not want to be encumbered by rank, for he had decided to write a novel that reflected war from the ground up. With his educational background he knew he would be around officers enough to understand their roles.

Mailer took pride in his map reading, but a soldier was not supposed to exhibit any skill. When Mailer blurted out the right answer in a map-reading class, he realized he had "fucked up completely. I'd broken the rules, and all the other guys turned around and glared at me." It had to remind him all over again of that nice Jewish boy, the "premature expert."

By January 1945 Mailer found himself in the Philippines on a mopping-up operation. This is where he met the men of the 112th Cavalry out of San Antonio, Texas. They were a tough crew of battle veterans, who did not think much of educated "Jewboys." Mailer, like the rest of his friends, had to stand constant abuse. "We can't all be poets," one officer sneered at him. Mailer's defense of himself was remarkable. He started to imitate the dialect of his Southern persecutors and actually developed a fondness for it, as he had for the snobbish tones of Harvard Yard. Adopting another dialect represented another way of identifying himself with the outside world and of integrating it into his own personality.

Mailer adjusted with the help of a new friend, Francis Irby Gwaltney, an Arkansan who also had aspirations as a novelist. Gwaltney liked Mailer's gentleness and regarded his friend's subsequent reputation for aggressiveness as a terrible burden to bear for a basically sensitive man who wrote his wife long letters four or five times a week and his mother shorter ones because he did not want to worry her. Gwaltney hated officers even more than Mailer did, and he could not abide their anti-Semitism. A much more physical man than Mailer, Gwaltney actually struck an officer once. He felt for his uncomfortable and inept army buddy but shared his lust for experience he could use as a writer.

Mailer's first job as a telephone lineman ended when the wire sergeant (feeling intimidated by his intelligence) got him reassigned. A poor typist, he was given another desk job as an interpreter of aerial photographs, getting a "general's eye view" of the war while he read Spengler's *Decline of the West* and *The Infantry Journal.*

Finally, Mailer got up his courage and requested a transfer to an intelligence and reconnaissance unit, so that he might see some real action. It was not an easy decision:

> *I was brought up on those war hero novels. Of course, all the war ideals you had were quickly lost about a week after you got into the Army. But all the time I was overseas I had these conflicting ideas—wanting, the way everyone else did, to get the softest, easiest job, to get by with the least pain—and also wanting to get into combat and see it. The only time I could make up my mind was the time I asked to go to Recon.*

Patrol in the Philippines meant slogging each day under a fierce sun with a heavy pack, having the runs, feeling chronically exhausted, suffering from jungle rot and viruses, certain that he would die, and no longer caring much what happened. He saw just enough action to feel he could write convincing war scenes. Gwaltney, who knew his friend could not see to shoot worth a damn, thought it was a miracle he survived the war.

AN EXERCISE IN HUMILITY

When the Pacific war ended on August 14, 1945, Mailer was shipped with the occupation forces to Japan. While Fanny fretted and wrote letters demanding that her son be sent home, he became a cook. It took Mailer a while to develop his technique for separating eggs, which consisted of breaking an egg, positioning it on a cutting board, then tilting the board as he edged the yoke with a meat cleaver, trying to prod it to roll down the incline away from the egg white.

Mailer and Gwaltney palled around and considered going to a brothel—an idea the Southerner took matter-of-factly while his friend worried—even writing Bea for permission, which she gave with the pointed comment that she would wait. In Gwaltney's memory, they made quite a pair, "looking a bit like high school seniors slipping into a burlesque house, Gwaltney spruce and towheaded, Mailer shy and runty."

Mailer's feelings were later summed up in a story, "The Language of Men" (1951)—about an army cook, Carter, lonely for his new bride and longing to go home—that contains one of Mailer's most nakedly autobiographical passages:

> *He became aware again of his painful desire to please people, to discharge responsibility, to be a man. When he had been a child, tears had come into his eyes at a cross word, and he had lived in an atmosphere where his smallest accomplishment was warmly praised. He was the sort of young man, he often thought bitterly, who was accustomed to the attention and the protection of women.*

Mailer later said that he was "a modest young man" when the war was over, having realized his four years of taking himself seriously at Harvard did not do much for him after the army had shown him he had "little to offer next to the practical sense of an illiterate sharecropper." A rite of passage, a declaration of manhood, had turned into an exercise in humility.

THE BOOK OF A YOUNG ENGINEER

Mailer got out of the army in May 1946 with the scaled-down ambition of writing a short novel about a patrol, having gotten the notion from books such as John Hersey's *Into the Valley* and Harry Brown's *A Walk in the Sun*. He began with a chapter introducing the characters, and soon chapters accumulated, with the author becoming annoyed at how long it took him to get to the patrol. In two months of writing in a bungalow in Provincetown, Massachusetts, he had a total of about two hundred pages: fifty thousand words. He worked methodically every day, compiling a huge dossier for each character and other files full of notes. There were even charts keeping track of characters and scenes. As Mailer later noted, it was "the book of a young engineer" who made sure everything was welded and riveted securely into place. He liked to create workrooms for himself, small enclosed spaces where he could shut a door and feel entirely alone with his book. Bea observed his absolute devotion to a rigid schedule as he added data about his characters to index cards that he would shuffle when he needed to alter the structure of his novel.

At the end of the summer they moved back to Brooklyn, finding a two-room apartment on Remsen Street just around the corner from his parents' apartment building. Conditions were rather crowded, so he located a garret down the block where he could write about twenty-five pages of first draft each week.

As usual, not only Mailer but his sister concentrated on his work. Many of Barbara's classmates at Radcliffe, including Alice Adams and Alison Lurie, who would become writers themselves, would hear about her "wonderful" brother. Attending a party in late 1946, Lurie noted that Norman seemed so joyous and such a contrast to the gloomy writers she had known. Next to Norman and Bea, Barbara seemed "subdued." To Mark Linenthal, who returned to Harvard after the war, Barbara (who was living in the Co-op), seemed a "quiet, serious girl" who lived by her brother's values.

Barbara might be content with this subservient role. Bea was not. A brash Adeline Lubell Naiman, a recent Radcliffe graduate, persuaded Little, Brown to give her a job as an editor. Naiman then arranged a tea party at which Norman would be present. She wanted him to meet a friend of hers at *Harper's Bazaar* who might be interested in writing about him. Naiman found Bea a "disappointment." Absorbed in discussion with Norman, Naiman realized that Bea resented the lack of attention. Even then, before the great success of *The Naked and the Dead*, Bea impressed Naiman as angry, although later she was sympathetic to an accomplished woman who must have found the lionizing of her husband tiresome. At the same time, Naiman thought of Bea as "so wrapped up in herself" that she probably did not see other women as "competition."

Bea, beginning to be overwhelmed by the size of her husband's ambition and discipline, decided to write a novel herself. Fanny, among others, interpreted such actions as just another sign of Bea's competitive and divisive nature, which Fanny deemed a family trait. In retrospect, Fanny took a very tough attitude toward Bea and her family. Although she praised Bea's mother as a "bright, capable woman," she criticized her for not being more of a "mother and housewife." As Fanny put it, there was "no binding attraction" between Bea's parents, no real love, which was, in Fanny's view, what made a family thrive. Instead, Bea's mother sought "the limelight" and was "very aggressive, more than Bea even." Of the whole Silverman family, Fanny commented: "Everybody pulled in a different direction." Fanny's niece Osie claims no one in the Mailer family really liked Bea, not even Barney. Fanny called Bea the "world's worst housekeeper," who liked to surround herself with "*dreck*" and who "never planned for anything."

When Alice Adams visited Bea's family in Chelsea, Massachusetts, she met Bea's mother, who was "fat and rather noisy and awfully nice to me." Mr. Silverman left no impression at all. To Adams, the recent talk about Bea's shrillness seems "revisionary." She found Bea relatively "liberated," although Adams cites Bea's reference to herself as a *natansika*, Yiddish for "someone who dances behind."

Others thought that Bea tried to identify with her husband's work. When the talk turned to writing, however, she found it difficult to be as articulate as Norman, and she has subsequently confessed that all the attention paid to him shook her confidence in herself. On several occasions she tried to counter his influence by acting drunk and showing off on the dance floor. Her political pronouncements were also becoming more strident, as if in compensation for the fact that her role in the marriage was becoming decidedly more passive. Usually her husband shrugged off her outbursts; she still seemed to have a magnetic power over him. Adeline Lubell Naiman thought Norman was sexually addicted to Bea and that she was the "first real woman" who had made it possible for him to fulfill his fantasies. Like Fanny, Bea abetted Norman's hunger for fame. The two women would sit through many evenings as he read passages from his manuscript.

Having abandoned the idea of writing only about a long patrol, Mailer faced the prospect of editing a huge manuscript. He wrote to Gwaltney, exaggerating his predicament: What was he going to do with three hundred thousand words, half of which were "fuck piss cock shit cunt. Nothing more painful than reading your own crap." Later Mailer would say that he never actually used the word *fuck* in his manuscript.

During the editing, Norman turned to his cousin Cy for help, showing him sections of manuscript. Cy picked on the novel's first sentence: "Nobody could sleep on the night before the invasion of Anopopei." The opening was cumbersome, not direct enough, and Norman tried to say too much. To Cy, it sounded like a bad lead in a newspaper story. How about, instead, something much simpler: "Nobody could sleep."

The very brevity of the statement would launch readers into the scene. Norman adopted Cy's suggestion at a lunch meeting, where they also came up with the idea of using *fug* instead of *fuck*, since Cy (already acting as Norman's attorney) thought that stronger language might provoke prosecution for obscenity.

It was characteristic of Mailer to seek literary and legal assistance within his family. To Shirley Fingerhood, who worked for Cy Rembar, Mailer and Rembar were more like brothers than cousins. Cy was the family attorney, handling contracts, watching Mailer's money, and representing a nursing agency Fanny had started.

For additional help on his manuscript Mailer turned to a new friend, Charles Devlin, a "black Irishman" who had a room in the building where Mailer wrote his novel. Although he never became a published writer himself, Devlin had an incisive mind and knew just where to cut the bloated manuscript and to sharpen and rearrange scenes for maximum dramatic impact. He could be honest to the point of cruelty, but Mailer admired him for precisely that quality. A professional himself, Mailer asked for nothing less than the truth about his book.

Another writer/friend, Norman Rosten, who lived on Remsen, commiserated with Mailer over the difficulties in getting published. Mailer used to say to him, "Hey, I've got to hang on to you. You're the guy who's been published." With two books of poetry in print, Rosten seemed to have a leg up on his contemporaries, Mailer and Arthur Miller, both of whom lived for a while in the same building. "They used to scowl at each other," discounting each other's talent, thinking (as Mailer later admitted in *Marilyn*) that the other guy would not amount to much. Rosten remembers it with a laugh: "They both have a sort of distrust of the rest of humankind that's in their work." To the cheerful Rosten, they were a "grumbly, suspicious" pair, although he found Mailer a likable and lively companion, a somewhat softer personality in the days before fame overcame him.

Mailer eagerly accepted Rosten's offer to introduce *The Naked and the Dead* to Ted Amussen, his editor at Rinehart. "Let's go and see him," Rosten remembers saying, "and the thing I like to remember about it is that we went on the subway holding the manuscript in boxes—I had half of it, he had half of it."

Actually, Mailer knew Amussen, who had expressed considerable interest in Mailer's earlier work but had not published it. This time, however, the editor, with the backing of the firm's head, Stanley

Rinehart, signed the author to a contract with a $1250 advance, considered quite large for a first novel. Mailer gloated over its acceptance, having gone through an agonizing period with Little, Brown during which various editors had caviled at the book's strong language. Amussen also considered Bea's novel, but she never bothered to make the revisions he suggested and shortly thereafter she abandoned the thought of becoming a published writer. By August 1947 with the editing of *The Naked and the Dead* completed, Norman and Bea prepared to set off for Paris to study at the Sorbonne, having saved money and taken advantage of their hundred-dollar-a month allotment under the GI Bill of Rights.

VIRTUES & VICES, LUSTS AND FRUSTRATIONS

In *The Naked and the Dead*, Mailer picked up almost exactly where he left off in "A Calculus at Heaven" while also returning to the theme of power and brutality that had bedeviled him in *A Transit to Narcissus*. The novel follows the fortunes of several soldiers, many of them clearly modeled after the author's army buddies. There is, for example, Wilson, the easygoing Texan who loves to drink and screw. Any number of Southerners could have served as Mailer's inspiration, although the stereotype is so broadly presented that it need hardly have been taken from life. Joey Goldstein reminded Gwaltney of Isidore Feldman, a Jew from St. Louis whom Mailer admired for his physical dexterity and strength and derided for his lack of imagination and Jewish insularity. Gwaltney thought that Mailer had put more than a little of himself into another Jew, Roth, who dislikes dwelling on Jewishness. Roth is college-educated and feels he is above ethnic considerations. He is also full of self-pity, complaining that his CCNY degree has not helped secure the good employment he deserves. Other characters—like Gallagher, the anti-Semitic Boston Irishman—derive from Farrell and other fiction Mailer had read. But Sergeant Croft, another Texan, has a meanness and intimidating force that comes directly out of the terror Mailer felt as a private.

The cast of characters in the platoon is an impressive geographical and ethnic study of America, of its "virtues & vices, lusts and frustrations," as Mailer put it in a letter to Gwaltney. It is also derivative (he admitted) of Dos Passos and other literary lights in his pantheon. What makes the novel come alive is the interaction between the characters as they try to drive behind the Toyaku line and prepare for a two-pronged attack that will annihilate the enemy. When they pit themselves against nature on the Japanese-held island of Anopopei, there is a sense of fate, of the irremediable nature of things that makes Mailer's prose, for the first time, grapple with a theme that is larger than the sum of his characters:

> Far in the distance they could see Mount Anaka rising above the island. It arched coldly and remotely from the jungle beneath it, lofting itself massively into the low-hanging clouds of the sky. In the early drab twilight it looked like an immense old gray elephant erecting himself somberly on his front legs, his haunches lost in the green bedding of his lair. The mountain seemed wise and powerful, and terrifying in its size.

The long patrol of a platoon, however, could not bear the weight of the great themes Mailer wished to introduce into his fiction. How to treat the army as an institution and the geopolitical significance of the war? In a second draft, a suggestion from Ted Amussen stimulated Mailer to add the officers, Lieutenant Robert Hearn and General Edward Cummings. Amussen had advised Mailer to make Lieutenant Brook (Hearn's precursor) "wealthier," and this is where Mailer got the "initial push" that resulted in the scenes between Hearn and Cummings. "And with Lieutenant Brook the book would not be getting good reviews now," Mailer insisted to Amussen, who reluctantly agreed to have his name mentioned in Mailer's acknowledgements.

Hearn is a Harvard man. Before the war he follows a routine in his first college year that is remarkably like Mailer's, spending "nearly all his afternoons in lab and his nights studying. He makes himself a schedule which charts everything down to the fifteen minutes he can allow himself to read the comic pages on Sunday morning, and the movie he can see on Saturday night." Hearn is stimulated by the literature he reads in the second half of his freshman year, even absorbing the same smells of the *Advocate* office—"of old furniture and old prints and the malty odor of empty beer cans in the aged rooms of the magazine"—that Mailer would later write about in a reminiscence.

Hearn, however, is more assertive and disenchanted than the Mailer professors at Harvard remember. One episode in the novel is based on Harry Levin's comparative literature course Mailer attended from time to time. In the novel, the lecturer describes the "deep significance" of the number seven to Thomas Mann in *The Magic Mountain*. Hans Castrop spends several years on the mountain; the first seven days in the novel are "given great emphasis." Most of the major characters, the lecturer points out, have seven letters in their name. An impatient Hearn, observing his fellow students piously taking notes, speaks up, calls the novel a "pompous bore," condemns its "German didacticness," and the "critical claptrap" it inspires—which leaves him "unmoved."

Years later, at a party, Levin confronted Mailer with this episode and told him that if he had spoken up as Hearn did, Levin would have agreed with him, for Levin did not care for Mann's numerology either. Mailer's reply amused Levin: "Okay, now it's your turn to take a crack at me."

Most striking is Hearn's emptiness and search for a new identity:

> *He has lived in a vacuum for eighteen years, cloyed by the representative and unique longings of any youth; he has come into the shattering new world of college and spent two years absorbing, sloughing off shells, putting out feelers.*

Hearn has had no experience commensurate with his longing to be an original and a rebel. He is aloof and (like most of Mailer's heroes up to this point) chary of being marked, of getting involved in the fate of others.

Hearn also has Mailer's scorn for authority. Like Bowen Hilliard in "A Calculus at Heaven," Hearn's prewar experience has been a record of failure: He has been unable to connect with other people or to live by his liberal principles. His superior, General Cummings, detects in Hearn a contempt for his fellow man that is a kind of incipient fascism. The authoritarian Cummings suggests that Hearn, stripped of his liberal cant, would in fact like to exercise power. The brutality of the army and its disregard of the individual is actually compatible with Hearn's arrogant personal attitudes, which are not much different from Paul Scarr's.

Mailer has acknowledged putting a part of himself in Hearn, the educated liberal bucking authority and identifying with the common soldier, wanting to be a part of the army, looking upon it as a test of his manhood but also acknowledging that it has brutalized him. When Hearn rebels against Cummings, deliberately mashing his cigarette on the immaculate floor of the General's tent, he is put in charge of a platoon—an assignment he welcomes but that puts him into conflict with men he must now discipline on a risky mission behind Japanese lines.

It is Hearn's conceit that he can mold his platoon into a unity of purpose without resorting to the tyranny of authority Cummings has applied to him. But he quickly finds himself isolated, for the men have become used to the harsh rule of their sergeant, Sam Croft, who maneuvers Hearn into an ambush in order to regain control of the platoon. The abruptness of Hearn's death recalls Mailer's first imaginative depiction of war in 1939, which is repeated in *A Transit to Narcissus*. Hearn is moving out of a hollow in the early morning, feeling he has overcome the dejection of the previous night, and enjoying himself: "A half hour later, Lieutenant Hearn was killed by a machine gun bullet which passed through his chest."

In creating Hearn, Mailer faced the possibility of his own death, that he would be ground up in the mechanisms of war, his life cut off suddenly, a victim of the long rise and quick fall of the tragic curve that Cummings has been reading about in Spengler's *The Decline of the West*. As Cummings speculates, "The fall is always more rapid than the rise. And isn't that the curve of tragedy; I should think it a sound aesthetic principle that the growth of a character should take longer to accomplish than his disaster."

Several critics have noticed Mailer's curious affinity for Cummings, the grand strategist. As Philip Bufithis remarks:

> The general sitting alone at night in his tent mapping out his attack strategy while the bivouacked men outside idly chatter and complain symbolizes Mailer's conception of himself as the cloistered artist. He identifies his own struggle to forge a novel from a collection of uncorrelated ideas and imaginings with Cummings' brooding efforts to design a battle plan from the diverse elements of a tired obstinate army. Cummings' mind—like the artist's—is demiurgic, for it recombines and reshapes the phenomena of raw reality to engender a meaningful, living, new reality. The creative will makes from lumpen formlessness vital form. General Cummings represents, then, Mailer's self-projection of himself as the romantic artist convinced that he is possessed of the ability to recreate the world.

Part of Cummings's power as an "artist" stems from his transcendence of his sterile Midwestern roots and the provinciality of family life. He has grown up profoundly influenced by his mother, who encourages and protects him even as he steels himself to follow his father's injunction to be a man and leave the maternal home. With his broad vision, Cummings is also markedly devoid of sympathy for others—as though his self-contained emotions are requisite to his exercise of power. He must stifle the woman in himself—as Mailer had to do, as the other soldiers in the novel do. The men in *The Naked and the Dead* are not fully human because they have trouble integrating their male and female sides. Red Valsen, for example, finds it impossible to commit himself in marriage to the woman he lives with or to express his love for her, for he associates home life with the diminution of the independent male self. Consequently, he feels isolated and unable to believe in any positive course of action for himself. In general, the men distrust women, cheat on them, and accuse them of betrayal. Women stand for all that is unstable, unreliable, and insubstantial. The worst insult Croft can think to hurl at his men is that they are "a bunch of women."

Cummings's aversion to human contact is similar to Paul Scarr's dread of physical contact and Croft's dislike of being touched. The result, as Andrew Gordon has noticed, is a novel with a very "narrow emotional range." While some of the men are capable of momentarily feeling for each other, the overwhelming mood—as in *A Transit to Narcissus*—is one of self-absorption. Not merely a novel about how the military machine crushes the human spirit, *The Naked and the Dead*, in Gordon's words, "seems to correspond not so much to the reality of masculine relationships as to the author's own psychological reality."

A BOY SCOUT AND A WRITER OF
UNMISTAKABLE IMPORTANCE

On October 1, 1947, Mailer turned in his revised manuscript to Rinehart, attended a family farewell party at his mother's apartment, and set sail with Bea on the *Queen Elizabeth* for Europe. Aboard ship he wrote to Gwaltney, complaining about English food, the dreariness, and all the patriotic talk. He was feeling rather ornery, and it upset him that Bea was sleeping. She was no longer exciting in bed, and he speculated that no couple could live together very long without boring each other.

He was so out of sorts that he even took after his hero Hemingway, making fun of the delicate bedroom dialogue in the novels and comparing it to the "grunts and curses" that punctuated his intercourse with Bea. The trouble with Hemingway, he confided to Gwaltney, was that "he never had a decent fuck in his life." His own novel was still very much on his mind. It was an "antiwar job," he told his friend, with a general as his heavy, a "beaut of a villain—a homo, a reactionary, a sadist." He was expecting to be branded a Red and worse things, but the name he gave to himself was Jew Radical.

"The chances are that there's not a single general in the U.S. Army who's like him," Mailer later admitted when asked about a real-life model for Cummings, but the author maintained that Cummings represented a position that had its adherents in the American military. In fact, the year Mailer spent writing *The Naked and the Dead* had been, in Bea's word, "scary." With tensions between Russia and America already high, it seemed probable there would be another war. Heavily influenced by Henry Wallace's speeches calling for an accommodation with Russia, Mailer feared that war would seem like a welcome solution to the frustrations of diplomacy. He thought of himself as an anarchist whose army experience had soured him on any kind of collective action. He had come back from war far less idealistic and somewhat cynical about human affairs. His mother believed a "certain kindness, his softness" had been lost in the war, and some of his army buddies agree that he was scarred and rather caustic as a result of his service.

During the fall of 1947 Norman and Bea found a one-room, Murphy-bed apartment with a dark, high, metal-embossed ceiling in the quiet, reserved Hôtel de l'Avenir at 65 rue Madame, within walking distance of the Sorbonne. Mailer admired the city's beauty, but it lacked "juice." It was still recovering from the war and experiencing shortages with a somberness he found hard tough to take, especially since he did not have the challenge of a novel to occupy his time. The weak electricity affected the lighting and put a dim cast over everything. He longed for the "ballsy kind of noise and size and excitement of America." At first, it seemed incredibly cheap but also very lonely.

Moving from the hotel, the Mailers found a furnished apartment on the Left Bank for twenty-four dollars a month. It was dusty; it had mice but also a piano, which pleased Bea. With a living room, den, and bedroom, the apartment was bigger than their Remsen Street flat. The bathroom had a toilet and sink; the bathtub was in the kitchen, where on their first bath together they were nearly asphyxiated by the gas water heater. They much preferred going to the public baths once a week as the Parisians did.

"We were all living on the Left Bank and trying to relive the twenties" of Hemingway and Fitzgerald, Stanley Karnow recalls about his Harvard classmates:

> *Mailer was a lot different from us. He was very diligent—a guy who was a real writer. There was a workmanlike quality about him. We knew about his novel,* The Naked and the Dead. . . . *One of the things that struck me was the middle class quality of his life. We were all living in cheap hotels without bathrooms, eating in dumpy bistros and so forth. He was married and living comfortably in an apartment. He seemed a lot older and a lot more stable.*

Karnow remembers that Mailer liked to consort with people like Stanley Geist, an erudite friend with a "no kidding quality"—who struck Karnow as perhaps having an ambition to become the next Edmund Wilson. Bea seemed very much devoted to her husband and in the background.

Geist, a Harvard graduate a few years older than Mailer, was impressed with the fact that Mailer was "a little less stuck on literary mythology than other people." He introduced Mailer to French novelist Jean Malaquais, who quickly became one of Mailer's mentors.

Mailer had no intention of becoming an expatriate or of trying to relive the life of Hemingway and other writers of the 1920s. He was intensely interested in contemporary affairs. Mark Linenthal, who had been a navigator on a bomber shot down by the Nazis and who had been put in a Nazi prison camp, fascinated Mailer with a perspective on war different from his own. Though Mailer was, like other Americans, intrigued with Sartre and Simone de Beauvoir, he showed no evidence of having read these authors, and it would be some years before he would develop his own brand of existentialism.

Alice Adams remembers that her husband, Mark Linenthal, brought the Mailers home one day after registering for classes at the Sorbonne. Adams noted Norman's "apologetic" tone about their maid: "Of course I wouldn't let Bea have a maid if I didn't know she could handle it all herself," he remarked to Adams. Both Norman and Bea were trying to pick up French, and to Adams Bea seemed the more successful of the two, becoming in her use of French "elegant and rather haughty, less proletarian whereas in English she made a point of being vulgar." The Mailers seemed "extremely happy" to Adams, with Bea quite content to play the housewife.

Stanley Karnow's friend Kenneth Lynn remembers that "there were a whole bunch of us from Harvard in Paris that year and we saw one another frequently." Although not a close friend of Mailer, Lynn had a few friends who were, and he and Mailer met several times at parties, lunches, and dinners. Lynn recounts that Mailer seemed to be very interested in politics but knew little about it: "He said to me, 'The other day you said that millions of Soviet citizens had died in a forced collectivization of the Ukraine. How do you know that?' He had never heard this idea before. He was staggered by it."

Lynn was surprised, in turn, having known about it for half his life. How could Mailer not know this and yet still be interested in politics? To Lynn it seemed naive—not self-deluding but just "plain ignorant."

Lynn found Mailer a "very nice guy" and even "gentle." Bea had very sexy legs, in Lynn's estimation, and was "very conscious of her sexuality." Mailer gave Lynn the galleys of *The Naked and the Dead*, and Lynn took note of the "demonic, crack the whip sexuality of it. This nice easygoing guy had some deeper currents in him." The sexuality and the frank talk, however, "was sort of the style of all of us," Lynn points out: "Men and women alike—as opposed to the way we talked in Cambridge—were all into 'shit, piss, fuck.' " Mailer was not much of a drinker in Lynn's memory of those days:

> *I never saw any hand wrestling—these Hemingwayesque signs.* The Naked and the Dead *seemed to me then, and seems to me now, very indebted to Dos Passos, and we talked about Dos Passos. He wanted to talk about Melville and* Moby Dick. *Hemingway's name would have come up, of course, because of the Paris setting, but he did not bulk very large. The idea that Norman Mailer was a vest pocket Hemingway—I would not have said that of him.*

Mailer might have seemed older than his Harvard friends, but in fact he was about the same age as most of them and just as concerned about his relative lack of worldly experience. Compared to Hemingway and Fitzgerald and a whole previous generation of writers, "we were all second hand in Paris and always conscious of it," Lynn concludes. If even Dos Passos, a well-traveled man, had failed to encompass the country in his trilogy *U.S.A.*, then how could Mailer hope at his age to do it? Lynn wondered. He suspected that sex loomed so large in *The Naked and the Dead* because Mailer did not know "fuck-all about anything else."

Mailer's grasp of politics and of the novel he had just written began to change under the mentorship of Jean Malaquais, the novelist and Marxist who would later translate *The Naked and the Dead* not out of any love for its style but, frankly, for the money. At first, Mailer was put off by his new acquaintance, for Malaquais regarded Mailer as terribly naive, something like a "Boy Scout or a young kibbutznik." Mailer, on the other hand, told his wife that Malaquais was "one of those arrogant, cocky Frenchmen." Mailer did not want to hear from Malaquais that the Wallace campaign was a sham, infiltrated by Stalinists, and hardly the harbinger of a new political order.

Yet Mailer seemed mesmerized by the vigor and subtlety of Malaquais's thought. Malaquais could anticipate and formulate an opponent's position as deftly as his own with a power that made "the veins in his forehead . . . throb as though to demonstrate that the human head was obliged to be the natural site if not the very phallus of Mind." A very masculine figure with his "rugged face and mighty brow," he tore apart both Mailer's style and his politics.

Rather than attend his classes at the Sorbonne, Mailer preferred to be schooled in Malaquais's European interpretations of the war, which destroyed his young protégé's anarchism and made him take an interest in societal institutions. To Malaquais, Mailer seemed "eager, touching, romantic" and rather "uncouth"—a Brooklyn boy who could not speak French but who endeared himself to Malaquais by coining a French phrase and then mimicking himself.

After a year in Paris, Mailer wrote Norman Rosten in his usual bantering fashion asking why he should "waste a postcard" on him. They were too expensive now that "all the fucking Americans are here and the stores want a hundred dollars for a Picasso original." Mailer blamed this changed state of affairs on "Marshall Plan imperialism." Switching to a discussion of *The Naked and the Dead*, Mailer told Rosten he knew it was a "Marxist book." Everyone was writing to tell him so, even though he was an anarchist when he wrote it. "Naturally, I'm too fucking stupid to know," Mailer concluded. He disagreed with Rosten's assessment that the novel was too long. Rosten had been swayed by editors too much, Mailer pointed out. This is an argument Rosten remembers, for Mailer often urged him to listen to his "inner voice." In his letter, Mailer argued in favor of long books. Even the "boring sections of a work gave depth and verisimilitude." Mailer was not writing to beat *Time* magazine deadlines. "Go cut your own stuff. I'm spreading myself around," he wrote Rosten. Then he concluded the letter with a typical, tender flourish: "Thanks for the picture of Patty [Rosten's daughter]. In twenty years when I am cynical and sick, due to the contradictions of the capitalistic, acquisitive society, I shall look her up as something sweet and fresh and lovely."

When the galleys for *The Naked and the Dead* arrived, the Mailers developed a game in which Bea played the easygoing Southerner, Wilson, and Norman played the sadist Croft. They went so far as acting specific scenes, with Norman enjoying the opportunity to run around, yell, and bully everyone like a "southern son of a bitch." At times like this, Norman and Bea seemed very close, and the worrisome evidence that she was beginning to find his growing celebrity a trial faded in importance. If he could be truculent, she could be the commissar, dismissing him with phrases like "Tough shit, Norman" and "Don't be ridiculous." She acted like his equal and sort of like his conscience.

In April 1948, Fanny and Barbara arrived in Paris. They would be joined soon by Barney, who had been working for two months as an accountant in Poland for a Jewish relief agency. Barbara Probst Solomon, who got to know Fanny and Barbara Mailer on the ship, met Norman and Bea on the Cherbourg dock and was struck by "how close they were." To her it "seemed a wonderful marriage." If anything, Bea seemed more intimidating than Norman, but they were a perfectly mated twosome. "I've never seen Norman with any of his wives act so 'couple-y' again," Solomon asserts. Soon, however, Solomon saw Bea's "overbearing" and "competitive" side and her attempts to cut him down to size, as though she were saying, "I'm the butcher's daughter, the smartest girl on the block" who would shape up Norman, "the spoiled boy."

Of course, it would not be easy for any of Norman's women to please Fanny. Adeline Lubell Naiman, who roomed at Radcliffe with Bea's sister Phyllis, got to know Fanny well and to love her. "Everything she said struck me with absolute delight," Naiman recalls. As "the nice Jewish girl," Naiman became one of Fanny's favorites, but Naiman is quick to say that Fanny never understood Bea and probably liked

Naiman so well because "I was no threat to Norman's marriage or to her ownership of Norman."

Mark Linenthal liked Barney and Fanny when they visited Norman and Bea in Paris. The were "welcoming . . . and very *en famille*, though they weren't totally approving of Bea, which surprised me." According to Linenthal, Mailer would sometimes criticize Bea in his parents' presence just to get them to defend her. Alice Adams, on the other hand, believed Bea and Barbara shared a real "sisterliness."

Writing to Ted Amussen on May 10, 1948, Mailer noted that his life in Paris was "getting too enjoyable." He feared the possibility that he could spend five years there "without any pain at all." So he and Bea had arranged their "own little deus ex machina in the form of a steamship passage in August." Mailer knew that the world had changed for them that spring when his novel received glowing reviews and a well-organized advertising campaign. Although he had expected recognition, he was dumbfounded at finding his work at the top of the best-seller list. At first the news from New York provoked much hilarity. While he fancied his work as "the greatest book written since *War and Peace*" he did not really take himself that seriously and wondered whether he had somehow cheated in writing the book to make it more palatable for a popular audience.

There was a happy, exhilarating moment—just before the full force of Mailer's fame hit them—when Fanny, Barbara, Bea, and Norman took off for a trip to Switzerland by car (Dave Kessler had wired money for its purchase). In the early summer of 1948 they crossed the Alps to Como, Italy. Bea remembers that as they maneuvered through one "particularly precarious mountain pass," Fanny cried, "If anyone ever told me I'd be crazy enough to come on this trip, I would have told them it was impossible."

Shortly after this trip Barney, usually so self-contained and modest, said to Bea one evening in Paris: "You're going back to America, Norman's going to be famous, and you're going to have a lot of competition." According to Barbara Probst Solomon, "Bea paled visibly." For good measure, Barney advised her to improve her wardrobe and cultivate a more "glamorous" look.

Yet in Paris Mailer felt as though he was just beginning to learn how to write. He knew next to nothing about style, even though *Newsweek* and other magazines were hailing him as "a writer of unmistakable importance." He wanted to believe the good reviews, but he felt like "a bit of an imposter." Success gave him enormous energy, but much of it was wasted because there seemed to be nothing left to write about: "My life seemed to have been mined and melted into the long reaches of the book." Characteristically, he thought of his predicament in terms of having to create a conflict—another long patrol—in which he would break through to a new identity:

> *Success had been a lobotomy to my past, there seemed no power from the past which could help me in the present, and I had no choice but to force myself to step into the war of the enormous present, to accept the private heat and fatigue of setting out by myself to cut a track through a new wild.*

It was not surprising, then, that in his next novel he would create a narrator who literally cannot remember his past and who has to create out of the materials of the present a whole new style of life.

3.

BARBARY SHORE (1948–1951)

ROUGH TIMES FOR LITTLE NORMIE

Before Norman and Bea left Paris for New York in the summer of 1948, Norman had a taste of celebrity. An American student cornered him, asking a lot of boring questions. It made the novelist uneasy. Having met this same student a few weeks earlier at the Sorbonne, this new encounter had a "sinister" quality for Mailer, as if he was being spied upon. He wanted to be recognized and would enjoy the attention accorded him on his return to the States, but he was uncomfortable with the feeling that he was now a part of other people's fantasies and that they might be responding to an image of him that was nowhere near the mark. Writing to Gwaltney about this incident, Mailer was at pains to sound as though nothing had changed, referring to himself as "your old ass-hole buddy" and suggesting to Gwaltney's wife, Ecey, that she should not stand in "awe" of him since her husband could "probably beat the shit out of him."

Mailer worked at keeping his life unpretentious, returning in midsummer to the same Brooklyn attic where he had written *The Naked and the Dead*. To Bea, "Norman was always living out his bohemian fantasies."

To him, it was surely a way of remaining grounded in where he had come from. That fall he seemed "new and fresh" and still naive to fellow novelist Calder Willingham, who met him for the first time. Mailer dressed very casually for most occasions, showing up without jacket or tie, in a "faded tan sports shirt, baggy pants, and scuffed shoes" for the party his publisher threw for him. One interviewer claimed "it was still possible to see the traces of an earnest adolescent" on the twenty-five-year-old novelist's face.

The interviews, the parties, the reviews were overwhelming and seemed "unreal" to a writer who had not yet figured out what to do next. Accustomed to being an observer, now he had to delight and to entertain an audience. He wanted to believe the great reviews, but it embarrassed him to be treated like "a movie queen," and he refused to be photographed for *Life* magazine, declaring it was "much better when people who read your book don't know anything about you, even what you look like." He made light of his distress but also allowed himself a rather telling remark about his self-image: "These are rough times for little Normie."

Rough times as well for Bea. According to Norman's cousin Osie, on the return to New York from Paris, Bea tried to back out of this new world, objecting to Norman's seeing the reporters who were waiting for him and generally sulking over his celebrity.

The Mailers coped with fame by visiting the Gwaltneys. August in Arkansas proved a relief from the limelight. In fact, the Gwaltneys were impressed by how little Mailer had to say about his fame. Norman acted like he wanted to be one of the boys and would go out to toss a ball with a neighborhood kid. He relaxed by going stream fishing, playing cards, and just loafing around the house. This new country appealed to Norman, who responded well to Fig's challenge to climb a tree—although Ecey thought the two men acted like little boys. She remembers how aggressive Norman got on one occasion while they were drinking and playing cards, slapping them down, snapping at Fig, and "goading" him. Fig, usually such a cool character, started to say, "Well, you goddammed—" and abruptly halted. "Go ahead and say it, go ahead," Norman rejoined. Very slowly Fig said, "Jew." Ecey regarded this incident as a test, in which Norman kept boring away at his friend, trying to get at the rawest and deepest feelings that were hidden by his smooth exterior.

On a cotton plantation Norman seemed embarrassed by a girl in a shabby dress whose pubic hair was visible between the buttons. In college he had written a story about exploited cotton-pickers; these people seemed to live relatively pleasant lives with their small homes and neat gardens. Yet Southern manners troubled him. He could not understand why they were polite even to the people they disliked. He also detected a meanness in Southern faces. They were "scary" and "hard" and intolerant. Southerners could be just as rude as curt Northerners. For example, drawling out an expression like "W–e–l–l, I don't know 'bout that" was just "a kind of insolent, *slow* arrogance." Norman made these observations, however, in a spirit of discovery and had much praise for the peacefulness and stability of the land. He liked to practice his Southern accent, announcing, "I think I've got it figured out. All you have to do is put 'little ol'' in front of everything—'That little ol'' chair, this little ol' plant." Bea did not like the idea of her husband going Southern: "Norman, they think fucking is a sin," she reminded him.

Sharp-tongued Bea usually deferred to her husband, but she came out with startling remarks: "Oh, Norman, you look like a jerk with your glasses on." She seemed totally uninhibited, and her profanity shocked Ecey. When one of Ecey's friends complimented Bea on her pretty eyes, Bea replied, "What the fuck, you do too." When Bea suffered from a stomach upset, she complained, "My asshole hurts." Ecey suspected that Bea reveled in startling people, and Norman (who did a much better job of controlling his cursing) humored her and made no scenes. The Gwaltneys might have been taken aback by Bea, but Fig later claimed they loved her for her strong character. She seemed "somehow both vulgar and innocent" when she dressed for bed and asked, "Norm, do you want to fuck me tonight?" She had a "devilish and healthy" smile.

Back in New York by the end of August, Mailer announced in an interview with the New York *Star* a change in his politics. *The Naked and the Dead*, he suggested, was "negative" in the sense that it had been written by an anarchist who deeply distrusted all organizations. He had worked in isolation in a Brooklyn room and had a grasp of politics no more profound than what he could get out of the newspapers. Now he believed in "collective action." He had decided to join the Henry Wallace presidential campaign, which had staked out an accommodating stance toward the Soviet Union, rejecting the Cold War positions of both President Truman and the Republican candidate Thomas Dewey. Like many of Wallace's Progressive Party members, Mailer seemed much tougher on his own country's foreign policy than on the Soviet Union's:

> *Italy is pretty bad right now, a pretty ugly country. The Marshall Plan definitely is keeping in power the smartest, dirtiest, old-time politicians, the broken-down aristocracy that would normally have been kicked out. Italy would be better off under communism than under the kind of very bad capitalism they have there. You don't have to be a Communist to see that.*
>
> *About France and England, I don't know. As far as the countries of eastern Europe go—like Poland, where they had one fascist dictator after another—they're better off. Czechoslovakia—I don't know what the score is there.*

Mailer's shifting political attitudes could best be characterized at this point as those of a fellow traveler, for he apparently had little idea of Stalinist terror or of how preposterous his comments on Eastern Europe were. Like many fellow travelers of his time, he saw the Soviet Union as the great antifascist bulwark.

By October 23 Mailer had made eighteen speeches for Wallace and planned to give another dozen. A poor speaker, he usually faltered nervously through his public appearances. On a two-week campaign swing through Hollywood, Mailer made a rather disheveled impression in casual shirt and slacks, untied shoe laces, and socks that always seemed to be around his ankles. Shelley Winters liked his unassuming quality. He enjoyed himself, he wrote Gwaltney, even though Los Angeles seemed to him the "ugliest city in the world."

In October Mailer met Mickey Knox, a guest at Gene Kelly's house. Knox, an actor from Brooklyn, "hit it off immediately" with Mailer, and the two became friends and later collaborators on a screenplay. Knox, in fact, was one of the few people in Hollywood Mailer got to know well, although he met the big names such as John Huston, Fredric March, and Humphrey Bogart. Knox remembers a Mailer nervous about speaking at Wallace rallies and unconcerned about his appearance. "For Christ's sakes, Norm, wear socks over your calf," an irritated Knox would say as he watched Mailer constantly pulling them up.

"Norman was very full of himself," one of his acquaintances at the time puts it. At a Progressive Party rally in Yankee Stadium an excited

Mailer turned to his companion and said, "When they put the spotlight on me, I'm going to stand up and say that I'm joining the Communist Party tomorrow." He said nothing of the sort when the spotlight turned to him, but his mood typified his flamboyant attitude. On occasion, Mailer could be quite "volatile." At a party a German journalist made a disparaging remark to a French woman about how he remembered French women during the German occupation of France, and "Norman hit the ceiling and really lit into the guy. It was very nice to watch. He was full of spirit."

Mailer's politics underwent substantial changes between August and October 1948. Wallace failed to catch fire with the public, and Mailer slowly and reluctantly heeded Malaquais's diatribes against the American Communist Party. Mailer shocked many pro-Soviet Progressives when in a speech in Hollywood he attacked both the Soviet Union and the United States as destructive imperial powers employing tremendous concentrations of economic and military force. The Soviet Union was no longer exempt from the excoriating analysis of power politics Mailer had given in *The Naked and the Dead*, where General Cummings argues that the history of the twentieth century should be viewed as the development of great nationalistic power blocs. Cummings avers that war is nothing more than the struggle for supreme power. Without Malaquais's Marxist analysis suggesting that the Soviet Union had perverted and stifled the idea of international revolutionary socialism, the Mailer of *The Naked and the Dead* had concentrated on the faults of the American system.

At the Cultural and Scientific Conference for World Peace at the Waldorf Astoria in late March 1949, Mailer announced his new politics in most dramatic fashion. At this controversial event (attended by such stellar fellow travelers as Lillian Hellman and F. O. Matthiessen and attacked by such anti-Communist liberals as Norman Cousins and Dwight Macdonald) a "white-faced" Mailer, the darling of an audience who had been calling out his name, announced, "I have come here as a Trojan horse." He denounced the idea of peace conferences. They did no good so long as the United States and the Soviet Union continued to converge toward the same point: totalitarian state capitalism. Mailer was loudly booed. Lillian Hellman, who had just gotten to know him after her enthusiastic but aborted effort to adapt *The Naked and the Dead* as a play (too many characters, too much action), deplored Malaquais's influence on him; to her Malaquais was "probably a phony." Irving Howe, much more sympathetic to Mailer's new politics, nevertheless found Malaquais "opinionated, cocksure, and dogmatic" but also "very smart in his limited way." Howe suspected that Mailer had simply exchanged one kind of orthodoxy for another; neither Stalinist nor liberal, he veered toward the Trotskyist line.

Howe now calls the conference "the last hurrah of the American pro-Stalinist cultural community." Mailer's "third camp position—a plague on both your houses" delighted Howe and others who had come to challenge the conference's organizers. But Mailer's own views, as Howe would later make clear in his review of *Barbary Shore*, were somewhat "dubious and undeveloped." When Mailer finished his speech, Howe remembers going up to congratulate him:

> *Then there occurred one of those characteristic Norman incidents, which make you uneasy with him. I said to him, "Mr. Mailer, I think you've made a very honest speech." He said to me, "Oh, nobody's honest." That was forty-one years ago. I remember it as though it were yesterday. And I felt a slight chill.*

At the Waldorf, Mailer gave the gist of the case he would put to his readers in his new novel, *Barbary Shore*, a draft of which he had begun shortly after Wallace's defeat in the November election. It could not have escaped Mailer's attention that *Barbary Shore* would be unpopular and subversive of the very success engendered by his previous work, which was so knowing in its portrayal of human character, so bold in its claim to have analyzed a whole society.

SECOND-NOVEL PANIC

Mailer's changing politics reflected no stable point of view. As soon as he had permitted himself to think like a collectivist, he was lost. All of his energies had been put into opposing organized authority. He had no clear alternative to the fascism espoused by General Cummings. Liberal Lieutenant Hearn had been the General's opponent, but just when Hearn was put in charge of a platoon and was beginning to see how much he enjoyed commanding men, Mailer had killed him off. Many years later he admitted, "I wasn't altogether sure in my heart that I knew what to do with him, or knew how to bring him off."

In Paris Mailer had written about fifty pages of a novel entitled *Mrs.*

Guinevere, a take-off on Sally Bowles in Christopher Isherwood's *Berlin Stories*, but the work went nowhere and he dropped it. Immediately after the Wallace defeat in November 1948 he had traveled to Indiana, hoping to collect material for a novel about a labor union. But he and Bea hated the Middle West, and when he settled down in Jamaica, Vermont, for a month of preparation to write the novel, he discovered he knew nothing worth saying about labor unions. In what he later called "second novel panic" he returned to *Mrs. Guinevere* and found the germ of an idea that would develop into *Barbary Shore.*

This fumbling period is reminiscent of what Mailer went through while writing *A Transit to Narcissus.* Although he wanted to take on society and its institutions, his experience had been inadequate to the task. *The Naked and the Dead*, on the other hand, derived from an environment he had internalized and made his own. As he later put it: "The army was the only milieu I ever had. It was like living in a society where rumor has the same validity as fact, like a tight community where you can weep about people you never saw." Mailer had not discovered another milieu to which he felt personally connected, one that affected his sense of himself.

From January to May 1949 the Mailers settled into the quiet of Vermont, watched the snow fall, avoided the "village literary teas," and waited in vain for the new novel to take shape. Turning over in his mind a fiction that would be an amalgam of Kafka and Marxist dialectics, Mailer wrote Gwaltney about *The Castle* and its fairy-tale quality. He identified with Kafka's hatred of bureaucracy and the bewildering way individuals get caught up in it. By May he had a draft of half a novel with a hero who mirrored the confusions in himself. It had no plan. There were no index cards or charts—no trace of the young engineer. Indeed, he wondered whether he could make this strange book cohere. It rather frightened him, and he looked for a change of scene that might stimulate him to finish the remaining portion.

LOTUS LAND

Mailer interrupted the writing of *Barbary Shore* in the summer of 1949 with a trip to Hollywood. As an undergraduate he had dreamed about becoming a screenwriter. Now Hollywood would provide, if nothing else, a good background for one of his later novels. While Norman set things up in Hollywood, Bea stayed for a short time in Chicago with Adeline Lubell Naiman, who remembers Bea "in her radiant prime, pregnant," and probably hoping the baby would hold everything in place." What she really thought eluded Naiman, since Bea did not take her into her confidence.

With Bea, now seven months pregnant, Norman moved into a small, unpretentious house in the hills overlooking Laurel Canyon. It was a "very quiet and sylvan setting" in which they could behold "that horrible city that lies below us," Mailer wrote the Gwaltneys, sending them "Love from Lotus Land." He basked in Bea's "beautiful pregnancy," but he worried about whether he could finish his novel in a town where writers walked around "on their hands and knees, not knowing where their next job is coming from."

To Norman Rosten, Mailer sent a hilarious letter, describing his home and his "horse of a Belgian police dog, Herr von Ritter who always has a hard-on and thinks Bea is prime meat." Mailer said they were hoping for a girl, for they all had seen enough of the "massive dong of Herr von Ritter." Mailer admitted he had doubts about the quality of his new novel, but he enjoyed telling Rosten about the baby inside Bea, pushing her around with, no doubt, a clenched fist—"the militant little bugger."

Susan Mailer was born on August 26, 1949. Mailer wrote the Gwaltneys:

> I've been running to the hospital, dicking around, getting bawled out by my wife who acts infinitely superior to me now, and just generally suffering. . . . Bea has become the Mother. Never sleeps at night, pushes me around. I just carry a fucking guilt complex all the time. . . .

For once, Norman was not the center of attention. But he was delighted with his daughter, writing the Gwaltneys later in the year: "Susan is cute, and laughs a lot, and looks a little bit like me in spite of being cute."

Barbara came for a visit that summer, as did Fanny and Barney. Mickey Knox, now one of Norman's close friends, was amused by Barney's penchant for "pinching all the girls." He even "made a play" for Knox's wife Georgette and tried the same thing years later with Knox's second wife, Joanne. Barney was a grabber. Knox admired Bea, but she also troubled him. She liked the attention her celebrated husband brought to both of them but she also seemed annoyed by it. She had a habit of correcting him, as if to remind him of his place, and to assert her own rights. There was something "timid" and "sweet" about Mailer, Knox recalls, and Bea knew how to go to work on his vulnerability.

While Mailer struggled with his "experimental, tricky" novel, he also tried his hand at a screenplay, inviting Malaquais and his wife to stay with him and Bea. Malaquais had experience as both an assistant director and scriptwriter and soon became Mailer's collaborator on an original screenplay (a take-off on Nathanael West's *Miss Lonelyhearts*) commissioned by Samuel Goldwyn. Malaquais remembers being ushered with Mailer into Goldwyn's living room (lined with "dummy books") to meet the mogul, dressed in a bathrobe. Goldwyn lisped while he pushed his false teeth into place. Malaquais regarded the whole scene as "high comedy." They were to get fifty thousand dollars, which included revisions, and three offices (one for secretaries), but nothing came of the deal because the writers refused to allow others to change their script. Mailer would double up with laughter when he repeated Goldwyn's judgment on the script: "There'th not enough hearth." A few years later, Mailer admitted to an interviewer that the script "stank. It was half-art, half-commercial, the sort of thing you can delude yourself about for a long time."

Bea observed her careful husband: He did not plunge into the heady atmosphere of Hollywood. He had other offers to write for the movies but turned them all down. He enjoyed meeting the stars, attending many parties, but he did not identify with his new acquaintances. Mailer doggedly refused to play the Hollywood hotshot. "Norman, get a haircut or people will think I'm not paying you enough money," Sam Goldwyn advised him. Mickey Knox thought Mailer wanted people's good opinion and worried whether he would become the target of Dorothy's Parker's wit—as everyone sooner or later did. (Not to worry, Lillian Hellman counseled: "It will amount to no more than the compliments she's just given you.")

Shelley Winters remembers Mailer's "great, piercing blue eyes" and the way he coached her for an important role in *A Place in the Sun*, an adaptation of Dreiser's *An American Tragedy*, which Mailer called "*the* American success story." He spoke with Winters (trying to overcome her "blonde bombshell" reputation) as a colleague and went over the novel in detail. He had such affinity for Dreiser's story of a poor boy who craves wealth and glamour that she thought of him as Dreiser's protégé.

And no wonder, since Bea had written the Gwaltneys about Norman's success, boasting that he could easily be elected borough president of Brooklyn and that "all our local bourgeois mothers no longer want their sons to become doctors and lawyers. 'Go to your room, Sonny,' they tell their offspring, 'and write a book like Norman Mailer did.' "

Mickey Knox, picked to play a boxer in a movie, went with Mailer to the gym three times a week for enthusiastic workouts. Mailer loved the feel of new muscle, he wrote to Gwaltney: "You wouldn't stand a chance with me now, you po-o-or white-headed baboon. Bea says I've finally achieved my ambition, and I look like a truckdriver. 185 pounds of muscle and shit." Like Knox, Mailer enjoyed preparing for a new role. Movies intrigued him "inordinately because the question of identity is so vivid in them. Movie stars fascinate me. Their lives are so unlike anyone else's," Mailer has admitted.

During his Hollywood days, Mailer was courted as another one of those Eastern writers who had come to conquer Hollywood. It was Mickey Knox who brought *The Naked and the Dead* as a property to Burt Lancaster (who wanted to play the role of Lieutenant Hearn). With his cousin Charles Rembar as his attorney, Mailer got script approval, but neither Lancaster nor his producer, Harold Hecht, provided a version of the novel that pleased the author, even though they enjoyed dealing with this "brilliant" writer who insisted on "creative control" of the picture.

Mailer would later admit that in Hollywood he became "much more macho. . . . I suddenly felt like a strong man." The real trouble with Bea began in this formative period. Bea tried to paint, to be creative in her own right, but she had few friends of her own. She and Norman quarreled and even exchanged blows, and their incessant profanity set Malaquais's teeth on edge.

Fanny believed Bea envied her husband's celebrity. She had no sympathy for her depressed daughter-in-law, who had become bored with motherhood after the first few months and looked for an outlet of her own—something to match her husband's dogged daily routine of writing from the early morning until 1:00 or 2:00 P.M. She read Simone de Beauvoir and incorporated many feminist ideas into her unsatisfactory novel. Mailer has admitted living with "a premature Women's Liberationist." He called her a "very strong woman"—in fact "stronger" than he when they had married. She had expected to work very hard to support her husband while he wrote his books. If *The Naked and the*

Dead had not been such a success, "we probably would have been a happy couple of that sort, she the strong one, I the gentle one."

Although Mailer appeared to adjust to the heady new atmosphere, Shelley Winters thought that both he and Bea were "a little intimidated" by it and had trouble adjusting to its mores. At one Mailer party, she remembers Bea setting up "little TV tables and putting out a big spread—big hams and turkeys—stuff like Norman still serves at his parties—baked beans, potato chips. It was good but like a picnic, not elegant food like squab and quiche that was usually served in Hollywood."

Saul Chaplin, who socialized with Mailer during his Hollywood stint, believes it is remarkable that Mailer made no great impression: "It wasn't like he was the life of the party or always on or had strong opinions, nothing like that. . . . He was reserved, spoke quietly, and was pleasant to be around. He seemed nothing like the Norman Mailer who has since emerged."

By June 1950 the Mailers had had it with Hollywood. Although Norman had completed a draft of *Barbary Shore*, he felt it was chaotic and reflective of his wild Hollywood year. With his usual discipline he had churned out three pages a day, but they had been done in "literal terror" and great doubt, for the novelist had lost his sense of direction. *The Naked and the Dead* had been such a consciously controlled book, and now "for the first time" he had become "powerfully aware" of his unconscious, which seemed to be breaking down his effort to control the book and to have "little to do" with him. He and Bea decided to return to Provincetown, where a good part of *The Naked and the Dead* had taken shape.

MURDER, SUICIDE, INCEST, ORGY, ORGASM, AND TIME

In Provincetown Mailer did not carry himself like a celebrated author. His friend Nat Halper marveled at how young Norman still seemed, asking him naive questions like "How do you work parallels in correspondences?" Halper had also heard things about the tension between Norman and Bea and that Norman suspected her of spreading the word that he was "no good in bed." At the same time, Robert Gorham Davis and his wife visited the Mailers in Provincetown and remember them as happily married, with "little Susan crawling between them on the floor."

Larry Alson, who met and fell in love with Barbara in the summer of 1949 after she had returned from visiting the Mailers in Hollywood, liked Bea. He later realized, however, that she had a "chip on her shoulder," the result of considerable tension. He and Barbara left for Europe in the summer of 1950, while Norman and Bea were in Provincetown. Once in Europe, they married—in part because Barbara did not want to explain to Fanny her reasons for living with a man. Alson's father, an accountant with some reputation in the Jewish community, proved acceptable to Fanny: "proper middle class, no question," Alson explains.

A severely depressed Bea returned to playing the piano and painting when they moved to Putney, Vermont, in the autumn. She remained "absolutely miserable" in spite of all the interesting people who wanted to associate with her husband. She had no life of her own.

Mickey Knox noticed that in Vermont Norman got into the habit of going to New York City alone. Knox did not know about the faltering marriage, but the signs were there: a quiet, "despondent, suffering" Mailer, "withdrawn and gloomy."

When Norman Rosten visited Mailer in Vermont, Mailer had completed a "second draft of the albatross," but he remained hard at work each morning on revisions. He enjoyed his year-old daughter, but his marriage and his work depressed him. He expected *Barbary Shore* to raise a "shit storm." The writing itself had been torture and somewhere in the middle of it he had lost the dreamlike rhythm; his mood had been broken, he later realized, by the "disaster in Hollywood." To Calder Willingham a dejected Mailer confided: "I'm going to stay here in Vermont building stands for power tools for the rest of my life."

Mailer has described the writing of *Barbary Shore* as a slow, excruciating birthing process, with nothing like the rush of words that had made it seem as if *The Naked and the Dead* had written itself. *Barbary Shore* "came out sentence by sentence." He refused to repeat himself or to write the sequel he called "The Naked and the Dead Go to Japan," but his first published novel had set a precedent; every subsequent work had to take on a subject larger than himself and his background. His own past, he asserted, had become "empty as a theme." He resisted writing about "Brooklyn streets, or my mother and father. . . ." Nevertheless, as

Mailer acknowledged many years later, *Barbary Shore* evolved into his "most autobiographical novel."

Why not? Thomas Wolfe, one of Mailer's adolescent favorites, had created literature out of autobiography and family history. James T. Farrell, another important influence, had set his work in his own backyard, so to speak. All Faulkner had needed was his little "postage stamp of native soil." The other Jewish writers of Mailer's generation have seen nothing ignoble in sticking close to home. Yet Mailer's dream of literary greatness seems founded on rejecting his past as a subject. When he looked at his childhood and adolescence, all he saw, in Richard Poirier's words, was the "Jewish boy blob," with nothing romantic, heroic, or adventurous to write about.

On the unconscious level, however, Mailer busily transformed his novel of political disillusionment into a family romance reflecting precisely those personal conflicts he thought were beneath his novelist's concern. Not only is *Barbary Shore* set in Brooklyn, but also it takes place in the house in which Mailer had written *The Naked and the Dead*. In his small, close room, Mikey Lovett, the novel's narrator, tries to write his novel. It is not going well. It is about "an immense institution," and writing it feels like "burrowing at a mountain." He is Mailer's age and he suffers from amnesia, having—like his creator—no sense of the past that can help him cope with the present. Lovett has been wounded. He knows this because of the scars on his body. He suspects he is a war veteran, but that experience (whatever it was) has only served to make him feel displaced. As his name suggests, Mikey Lovett is still an adolescent in search of love, on a quest for commitment and belonging. In his novel, a hero and heroine have passed through the institution and meet only after they have "escaped" it and have found themselves "capable of love." Lovett's problem is his author's: How to place himself in the contemporary world? What must he do to become a man?

Yet Lovett's impulse, like Mailer's, is not to engage himself directly with the world but to secrete himself in a garret that has been passed on to him by a fellow writer who suggests that the landlady, Guinevere, is a "nymphomaniac" capable of providing Lovett with more adventure than he can handle. In fact, Norman Rosten (who sublet his room to Mailer) remembers that Mailer affectionately called his landlady Guinevere— "a saucy lady, sassy, lively, with an Irish quality." In her early thirties, a flirt, "stacked" and "slovenly," she would come into Mailer's room dressed in a housecoat, accompanied by a small child, and make the bed in a provocative way (Rosten remembers her "sticking her ass in your face") while engaging in small talk with Mailer and Rosten or Charlie Devlin. "We were all trying to figure out how we could seduce her—this sweet-tempered lady—to get her in one of those rooms while she was alone. If she only knew the plots of these plots against her!" All three writers had lived in the house, but none of them (so far as Rosten knows) ever took Guinevere to bed.

The details in the novel are a facsimile of life—including Guinevere's husband, McLeod, whose dry laugh, self-contempt, incisive mind, and air of mystery are modeled on Devlin. McLeod becomes a mentor for Lovett as he recapitulates the history of revolutionary socialism in the twentieth century. But McLeod's politics are Malaquais's, not Devlin's— McLeod repudiates his former Stalinism, condemns American capitalism, and promotes Trotsky's notion of internationalism: The revolution must be carried to every country and not confined to "the land beyond the sea," as Russia is called in the novel.

Mailer later confessed that he put "Malaquais's philosophy in Devlin's body," and Devlin broke with him because of it. In *Barbary Shore*, father and son, mentor and acolyte, try to claim Guinevere's love, for she represents not only the solace of the flesh but the down-to-earth and maternal qualities these men forsake in their abstract concern with politics. Guinevere lives day by day. She keeps a house, raises a kid, and still manages to remain endlessly appealing whereas the men are isolates, timid and frightened or chastened by experience.

Guinevere is one of the most attractive characters Mailer has created. She is alluring and yet she has a strong sense of herself. She has no mind for politics, but her lack of interest has a way of making the men's concerns seem childish. She is vulgar and materialistic and talks like the Hollywood producers Mailer distrusted, but her directness is refreshing in the midst of so many pages of political speechifying and idealistic sentiment. When Guinevere speaks, the novel comes alive. Mailer has never written anything funnier than her detailed proposal to Lovett that he base a screenplay on her story about the love life of a doctor: "He's got the biggest whang on him in the whole town and maybe he don't know it."

Barbary Shore is a parody of an Arthurian romance, with Guinevere, a former burlesque queen, the center of everyone's attention—including the Trotskyite Lannie, a female Lancelot who makes love to her, as does Hollingsworth, a government agent in pursuit of McLeod because of his

Stalinist record, which apparently includes the murder of at least two men. Never having subordinated her humanity to an ideology, Guinevere is the least repressed character in the novel. She is not simply outspoken. She is comfortable with herself in a way that the other characters covet. They are wildly inconsistent: Hollingsworth's task is to trap McLeod, to make him confess to his subversive past, yet Hollingsworth also admires McLeod's heroic qualities, his singleness of purpose and ruthlessness. Similarly, Lannie has a divided opinion of McLeod. She is drawn to his faith in international socialism, yet she condemns him for his Stalinist past and for the part he played in the events leading to Trotsky's assassination in Mexico.

On a strictly political level, the novel is a mess that reflects the author's own ideological confusion. On an emotional level, Guinevere is the magnet that holds these disparate personalities together, the mother who presides over this divided house.

Andrew Gordon suggests that *Barbary Shore* gave Mailer the opportunity to "grow up again" in Brooklyn. In the fiction, the strong mother and the weak father appear, but with a difference: McLeod has Barney's fastidiousness (he proposes that he and Mikey share the chore of keeping the bathroom clean), but he is meant to grow in stature as he transfers his allegiance to revolutionary socialism to his "son," Mikey. McLeod, unlike Barney, has style and substance. Or as Mailer later put it, he thought of McLeod in terms of Malaquais, who had never been a Communist and yet had about him "a quality . . . which was pure old Bolshevik." Like Barney with his South African background and demeanor that caused his son to think he looked like a "colonel from the Bengal Lancers," McLeod is an exotic; there is something foreign about him—as Hollingsworth suggests in his insistence that McLeod is actually a "certain Balkan gentleman" involved in revolutionary intrigues abroad.

Mailer felt disabled by his childhood: It did not equip him to be the man he wanted to become. Like Mikey, he had been deprived of his true identity. But both the fictional hero and his creator shrink from action. While Mikey fantasizes about bedding Guinevere, it is the crude Hollingsworth who actually succeeds with her. Modeled after the pushy, intrusive American in Paris who had plied Mailer with so many questions about his work, Hollingsworth represents the threatening violation of individuality that Mailer seemed unable to combat. Mikey is passive; he waits in his room for Guinevere to appear and then visits her only when he feels she has reneged on her lover's promise. At times he is a self-pitying whiner—as Mailer in his worst moods has been.

Lovett is a projection of Mailer's problem with aggression. Beginning with *A Transit to Narcissus*, the Mailer hero fails to cut a figure in the world because of his fear of violence, of what might be done to him, or of what he might do to others. Denying himself the use of force, however, makes the hero lifeless. He has a voice but not a convincing character. He is, like Mailer's father, afraid to get his hands dirty. Thus each Mailer fiction is about the hero's quest to fight the barbarians and about his simultaneous reluctance to sully himself.

The author would have us believe that McLeod's rekindled faith in revolutionary socialism is itself a heroic act. He is the old, pure Bolshevik passing on his dream to Lovett. McLeod has admitted his sins, shrived himself, and is owed—so the logic of the novel goes—a tribute. He is now his own man, an agent of neither side in the Cold War. But McLeod has done nothing—except steal what is referred to as "the little object," which critics have variously interpreted as "the grail" of the book, the idealism Hollingsworth has tried to destroy, or, more literally, as an actual thing (like the secret of the atomic bomb) which deprives both America and Russia of the absolute power they seek.

The novel's ending, as Irving Howe has pointed out, is offensive:

> *It is one thing to say that capitalism and Stalinism are both reactionary societies and that a political identification with the first may lead to a political victory of the second; but it is sheer cant to suggest that the absolute dictatorship of Russia and the limited but real democracy of the United States are, or are soon likely to be, "two virtually identical forms of exploitation."*

The tone of "pious, apocalyptic certainty" in the prose could only be taken by a writer who, Howe says, "has come to his radicalism a little late; he does not really know in his flesh and bones what has happened to the socialist hope in the era of Hitler and Stalin, and that is why he can refer so cavalierly to democracy and carry on like a stale pamphleteer." Howe admires Mailer for his courage in writing an unpopular book, but his "relation to his material, like his presentation of it, is not authentic. Otherwise he would not seem so sure."

This astute analysis is as much a biography of the writer as it is a criticism of his work. Although McLeod is a murderer and has been willing to sacrifice humanity to ideology, his sentiments, his repentance are supposed to be honored. Mailer tries to get away with this by making Hollingsworth a cretin, yet Hollingsworth is right to ask what McLeod has done to earn his air of superiority. If Hollingsworth is given his due in such exchanges with McLeod, he also has to bear the burden of acting out all of the perverse desires that plague McLeod and Lovett, so that it is Hollingsworth who is shown mistreating women and who ultimately kills McLeod and steals Guinevere at the end of the novel. As Andrew Gordon suggests, this is Mailer's way of preserving his pristine heroes. Given Lovett's coveting of Guinevere, it is remarkable that he demonstrates almost no hostility toward McLeod. The explanation is that Hollingsworth is Lovett's "proxy, he acts out Lovett's fantasies and wards off any blame that might accrue to Lovett." Like Lieutenant Hearn who mashes a cigarette on General Cummings's immaculate floor, Hollingsworth (behaving like a defiant son) dirties the fastidious McLeod's floor by dumping pencil shavings on it.

In *Barbary Shore*, Mailer the anarchist and antimilitarist wars with Mailer the rationalist and revolutionary socialist. The haunting, phantasmagoric first third of the novel is by far its most convincing part. Mailer captures, as Norman Rosten notes, the personal and political confusions of the time: "He puts you through all the political formats, trying to find out where you are. In that way the book was a little confusing—you didn't quite know who or what anything was. But it had a magnetic, mysterious appeal at the time because in '51 everyone was screwed up that way. No one quite knew what one was doing."

In the novel's first historical parable Lovett describes his fantasy of a plump, complacent, middle-aged traveler who is anxious to get home. He is tired and "depressed" after a long trip and suddenly shocked to find that while he recognizes the city in which he travels as his home, "the architecture is strange, and the people are dressed in unfamiliar clothing," and he cannot read the alphabet on the street sign. He tries to calm himself in the belief that he is dreaming, but Lovett shouts "this city is the real city, the material city, and your vehicle is history." The fantasy aptly conveys the novel's contention that man thinks he knows the course of his life, thinks that he can read the signs of history, when in fact what he has taken to be so familiar, so easily understood, is elusive, strange, and terrifying. As Mailer sums it up in *Advertisements for Myself*, *Barbary Shore* was his first "attempt [at] an entrance into the mysteries of murder, suicide, incest, orgy, orgasm, and Time."

THIS EVIL-SMELLING NOVEL

As Mailer had predicted, *Barbary Shore* received bad reviews. One reviewer advised his readers to drop "this evil-smelling novel" into the garbage can. This hyperbole amused Mailer, but he did not think it funny of *Time* to call *Barbary Shore* "paceless, tasteless, and graceless," and he rued *The New Yorker*'s evaluation of his book's "monolithic flawless badness." By Mailer's count, "the reviews ran in the proportion of fifty which were bad to five which were good." It did not help matters that his work appeared just after the Chinese had invaded Korea, sending the nation into another fit of hysteria over the Communist menace. Mailer knew, of course, that his novel had grave faults, but in a different climate he would at least have gotten a more charitable reception.

It was too early for Mailer or for his critics to see that they were responding to a dangerous side of his character, one that would become more apparent in later books and in public appearances: He took the word for the deed. By his own admission, the last third of *Barbary Shore* "collapsed into a chapter of political speech and never quite recovered."

During the Wallace campaign, Angus Cameron, an editor at Little, Brown and Massachusetts state chairman for the Progressive Party, distrusted Mailer's ideas; they tended to take on a life of their own. He willed them to power, and endowed them with a mystical quality that contradicted his Marxist brand of materialism. Mailer lacked a sense of the pragmatic, of "cause-and-effect relationships." Cameron's concerns were prophetic: *Barbary Shore*, ostensibly written by a revolutionary socialist, actually succeeded in destroying Mailer's belief in the laws of history. He had set out to write a novel questioning the confident design of *The Naked and the Dead*, and he had accomplished his mission too well. He had begun to doubt his mastery of the novel form and to attack the premises on which he had built his life.

4.

THE DEER PARK
(1951–1955)

THE OLD FIGHTER

After the publication of *Barbary Shore* in the spring of 1951, Mailer looked for a new adventure. Although he seemed "depressed, moody, and withdrawn" to Mickey Knox, to others he remained the brilliant young author with a "growing braggadocio" and his own court. Bea had no intention of humoring him, and their marriage disintegrated as each of them turned to other lovers. According to Rhoda Lazare Wolf, he ended the marriage by proposing, "You go out and fuck and I'll fuck."

Forsaking Vermont for Greenwich Village, Mailer looked up Dan Wolf, whom he had met through Malaquais a few years earlier. One night at Wolf's apartment, Mailer had him place a call to Adele Morales, a Spanish-Peruvian painter. Wolf had gotten to know Adele through his friend Ed Fancher, who had met her in the New School cafeteria in 1947. She was then twenty-one and exploring the world of art, taking every "esoteric" art-appreciation course that appealed to her. Ed had helped her to find an apartment on Sixteenth Street, and she began to make friends in the Village. Later she would describe her exultation in these years as akin to the scene in *Saturday Night Fever* driving across the Brooklyn Bridge and getting that feeling of "freedom and adventure." She had come from the Bensonhurst section in Brooklyn. Dan Wolf told her about Mailer, and when he finally called her, she felt she had known about him for years.

This sensual beauty may have had a special aura for Mailer, since she had just broken up with Jack Kerouac. But it was 1:30 A.M., she was tired and did not want to come over, even though Mailer was quite willing to pay her cab fare. Then he got on the phone, Morales recalls, and "quoted a beautiful line from Scott Fitzgerald . . . about adventure and getting up and going out into the night, and that did it." She was amused and intrigued. Her affair began immediately with this "very shy" man who captivated her with his talk and doubted that he was "physically attractive" to women—although Morales thought "he was enormously sensitive and good-looking. Very slender, and he had a nice body." She quickly identified with Mailer's ambitions and with his hurts. When the terrible reviews of *Barbary Shore* were published, she felt they upset her even more than they did Norman, making her cry because they seemed so vicious and personal.

Mickey Knox speculates that perhaps with her Latin background Adele seemed "exotic" in comparison to Bea. Mailer later singled out her "elemental and primitive" qualities that he believed came from her Indian background. Knox liked her immediately. She seemed so "nice and natural," not the "tough" woman of later years, the one who gained "a lot of muscle through Norman." Adele had an interesting father. Knox admired his "dark chiseled features and high cheekbones, looks like an Indian who's walked out of the mountains of Peru, which in fact he did." He had been a professional boxer, and Mailer enjoyed going a few rounds with him. Adele's mother, on the other hand, was (in Knox's words) "a horror": "high-strung, nervous" and prone to make snap judgments. The first time she saw Knox she abruptly said, "You're an ex-con, aren't you?" Knox remembers that she could be "mean and insulting." Not a physically attractive woman, she had tremendous fights with her two daughters, both of whom left home early.

On the Lower East Side Mailer found a loft in a run-down building he set about fixing up, declaring that he would do everything himself, including (to the amazement of an admiring Lillian Hellman) the plumbing. Adele thought that taking the loft on Monroe Street would be a "challenge." The size of it—you could ride a bicycle across it—the fourteen windows, the view of the water, and the bareness appealed to her. Writing to Fig Gwaltney, Norman described himself as the "emperor" of this big space that Adele, he claimed, was "terrified of." He created his life anew, shedding all vestiges of the nice boy married to Bea. Although he was happy with Adele, he also picked fights with her. When she asked him why, he replied: "I pick on you because Bea picked on me." To Shirley Fingerhood, who heard Norman say this to Adele, the affair had a staged quality to it, as if Norman were "practicing" on Adele, inventing her, imagining situations to test out his new persona.

In the summer of 1951 that persona absented itself from the family home in Brooklyn. Fig and Ecey Gwaltney, on a trip to New York, met Fanny and Barney for the first time. "Mrs. Mailer received us very graciously," Ecey recalls, "sort of like a queen mother, regal and ladylike, but I had no idea that she was such a power in the family." Norman had said very little about his parents, but Ecey sensed "some little hostility somewhere in Norman's feelings" about his father. He would sort of laugh when he spoke of Barney's love of talk and dapper clothes. Ecey imagined there might have been a hint of disappointment behind Norman's words about his father. The Gwaltneys marveled at how Norman maintained his "intrigue" with Adele while keeping up appearances with Bea in front of his parents. Ecey speculated that a part of him enjoyed the drama of it. Ecey teased Norman about Adele: "She shaves her legs, why doesn't she shave under her arms?" " 'Cause it gets me hot," he replied. To Ecey, Bea seemed contemptuous of Norman's fling with Adele and treated her husband as less worldly and sophisticated than she. Bea remained her usual outspoken self. Ecey remembers a typical incident: "Susie came walking in, and she was scratching herself. Bea said, 'What's the matter, honey? You got sand in your pussy?' " Most of the time Norman ignored Bea's vulgarity, but he could not help expressing his irritation on a hot day when Bea stripped off her blouse in front of the Gwaltneys: "Bea, why don't you just take out one of your tits and show us?" he asked. When Adele came by for a small package she had left, Bea quipped: "Oh, she forgot her Ortho gel." On a visit to Long Branch, Bea remarked to Ecey: "I don't need this Adele who has fifteen orgasms at one time." Bea suggested her marriage foundered after the birth of Susan, when the sex had gone bad. Highly critical of her husband's literary politicking and socializing, of the salon he created for himself in the village, she angrily contended that he depleted valuable energy. Ecey felt Bea envied Norman.

While Mailer did not tell his parents about Adele, he took his sister,

Barbara, into his confidence. According to Rhoda Lazare Wolf, Barbara would never think of having a party without inviting her brother, and in 1951, when Barbara and Larry Alson were living on Riverside Drive, they gave a party at which Rhoda got her first look at a "stunning" Adele. Rhoda remembers spending most of the evening on the floor talking with her and feeling the tension provoked by Bea's appearance with Steve Sanchez, a small, "dark-skinned," intense man with a look that tended to startle women. Larry liked Steve and noticed that his macho flare gave him a certain mystique. He seemed, in other words, the male counterpart of Adele Morales.

At their Lower East Side loft, Norman and Adele hosted many parties, bringing together not only writers and painters but also groups of unlikely guests, as if in a deliberate attempt to create an unusual event. It was a bad neighborhood (on Monroe Street, close to the Manhattan Bridge), but it did not stop visits from the likes of Lillian Hellman dragging her fur coat along the filthy steps up to the fifth floor. John Aldridge, author of an influential critical study, *After the Lost Generation* (1951), became a Mailer friend and was invited to engage in the new Mailer sport—arm-wrestling—which the two men agreed to forgo when they realized that anatomically they were not a good match (the tall man and the short man had trouble interlinking arms).

The most dramatic incident of this period came about when a gang of toughs invaded a Mailer party. The doughty host came forward and was attacked with a hammer. At the sight of his head streaming blood, Adele screamed and advanced on the intruders, who quickly left. According to one witness, Norman was "knocked cold," although he later claimed to have taken two hammer blows and had been ready to fight on. Adele liked this version as well, conceding only that a "dazed" Norman might have gone down on one knee but had recovered immediately, "the old fighter." He concealed the incident from his mother, telling her he had banged his head in a taxicab accident. Mailer eventually gave up the loft, even though it put him ahead of his times and enhanced the daring image of himself he now cultivated.

Mailer spent the summer of 1951 with Adele in Provincetown partying and trying to get a novel started. Fay Mowery (later married to Roger Donoghue, a Mailer crony) remembers meeting Norman and Adele, whom people knew better than Norman—primarily because of her relationship with Jack Kerouac. Fay found Norman "absolutely delightful" and "great fun to be with," although just one of several writers like Tennessee Williams (enjoying the success of *A Streetcar Named Desire*). Mailer did not by any means attract special attention.

Edith Begner, who became friends with Norman in Provincetown, had befriended Adele in 1949–1950 when they were doing window displays in Brooklyn. Adele, in her view, was a radiant and "pliable" woman, rather "sponge-like" in her capacity to absorb other people's ideas and styles. Begner did not think that Adele had a life of her own, and soon saw her being fed into the Mailer "machine" and thoroughly taken over by his habits. Nat Halper, a longtime Mailer friend and Provincetown resident, saw another side of Adele: He believed that she—known for being "very, *very* good in bed"—had restored in Norman some of the confidence Bea had undermined.

March 11, 1952. "Adele is fine," Mailer wrote Fig Gwaltney, "and things go on pretty much the same. Bea and I are now divorced, and she's about to marry Steve [Sanchez] in Mexico. Feels funny to think of myself as ever being married." Bea had taken Susan with her and that depressed Norman. Still trying to start a novel, he felt some pressure from Adele, who wanted to get married. In the aftermath of a divorce, he doubted his suitability for marriage.

Barbara told Shirley Fingerhood (who worked for her cousin Cy Rembar) that Norman and Bea's divorce had devastated her. Barbara had been thrilled to be adopted into Norman's circle after his marriage and to see that his childhood bond with her had not been broken. Bea had been an exhilarating companion. Then the divorce had smashed Barbara's confidence in the permanence of family life, and the world seemed a much more unstable place.

Adeline Lubell Naiman suggests Norman had married Bea as a boy and had gone from nowhere, so to speak, to the overwhelming experiences of war and success. "There wasn't a movement from Bea to Adele. There was a gap." Mailer had itched to get out of the marriage.

THE BIG LEAGUE

Other Mailer friends such as Norman Rosten escaped his physical challenges and encounters. "Perhaps he respected my superior poetic sensibility," Rosten jokes, "He knew I was a handball player and this was not his idea of an American sport." Hedda, Rosten's wife, pointed out that Mailer could be at ease with the "other Norman" since poetry was not a field he would ever seriously enter. The two Normans would joke about what they should call each other, about who should be Norman One and so on. Mailer signed one of his letters to Rosten "Norman Zero."

If rivalry with Rosten was entirely in jest, Rosten realized it was not so with other writers. Mailer would say, "Jesus, there's two books coming out. I wonder how I'm going to make out—there's Irwin Shaw's *The Young Lions* and there's Jim Jones. . . ." Mailer knew the market, Rosten recalls. Like Arthur Miller, he had an instinct for it—"the ultimate audience"—in a way that "we poets, who counted on a couple of square blocks of a city, did not."

Mailer had a major reputation to protect. No one knew better than he what an impact he had on other novelists. They took their measure from him and sought him out. He was the man to beat.

At the same time, Mailer evoked as much admiration as envy. "I was just knocked out by *The Naked and the Dead*," William Styron remembers. In his own words, his first novel, *Lie Down in Darkness*, had on a "modest level . . . done well critically and commercially," and he was "very happy with it." Through "the literary network" Styron heard that Mailer wanted to meet him, and Styron assumed he was "casing the competition." Styron first met Mailer at a lunch with Calder Willingham and Vance Bourjaily arranged by Robert Whitehead, the theatrical producer, who wanted them to write plays. "Impressed and awed" by Mailer, as he had recently been with James Jones, Styron found himself in their company in the Village ("maybe four or five times") in 1952.

In the first year of this threesome there was much to share and respect. Styron recalled: "There was tremendous excitement about being a young writer in those days, and of taking part in a shared destiny." The rivalries and jealousies of the literary community that make Kurt Vonnegut describe writers approaching each other with the "edgy mistrust of bears" seemed suspended. Styron later thought it had been naive, perhaps even dumb, to imagine that there could a "moratorium on envy" and that he and Mailer and Jones could be generous with each other, establish a camaraderie, and find their illustrious places beside their masters, Hemingway, Faulkner, and Fitzgerald. At the time, however, there seemed to be "glory enough to go around." At one of those gregarious Village gatherings Styron put his arms around the shoulders of Mailer and Jones and announced: "Here we are, the three best writers of our generation . . . !" The special bond between them was enhanced by their feeling that they had been fortunate to survive the war. Styron believes that they were all facing "a convenient point of reckoning, a moment to attempt comparisons."

George Garrett, a Jones biographer, notes that Jones "really thought he was living and working in approximately the world inhabited by Hemingway, Faulkner, Fitzgerald, Wolfe, Steinbeck, and Dos Passos." These writers had yet to learn what Garrett calls the "hard facts" of the publishing world and of literary politics, bleak truths they were all spared by early success. Jones, after all, had started his career with the great Scribner's editor Max Perkins.

In New York in February 1952 to accept the National Book Award for *From Here to Eternity*, Jones wrote to his mentor, Lowney Handy, fondly describing one of those long evenings of dinner and drinks with Styron that stretched into the dawn. Jones had prolonged his stay in the city just so he could meet Mailer, who turned out to be "a hell of a fine guy." Mailer's first reaction to Jones and to his book was virtually identical to Styron's:

> It knocked me down and half knocked me out. I thought it was an extraordinary book. I had a sinking feeling, "Well, you're no longer the most talented writer to come out of World War II. You've been replaced." Extraordinary sensation. I've always felt I understood kings losing their crowns ever since. . . . I once wrote a one-act play about Eisenhower and Khrushchev called "Buddies." They were the only equals in the world so they had to become friends. In a way Jones and I were the same. We had the same kind of experience, both young, both had written war novels, both had enormous receptions for their books. So in a certain sense we felt like the touchdown twins.

For a time, Mailer and Jones were fortunate to have Styron between them. They respected him, for he had a literary elegance that eluded them and he deferred to their raw force as writers and personalities. Jones had star quality. "Moving about at night with him was like keeping company with a Roman emperor," Styron remembers. In his genial fashion, Styron would excuse himself from arm-wrestling matches with Mailer: "You're stronger than me, Norman. It's not my idea of fun."

With Mailer and Jones, of course, there had to be arm-wrestling and other contests of strength and shrewdness. Mickey Knox remembers that in 1952 and 1953 he used to join Mailer, James Jones, and William Styron for drinks at the Eighth Avenue bars. They enjoyed playing liar's poker, with Jones losing constantly, Mailer usually winning, and Jones complaining, "You damned Jewboys!" Mailer favored arm-wrestling and did well, according to Knox, because of his strong shoulders. Knox remembers one match, "real late in the evening," when Mailer succeeded in getting Jones's hand to within three inches of the table. Jones was a much bigger man, and he had been a boxer in the army. Knox remembers that it seemed impossible for Jones to recover his position, yet a look of "sheer determination, of fear, a wild kind of look, either close to death or close to violence" came over Jones as he forced Mailer's hand back up. The two men stood that way for a long time—maybe a minute, maybe as much as five minutes, before they decided to call it a draw. "It wasn't pleasant, and suddenly things got very quiet," Knox concludes. He did not feel good about it, having "pushed" Mailer and Jones into it, saying something like "this is the showdown." Knox believed that "something went out of their friendship right there and then . . . and it was pretty awful to watch."

If Mailer had willed himself into the role of champ, Jones looked and evidently took naturally to the role of warrior/writer. Styron summons the effect of Jones's dust-jacket photograph: "Was there ever such a face, with its Beethovenesque brows and lantern jaw and stepped-upon-looking nose?" Jones had enlisted in the army, joined the infantry, seen combat on Guadalcanal, and had sustained a serious head wound. He had killed a Japanese soldier in hand-to-hand combat. With nearly five years in the service, he was the genuine article. It was no effort for Jones to carry himself with "physical ruggedness and a cocky, athletic swagger." He had "something of the charisma of a heavyweight boxing champion," observed Seymour Krim. Mailer had to feel like the pretender.

It is clear from the correspondence that developed between Mailer and Jones that they had great affection for each other. "Just to tell you I love you a little, you fucking bully," Mailer said in one of his letters to Jones, which he signed "Brother Norm." Mailer joined Jones in being utterly serious about fiction in a way that "now seems [to Styron] a little old-fashioned and ingenuous, with the novel . . . in magisterial reign . . . as sacred mission, as icon, as Grail." Mailer and Jones would pump each other up: "Every fucking pulse in you is a writer, and no matter how hard it comes, and how slow, nothing will stop you till you croak," Mailer wrote Jones. "You know out of all the people Ive met, Ive only met two REAL writers besides myself, and thats you and Billy [Styron]. . . . If either of you fails, its like part of me fails too; and I'm sure that both of you feel that of me," Jones replied, assuring his friend, "I love you too."

In the end, who could live up to this holy of holies? Sensing the dissolution of their imagined literary situation six years later, Mailer would have to invent a pretext for their disaffection, accusing both Styron and Jones of abandoning their youthful ideals—the religion of fiction—even as he struggled to produce a novel worthy of Fitzgerald.

"THE MAN WHO STUDIED YOGA"

By the winter of 1951–1952 Mailer had become thoroughly demoralized about his writing. For a month he had worked at "a rather mechanical" novel about Hollywood before dropping it. Then he turned to short stories, writing ten in a few weeks and spending no more than a day on most of them. They were all right, but they did nothing to "raise the house an inch or two," as he later put it in *Advertisements for Myself.* A few of them were set in Japan right after the war, and they marked, in his opinion, "the only time I took a retreat in my work." The stories required only a little investment of his time and almost no risk during a period when he could only come up with "disconnected thoughts" about a novel.

The turning point was a party he had arranged to entertain an editor of a woman's fashion magazine considering one of his stories. Detecting no rapport between them, Mailer thought her "condescending." He resolved to think no more of literary politics. The next morning he woke up with the idea for an ambitious eight-part novel about a "mythical hero," Sergius O'Shaugnessy. But he would begin with a prologue about "a small, frustrated man, a minor artist manqué." O'Shaugnessy would "travel through many worlds, through pleasure, business, communism, church, working class, crime, homosexuality and mysticism." Like Joyce, Mailer would play with time and human character:

Eitel and Elena, for example, would be forty-five and twenty-five in The Deer Park, *and Sergius would be twenty-three, but later in the working class novel, Elena would be a girl of seventeen having her first affair with Sergius whose age would have come from twenty-three to forty. So the past for one would be the future of another.*

Mailer feared that he was no writer at all. He had considered becoming a psychoanalyst, going into business to gather material for a novel, or "working with my hands for a year or two." Yet he had conceived a scheme that could only be accomplished by a great novelist. Nothing could seem to be more self-defeating, especially since he had repeatedly failed (with the exception of *The Naked and the Dead*) at rendering social reality. Now he presumed to create a hero who would take on several institutions at once! Nevertheless, Mailer's plan suited the intrepid identity he wanted to forge for himself. An eight-part novel obviously surpassed the reach of *The Naked and the Dead*. The new project would also surpass *Barbary Shore* by dealing not just with the strangeness of one historical period but also with the phantasmagorical nature of time itself, with the way the writer's imagination can recreate but also displace periods of time, flashing backward and forward between ages as Virginia Woolf does in *Orlando*. Still a young man himself, but one who believed he inhabited several ages at once—behaving sometimes like a mature man and at other times like an adolescent—Mailer had to insist on the writer's power to transcend time and the ages if he was to get out of his rut. As a literary conception, his new work might turn into folly, but it had the merit of renewing faith in his imaginative powers. Nothing was beyond him.

Wisely, Mailer began with the prologue, accomplishing a masterful piece of fiction and regaining his confidence before writing the first novel of his eight-part epic. "The Man Who Studied Yoga" concentrates on Sam Slovoda, "an overworked writer of continuity for comic magazines" who never seems able to organize, to find the proper form for the novel he has been meaning to write for some years: "It is so complex. Too loose, thinks Sam, too scattered."

Much of the story's fun is to be found in the confidential yet elusive and reserved tone of the anonymous narrator: "I would introduce myself if it were not useless. The name I had last night will not be the same as the name I have tonight. For the moment, then, let me say I am thinking of Sam Slovoda." Is the narrator meant to be taken as one of the author's personae? Is this why the narrator's name changes? A new name for every new story the author writes? This narrator has an existential identity (no references to his past or future) reminiscent of *Barbary Shore*. But in his engaging drollery the narrator of "The Man Who Studied Yoga" is far more provocative and convincing than Mikey Lovett. The narrator's turns of phrase, his light, deft irony suggest the very mastery of character and circumstance that eludes Sam. As Andrew Gordon suggests, "The anonymous narrator acts as curative, as therapist for both the tale and its hero." Or as Frederick Busch puts it, "The narrator is Sam's *alter ego*, his other self, waiting to be born." If the narrator finds Sam fascinating, it is for the same reason Mailer does: Sam's is a "story of a man trying to give birth to himself."

A wonderful teasing undercurrent in the narrator's comments creates a fascinating sensation of being immersed in the immediacy of Sam's experience—not by an omniscient intelligence but by a literary mind literally "thinking" of the character at hand. "I know what Sam feels," the narrator says matter-of-factly. One might suspect the narrator is Sam's psychiatrist: "It is just that I, far better than Sam, know how serious he really is, how fanciful, how elaborate, his imagination can be." But the story also contains considerable skepticism of psychoanalysis and of psychiatric jargon.

"I mock Sam, but he would mock himself on this," the narrator notes in describing Sam's "secret conceit that he was an extraordinary lover." Certainly the narrator has much of Mailer's divided sensibility, for he adds: "One cannot really believe this without supporting at the same time the equally secret conviction that one is fundamentally inept." The narrator is a self-described romantic, as Mailer surely is, and both sympathize with "the antagonism [Sam] feels that Eleanor [his wife] has respected his private talent [as a lover] so poorly, and has not allowed him to confer its benefits upon more women."

Sam is not Mailer, of course, but he can be regarded as a fiction Mailer has drawn of himself, for Mailer has lived Sam's bohemian fantasy of an unheated loft-life and suffered the sexual disenchantment of a wife who has questioned his manhood. Sam is Mailer's effort at literary psychoanalysis, and the story reflects Mailer's belief that he can diagnose himself better than any psychiatrist could.

"The Man Who Studied Yoga" is about a man in midcareer who questions his accomplishments and his maturity. He has opinions on most of the subjects of interest to Mailer, but his insights are never acted on, and the narrator is sympathetic but disappointed in him. Sam knows he lacks "energy and belief," but he plans "to write an article some day about the temperament of the ideal novelist," which is linked in his mind with a conception that it is not possible to

> have a hero today. . . .a man of action and contemplation, capable of sin, large enough for good, a man immense. There is only a modern hero damned by no more than the ugliness of wishes whose satisfaction he will never know. One needs a man who could walk the stage, someone who—no matter who, not himself. Someone, Sam thinks, who reasonably could not exist.

Sam is ruminating, of course, on Mailer's prescription for the perfect novelist, the one Hemingway tried to become.

Rather than recklessly taking on the subjects that bemuse him—sex, politics, psychology—Sam is reduced to watching a pornographic movie with his wife and friends, and after a second viewing alone with his wife, he makes love with her passably well but in a passive way that characterizes a life that in trying to avoid pain succeeds "merely in avoiding pleasure."

"The Man Who Studied Yoga" is a story told by Alan Sperber, one of the guests invited to watch the pornographic movie. Alan describes Cassius O'Shaugnessy, "an absolutely extraordinary fellow" with an "amazing career" which includes having served "in France with Dos Passos and Cummings." As "one of the founders of the Dadaist school," said to be an influence on T. S. Eliot, a monk and a Communist, a Trotskyist, an anarchist, then a pacifist imprisoned during World War II and a companion of gangsters before going to India to study yoga, he appears to be a parody of Sam's ideal artist-activist hero as well as of the "mythical hero" of Mailer's own eight-part odyssey.

Sperber's story heads toward the ultimate mystical revelation of what Cassius learned from contemplating his navel in India, where it seemed by giving "a counter-clockwise twist" his navel would unscrew and he would receive "the reward of three years of contemplation." But the effect of this unscrewing is comically inconsequential: " 'Damn,' said Cassius, 'if my ass didn't fall off.' " Alan has told the story to achieve the maximum degree of suspense and uncertainty in an audience of friends who cannot fathom what he is leading up to. The punch line is irritating, for they are impatiently awaiting the showing of the pornographic film.

The story's denouement is unsettling because their intellectual pretensions are burlesqued. They would just as soon see a dirty movie where the revelation is not metaphysical but merely ridiculously physical.

"The Man Who Studied Yoga" exposes postwar America's "wasting of productive energy," a theme Mailer began to develop in the early 1950s in a series of nonfiction articles. In "The Meaning of Western Defense" (1953), for example, he decries the "psychological contradictions" driving Americans into "more passivity, anxiety, hysteria and guilt than the passivity, anxiety, hysteria and wasteful obsessions of the Soviet." The "inner crisis" of Americans Mailer speaks of in "The Meaning of Western Defense" is dramatized in "The Man Who Studied Yoga," in which habit-ridden Americans exhibit accelerating "sexual tastes," fill themselves with "onanistic substitutes" like the pornographic film, and then are riddled with "guilt and anxiety."

This portrait of American ambivalence is Mailer's own dilemma writ large.

DISSENT

The year Mailer wrote "The Man Who Studied Yoga" (1952) Irving Howe established a new journal, *Dissent*. Raising money and assembling a staff of editors, Howe wrote to Mailer and then met him at the Oyster Bar in Grand Central Station. Mailer was extremely cordial even though Howe had severely criticized *Barbary Shore* for its "element of the intellectually jejune." (Howe would always find Mailer above petty quarrels and grudges.) Howe outlined to him "the idea of a non-party, non-ideological magazine of the left which would go against the dominant trends of the time. . .and attack McCarthyism more vigorously than some of the others in the intellectual community." Mailer agreed to become an editor and to contribute occasional articles. "We were more political in the traditional sense than he was," Howe observed, "but he was nice to have around."

Mailer would gradually drift away from *Dissent*. Howe puts it: "He was not the kind of man who is going to stick to anything for very long. He had his own interests," Mailer kept his name on the masthead and clearly sympathized with any group that wanted to be independent of the liberal cant, the political hysteria, and the conservatism of the times.

Dissent would, in fact, be the first to publish his most important essay, "The White Negro."

Mailer would always pride himself on being a maverick, so individual that he could avoid the stereotyping and intimidation by the institutions of the time that were stifling dissent. A year after the founding of *Dissent* he dealt with an attack on his father with great shrewdness and humor. During a Civil Service Commission check, Barney Mailer, working as an accountant for the U.S. Army, was identified as a security risk. Doubts had been raised by Barney's association with a "concealed Communist"—his son, Norman. Barney thought the charge preposterous and turned the matter over to Cy Rembar, who collaborated with Norman on an affidavit they hoped would squelch the allegation and expose the "silliness of the case." Mailer addressed himself to two questions: Did he have any influence over his father and was he (Norman) a concealed Communist? Mailer characterized Barney's temperament as "conservative" and "stable." He had never tried to influence his father, to learn about his work, and Barney had never shared information about his job with his son. Indeed, they disagreed politically—not an uncommon phenomenon between fathers and sons, Norman pointed out. Moreover, did members of the loyalty board think their children had enough influence over them to lead them into "activities or attitudes unnatural or repugnant" to their own outlooks and temperaments? The charge of being a concealed Communist made no sense, since Mailer had written and spoken openly about his political beliefs. He had been called various things—an anarchist, a Trotskyist, a splinter socialist—but so far as he could see he had had no political influence on anyone. And how could he be serving the Communist Party when much of his writing had attacked its dogmas? Mailer suggested that if a secret recording device were to be put in his parents' home, not much evidence of political conversation would result. He ended on a comic note, producing a sample of a rare family conversation about politics that he hoped would make the charges against Barney seem ridiculous:

> NORMAN MAILER: *I think the whole thing in Korea is hopeless. It's a pilot-light war. Ignorant Americans and Orientals are just butchering each other.*
>
> I. B. MAILER: *I don't know where an intelligent boy like you picks up such idiotic rubbish.*

> *FAN MAILER (the mother): Don't call him an idiot.*
> *NORMAN MAILER: Well, he's not so smart himself.*
> *I. B. MAILER: I never talked to my father the way you talk to me.*

The affidavit was successful. Barney did not even have to attend a hearing.

LORD FAUNTLEROY

Mailer the radical was only one side of the man. Norman took Adele to Provincetown for the summer of 1952 and surprised Nat Halper by how "humbly" he asked permission to bring Adele for a visit. This courtly behavior puzzled Halper until he realized "there was a part of him that was still a young boy even as he was consciously becoming a macho figure." Mailer had been taught not to "intrude on people" and not to "disoblige" them. This gentlemanly code, as Halper saw it, derived from a "different tradition, back to Lord Fauntleroy."

The refined, romantic side of the man clearly came from Barney, but by itself this code was stifling and unproductive. It put Barney in an extremely passive position, since he could not deign to do business with the rough world Fanny confronted so heartily. As a result, Barney could seem both hapless and irresponsible, and there would be times when his outlandish behavior perhaps compensated for his ineffectiveness and provided an escape from his gentleman's role. Barney, no less than Norman, needed his outlets. When Shirley Fingerhood met Barney in the early 1950s, he struck her as a "somewhat broken" man, with a "subsidiary" role in the family and a tendency to get in trouble over gambling debts. He was reputed to have lost his clients' money, and on one trip to Mexico with Fanny to see their granddaughter, Susan, he evidently got "heavily in hock," according to Larry Alson. Adeline Lubell Naiman remembers Norman swearing her to secrecy about Barney's gambling, as though he were telling her "why he was angry with his father." Barney was something of a drunk and "sort of a braggart," which seemed "unforgivable" to Naiman.

By the early fall of 1952 Mailer wrote to the Gwaltneys refreshed from two weeks in Provincetown and obviously pleased that he had 140 pages of a new novel in the works. Yet he could not seem to stand still. The writing proved difficult (the subject was Hollywood) and he quarreled with Adele. Should he commit himself to this woman who had, in Halper's words, "pretensions to secret, primitive knowledge"?

After a "slight falling out" with Adele, Mailer felt he had to get away from the city. So he and Mickey Knox set off by car to California, where Mailer was going to investigate the possibility of writing another screenplay. Mailer made less than an ideal traveling companion, getting into an argument with Knox about the route they were to take in their detour to Arkansas to visit the Gwaltneys. With Knox driving and Mailer reading the map, they went a hundred miles out of the way and fought over whether the driver or the navigator was at fault. They did not speak to each other for two days.

Mickey Knox liked Fig Gwaltney's easygoing country manners, and he tried to stay out of the way as Mailer and Gwaltney discussed writing. "It was their night," Knox puts it. Back on the road and heading into Arizona, Mailer asked Knox if it would be much of a detour to visit Palm Springs. Knox later felt that Mailer had this on his itinerary all along, for in *The Deer Park* he describes Palm Springs perfectly: "He had everything right—the architecture, the vegetation, everything. . . .We couldn't have spent one hour there."

In Hollywood Mailer met with several actors and directors. Knox thinks that Mailer may have used John Huston as a partial model for the character of Charles Eitel, the director in *The Deer Park*, who must pit his talent and integrity against the cowardly, commercial milieu of an industry quickly caving in to political pressures that result in blacklisting.

The Hollywood interlude ended uneventfully but served its purpose, for by the end of 1952 Mailer had a complete draft of *The Deer Park* to show Stanley Rinehart. But the editors at Rinehart had their doubts about the book's coherence and secured Mailer's permission to show it to John Aldridge for a critique. On the understanding that Mailer would not see his remarks, Aldridge wrote a four-page negative report on the crude state of the manuscript and its "dull, mechanical, monotonous, [and] passionless presentation of experience."

Aldridge liked Mailer, but he had tried to take an objective view of a book not ready for publication. In retrospect, the critic takes a rather wry attitude toward his high-minded dismissal of Mailer's work, although he has not altered his opinion very much. To Aldridge's consternation at the time, the editors gave Mailer his report and used it to reject the manuscript. Naturally, an angry Mailer wrote Aldridge, comparing his methods to General MacArthur "delivering harsh pronunciamentos from your high and lonely peak, deriving your pleasure, I suspect, from the bitter notion that you've been true to yourself and hang the consequences." There were more exchanges, with Mailer calling his manuscript a first draft and Aldridge answering he had not read the book on that basis. Remarkably, Mailer announced a halt to the bickering, simply admitting their difference of opinion and resuming their hitherto cordial relations.

Mailer was nevertheless shaken by the reception of his new work. In a letter to the Gwaltneys he admitted that the novel did not satisfy him. The characters were not right, and he would have to do a complete rewrite. In April 1953 he was still hard at work, spending all day on the new version and complaining to the Gwaltneys about how "brutal" it was to write. He and Adele were preparing to visit them. Mailer reported to Fig on Adele's attendance at art school full time, producing eccentric abstract expressionist canvases, which, he thought, showed some improvement.

Bea had moved to Mexico, where she had married Steve Sanchez and was studying in medical school. Norman dreaded a visit he knew he had to make in order to see his daughter, Susan. On the way there in the spring of 1953, he and Adele stopped to see the Gwaltneys. Norman liked to play the Southern gentleman, reassuring them that Adele "will have a wedding ring for your friends," but Ecey was never certain when he was "going to be conventional and when he wasn't." Norman shocked Ecey when he "bopped" Adele on the arm during a quarrel. People did not hit each other in Ecey's set, and she disliked this physical expression of anger. Compared to Bea, Ecey found Adele uneasy in the South and speculated that it might have something to do with her dark skin. In Ecey's view, Adele always brought things around to the subject of sex. Adele wanted to know all about Ecey's sex life, if she had had an abortion, if she had fucked Fig before their marriage. Sometimes Norman got irritated with Adele's obsession with her own body: "You're always worried about your fucking period. Let's don't talk about your period all the time."

On the way to Mexico to see Susan, Norman and Adele stopped in New Orleans to attend a party at which they met Patti Cozzi and Woody Leafer, who introduced Mailer to peyote. When Norman began to hallucinate about Aztec human sacrifices, Adele got frightened, vowing never again to try such stuff. He wanted to vomit and was sick for a whole day. Cozzi remembers Adele during this short stay as a "very sweet, nice person."

Mexico, Mailer wrote the Gwaltneys in July, calmed their spirits. They had spent the last two weeks traveling with his sister, Barbara, and her husband, Larry, around the country. Norman loved the contrasts between jungles and valleys and mountains, "the long lonely vistas of the Southwest," and the "incredibly beautiful towns"—some of them more exquisite than what he had seen in Europe. Driving was an adventure: "It's a fabulous drive through deep canyons, hairpin curves, terrific descents and ascents, etc." It was exhilarating but exhausting, since one could go a hundred miles without more than a two-hundred-yard straightaway. "You get a stroke passing some of those trucks." For fifty-five dollars a month they got a place at the Turf Club, just outside of Mexico City "in a pretty little canyon." The house was a little strange, with a kitchen, bathroom, and a living room "shaped like a semi-circle with half the wall of glass, and a balcony bedroom." He and Adele joined Barbara and Larry in Acapulco for a few days, where he admired the "high jungle cliffs falling from the rocks into the sea." His first experience with deep-sea fishing excited him, and he managed to pull in an eighty-five-pound sailfish almost nine feet long. Although he had hoped to work some on his novel, he felt so relaxed and mellow that he hardly touched it.

In December 1953 Susan came to New York for a visit, and Mailer reported it to Fig Gwaltney:

> *Susy is getting more like Grandma every day. It's really funny to see the two of them together. Same determined mouths, same stubborn little chins. She's getting a little spoiled to my taste what with the relatives all gushing over her, so that the other day at the dinner table hearing her perform like a little trained pig, I said: Susan, do me a favor. SHUT UP. Susan: You are too serious, you make me sad. Norman: (furiously) You heard what I said.*
> *(Silence)*
> *Susan: (after three minutes) Why do you say "Shut up?" Why do you not say "Keep quiet?"*

Mailer continued to struggle with the manuscript of *The Deer Park*, taking time out to write long letters to Fig Gwaltney, appraising Fig's writing as well as giving progress reports on his own. Mailer called Gwaltney a "natural born writer" but also accused Fig of sloppiness and not working hard enough, not revising enough. Although Mailer occasionally sounded pompous, he almost always tempered his criticism with some kind of self-deprecating comment that told Gwaltney he could take or leave the advice. He also confided to Gwaltney his worry over not having found a subject for his own next novel.

On February 23, 1954, Mailer wrote Gwaltney about Adele's lovely "productive" period. She had completed "five lovely canvases." By April they were considering marriage, and Mailer contemplated ways to "skip all the family crap." On April 19 they were married at City Hall with his parents "in attendance." It was a very casual affair: no flowers, no big announcements. Although he had been telling friends about the impending marriage he had been reluctant to go through with it, sensing that marriage would give an eager Adele a new hold on him.

An unhappy Fanny held her tongue—until the day she and Adele went to Saks to buy a "hostess gown" for Adele. In the fitting room, Fanny exploded when she discovered that her new daughter-in-law did not shave under her arms. Barney, on the other hand, seemed delighted with Adele, teasing her and doing his "little flamenco" dance for her and laughing. Yet he was punctilio itself and frowned on anything he deemed improper, except for his gambling losses, which Adele suspected Norman of having to cover. Fanny refused to pay her husband's debts, and when a crisis neared, with several gambling partners threatening Barney, Fanny intervened, telling them that she would go to the police and expose all of them if they did not leave her husband alone. She recognized that gambling was Barney's "ruination," but she concluded that "at heart he was very honest and always treated me like a lady." For father and son, the role of Prince Charming—if not wholly satisfying to them—served nevertheless as an indispensable part of the Mailer identity.

Nearing the summer of 1954, Mailer had completed another draft of *The Deer Park*, which was accepted by Rinehart with little enthusiasm, although Mailer's editor, Ted Amussen, was "high on it." Exhausted by his ordeal with the manuscript and suffering from a "lousy liver" (probably the result of getting jaundice in the Philippines and drinking too much), he set off with Adele for another summer in Mexico. Emulating Hemingway, he became obsessed with bullfighting, an aficionado of the "passes" who contemplated getting into the ring himself. To relieve his depression over *The Deer Park* he began smoking marijuana in earnest; it provided him a sense of renewal just when he felt most jaded.

Sometimes, however, the pot turned him ugly, and a streak of violence and sexual adventuring began to appear. Making the acquaintance of a man who had been imprisoned for killing his wife, Mailer wanted to know all the details, about how it felt right after the man shot her. Later that winter, he would become engrossed in the story of one of William Styron's friends, who had stabbed his girl. Happening to walk into the kitchen as Adele picked up a large knife to slice a salami, he noticed the knife accidentally pointed at his stomach and said, "You don't dare, baby." The tough talk had become habitual for a man who had had few opportunities to be "one of the boys." When two of his friends started reminiscing about their youth, telling lurid tales about a "gang bang" and a "penis-measuring contest," a silent Mailer finally blurted out, "Christ . . . I was going to Hebrew School every afternoon."

PSYCHIC OUTLAW

The trouble started in the fall of 1954. Stanley Rinehart had finally read the new version of *The Deer Park*, and he was shocked—especially by a scene that depicted (rather obliquely) Bobby, an aspiring actress, performing fellatio on movie mogul Herman Teppis. Rinehart worried about the reaction of his mother (the novelist Mary Roberts Rinehart, then in her late seventies). Mailer had abandoned his subtitle, "A Search for the Obscene," and his work by today's standards hardly seems pornographic, yet it would offend and worry more than a half-dozen publishers who rejected the novel—not so much because of its language, which was less profane than *The Naked and the Dead*, but because sex and the talk of sex became such an important theme.

At first, Mailer agreed to make changes in the scene. He could tell how deeply Rinehart had been offended. Tired after his long labor on *The Deer Park*, he hoped to recuperate enough to put together ideas he had for two novels—one on bullfighting and the other about a concentration camp. Yet it hurt Mailer's opinion of himself to give in, so after thinking about it for a day he called Ted Amussen to explain he would not change a word. When Amussen met Mailer to explain Rinehart's decision not to publish the book, Mailer tried to talk him out of it. Seeing it was no use, he threw down some change on the table saying, "Okay, you son of a bitch, that's the end of that" and walked out.

Severing the connection with Rinehart meant not only suffering the anxiety of getting another publisher but interrupting plans for a new novel as well. Not only did several publishers decline to publish *The Deer Park* but such prestigious figures as Bennett Cerf campaigned against it, implying that the book would be harmful to the publishing community. Mailer was astonished. How could he ever have thought publishers were "gentlemen," that they actually liked him, and that they would honor his ideas even if they did not like them? Mailer had his own misgivings about *The Deer Park* and wondered whether it might not be a minor work, but where were the great editors like Max Perkins who would stand by an author for the sake of future work? Suddenly Mailer felt like an adolescent whose illusions had just been shattered. He was the victim of an extraordinary innocence: "The fine America which I had been at pains to criticize for so many years was in fact a real country which did real things and ugly things to the characters of more people than just the characters of my books."

Acting as his cousin's attorney, Cy Rembar challenged Rinehart's contention that the novel was "obscene" and therefore unpublishable. Rembar offered to "test the issue in a suit for the advance of royalties." Confronted with legal action, Rinehart "held to his position, but . . . paid Mailer for the privilege of not publishing his book," Rembar notes.

The shift in Mailer's character at this point was remarkable. He began to enjoy his status as outcast, reveling in the murderous feeling of a "psychic outlaw." In a letter to the Gwaltneys (February 15, 1955), he confessed: "It feels good to feel mad. . . . I had been needing a kick in the ass, and the result is that I've been liking myself better because I discovered I was still a fighter." Physically ill with his liver complaint, psychically low as a result of trying to maintain an image of the successful and popular author through the debacle of *Barbary Shore*, Mailer finally let go and allowed himself the pleasure of becoming a bad boy. Egged on by the feisty Adele, he prepared himself to "take on the world."

As rejections of *The Deer Park* accumulated, Adele remembers Norman ranting, "Those motherfuckers. I'll show them." To Adele, her husband was on the "firing line." *The Naked and the Dead* was "a tough act to follow," and a "lot of people" were waiting for the "Boy Wonder" to "fall on his face." Of course, he had his share of supporters, but either way he confronted tremendous pressure.

Mailer praised his wife's fighting spirit to his friends. Adele says she did what she thought her man wanted. The first five years of her marriage were hectic; they always seemed to be moving. They had perhaps five apartments in ten years, Adele recalls. They were in search of something, but she could not say in so many words just what it was. They could not seem to settle down. They had the money to own property, but both of them shied away from it. Rhoda Lazare Wolf describes Adele as both "follower and leader." Adele had neither the desire nor the power to check Norman's excesses.

Things seemed almost too easy when Walter Minton at Putnam agreed to take *The Deer Park* as Mailer had written it, believing the controversy over its obscenity would increase sales. Mailer seemed rejuvenated by a "ferment of ideas," writing every day in a journal not for publication but just to discover what he thought. Writing, which had become an obligation, had depressed his spirits over the past eight years; now he wrote for the sheer joy of it.

As Mailer's view of himself changed, as he became more aggressive, he began to doubt that he had done justice to his narrator-hero in *The Deer Park*. Mailer said he had to revise *The Deer Park* one more time, "ripping up the silk of the original syntax." The novel, in short, would have to be made of much rougher material—as would its author if he was to survive the publishers and critics.

The Deer Park, then, continues *Barbary Shore*'s quest for a heroic identity. The narrators of both novels resemble Paul Scarr in *A Transit to Narcissus* in that they are on journeys of self-discovery, in which they must shuck off their timid selves. O'Shaugnessy shares Lovett's sense of uncertainty and estrangement: "I was never sure of myself. I never felt as if I came from any particular place, or that I was like other people." He speaks for a Mailer who had always felt outside of Brooklyn and could never measure himself within its precincts. As he puts it in *Advertisements for Myself*, "for Brooklyn where I grew up is not the center of anything." Only his work could put him at the center of things; only a courageous novel could make up for being a Brooklyn boy.

O'Shaugnessy is more self-aware, more active as a writer than Lovett is in *Barbary Shore*, where his writing is a given but is not really explored. *The Deer Park*, on the other hand, is the product of Sergius's imagination: It represents his coming to terms with himself and his

world. Although his friendship with Charles Eitel, a blacklisted Hollywood screenwriter and director, is reminiscent of Lovett's friendship
with McLeod, Eitel's story is framed in Sergius's words, and when Eitel
speaks it is in the context of O'Shaugnessy's critical point of view.

Eitel has been a Communist sympathizer, a fellow traveler whose
presence embarrasses his motion-picture bosses. He then alienates them
by refusing to cooperate with a congressional committee investigating
subversives. Eitel turns from Hollywood with the hope that he can
recover his talent honestly as an artist but finds that the great film he had
always dreamed of creating has been corrupted by his absorption of the
cheap techniques of commercial filmmaking. He takes heart from his
affair with Elena Esposito; it makes him feel he can conquer his doubts
and produce an original script. When the lovers waver in their loyalty to
each other and fail to put trust in their love, Eitel capitulates to producer
Collie Munshin by agreeing to testify about his Communist past and to
construct his film according to Hollywood conventions.

In O'Shaugnessy's view, Eitel does not have the courage of his
convictions. In spite of considerable intelligence and absence of cant,
Eitel lacks the fortitude to stick with his original script, which is based
on West's *Miss Lonelyhearts*—as was Mailer's and Malaquais's script for
Goldwyn. Eitel is scared to go it alone, he realizes, when to his astonishment Elena leaves him. Eitel loves her but cannot seem to help taking a
superior attitude toward her as he does toward nearly everyone except
O'Shaugnessy, who may be able to avoid his mistakes. Elena is a failed
dancer of limited intellectual gifts, yet she proves to have more strength
and dignity than Eitel, rejecting her dependence on him even though the
alternative she faces—going to live with the pimp Marion Faye—puts
her in a worse position. Elena makes what Mailer might call an existential choice, forsaking the status quo for an uncertain but at least open-
ended future. Continuing to live with Eitel only closes off Elena's
possibilities and makes her feel small, just as Eitel's surrender to
Munshin diminishes his opinion of himself. This love story—the best
Mailer has ever written—obviously corresponds to his own wrestling
with Hollywood, with popular success, and with his desperate efforts to
create a heroic sensibility. It is also a love story that his narrator,
O'Shaugnessy, creates based on surmise, on his observation of the
characters, on what they have told him, and—most importantly—on his
will to find a meaning in the story that will help him live his own life. For

as Eitel loves and loses Elena, and as he gradually turns his original
script into a Hollywood cliché, O'Shaugnessy's own life story—from
orphan to war hero—draws Hollywood interest. He is sorely tempted to
sell his biography (sell himself, in effect) to the studio, where he may
also become a film star. What prevents him from doing so is the example
he has made of Eitel:

> *"For you see," [Eitel] confessed in his mind, "I have lost the final desire*
> *of the artist, the desire which tells us that when all else is lost, when love*
> *is lost and adventure, pride of self, and pity, there still remains that*
> *world we may create, more real to us, more real to others, than the*
> *mummery of what happens, passes, and is gone."*

Sergius goes on to imagine that Eitel equates the creative act with
Sergius's rebellion, with the "small trumpet of your defiance."

Sergius invents an Eitel from whom he can learn, and his lessons are
facilitated by his relationships with many of Eitel's lovers and friends.
Sex star Lulu Meyers, for example, has been married to Eitel but now is
free to engage in an affair with O'Shaugnessy, which she eventually
terminates, much to his despair. Yet from Lulu he learns what it means
to become the ultimate Hollywood product. Lulu is an exhibitionist; she
is dedicated to the craft of acting and yet she relishes glamour roles; she
scorns publicity and yet she is responsible for the best gossip items
about her. Above all, she is characterized by her mastery of the camera,
so that every photograph of her is a work of genius. Entirely a captive of
her stardom, she is a good example of what O'Shaugnessy might
become if he turns his life into a Hollywood script.

In his final revision, Mailer tried to give a hard, clipped edge to
O'Shaugnessy's words to suggest he has avoided the extremes of self-
pity and self-aggrandizement that characters like Lulu tend to indulge
in. The Putnam version uses fewer adjectives and replaces the rather
elegant phrasing of the Rinehart draft with more direct and concrete
talk.

If the novel's milieu, Desert D'Or (closely modeled on Palm Springs)
is like Louis XV's Deer Park, that gorge in which innocents like
O'Shaugnessy are engulfed, he barely escapes the gorge by imagining
for himself the lives of its victims, of its pimps and prostitutes, of its
sultans and sycophants, and forges a style of his own. At his best

O'Shaugnessy "invents his thoughts (the way Ishmael rendered Ahab),"
suggests one critic. Yet many readers of *The Deer Park* remain unper-
suaded by O'Shaugnessy's character. How can he be a believable hero
when he escapes virtually unscathed? He never really makes a false
move or does anything to truly damage himself. He resists temptation all
too well by simply perceiving the mistakes of others. Compared to Eitel,
Sergius is untested. He is a gentleman adventurer, with the emphasis
still on the gentleman. He is like Mailer's childhood adventure heroes,
who cannot get hurt.

This tender, self-protective quality was an aspect of Mailer's youthful
self that he had tried to explore and to exorcise in *A Transit to Narcissus*.
In *The Naked and the Dead*, Hearn is removed from the action before he
can be truly tested. In *Barbary Shore*, Lovett has even less opportunity
to find out what kind of man he is. Instead, the powerful characters are
Croft and Hollingsworth, both of whom express a violent energy that
Mailer is unwilling to invest in his ostensible heroes. In *The Deer Park*
Marion Faye performs a similar function for Sergius O'Shaugnessy. As
Robert Solataroff recognizes, Faye is "the secret hero of *The Deer
Park*." He is Sergius's dark twin, the antisocial antihero who rejects
romance in favor of pimping, who lets loose his murderous instincts in
his degradation of women, taking Elena away from Eitel in an ugly
episode that deflects O'Shaugnessy's own sexual interest in her.

Faye is not without his sensitivities. He recognizes the true artist in
Eitel and castigates him for commercializing his genius. Faye tries for
his own kind of integrity, not pretending to be altruistic or compassionate. He treats Elena badly to prove to himself that he is devoid of
sentimentality and hypocritical feelings about love, yet he comes to
realize that he has his limits, that he is not devoid of feeling for Elena or
for Eitel. Why else would he care that Eitel has sold himself to Hollywood? In Robert Merrill's words, Faye attains a kind of "perverse
integrity," knowing what "he does *not* like," but he is unable to present
a positive alternative, a counterculture.

Sergius and Marion have a common root in Dorothea O'Faye (a
former Hollywood gossip columnist), Marion's mother, and Sergius's
protectress when he first comes to Desert D'Or. She is a sexualized
Jewish mother who holds court, playing the same games night after
night with the same cast of characters—who are rather like the repetitive clichés of Hollywood scripts. Dorothea presides over her house in
Desert D'Or like a queen, possessive and aggressive and reminiscent of

Guinevere in *Barbary Shore*, but both Sergius and Marion escape Dorothea's clutches. Sergius becomes Eitel's protégé while Faye rebels against his mother and her Hollywood society by establishing his own house with his own call girls. He goes against the grain of conventionality while Sergius is allowed to slip through it by becoming an artist, avoiding the worst assaults just as he did when he was a prizefighter, hoping he would not catch a blow to the head that would mar his looks or his brains. Faye, Sergius's surrogate, suffers the fate Mailer would not inflict on himself or on his nice hero: Faye, his arm locked around his head in pain from a car accident, is put in prison for not having a permit for the gun in his glove compartment. As Mailer's incipient hero, Faye loses consciousness thinking the year in prison will give him "more education."

In spite of declaring himself a "psychic outlaw," Mailer did not make Marion Faye his hipster hero, even if he subsequently accorded him the status of *The Deer Park*'s "evil genius." Mailer succeeded somewhat in beefing up O'Shaugnessy's style, but he recognized that "not enough happened" to Sergius in the second half of the book. It was too late to do another rewrite. Instead, he worked furiously, making changes in the Rinehart galleys, which Putnam used after putting off publication from the summer to the fall of 1955. A wreck because of the "pot, with benny, saggy, Miltown, coffee, and two packs a day" that kept him going, he did not have the stamina to attempt the novel of a much more ambitious Sergius O'Shaugnessy who would have accepted Hollywood's offer and who would have had to deal with the corruption that Faye confronts.

On August 25, 1955, Mailer wrote Jones about finishing his rewrite of the galleys: "I'm empty, vitiated, flat, bored, wrung out rag-like, and all the other states that I guess you know as well as me." He was in a "real post-delivery physical depression now." He asked for Jones's professional opinion and could not help bragging that *The Deer Park* would make Jones envious. It surpassed *The Naked and the Dead*—"smaller but deeper," Mailer thought. Jones's competitive instincts would be aroused, as Mailer's had been in reading *From Here to Eternity*. He went on to say that he and Jones and Styron were family. They could rival each other but would band together when others attacked their work, for "our books clear ground for one another."

The Deer Park sold fifty thousand copies and received more negative than positive reviews. In his own mind, Mailer associated the "middling success" of his novel with his failure to work through to a complete vision of the artist as outcast. He did not remain true to his faith in the writer who often "works best in opposition" to his society. In his secret heart of hearts, he had wanted another best-seller and the literary community's approval. This is why Eitel's story of conviction and compromise had meant so much to him. Now he vowed that his next effort would be the "proper book of an outlaw."

5.

ADVERTISEMENTS FOR MYSELF (1955–1959)

THE VILLAGE VOICE

Even the best reviews of *The Deer Park* tended to be mixed. Malcolm Cowley, for example, suggested that although Mailer was "not a finished novelist," he was "one of the two or three most talented writers of his generation." But he had not yet lived up to his potential. He felt depleted and could not sleep. He smoked too much. Mickey Knox introduced Mailer to a doctor who prescribed Seconal, which Mailer took with bourbon. Soon he could not sleep at all without the pills and blamed the doctor, a man Adele thought got a kick out of treating the literati and quoted Shakespeare when Mailer visited the office.

Another kind of writer might have retreated from the action, started a novel, or given himself a fallow year. A restless Mailer, "like an actor looking for a new role," he later confessed, regarded silence or working in solitude on a novel with fright, for his confidence had been shaken. He had Mickey Knox visit bookstores, posing as a buyer, to question salespeople about *The Deer Park*. In Knox's view, his friend, "running scared," wanted to know why his novel was not a bigger seller.

Mailer began to conduct what he called a "self-analysis." He would

pick up accents and try them on himself. He recorded himself and
studied the nuances of his voice. Sometimes he would go into a "deep
personal state," sitting by himself for hours apparently lost in thought.
He even built a kind of isolation booth—carpeted and soundproofed—
to which he would go to scream. He got into fights on the streets and in
bars—on one occasion seriously damaging an eye after a fight with a
sailor who had called his poodle a "queer." Like many of Mailer's
friends, Adele considered his behavior disgusting and absurd. It was
especially ridiculous, she thought, that he should hand over two poodles
on a leash to one sailor as he fought with another. By what kind of rules
did her husband think these men lived? She thought he derived some
kind of pleasure out of these encounters. Jean Malaquais believed that
some part of Mailer "*wanted* to be beaten up."

It was as if Mailer was trying to rip away the remaining protective
layers of that "Jewish boy blob" and get down to the bone, exposing the
dark core of his soul, forsaking his privileges, and learning to survive on
his own. He was deadly serious—even though his aspirations would
continue to have a postadolescent silly side.

Mailer risked his reputation by behaving so foolishly, but in his own
mind it would be worse to reverse course and start a novel he had no
faith in. He needed another kind of forum for his budding ideas, one that
by its very nature allowed him to experiment without having to combat
the heavy judgments of book reviewers. He had bought a thirty-percent
share in a new newspaper, *The Village Voice*, run by his friends Dan
Wolf and Ed Fancher, which was meant to be a kind of European,
underground vehicle for writers. At first he had shown no interest in
the paper's operation, but by late 1955 Mailer was attending editorial
meetings.

By January 1956 the paper was losing a thousand dollars a week.
Mailer offered to write a weekly column to boost circulation. There had
been disagreements about the paper's focus, with Fancher and Wolf
resisting Mailer's call for an all-out attack on society even at the cost of
alienating advertisers. The column was a kind of compromise; in it,
Mailer could have his way, launching his "private war on American
journalism, mass communications, and the totalitarianism of totally
pleasant personality."

In his first column Mailer made sure he would start a fight by insulting
his readers, calling the Village "one of the bitter provinces" full of
"snobs and critics," who had turned "venomous" from "frustrated am-

bition." His theme, reminiscent of "The Man Who Studied Yoga," lacked the ironic, playful, and self-critical suppleness of that story's narrator. Mailer wanted an enemy and declared that for him to have a real impact on the Village he would have to be "actively disliked each week."

If Mailer had wanted to do his own market research to find out what Villagers thought of him, he did not have to wait long for a response. After his second column, in which he had condescendingly warned his audience that reading him would be difficult, negative letters arrived calling him such things as an "adequate journeyman writer" suffering from "illusions of grander," a "narcissistic pest," and a whiner. Parodied and pilloried, he certainly got the attention he sought. There were a few positive responses Mailer regarded as "a favorable turn at the front," for he fancied himself involved in a war, creating conflicts that would stimulate new material for his fiction. Fighting readers about his ideas was a form of action that gave him a sense of dangerous reality and compensated for what one of his readers shrewdly identified as "a sense of your having been hurt and misunderstood too many times." Past the "point of polite intellectual rebuttal," he now used his "pen like a hammer," the reader suggested, noting the pathos in his ploy: "I have a suspicion that the man behind the mask is basically an abnormally tender and sensitive person; it's too bad the world isn't nicer to sensitive people," the letter concluded.

Predictably, Mailer attacked conformity and everything that conspired to support the status quo. He affirmed the authority of the novelist, who prized individuality, who explored human emotions, as opposed to the psychiatrist, who favored a jargon that obscured and diluted the force of human feelings. "Man is a rebel," Mailer affirmed, quoting Robert Lindner, one of the few psychologists he respected. Psychoanalysis crippled its patients, Mailer contended, by trying to make them "adjust to the warpings of an unjust world."

By his sixteenth column, Mailer had found his way to a set of terms, the Hip and the Square, that encompassed his either/or, Manichean view of the world—a distillation of what he had been working toward in *The Deer Park*. The squares, of course, were the conformists, the great middle class that thrived on received opinion and attenuated sex—like the grouping around Sam Slovoda. The hipsters, on the other hand, were more elemental and without intellectual pretensions. "Hip is based on a mysticism of the flesh," Mailer declared. It was not rational like French existentialism but rather depended on impulse and spontaneity.

The hipster did not know where he was going, but he knew he had to be on the move, braving new experiences rather than settling for what he already knew. For a writer nearly out of his mind with worry about the course of his own career, who recklessly reached out for any new experience that might prove therapeutic for his art, the concept of Hip seemed like his salvation.

By his actions, Mailer the artist could change the nature of reality, bringing his own special attitude toward it—as he had argued in his essay "David Reisman Reconsidered" (1954), first published in *Dissent*. The hipster had the sensibility of a novelist making up things as he went along rather than accepting the language and the perceptions of others. Above all, the hipster had a unique style. He had the autonomy that Mailer desperately wanted for himself. This was undoubtedly a male principle, for Mailer held up Hemingway as a forerunner—a man who measured all of reality in terms of his tremendous prowess and appetites, a man with enormous flaws but who had not shied away from testing himself against the big world.

At the moment Mailer despaired of his ability to write a great novel, he wanted to take on the world. His nearly hysterical intransigence gave his struggling *Village Voice* partners (short-staffed and still losing money) fits. He handed in at the very last moment columns that were often twice as long as expected, which necessitated tearing apart the paper to create more space. Sometimes an advertisement had to be dropped to accommodate a long column. Mailer would brook no editing of his words, and he expected them to be perfectly proofread by Fancher, Wolf, and John Wilcock—the one staff member who had significant newspaper experience. Wilcock, who decried Mailer's "lack of professionalism," bore the brunt of Mailer's tirades against the typos.

After further angry episodes with his *Voice* partners, Mailer bowed out of the operation with a financial settlement. He had made a public spectacle of himself for the first time and did not seem to regret it. In a farewell column, he noted that he had wanted the *Voice* to be the first "Hip newspaper" in New York and now had to withdraw because of basic disagreements with the editors, but after four months he had found his subject, "The Hip and the Square," and he "wondered in which form some of us will swing into communication again." The jazziness of a phrase like *swing into communication* indicated a temperament searching for a more limber style, less self-consciously literary, more like a man who had to admit he was improvising as he went along.

The *Village Voice* period took a heavy toll on Mailer. Styron and Jones did not like *The Deer Park* and could not understand why Mailer was wasting himself on journalism. Styron remembers the novel in manuscript. He had "mixed feelings. It seemed claustrophobic to me. There were wonderful scenes," obviously the product of a great talent. Mailer had by no means "disgraced himself," but Styron could not muster any real enthusiasm. Jones, who had such wonderful support from Scribner's, could not believe Mailer's contention that Scribner's lacked the guts to publish the book because of the "sex in it." In an angry note to Mailer that he decided not to send, Jones observed that this was the first time he had ever been disappointed in Mailer and doubted his integrity. Jones leveled with his friend: the book "wasn't good enough" for Scribner's. "It's you who lack the guts, my friend. The REAL kind. MORAL guts. Grow up, boy! In friendship, Jim." In the letter Jones did send (dated March 31), his tone was hardly more conciliatory, for he repeated in slightly milder form the same points and added: "though Ive read the galleys and the finished version, I dont see how you helped it very much."

Jones was quite angry with Mailer on other counts. On February 29, 1956, Mailer had sent him a letter alleging that he had it on good authority that Jones had been trying to start a feud with him and advising him to save his energy for his real enemies. On March 5, Jones replied to say that he had no interest in starting a feud, "literary or personal." Mailer had it wrong: Jones's opinion of him was not "unprintable," although there was no denying that his feelings had cooled. Jones could see that their paths as writers were diverging, but that did not mean they were adversaries. Mailer could rest easy on that score, although Jones believed that he had "someday . . . better learn to distinguish between truthful 'sources' and untruthful ones."

The source, evidently, was Jerry Tschappat, a writer who had been groomed by Jones's mentor, Lowney Handy, a charismatic and rather high-handed leader of a writers' colony notorius for running young writer's lives—including diet and other personal matters. Jones would later have his own falling-out with Handy, but at the moment he defended her and criticized Mailer for interfering with one of her writers—Mailer got Tschappat a publisher before Jones felt he was ready to publish and implied that Jones himself needed help in freeing himself from Handy's clutches. Jones wondered if it had ever occurred to Mailer that Jones might need the discipline she provided and that she kept him from wasting his talent in drinking and fucking sprees?

Mailer replied on March 22 in a rough but still friendly tone. Judging by Jones's long letter, Mailer felt confident in saying "deep in that crusty, fucking heart of yours you probably have the same kind of warmth for me that I have for you." He did not think much of Jones's "crappy half-assed theories" about his engaging in a conspiracy to spirit Jones away from Handy. If that is what Jones really thought, then Mailer's advice was to "just go take your cock and shove it up your own ass, because you're fucking yourself out of a friendship anyway." Jones could not know what Mailer was actually doing, and he was quite mistaken about Mailer's love for the literary life in New York. His views were the same as Jones's, Mailer claimed, signing himself as "Yours, you dumb benighted asshole of a writer, Norman." Enclosed with the letter to Jones was another from Mailer to Jerry Tschappat, explaining he did not want to hear stories about Jones and Handy.

Jones replied to Mailer on March 31, expressing gratitude for both letters. He was still sore about Mailer's relationship with Tschappat and went on for several pages defending Handy's treatment of him. He hastened to assure Mailer that "I still believe there are great books in you. *Great* books. If you can ever get them out. But I certainly doubt very much if youll ever do it while writing a fucking column for the *Village Voice*." Of course, Jones expected a "rebuttal" from Mailer:

> Always remember, if you cant find a psychiatrist for the *Voice*, you always have me. Except I wont let my vanity spread so much as to print our arguments in the *Voice*. I want to be a novelist, not a political and moral essayist. Sorry. A dig. But you got it coming.

Having written through his wrath, Jones admitted, "I still love you." Mailer was an "old brother" whom he invited to come see him "if you think you can stand it."

Styron and Jones were not alone in thinking that something had gone seriously wrong with Mailer. During the *Village Voice* period, Lyle Stuart had lunch with Cy Rembar and complained that Mailer was "throwing away a certain talent" by playing to the *Voice* audience to prove "how bright and brilliant he was." If only Mailer would continue in the tradition of *The Naked and the Dead* he would become a "latter-day Charles Dickens, a readable writer who had something to say and could say it," Stuart told Rembar, who was sympathetic but certain he "couldn't do anything" with his cousin. This seems to have been a time in Mailer's life when his family uncharacteristically had little influence on him. Larry Alson recalls that he and Barbara were moving in social circles quite different from Norman's.

Of course, the family still had an involvement in his affairs. For example, Norman always had a place for his father. Walter Minton (Mailer's publisher at Putnam) remembers that between 1956 and 1961 he would get periodic visits from Barney, who did Norman's accounting. Minton liked him, thought of him as "street-smart" with a "no bullshit, dollars and cents attitude," but "always polite." With the whole Mailer family behind him, Norman had enormous support even in his worst periods, but that did not seem to salve the deep hurt he projected aggressively onto others.

Mailer had started to isolate himself from his fellow writers. There had been a time when he would not brook any bad words about Styron. For example, Larry Alson, who had met Styron in the Village and first introduced him to Mailer, notes how stoutly Mailer defended Styron to Jones, who had expressed some doubts. No, Mailer insisted, Styron was in their "class." A different Mailer now got together with Styron to make fun of passages from Jones's *Some Came Running.* "Somebody told Jim," his wife Gloria says, "and he was hurt and mad about that," although he could never quite sever the "bond" between himself and Mailer.

To Mickey Knox, James Jones was a competitive writer, but it seemed to him that Mailer was a much worse case. Jones, at least, developed long-term relationships with fellow writers Irwin Shaw and William Styron. Mailer, on the other hand, seemed to go out of his way to offend writers—snubbing Shaw in a restaurant while Knox stopped at his table to say hello. Gloria Jones, adds: "Jim was very competitive . . . but I don't think Jim was competitive with Norman. His letters to Norman don't show that."

A REAL SWEET OFAY CAT, AN UNEMPLOYED AND UNEMPLOYABLE HAMLET

Mailer thought he had made a mess in writing for *The Village Voice.* He decided to take Adele to Paris. She hoped the trip would be a "delayed honeymoon." She remembers it as a lonely, tense time, with her husband "very nervous," drinking heavily, and suffering from insomnia. They could have seen James Jones, but Mailer avoided him, knowing that Adele found Jones "a parody of the chauvinistic macho type . . . adolescent and silly, almost laughable."

Adele may have been more of a problem for Mailer than either of them wanted to admit. Adeline Lubell Naiman, who had believed so early in the genius of the author of *The Naked and the Dead*, had a falling-out with Mailer shortly before the Paris trip when he accused her of hating Adele. Naiman saw that the marriage was failing and that Mailer lashed out at others and accused them of things that Naiman suspected he felt himself. He attacked Naiman for treating Adele as an intellectual inferior. She asserts she felt nothing of the kind but understood Mailer's charge as a projection on her of the "snobbery that he was sure people must have been feeling toward Adele." Naiman concedes she had some difficulty communicating with Adele but that she liked her and on occasion felt they had achieved a kind of rapport. But Mailer remained unconvinced, and his violent criticism brought her to tears. She felt he had broken a trust between them. He had always treated her with such care and sensitivity. Now she suspected him of using her to work out his own internal conflicts. She vowed never to see him again.

In Paris, Mailer slowly weaned himself away from cigarettes, Seconal, and Benzedrine and tried to write. It was unnerving to discover that the words would not flow, and he began to suspect that he had "burned out" his talent. Very little writing got done during the spring sojourn in Paris. One of his friends there remembers that he was especially concerned with the "problems of writing pornographic novels." He took a very studious approach, exploring the possibility of sustaining interest while the same thing went on page after page. It was a craft he seemed bent on mastering—as he made clear in an incident at Jean Malaquais's studio. In front of Adele, Malaquais and his wife, and another couple, Mailer announced he would read aloud certain passages from a pornographic novel he had picked up in Paris. It seemed very much like a literary exercise—not merely a means of shocking the company. But it was also a kind of test—a challenge to Malaquais to let him do it. Pushing things to the limit and building up the drama of the evening, Mailer said to Malaquais: "If you let me read this out loud, I'll give you a thousand francs." Malaquais said, "What if I don't?" To which Mailer rejoined, "Well, then you have to give me a thousand francs." Without saying anything, Malaquais reached into his pocket and handed Mailer the money and the passages were not read. The episode seemed trivial, yet it captured the tension of the period. Adele seemed to be looking forward to it "in a kind of squirmy way, the woman I was with was on the verge of being shocked, and Malaquais appeared to be rather straitlaced about it," Mailer's friend remembers.

That spring in Paris Mailer met James Baldwin, who reacted ambivalently to a Mailer who liked to think he was cool, a hipster. They recognized each other's talent, yet they could not break through a certain posturing. They took positions. Baldwin deplored Mailer's emphasis on the hip sensuality of blacks, and Mailer suspected Baldwin of merely trying to protect "the Negro people." Each writer condescended to the other. Jean Malaquais thought Baldwin "a confounded snob," a name-dropper who took every opportunity to prove he was more "elegant" and "European" than Mailer. Baldwin, on the other hand, thought that Malaquais "patronized" Mailer "enormously" and did not take him seriously as a writer, which Baldwin did. But Baldwin could not buy Mailer's pretensions as a swinger. The Negro jazz musicians Mailer befriended did not for a moment consider him hip: "They thought he was a real sweet ofay cat, but a little frantic," Baldwin concluded.

On a visit to Arkansas in the summer of 1956, the friendship between Fig Gwaltney and Mailer became strained when Fig made a remark that Norman took as a slight to Adele. He turned on his friend, accusing him of being afraid of Adele, knowing that she was "too much woman for you." Fig could not get over the fact that his friend would attack him in his own home. For a whole evening "he just put us through the wringer," Ecey recalls. Although Norman tried to patch things up in a letter, Ecey believes that Fig could not forgive him. As she puts it, "Many people have indulged him [Mailer]—I have—but not Fig."

By the fall of 1956 the Mailers had decided to move to a farmhouse in Connecticut, where he could quietly work but still be in touch with the literary community around Washington and Roxbury, which included William Styron and James Jones. The change of scenery seemed to perk him up. Around this time he sent one of his bantering letters to Norman Rosten, inviting him to come and enjoy the skiing, especially since Rosten knew Marilyn Monroe, married then to Arthur Miller, "and me and my friends we've always wanted to meet Arthur Miller."

Mailer gained weight. At 175, he was a good thirty-five pounds over what he had weighed in the army. Next to his desk in the barn, he had

light and heavy punching bags for workouts and he started boxing
regularly with Adele's father.

Numerous times Mailer challenged his friends to boxing matches.
Chandler Brossard, a better boxer than Mailer, refused to fight and
attributed his friend's hostility to his inability to write. Brossard looked
upon Mailer in this period as "an unemployed and unemployable
Hamlet."

At one point Mailer even tried to instigate a fight between Adele and
John Aldridge's wife, Leslie. He was evidently more successful with
Bennett Cerf, who obliged him by duking it out in the flower beds
outside the house after Mailer had said, "You're not a publisher, you're a
dentist." This openly confrontational stance deeply offended Fig
Gwaltney, who would not indulge his old army buddy in such antics.
Mailer's behavior was "insulting and crassly adolescent," and Gwaltney
resented his friend acting as though anything he said was "an utterance
of God . . . so let's just stop this second-coming-of-Christ routine," he
said in a bitter letter.

Chandler Brossard noticed that if you did not take note of Adele, she
"had no use for you." When she tried to provoke Brossard, his lack of
interest infuriated her. When her abrasiveness got on Brossard's nerves,
Mailer seemed amused but suggested to his friend that "I'll take her
outside and knock her down a few times." In fact, he did no more than
draw her aside and make an angry show of lecturing her about her
behavior. Adele was a sore point. She was provocative and game for
any gambit her husband proposed. Soon, however, she initiated her
own contests, and friends noticed the tensions increasing between husband and wife. To make matters worse, Mailer sensed that some of his
friends did not take to Adele and he became increasingly defensive
about her.

John Aldridge, also part of the Mailer–Styron grouping, saw Adele in
Norman's shadow. She was, in his words, "clay to be molded." But then
everyone, in a sense, was subordinate to Mailer. Styron, for example,
seemed appealing to Aldridge only in the company of Mailer. Aldridge
calls Styron a consummate literary politician, a "good ol' boy" a little
too pleasant with everyone. His attitude amounted to a kind of "impenetrability." Eventually, Aldridge speculates, Styron saw Mailer "usurping his turf." After all, he had come to Connecticut first, and now he had
been displaced by a new king of the hill, so to speak.

Nat Halper visited the Mailers in Connecticut and was dismayed at how deeply Norman had gotten into literary politics, joining Styron in trashing James Gould Cozzens (*By Love Possessed* had just appeared)— as though Mailer and Styron were brothers bound together "against the enemy." Then later that evening Mailer attacked Styron for playing the literary politician.

Larry Alson and others heard rumors about the Styrons spreading the word that Adele was a lesbian. Referring to this period much later, Adele said of Rose: She was "a very strange gal. I didn't like her and didn't get along with her. She was a pain in the ass, that's all." Both Larry and Barbara thought her brother confused. Larry still recalls with astonishment the time Norman called his home and asked, "Is my wife there?" When a perplexed Alson said, "What?" Mailer replied, "Is Barbara there?" Larry was stunned. Barbara tried to persuade Norman to see a therapist.

Somehow during this disruptive period in Connecticut, Adele managed to have her first successful pregnancy; in her words, she "loved it." On March 16, 1957, Danielle ("Dandy") Mailer was born. Both parents had wanted the baby. In fact, Norman was "crazy" about it, Adele remembers. Fanny and Barney, the doting grandparents, took the train on the weekends to see the new family in Connecticut. Lyle Stuart, who visited the Mailers shortly afterward, remembers a happy family scene. He and Mailer took home movies of Susan playing in the snow with her father's "large standard poodle."

After the euphoria of the birth, however, Adele began to feel isolated. She had her studio and had started acting lessons, but she missed the New York parties—as did Norman. That summer Mailer angered his wife and Jack Begner, a friend and Provincetown doctor, by refusing to allow his infant daughter to be vaccinated. Begner lost patience with Mailer's crackpot theories about "holistic medicine" and told him, "You're not only a menace to yourself, you're a menace to your child." An upset Adele later took the child for the shots.

Walter Minton, Mailer's publisher, shortly thereafter witnessed a scene between Norman and Adele that epitomized a relationship turned confrontational. Stuck behind a slow-moving car in the Lincoln Tunnel, Adele urged Norman to pass, yelling, "You're chicken, you're scared. You're always telling me not to be afraid. Now you're scared!" Swerving around to pass the car, Mailer put himself in the path of an oncoming truck that just had room enough somehow to miss him.

"THE WHITE NEGRO"

Mailer's antics in these years had much to do with the changes in consciousness inspired by Allen Ginsberg, Jack Kerouac, and the rest of the so-called Beat generation. Although Ginsberg looked askance at Mailer's "macho folly," he still regarded him as a kindred spirit doing battle with the repressive and the square. If Mailer had started as a disciple of Dos Passos, he recognized, in Barbara Probst Solomon's words, that he was "on the wrong train." Like the Beats, he wanted to be on the cutting edge and saw them as his competition.

The new Mailer favored the psychology of Wilhelm Reich over that of Sigmund Freud. Where Freud emphasized the individual's adjustment to society, Reich touted sexual energy and the virtues of the orgasm. Mailer constructed what Reich called an "orgone box" designed to imbibe psychic energy. It looked like a huge and handsomely polished Easter egg within which Mailer would enclose himself, feeling at one with the new currents he felt were going to sweep society. In a similar vein, he rented a saxophone in order to "honk" along with the music of Thelonious Monk. Although he could not play the instrument, Mailer believed he was in tune with it, that he was "hip."

Unable to write another novel, Mailer decided to adapt *The Deer Park* for the stage. It gave him an opportunity to cast Marion Faye as the main character and to emphasize the darker elements of the novel that were obscured by making O'Shaugnessy its narrator. In the play version, both Faye and Eitel have been in prison, and Mailer's theme becomes "the nature of failure, both social and private." Changing the setting from Hollywood to hell emphasized the metaphysical status of his characters, who had become untrue to their own natures. At Actors Studio, the play went through a series of "semistage readings" under the direction of Frank Corsaro. It had dramatic power, but the script was diffuse and Mailer overwrote for the actors, not trusting them to supply their own emotions for the roles. Dissatisfied with Anne Bancroft, he suggested that Adele try the part of Elena Esposito. With no stage background, it took Adele some time to grow into the role, but Adele had Elena's sexuality and feistiness—and Elena's concern that she could not hold her own with the intellectual types. Eventually Mailer withdrew the play from production, realizing he had not achieved the right theatrical form for his reworked material.

Adapting his novel for the stage had been a false start, and Mailer knew he wanted to make a statement that would express his newfound grasp of social reality. To do so, however, entailed a tremendous risk, since he would have to speak in his own voice and to take responsibility for his reflections in a way that a novelist can avoid. Writing "The White Negro: Superficial Reflections on the Hipster" (1957) was not only difficult, it was frightening, Mailer has admitted. He was making something heroic out of the very antisocial elements most law-abiding citizens loathe. Even Irving Howe, excited over this "brilliant piece" and eager to accept it for publication in *Dissent* (it was a major scoop for a little magazine struggling to survive), disapproved of certain elements in it—particularly the following passage, which has provoked the wrath of several Mailer critics:

> *The psychopath murders—if he has the courage—out of the necessity to purge his violence, for if he cannot empty his hatred then he cannot love, his being is frozen with implacable self-hatred for his cowardice. (It can of course be suggested that it takes little courage for two strong eighteen-year-old hoodlums, let us say, to beat in the brains of a candy-store keeper, and indeed the act—even by the logic of the psychopath— is not likely to prove very therapeutic, for the victim is not an immediate equal. Still, courage of a sort is necessary, for one murders not only a weak fifty-year-old man but an institution as well, one violates private property, one enters into a new relation with the police and introduces a dangerous element into one's life. The hoodlum is therefore daring the unknown, and so no matter how brutal the act, it is not altogether cowardly).*

Many readers have regarded this passage as very dangerous irresponsible nonsense and have been repulsed by Mailer's willingness, on any level, to view this murder as "not altogether cowardly." His harsher critics will not stand for the idea that he is merely hypothesizing in the interests of advancing his argument and exploring material out of which he will create fiction, although, as usual, that is exactly what he is doing—thinking in such a way as to lay bare the groundwork of his fiction and of the arguments that may be held against it.

In trying to describe social reality Mailer creates a myth akin to another myth he invokes in his article: "the Faustian urge to dominate nature by mastering time." To speak of a "Faustian urge" is to use myth to explain reality. "The White Negro" is white, or Western man, who sees in the Negro the reverse image of himself. Faustian man has conventionalized existence and made it conform to his rules; he has murdered individuality and collectivized society; he has, in the twentieth century, created the concentration camp. The hipster rebels against the atomic universe of instant death and seeks some new source of energy that may provide him with the courage to be unconventional. "So it is no accident that the source of Hip is the Negro for he has been living on the margin between totalitarianism and democracy for two centuries," Mailer argues. Not having the secure identity most whites have taken for granted, the Negro has had to live in the moment, and his music, jazz, has expressed an improvisational spirit and distrust of socially monolithic ideas that has attracted generations of white artists to the urban centers of Negro culture.

Mailer wants to abolish moral categories not because he is against morality but because he rejects categorical thinking of the type exemplified by the social worker Louise Rossman in "The Man Who Studied Yoga," who is "a touch grim and definite in her opinions." People like Louise devour and deaden the world by categorizing it, by listing its contents and reducing it to what can be catalogued. Mailer as a novelist and social thinker, on the other hand, wants to create his own fluid context and believes there are individuals in society, white and black alike, who are attempting (not always consciously or consistently) to subvert the status quo. Occasionally he quotes these antiauthoritarians, since it is in their style, their feeling for nuance, that they are liberated from stultifying societal norms. "That cat will never come off his groove, dad" is as close as Mailer can come to the "Hip substitute for stubborn." Stubborn, however, implies fixity, and there is nothing static or staid about the hipster or about his world view, which implies (Mailer believes) a dynamism that the categorical squares cannot compete with: "Even a creep does move—if at a pace exasperatingly more slow than the pace of the cool cats."

So the last thing Mailer wants to do is to dismiss from his view people who might possibly be rebelling—like the hoodlums who beat in the brains of the shopkeeper. What Mailer advocates is, he realizes, a dangerous point of view—but not because it is immoral. What is truly dangerous is that he is proposing the abandonment of stationary values. Only a writer who sees the primary evil as the "collective violence of the state" could suggest "it takes literal faith in the creative possibilities of the human being to envisage acts of violence as the catharsis which prepares growth."

There is no question that Mailer's emphasis on Hip gives it an importance it might not otherwise have had, but that has been his point all along—that the novelist fastens on precisely those crucial elements that sociologists cannot adequately measure and dare not imagine without the data at hand. He risks much more than the sociologist or the historian because he wants to describe not only what is there but also what might be there or what might emerge with the provocation of a first rate novelistic disposition.

"The White Negro" created a sensation. Malaquais called the essay "a gorgeous flower of Mailer's romantic idealism." Interviewers wanted to know if Mailer was promoting Hip as a way of life. When Richard Stern put this question to him in an interview at the University of Chicago in the spring of 1958, Mailer suggested that he was attracted to Hip because it helped him articulate his feelings about contemporary life. "The notions of Hip enlarge us," he claimed, and brought back into the culture a "romantic spirit" that had "dried up."

Mailer's interviewers continued to struggle with the implications of "The White Negro," curious as to how far he expected himself or others to go with the concept of Hip. He, in turn, recognized that to be hip posed a "threat" to some readers:

> They feel that if they admit that I'm right about the hipster, then they have got to go out and become a hipster themselves, which is something I'd never ask of anyone. I just ask that the hipster be considered at least as interesting and serious a person as a young congressman.

Mailer claimed he was himself a "middle-aged hipster. I've turned terribly philosophical and mellow but still that's what I am."

The hipster was a way of psyching himself up, for Mailer viewed the hipster as competing for existence and for a vision of himself and of eternity. To the question of whether Mailer was naturally a hipster or did he have to work at it, the cagey writer only laughed and called his *Mademoiselle* interviewers "charming." But it was a fair question for the curious who wondered how much trouble Mailer had put himself to in dressing up what Richard Stern called his "pretty notion" of Hip.

In 1961, four years after "The White Negro," Mailer conceded that the essay was "no longer true." Or rather, it "wasn't true enough," for there were fewer White Negroes than he had imagined, and he may have killed the concept of Hip by prematurely aggrandizing it. Rather than keeping silent and allowing hipsters to grow into a force that might conceivably have changed society, Mailer had pushed Hip ahead of its time: "I advanced my career at the expense of my armies. As a general, you see, I gained strength and lost troops"—a hip away of putting it, for he spoke as though his words were more than metaphorical, as though he were in tune with revolutionary elements of society.

Mailer had not really abandoned his hipster hero and, in fact, ended his *Mademoiselle* interview declining to specify which things in "The White Negro" he no longer endorsed: "I don't know that I want to lose any more troops. I've said enough." He implied, in other words, that there were yet other battlefields on which he would test out his conceptions of hip heroism.

EMOTIONAL SWORD-TWIRLING

Few of Mailer's contemporaries understood the importance of "The White Negro" in his development or were prepared to accede to its pronouncements. James Jones, who had just received Mailer's mixed review of his new work, *The Pistol*, wrote on March 18, 1958, to say he could not agree with

> *your quasi-religious-philosophical points. . . . Hipsterism is a good illustration of a swiftly accelerating decadence, like a good many other things. But I can't honestly see it as a new method of approach to "the full living" that intellectually guided revolution failed to achieve.*

Nevertheless, Jones found it a pleasure to read the essay and to see that Mailer was "pushing out and not drawing back in, and that can only help a writer's work."

Jones realized that Mailer's acting out of his "quasi-religious-philosophical points" put a strain on their friendship. Jones also complained about Adele's provocative behavior—her "trying to get my goat over this or that thing," intimating that she had heard the most "unflattering" things about him and could tell him what people "*really*" thought of him if he wanted to know. When he said "sure," he would like to know, she had become "coy," suggesting it might upset him "too much." Adele had behaved similarly with his wife, Gloria, and Jones had ended the evening because he did want a "belligerent hassle, possibly a great verbal fight."

Jones had sensed that Mailer wanted a fist fight, and he made it plain that he would never engage in one, since he had no desire to find out which of them could "whip" the other. Anyway, "it would give Adele too great a happiness." Jones was sorry if his words irritated Adele and added that she was a "remarkably sweet gal when she's sober and I like her." So did Gloria. Jones missed their company for the rest of the evening, but "at least it was quiet and without any emotional sword-twirling."

Two days later Mailer fired off his reply. Jones was used to dealing with "parasites" and could not believe that a writer like Mailer only wanted his friendship. Mailer had taken a big chance by letting down his guard with Jones, and Jones had just proved that Mailer had better trust his "sour instincts" more than his "few remaining generous ones." He did not know what Adele had said to Gloria and could only point out that Adele liked her and was "bewildered" by their sudden departure. Evidently the Joneses did not understand Adele's kind of "heavy kidding" and "teasing." She intended no insult. If Adele had complained about Gloria or Jim, Mailer would have "told her to stick it up her ass." It was better to take "a little crap" than to risk ruining a friendship. Essentially, Mailer accused the Joneses of being oversensitive and walking out over a "couple of remarks." As for a fist fight, it had never entered Mailer's mind: "I wouldn't get into a fight with you unless I were ready to kill you, and I always instinctively assumed that was true for you." As for Adele enjoying such a contest, she relished "the pretense of violence," not the real thing. If Jones wanted to see Mailer, he would have to make the trip from Marshall, Illinois. The last thing Mailer wanted was "a farce of letters back and forth." This exchange did not end the friendship, but it could not be resumed on the old basis.

Styron recalls his estrangement from Mailer haltingly, grasping for the memory of what actually happened, and trying to be true to the baffling end of a friendship:

> *It was almost the day my second daughter, Polly, was born [March 1958] . . . when the letter [from Mailer] came . . . saying (it was sort of like the paranoid voice of Senator McCarthy): "Sources closer to you than you may suspect" —of course it plants a terrible suspicion in your mind as to who the source was—"have told me you have been making atrocious*

*remarks about my wife Adele." And then it went on from that to bluster
and threat. . . . It was just right out of the blue. There had been no
preliminaries. It was just like a lightning bolt, and I was really devastated. I'll never forget it. Because here was a man I thought I was very
friendly with. . . . It was the sort of thing you don't expect friends to
do. . . . If they're friends—well, if they have some terrible problem with
you, they will approach you and say, "Let's get to the root of this." They
don't send you a kind of murderous letter. . . . It was profoundly upset-
ting and depressing.*

Styron still cannot say what went wrong. "I think he was in some sort of
bad state himself. . . . I think he was desperately unhappy. I have never
pursued that. I have never felt it was necessary to nail that down."

The rumor was that Styron had alluded to Adele's lesbian tendencies.
As he recalls:

*A lot of people didn't like Adele. She was aggressive. She was out of
her—you know—I think a lot of people thought she wasn't a lady. I liked
her, but she'd get drunk. I think a lot of people regarded her as
common—or whatever the word is, and she just didn't fit in, a big
aggressive broad . . . and people were put off by her. It may have been
indeed—I suspect it was true—that I probably uttered something about
her like a lot of other people did and it got back to Norman.*

Mailer's personal and literary sense of himself were at a precarious
point, and Styron's gossip about Adele (if that is what it was) maddened
him. Mailer had become increasingly disenchanted with what he regarded as Styron's literary politicking. Unlike Adele, Styron's wife,
Rose, was the perfect hostess, smoothing the way for her ambitious
writer/husband. As much a politician as Styron, Mailer nevertheless
prided himself on never kowtowing to important people. Taking his
revenge in print, Mailer would later refer to Styron as "oiling every
literary lever and power which could help him on his way."

THE ARTIST IN TRANSIT INGLORIOUS

"The White Negro" was an undeniably bold piece of writing; it gave
Mailer the courage to take stock of himself. Counting from his first

undergraduate stories, he had been writing for almost twenty years. It was now time to plot the trajectory of his career in a collection of his work, brashly titled *Advertisements for Myself* (1959), in which he included "A Calculus at Heaven" (1944), the story that is a prophetic approximation of himself. An alter ego, the artist/poet Bowen Hilliard, a star of his college's literary magazine and a bitter critic of America, marries a promiscuous, outspoken woman who cannot paint, compose music, or write nearly as well as he. Their marriage fails when he sells out (not being able to make a living in the Depression, even though his art gains in strength) and goes to work for her father. He writes an autobiography, *The Artist in Transit Inglorious*, about his disillusionment with himself: "He felt that somewhere along the line he had missed not a turn so much as perhaps a flubbed traffic signal, stopping when he should have moved forward." Although Mailer had had the early success Hilliard had missed, much of Mailer's temperament nevertheless informed Hilliard's sense of how precariously he had always stood between failure and success.

If Mailer were to escape the fate of a minor artist like Hilliard, he would have to devise a new strategy for coping with his literary defeats and for promoting his genius. In *Advertisements for Myself* he collected much of his old and his new work, linking it together with italicized passages that summed up and commented upon his literary career. "It was a book whose writing changed my life. Let us hope that was conceivably for the better," Mailer wrote in a later edition of *Advertisements*. The serpentine style of the italicized passages was new: It wound back and forth between his past, present, and future in sentences that suggest an intriguing, often exciting, open-endedness. He is never altogether finished with his past, for his evaluation of it contains nearly as many interesting possibilities as does his promise of forthcoming work. Even when a particular sentence is not quite clear or fails to capture one's whole attention, he has loaded some part of it with a hint of richer insights that are in the offing, and just when he has gone too far in touting his talent, he withdraws into a qualifying phrase before one can attack his grandiloquence. In *Advertisements*, in a word, Mailer becomes his own critic/promoter, combining the seemingly contrary functions of creation and criticism.

Advertisements is divided into five parts: Beginnings, Middles, Births, Hipsters, Games and Ends. The use of plural endings is ingenious; one has to constantly re-evaluate which pieces are most effective, and multiple interpretations become de rigueur. The author, moreover, encourages shopping around. In "A Note to the Reader" he explains that there are two tables of contents: One lists the pieces in "roughly chronological" order and the other is for "the specialist" who wants to be guided by such formal categories as "short stories, short novels, poems, advertisements, articles, essays, journalism," and so on. The "Note" actually offers a third way of reading *Advertisements*, for Mailer lists in order of appearance "the best pieces in the book." The total effect of dividing the contents in so many different ways is to set up a literary marketplace and thereby to acknowledge that a writer's reputation rests not only on the quality of his work but on its variety and on the way that variety is received by the public.

The organization of *Advertisements* alone represents an extraordinary literary feat because Mailer both caters to and challenges one's reading habits. How clever of him, for example, to put into italics this acknowledgment of the idiosyncratic way people use books: *"Like many another literary fraud, the writer has been known on occasion to read the Preface of a book instead of a book, and bearing this vice in mind, he tried to make the advertisements more readable than the rest of his pages."* In this "Note" Mailer's references to himself shift from the third to the first person, simultaneously indicating his distance from and proximity to the material that is about to be sampled. He reads himself, so to speak, as one reads along with him.

Most impressive is Mailer's realization that he is addressing different kinds of readers with different degrees of tolerance and sympathy for his writing. Thus the italicized advertisements are studded with references to several areas of concern that are layered and distributed in what might be called a supermarket of styles: *"So the reader who is in haste to judge this possibility* [*that Mailer has* "a fair chance to become the first philosopher of Hip"] *had best skip ahead—those interested in what I was writing soon after* Barbary Shore *have only to turn the page."* It is outrageous that writing should be set out along so many corridors or aisles in separate displays, but this is how people are reading these days, Mailer implies, and there is an argument to be made for attending to all of the circumstances in which writing is communicated, or at least to as many of those different places and occasions as Mailer has the energy to address.

Advertisements is, as Mailer suggests in one of the headings for his second table of contents, the "biography of a style." How has his work, good and bad, gotten written? Through very hard labor, inspiration, and luck are the varying answers, with some of his best pieces having little relationship to the actual time it took to write them. And how does one assign value to his writing? He quotes negative and positive reviews of *Barbary Shore* in popular magazines, but he also quotes "a girl" in a class at the New School who said, "*Mr. Mailer! How did you have the nerve to put your name on that short story?*" His response is seemingly casual and evenhanded, but it also says much about the ambiguous status of literature: "*Well, I don't know but what she might be right. 'The Notebook' was written in an hour, and it's perfectly fair to take it seriously or decide it's a trifle.*" Mailer is not about to claim that our responses to literature can be certain or that one source is necessarily any more reliable than another. Nor is it always so easy to tell what is "serious" and what is not—not even for the author! Because of the grandness and modesty of his claims, he virtually ensures that his work cannot be dismissed no matter how many negative reviews he receives.

Mailer's excellent phrase *the biography of a style* captures the unique literary and extraliterary appeal of *Advertisements for Myself.* What happens inside and outside his writing are amalgamated by making his "advertisements" extensions of the pieces they preface. When he closes out his book with two stories, "The Time of Her Time" and "Advertisements for Myself on the Way Out," both part of the projected long novel mentioned several times in *Advertisements*, he is offering the final chapters in "the biography of a style." He is inviting readers to think biographically, for "Advertisements for Myself on the Way Out" is not a preface to a story; it is the story, and the "myself" is Mailer writing his biography by writing a story. "The Way Out" refers, in other words, both to Mailer's and the reader's way out of the book as well as to the narrator's way out of the story, which is also his way out of his own life. The time it takes to read the story, in other words, is identical to the time it takes the narrator to realize he is the "dead man on the floor."

Both stories are about Mailer's efforts to control time inside and outside of his fiction. At the end of "The Man Who Studied Yoga," Sam Slovoda is trying to fall asleep and the narrator gives "an idea to Sam. 'Destroy time, and chaos may be ordered.' " In "The Time of Her Time," the narrator, Sergius O'Shaugnessy of *The Deer Park*, has tried to live entirely by his own lights and to establish the time of his time, but as the title of the story implies he has not been entirely successful. Like Sam, he harbors a conceit that he is an extraordinary lover, and

O'Shaugnessy has been quite a sexual adventurer, even if he knowingly exaggerates his erotic gifts to women. He is Sam's hero, a man of action and contemplation—if setting up a bullfighting school in Greenwich Village and making acute observations on its inhabitants and on the nature of existence count. Obviously, O'Shaugnessy has not settled for Sam's middle-class mediocrity, and his violent streak is expressive of the hipster's effort to purge himself of the spineless socialized behavior Mailer deplores in "The White Negro."

But how seriously can O'Shaugnessy be taken? Is he as good as his word? Does he offer revelations that are superior to those of the artist-activist Cassius O'Shaugnessy or of the psychiatrist Jerry O'Shaugnessy in "The Man Who Studied Yoga"? Mailer may be parodying his own grandiose notions when he has Sergius O'Shaugnessy say in "The Time of Her Time," "over and over in those days I used to compare the bed to the bullfight, sometimes seeing myself as the matador and sometimes as the bull." But if Mailer is making fun of his hero, he also gives him a full and honest voice that honors the objective of his quest: to be the best at what he does in both the bullring and the bed.

The "her" of the story's title is Denise Gondelman, one of O'Shaugnessy's lovers. She is bright, Jewish, full of psychiatric jargon, and hostile to his hipster ethic. She has a steady boyfriend, but she has never had an orgasm. Her brief love-and-hate affair with O'Shaugnessy reflects her contradictory desires to be totally in control and to abandon herself to a moment of complete ecstasy, a moment that would take her beyond the categorical view of reality.

Although Denise is clearly related to characters like Louise Rossman in "The Man Who Studied Yoga," it is remarkable how much sympathy and respect the story creates for her. She is seen through O'Shaugnessy's relentless campaign to make her come, so that she seems frigid—even authoritarian in her judgments—yet Denise is a genuine quester; she wants to know what it feels like to have a climax, and she holds her own against Sergius's pride and masculine power-grabbing.

Sergius is just honest enough at the end of the story to see how misplaced much of his contempt for her has been. For she has much of his violence in her, even if she speaks in a language he cannot abide. It has been "the time of her time" because she has reached a catharsis through their violent intercourse in spite of her hatred of him. He has been under the illusion that "I was going to beat new Time out of her if beat her I must." In a way he has done that, but not by himself. As they part he admits to making the mistake of saying "I gave you what you could use." To which she rightly replies: "You don't do anything to me." There has been, rather, reciprocity between them which he recognizes too late in "the look in her eyes, that unmistakable point for the kill that you find in the eyes of very few bullfighters, and then having created her pause, she came on for her moment of truth by saying" that her psychiatrist told her that O'Shaugnessy's "whole life is a lie," for he has done nothing but run away from his own homosexuality.

Sergius does not deal with this parting shot except to label it as "her truth," which he matches with one of his own: "And like a real killer, she did not look back, and was out the door before I could rise to tell her that she was a hero fit for me." The language of this ending remains faithful to a hipster's vocabulary, which sees only dynamic, not static, truths ("she came on for her moment of truth").

The feminine pronoun in the story's title is a profound rewriting of the romantic, heroic quest stories that Mailer read in his youth. The feminine point of view does not displace the masculine one, but time—the mastery of time—is equated with the woman O'Shaugnessy tries to dominate. His failure to do so is Mailer's failure, for O'Shaugnessy's hipster vocabulary has been used by Mailer throughout *Advertisements for Myself.* "The Time of Her Time" thus completes the revision of *The Deer Park*, in which Mailer had gone only halfway toward revising O'Shaugnessy's language and character to portray both a tougher and more vulnerable character, a man more like Mailer, who is willing to admit defeat and fear and determined to conquer the weakness in himself.

"Advertisements for Myself on the Way Out" is the final, most elaborate joke Mailer has devised to comment on himself, the figure of the italicized "prefaces" to his writing, and on the selves of the narrators in his other stories. In "The Man Who Studied Yoga," Sam Slovoda dreams of a novelist-hero "who reasonably could not exist." The narrator of "Advertisements for Myself on the Way Out" offers several possibilities in lieu of a "name" that "eludes him": a "consciousness brought into being by the relations and mutilations of the exceptional characters I will introduce"; "an embryo eight instants old"; "the old house in which the end of this story takes place"; "the ocean and the sand dunes"; a tree; a dog. Existence, Mailer has argued all along, takes many forms and man should discard his Faustian arrogance and attune himself to all of them, including the possibility, as he suggests in "The Time of Her Time," that time itself is feminine.

In "Advertisements for Myself on the Way Out," a narrator without a name can be, for the moment, anyone and therefore capable of identifying with anyone's experience, a rich conception of existence that is viable right up to the moment the narrator realizes that he has been murdered in Provincetown by Marion Faye. Mailer has achieved what Sam Slovoda did not think was possible, a novelist-hero who "does not exist."

The important point for Mailer's narrator, as for himself, is to be able to "travel from the consciousness of one being to the emotions of another." As a dead man, the narrator is peculiarly attuned to the fact that our century is moving "toward its death, and the death of all of us." This awareness of death, properly cultivated, opens one up to a kind of animism that releases one from the Faustian imprisoned ego.

The universe is not linear; it is not a world of points and lines and planes, measurable surfaces and structures that contain and sum up human character and history. Instead, the narrator speaks of "travelling through the non-Euclidean present of space-time." Dominating the story is the metaphor of existence as an "expanding spiral of Being," so that the murder Marion Faye commits is connected to a nineteenth-century murder that also took place in his house, for the narrator believes in the "emotion of Being" that continues to reverberate in man and in the elements of nature for all time.

Provincetown is where, the narrator reminds us, the Puritans lost their way: "Without looking at the sun one could not point across the bay in the proper direction to Boston, Portugal, or the shores of Barbary. It is a place which defies one's nose for longitude and latitude, a cartographer's despair and a Puritan's as well." In such a place, one becomes dislocated and subject to a consciousness that turns in several directions at once—which is to say in no particular direction at all. One is connectionless, and in that state the narrator ruminates on the quality of his consciousness that remains—to borrow a phrase from "The White Negro"—in the "enormous present."

As in "The Man Who Studied Yoga," the final fiction in *Advertisements* is as much about its author as it is about its characters. For the dead man has left a list not so very different from the one Mailer supplies in *Advertisements* in giving his definitions of "The Hip and the Square." Many of the names on the dead man's list (a Negro, a movie star, an analyst) correspond to the subjects Mailer has covered in the book, and the linking together of seemingly incongruous and compatible figures gets at the protean and contradictory quality of existence discussed throughout *Advertisements*:

> *a fisherman*
> *an analyst*
>
> *a call girl*
>
> *a whore*
> *a businessman*
> *a mother*
> *a father*

The dead man lists everyone attending Marion Faye's party, "yet there were more items on the list than people present, and titles applicable to more than one, as if some of the guests contained several categories within themselves." This is Mailer speaking out of the dead man's consciousness, out of his own fiction-making capacities, out of, he believes, the source of creativity itself, which combines and transcends categories and which he has tried to uncover and explore in his *Advertisements*. "Am I already on the way out?" the narrator asks, Mailer asks, as creator and Godlike figure. "Yes God is like Me, only more so," the narrator speculates and affirms by his style, capitalizing *Me*. And his author, having begun a book that admits to his ambition to make a "*revolution in the consciousness of our time*" ends his final fiction with a narrator claiming, "I carry with me the minds of some of you." Style, Mailer implies in his concluding tour de force, has literally meant the writing anew of his biography.

6.

DEATHS FOR THE LADIES, AND OTHER DISASTERS (1958–1963)

THE AVENGER

In October 1962 Paul Krassner of *The Realist* interviewed Mailer and asked him why he was hostile toward women. Krassner had in mind "The Time of Her Time" and O'Shaugnessy's reference to his penis as "The Avenger." Mailer not only admitted his hostility, he suggested that "most men who understand women" had similar feelings, but they were incapable of admitting it: "I think most people walk around with terms like that in their unconscious mind. There're a great many men who think of their cock as The Avenger." To Mailer, O'Shaugnessy "happened to be enormously civilized. So he was able to open his unconscious and find the word, find the concept, and use it humorously, to himself." For many years (going back at least to *A Transit to Narcissus*) Mailer had been afraid of the violence within himself. It was wrong, he thought, to identify with characters like Croft, and yet Croft had won his "most secret admiration," Mailer admitted to Krassner. Now Mailer spoke openly, conceding that he had "*enjoyed*" O'Shaugnessy in "The Time of Her Time": "He was not altogether different from me. But he certainly wasn't me."

There is something ludicrous, Mailer knows, in his portrayal of O'Shaugnessy as the hipster with a swinging dick. But Richard Poirier reminds us that Mailer's point about Hip is that it is a form of adolescent behavior; it provides the opportunity to "grow up a second time," as Mailer says in "The White Negro." Like an unruly adolescent, the hipster is testing society's strictures, its pieties, and its forms of social control. Denise comes with Sergius precisely because he is, in his own self-mocking words, a "Village stickman."

Mailer's finest critics have recognized that pieces like "The White Negro" and "The Time of Her Time" are projections of his growing myth about himself. Andrew Gordon has pointed out that O'Shaugnessy is, in a manner of speaking, Mailer's own avenger, the substitute for the nice Jewish Brooklyn boy taught not to take on the big outside world, the world of filth and sex and untold dangers. O'Shaugnessy makes Denise come when he shoves his avenger into her ass and calls her a "dirty little Jew." The brutality of this violation gives Denise her orgasm. It is also a shock Mailer applies to his own sensitivities through Sergius—who defeats, in Gordon's words, "the dirty little boy in himself." The orgasm in such scenes makes a new time, annihilates past guilt over sex and other insecurities that have made Mailer and his male characters question their masculinity. As Gordon says of Mailer's fictional heroes, "they become clean by indulging in dirt." At least that is their conceit.

Denise, with her flat breasts, lean, tough body, and aggressiveness, is, in a way, O'Shaugnessy's competition. Their sexual encounter is staged almost like a fight, with Denise (exhibiting "the flat thin muscles of a wiry boy") returning for rematches and engaging in the taunting rituals usually associated with males. As the "dirty little Jew," she is closer in size to Mailer than is six-foot-four O'Shaugnessy. Indeed, the critic Howard Silverstein asserts that "Sergius, symbolically turning Denise into a male, buggers her." It is no wonder, then, that she accuses him of homosexuality or that some male readers of the story have turned it into their confrontation with Mailer. Denise, after all, is the bedtime version of O'Shaugnessy's showdowns with males—like the blacks who resent his move into their neighborhood to set up his bullfighting school. "The Time of Her Time" both celebrates and attacks male prowess.

Chandler Brossard, who visited the Mailers during one of their wilder weekends, describes their "constant, loathsome bickering" and how they worked in tandem, making hostile advances to him—almost as if they were competing for him or competing against themselves. On the

one hand, Adele seemed to be "aching for some awful scene," saying to
Brossard: "I like juicy, fuckable men. You're dry and unfuckable." After
Brossard told Adele that "if I were juicy and fuckable, the last person I'd
want to fuck is you. You bore the shit out of me," she replied, "Go fuck
yourself" and walked off with an air that said to Brossard she would be
back. Mailer, knowing of Brossard's reputation as a boxer, kept challenging him to a match. Brossard declined:

> "No, Norman. What you really want is for us to fall into each other's
> arms and cry and hug, covered with blood. That doesn't give me the
> slightest fucking kick at all and I'm not gonna do it."
> "You're funny, Chandler," he replied.
> "That's it, Norman. I'm not gonna do it. You have some need to do it, I
> don't," I told him. "It's a strange primitive notion. It kind of repels me
> because I don't like blood, and also it seems kind of homosexual to me."
> He laughed. He always fielded those things, you see. He heard you,
> but he never came back with a direct answer.

"The Time of Her Time" recounts the hero's search for an autonomy
Denise denies with her Freudian jargon that suggests Sergius is the
victim of certain repetition compulsions. She expresses, Gordon suggests, not only a masculine orientation but also a maternal drive. Like
the characters in "Advertisements for Myself on the Way Out," she
contains "several categories" within herself. She is a version of the
emasculating Jewish mother Mailer must conquer before she makes a
hash of his pretensions to independence. Denise comes armed with the
authority of her Jewish analyst, Dr. Joyce, and her Jewish lover, Arthur,
both of whom O'Shaugnessy must vanquish in his trial of her by
orgasm. They are the distant fathers—the authoritative Joyce and the
passive Arthur—that the orphan O'Shaugnessy must supplant in Denise's consciousness. They are also "projections, shadow figures in
Mailer's psychodrama," according to Gordon.

That psychodrama has to do with Mailer's feelings about growing up
unmanned and orphaned by a sense that he was not prepared to compete
outside the home. Before O'Shaugnessy is able to give Denise her
orgasm he has a premature ejaculation. Not only has he not commanded
her in this scene, he has returned to the helpless state of a boy who was
minded by nuns and grew up questioning his sexuality. O'Shaugnessy
then compares this defeat with his knockout in a boxing ring when he hit

the canvas and "watered the cup of my boxer's jock." Having sex is associated in his mind with proving himself competitively and with his fear that he cannot take control of such situations, that he is a passive "she." "The Time of Her Time" has been, in fact, Mailer's way of taking control while conceding the ambivalence of his feelings.

NORMIE THE HUN

Advertisements for Myself—especially "The White Negro" and "The Time of Her Time"—increased interest in Mailer's career, since he was exploring the roots of his own identity while claiming to lay bare the deep structures of society. No American writer before him, not even his model Ernest Hemingway, had so fused the invention of a literary style with the creation of a writer's identity. No one asked a Saul Bellow, for example, whether he really meant what he said in his fiction and behaved accordingly. Only Mailer treated literature as though it were life, as though in portraying a hipster in prose he had actually produced one.

The New York literary and intellectual community looked somewhat askance at Mailer's antics, but it also embraced him as its resident wayward genius. He never abandoned a certain boyishness or his gentlemanly—even courtly—manners even while proving himself a tough guy. He was still a part of society for all his cultivation of Hip. When he gave a sexually explicit talk at Brandeis, he was obviously "thrown" by the parting remarks of Joseph Israel Cheskis, a seasoned old socialist who said to his wife: "Esther, this kissing, shitting, fuck-ing, and sucking, it's an old business. Let's go!" Mailer eventually recovered from this dismissal, but Martin Peretz, who attended the talk, was impressed with Mailer's gentleness and the time he made for the young men who wanted to be included in his circle.

Both Diana Trilling and Norman Podhoretz met Mailer at a Lillian Hellman party in late 1957 or early 1958 at a time when "The White Negro" had made him an intellectual curiosity. Trilling sat on his left at dinner, admiring the respectful attention he gave to Mrs. Askew, the "dowagerlike" wife of an art dealer. That he should be so solicitous to a woman whom most literary figures in Trilling's experience would ignore impressed her enormously. She was not prepared, however, for his sudden turn on her, saying "Now, what about you, smart cunt?" Trilling laughed. It was so unexpected—"such a challenging greeting, so boldly flirtatious, it was so funny and outrageous applied to me"—and she reveled in the "wonderful" contrast between the way he had treated her and Mrs. Askew. They quickly became friends, each apparently intrigued by the other's personality and attitudes.

Norman Podhoretz, at one time a disciple of Diana's husband, Lionel, found in Mailer an intriguing alternative to what he now considered rather boring and stodgy liberal ideas about society. While he found much of "The White Negro" to be nonsense, he honored Mailer's iconoclasm, his willingness to take risks—even at the cost of appearing to play the fool. A few years later, Anne Barry, then Mailer's secretary, observed just how intense the friendship with Podhoretz would become. She remembers attending a party at the Podhoretz residence, where she saw the two Normans jousting with each other: "Competitive. Little ripples. Posturing, rooster behavior. Not only intellectual, though, but mixed up with the personal," says Barry. They would collaborate on letters to newspapers, debating the wording, and had other little projects, exchanges of phone calls, arguments about "lit-business stuff." On nights when he was up drinking Mailer thought nothing of calling Podhoretz for a go-round. Barry's impression is that Mailer treated Podhoretz as his intellectual equal, someone he could engage profoundly on the nature of being a Jew, a radical, a political person, and an artist. They had what amounted to all-night bullshit sessions at college.

As with Trilling, Mailer found in Podhoretz a mate against whom he could try out his more outrageous ideas while remaining accepted and even adored by New York intellectuals. Irving Howe has confessed that, like the rest of this group, he rather "spoiled" Mailer. Midge Decter, Norman Podhoretz's wife, attributed this special feeling for Mailer to the fact that he behaved like everyone's idea of a great novelist.

Trilling and Podhoretz would soon write two of the best essays on Mailer. Indeed, Podhoretz would show his piece to Mailer before it was published. Whether by accident or plan, Mailer had cultivated two opinion-makers who treated his work with a new degree of seriousness. When a nervous Adele—often uncomfortable around intellectuals—started to serve the Trillings something on the wrong plate, "Norman corrected her," Diana remembers, giving Adele "one of those looks that a husband might give his wife in some story in a woman's magazine in which the boss comes to dinner and she's not performing properly—that old scenario that he's not going to get his promotion."

At Provincetown in the summers of 1959 and 1960 Mailer assembled an entourage of boxers, writers, actors, and other artists. Outside the Trilling–Podhoretz–Howe intellectual court Mailer turned pugnacious, challenging his friends to arm- and thumb-wrestling, getting drunk and disorderly (resulting in one arrest), and engaging in what Seymour Krim calls "the shoulder-punching warmth of . . . barracksroom camaraderie." When Mailer first met Krim, he had a "crazy twinkle in his eye" and said he would not be able to start a new book unless he had a fight.

In the summer of 1960, Mailer began palling around in Provincetown with Roger Donoghue and sometimes Fay Mowery, a painter who would later marry Donoghue. Often, near the end of an evening, Mailer would become "aggressive and unpleasant," goading Donoghue (a former world middleweight contender) into sparring matches. Mailer threw some hard jabs while Donoghue would fight defensively; eventually he would jolly Mailer out of these confrontations. On more sober days, Donoghue would give him boxing lessons, and the rumor was that Mailer was teaching Adele how to fight. "Things did seem to be pretty heavy that summer," recalls Donoghue, who saw Mailer get "busted up" in an angry bare-fisted fight with an Irishman who was also a writer. This was literary life with a swagger.

Adele did her best to compete with her husband, "Normie the Hun." To get attention she acted the "pisser," chasing Seymour Krim around a room, threatening to cut off his tie with scissors. She knew that what really turned her husband on was to see women fighting. On one occasion she was successful in baiting Harriet Sohmers, an editor at *The Provincetown Annual*. While the two women rolled around "punching each other out," Norman joined his pals in egging the women on.

Irving Howe would occasionally see a different Norman Mailer during his Cape Cod summers in the early 1960s. Mailer would invite Howe and his wife for dinner. Howe remembers that

> *Norman would always come dressed in a jacket, which he never wore any other time. I never could decide whether this was partly a humorous put-down of his bourgeois socialist friends or a gesture of respect, or maybe both. He never discussed it. But he always amused me and touched me. And then there were stories about his violence which I had nothing to do with and knew nothing about—just gossip I don't want to repeat.*

Howe portrays a sympathetic, compassionate Adele at odds with the sensational accounts of her battles with Norman and others. Howe remembers with considerable gratitude that Adele took him by the arm at a time when he was feeling particularly low and marched him in to accept an award from the National Institute of Arts and Letters. She had a "calming and consoling" effect on a "nervous" and "jittery" Howe. He saw her a few times on Cape Cod and was very taken with "this extremely handsome woman. She had much more of a distinct personality than the other women I saw Mailer with. She was memorable."

James Baldwin was one of the few writers who really paid attention to Adele, listened to her, and identified with her vulnerability. Her husband, on the other hand, lacked a certain warmth and intellectualized everything, making even the simplest conversation a complicated affair for Adele.

For all their differences, Norman and Adele continued to make a family, happily welcoming the birth of their second child, Betsy Ann. On January 14, 1960, Mailer wrote Ecey Gwaltney: "We have another daughter Betsy Ann, 3½ months old now, and as cute as her father." Their first daughter, Dandy, was almost three, and "Sue is very much 10—a great kid, tough and cool with an air of pleasant gravity about her. She knows more about a lot of things than I'll ever know." He felt Adele had "changed quite a bit, but not in looks." And he tried to clear the air with the Gwaltneys (Fig had criticized *Advertisements for Myself* for its self-pity and "an occasional gleam of dishonesty"): "Maybe I'm pugnacious, but it's the only thing that relaxes me, and what I used to dislike about people in Arkansas, you included most of all Ecey, was that everybody was so fucking polite." He encouraged her to "really let go on me sometime." Holding back, he thought, was "bad for the blood and it's bad for character because people end up false—they become more and more sweet all the time and all the while they get more pent up." He hoped they would visit him in Provincetown and suggested they reread "Advertisements for Myself on the Way Out" to get a feel for the place—although how he supposed the raucous, murderous atmosphere of that story would appeal to the genial Gwaltneys is hard to fathom.

"EVALUATIONS—QUICK AND EXPENSIVE COMMENTS ON THE TALENT IN THE ROOM"

Advertisements for Myself accomplished the final break with Jones and Styron that somehow seemed necessary to Mailer if he were to remain true to his new style. When Jones wrote him on November 18, 1959, in praise of an *Esquire* piece, "The Mind of an Outlaw" (November 1959), detailing the ordeal of finding a publisher for *The Deer Park*, an edgy Mailer replied on December 1 that before he would answer Jones's letter "in kind," he would wait to see his response to *Advertisements* "because it may change your feelings toward me." Jones had "slugged" him "between the eyes" when Mailer most "needed and wanted" his friendship. It would be hard for Mailer to "trust him" until he saw some concrete evidence of Jones's good faith. The unforgivable fact, in Mailer's view, was that Jones had not been supportive while Mailer had tried to "hack" his way through "all sorts of second-growth shit." Rather than giving Mailer the benefit of the doubt and taking him at his word, at his "idea of myself," Jones had preferred to be swayed by the "opinions of others."

A week later Styron wrote Jones to say he had read "Evaluations— Quick and Expensive Comments on the Talent in the Room" in *Advertisements* and thought that he and Jones came off "rather well" in spite of Mailer's disparaging remarks about Jones's commercialism and Styron's literary politicking. Styron singled out the self-destructive and paranoid quality of the book and lamented the fact that Mailer did not put his energy into more fiction. Styron did not deny his talent and ranked himself, Jones, and Mailer as equals, regretting only that Mailer spent so much time "writhing in agony over recognition." This became a theme, as Styron noted, in some reviews of the book.

SUPERMAN COMES TO THE SUPERMARKET

The reviews of *Advertisements for Myself* that began to appear in early 1960 were mixed. No one—not even Mailer's publisher, Walter Minton—saw the importance of the book or considered it a breakthrough. The perceptive reviews and studies came much later, beginning with George Steiner's piece in *Encounter* (December 1961). Clay Felker, an editor at *Esquire*, had been impressed with an excerpt from *Advertisements* printed in the magazine under Mailer's title, "The Mind of an Outlaw." Caught in rather embarrassing circumstances, Felker suggested a whole new direction for Mailer's work. He had accidentally met Mailer for the first time in a jazz nightclub. Adele was in a rage, baiting her silent husband, saying things like "We're all shit; we don't add up to anything. You guys think you're significant, but it's all shit." Mailer only smiled and appeared to be getting a kick out of it. When Adele said she wanted to leave, Norman threw his keys on the table. She snatched them and left. To make conversation, Felker explored with Mailer the possibility of writing another piece for *Esquire*. Had Mailer ever considered doing something on politics—perhaps a report on the Democratic National Convention that summer?

Mailer was game to try a new form of writing, especially since several commentators were suggesting the upcoming election would be an important turning point in the country's history, but he was not at all certain about what approach to take.

While Mailer mulled over how he would cover the convention scheduled for mid-July, he and Adele spent another riotous summer in Provincetown. There was "boozing, fighting, a lot of fucking," as one participant puts it. The friction between Norman and Adele that Felker had glimpsed had taken on a pattern replicated in the Mailer circle: "*Everybody's* marriage was in trouble, and everyone was behaving outrageously. . . . We were all terribly Scott Fitzgeraldish, very dramatic and romantic and having high times," Jillen Howe remembers. She had met Norman through his sister, Barbara, and she obviously admired his "high energy"—fighting and drinking and writing every day. Both his recklessness and his discipline were amazing. It was a forced life in many respects, which was reflected in Mailer's injunction to a friend: "Do things that frighten you." That summer in Provincetown a story made the rounds about how he had taken on three blacks on Shankpainter Road and been severely beaten up.

Covering a political convention was quite a shift in tempo for this "psychic outlaw" who had not voted since 1948. Felker helped smooth the way with introductions to seasoned journalists like Max Lerner, who remembered Mailer coming on as the "brash initiate." Mailer made no pretense of being a reporter, and he was determined to do things his own way, taunting Lerner about his old-fashioned liberalism and acting like a boxer up on his toes, flicking out his arguments in quick jabs.

The highlight of the convention piece was to be Mailer's interview with John Kennedy. Adele could sense her husband's nervousness about it, although he acted cool when they arrived at Hyannisport. Kennedy's handlers were edgy, for they considered Mailer an unpredictable character. According to Arthur Schlesinger, Jr., Kennedy himself had no doubts about his ability to manage people and wanted to meet an author he claimed to have read. Other Kennedy intimates remember him suddenly balking and saying, "Why do I need an interview with Norman Mailer?" In truth, he had nothing to fear from a Mailer on his best behavior. Mailer dressed in a three-piece suit and spoke softly and courteously. Kennedy would get no opportunity to meet a White Negro.

The writer Peter Maas advised Pierre Salinger on the best way to prepare Kennedy for the meeting with Mailer. Kennedy should say that he had read Mailer and especially liked *The Deer Park*. Maas knew that for years Mailer had been irritated by people coming up to him and mentioning only his first novel. Even more important, Maas confided to Salinger, was for Kennedy to get the timing of the remark "just right." At the meeting, Kennedy walked up to Mailer to shake hands, saying, "Mr. Mailer, I loved your book . . ." As the pause lengthened, Salinger saw Mailer begin to bridle at the expected reference to *The Naked and the Dead*. "*The Deer Park*," said Kennedy, to Mailer's enormous delight.

No matter how Mailer turned it over, Kennedy's greeting made both himself and Mailer seem more impressive. Norman Mailer, and Norman Mailer's part in things, had received a presidential acknowledgement the writer had previously accorded himself only in "the privacy of my mind."

Journalists recognized the importance of "Superman Comes to the Supermarket" when it appeared in the November issue of *Esquire* about three weeks before the election. It is not just that Mailer, a controversial literary figure, touts Kennedy, making him seem glamorous and stylish—like a movie star, a great "box-office actor," to use Mailer's words; politics itself now has a romantic aura and the reporter expresses a multifaceted sensibility through which events are filtered. There is no pretense to objectivity; quite the contrary, the real story can only be fetched from the nuances of the scene, the drama of an extraordinary personality's engagement with events. Mailer is not outside the action but an integral part of the setting he describes.

Mailer slyly quotes "a writer one knows at the convention" who

suggests Kennedy is "your first hipster." The writer, one is tempted to
suppose, is Mailer himself, for he also has this writer call Kennedy
"Sergius O'Shaugnessy born rich." After years of having been pestered
about whether White Negroes exist, Mailer claims in his article to have
found one with the help of another writer's observation. How convenient
and how like Mailer to create a persona for Kennedy as he had created
one for himself. As Mailer quickly realizes, Kennedy has the right
makings for an adventurous, hip hero: a man of physical courage, "a
man who lived with death, who, crippled in the back, took on an
operation which would kill him or restore him to power." Out of Kennedy's *PT-109* heroism Mailer fashions an existential ethic, claiming
Kennedy is the kind of man whose action is existential "precisely
because its end is unknown." In politics, Kennedy has not played it safe,
choosing for a wife "a lady whose face might be too imaginative for the
taste of a democracy which likes its first ladies to be executives of home-
management." No doubt about it, Kennedy is daring: courting "political
suicide by choosing to go all out for a nomination four, eight, or twelve
years before his political elders think he is ready, a man who announces
a week prior to the convention that the young are better fitted to direct
history than the old."

Mailer portrays Kennedy as an authentic American hero, emerging
out of the slough of the Eisenhower years to recapture a dynamic sense
of the individualism that had made the country great before it had
succumbed to the homogenization of mass society. Using the past tense,
Mailer manages to make Kennedy a historic figure, destined to satisfy
the people's deep yearning:

> *It was a hero America needed, a hero central to his time, a man whose*
> *personality might suggest contradictions and mysteries, which could*
> *reach into the alienated circuits of the underground, because only a*
> *hero can capture the secret imagination of a people, and so be good for*
> *the vitality of his nation; a hero embodies the fantasy and so allows each*
> *private mind the liberty to consider its fantasy and find a way to grow.*

In short, Kennedy is the answer to the people's dreams; he makes them
feel more heroic. He made Mailer feel more heroic by seeming to justify
the writer's years of harping on Hip. "The White Negro" had brought
Mailer attention, but it had also isolated him, since so many critics
doubted the existence of White Negroes or considered them marginal

elements that would do no more than ruffle the fringes of society. With Kennedy, Mailer had a champion to groom; a man who spoke to society high and low as Mailer himself hoped to do. The very title of the article implies that there can be a reconciliation and synthesis of opposites: the Superman (both the popular comic-book hero and Nietzsche's world historical individual) and the Supermarket (mass, undifferentiated society). That Kennedy is able to secure the nomination in Los Angeles, the symbolic site for Mailer of America's descent into mindless uniformity, "packaged commodities and ranch homes, interchangeable, geographically unrecognizable," suggests the power of the candidate's personality to rekindle the dulled imaginations of the people.

Much of Mailer's rhetoric is just that—hyperbole. He is honest enough to admit that Kennedy's politics are conventional and not much different from the tired liberalism Mailer chastised Max Lerner for still espousing. But the thrust of the article, he later admitted in *The Presidential Papers*, was "forcing a reality . . . bending reality like a field of space to curve the time I wished to create." Mailer believed, in other words, that he was not reporting history but creating it.

THE TROUBLE

Kennedy became president in November by the narrowest of margins: A shift of about a hundred thousand votes would have given the election to Nixon. Mailer fancied that he had made a difference, tipping things in Kennedy's favor, making Democrats feel better about their candidate so that they worked harder for his victory. Like his claim that Kennedy remade his psyche in that five-hour, three-mile heroic swim from *PT-109* with a crew member hanging onto the belt Kennedy gripped with his teeth, Mailer's conceit that he had affected the consciousness of his time became a myth that took on a life of its own.

Mailer's first response to the myth was to gear up a campaign for mayor of New York City. In Manhattan, in the fall of 1960, he moved into an apartment on West 94th Street, where he seemed out of his element. He was cranky, depressed, wrought up—there was no telling which turn his mood might take. Adele noticed his exaggerated mannerisms, his switching of accents that took her by surprise. In the city, he seemed a "different person" to her, although they had been fighting more or less continuously for six months. Roger Donoghue believed that

Mailer was "fucking around a lot," and he had seen Norman and Adele turn one spat into a fist fight. Doc Humes, one of Mailer's Provincetown friends, saw his anxiety skyrocketing. He was "hunching his shoulders as though in expectation of a blow," talking like a Texan, badgering and nagging himself about unfinished work, and behaving as though "everything somehow related to him."

Mailer planned a big party for Saturday evening, November 19, 1960—his political coming out, at which he would announce his candidacy on behalf of the underprivileged and the disenfranchised masses of the city. He began to pester George Plimpton to invite power brokers like David Rockefeller of Chase Manhattan, so that there would be no mistake about his pull. Plimpton did his best, but it was completely unrealistic to expect corporation executives, city commissioners, and diplomats to show up. When Plimpton got to the party, he saw a rowdy crowd full of unfortunates who looked like they had wandered in off the street. Everyone seemed ill at ease—the disenfranchised as well as the intellectuals. The apartment was packed with two or three hundred people and tension mounted. When Plimpton arrived, Mailer hit him across the face with a rolled newspaper and demanded to know where the "power structure" was.

The atmosphere turned violent. Allen Ginsberg, not known for a harsh temperament, got so hysterical in an argument with Norman Podhoretz that Podhoretz backed off as if he expected the poet would hit him. A drunken Roger Donoghue took hold of an eight-foot-long table full of liquor and food and heaved it into the air. Mailer warned his good friend Barbara Probst Solomon to stay away from him. If provoked, he would really "let fly," he let her know in the surly tones of someone looking for a fight. After the event, Richard Gilman wrote about witnessing "fights quickly broken up in corners, sexual stalkings and contretemps, envies and jealousies staging themselves as group therapy." The columnist Leonard Lyons wrote that Mailer had prowled the party with a photograph of himself at the jazz club Birdland, where he had been arrested after a dispute over a check. "If you want to see it . . . try to take it from me," he challenged one of his guests. Jason Epstein of Random House turned down Mailer's invitation to box—as did Roger Donoghue. When Plimpton tried to edge away from a Mailer invitation to box, he got kicked in the leg.

As far as Mailer was concerned, everything had gone wrong. He was getting very, very drunk and indulging in self-pity, feeling that his entourage had let him down. To prove it was so, he staged his own psychodrama. At about 3:00 A.M. he ordered the small number of remaining guests to assemble into two lines—those for him and against him. Nobody moved. So he shoved nearly everyone, including Adele, into the line of his opponents. A few friends and the family maid, Nettie Marie Biddle, represented (in his mind) the remnant of his forces. While he muttered about treachery people slipped away.

At least one Mailer friend had seen Adele spend part of the evening with a girl in the bathroom looking "very cozy." There had been rumors and suspicions about Adele's bisexuality, and there is no question that on this particular night Mailer believed she had betrayed him. She had been baiting him, denigrating his work, and suggesting he had been an inadequate lover. By 4:30 A.M. nearly everyone had gone. Mailer had been out on the street chasing people and getting into scrapes. He walked into his apartment with a black eye, a bloodied face, and a bloodstained bullfighter's shirt. Versions differ as to what Adele said to him, and the incident is still so painful that she cannot discuss it. Evidently she sized him up and made a caustic remark. It probably did not matter if she said, "You look like you've been rolled by a couple of sailors in the back streets" or "You look like a woman with lipstick on your mouth." The point was that she did not recognize or accept him as her husband. He took out the two-and-a-half-inch penknife he usually carried with him. All Adele remembers of this moment is the funny look in his eyes before he stabbed her—once in the upper abdomen and once in the back.

Mailer said nothing. Adele was stunned and angry. Nearly as drunk as her husband, she kept muttering, "Things like this don't happen to people like us. They happen to black people in Harlem and to Puerto Ricans but not us. . . . I can't believe this." Doc Humes put her on a mattress and called a doctor, Conrad Rosenberg, who had her admitted to University Hospital at Second Avenue and Twentieth Street. Humes also called Mailer's sister, Barbara, and her husband, Larry Alson. They had left the party at 3:00 A.M. and had to return to Mailer's apartment at about 5:30 A.M. Barbara was shocked and not yet ready to speak with her mother. Instead she and Larry went immediately to Norman's apartment, finding his daughter Betsy there with the maid. Adele was already at the hospital. It was 8:00 A.M. Sunday, about three-and-a-half hours after the stabbing. One of the wounds was near the heart and the cardiac sac had been punctured.

At the time of the stabbing Mailer had been reeling, on the verge of passing out, and had groggily dismissed Humes after the doctor had left with Adele for the hospital. After lying down to rest, Mailer somehow made it to the hospital to inquire about Adele's operation, even instructing the surgeon about the incision he would find. Along with Barbara and Larry, Norman waited for Adele to come out of surgery, elaborating on one of his theories about how people got cancer. He claimed to an incredulous Larry that he had stabbed Adele to "relieve her of cancer." Larry had heard about Adele and the girl in the bathroom. Barbara thought it was "probably the most horrible day" of her life. Later it would be Barbara who ran around looking for lawyers to represent her brother.

Before the operation Mailer had somehow sneaked into Adele's hospital room and advised her not to talk with the police. The unconvincing story given at the hospital was that she had fallen on some glass. The hospital notified the police and by Monday afternoon Adele had confessed that her husband had stabbed her. She said she was afraid of him and begged the policeman who interviewed her not to allow Norman near her.

Larry Alson remembers that later that Sunday or perhaps the next day Mailer huddled with Roger Donoghue and a friend, a retired detective, who advised Mailer to skip town "until this whole thing cools off." It was like a "council of war," Alson notes. Mailer decided not to leave New York. According to Fay Donoghue, Mailer called her, saying he wanted to prove his sanity, which he would do by appearing on the Mike Wallace show. Now seeing the gravity of the situation, Mailer said to Donoghue that he should have "flattened" him when Mailer had challenged him to fight at the party. Visiting Fay at her apartment, Mailer seemed "very tense and talkative." When Fanny showed up in a taxi to collect her son, he had already left. Fay was impressed with Fanny's calm. "Intelligent and reasonable," she reiterated that the family very much wanted Norman to see a doctor. Throughout this period, Roger and Fay Donoghue never lost their sympathy for Mailer. They felt Adele had provoked him with her slighting comments at the party about his masculinity. She was ridiculing him on the one subject he had no sense of humor about.

On Monday morning Mailer appeared on the Mike Wallace television show. He announced his intention to run for mayor of New York City.

His solution to juvenile delinquency was to hold jousting tournaments in Central Park. Since a hood's knife was his sword, a symbol of his manhood, it would be better to find ways of channeling his violence than to take away his weapon. When Wallace commented on his guest's black eye, Mailer laughed, admitting he had gotten into "quite a scrape Saturday night."

After the Wallace show, Mailer and Mickey Knox drove around the city. It seem odd to Knox that Mailer would be so worried about retrieving from his apartment an open letter to Fidel Castro he had just written. Mailer was afraid to go home, thinking there might be cops there. Given the confrontation between the U.S. government and Castro, Knox thought that Mailer hoped to make "a real splash." In the car, Knox took Mailer's knife away from him, saying, "Norman, that's the one thing you shouldn't have on you." But Mailer took it back, insisting that he would not use it but that he needed it for "personal reasons." Mailer seemed calmer and more rational than Knox had seen him in a long time. Mailer adamantly refused to see a psychiatrist.

Mailer then showed up at his sister's. She advised him to see an analyst. Her childhood friend Rhoda Lazare Wolf thought she was "overcome" by the "tragedy" of Norman's marriage, and she doubts that Barbara could speak freely to her brother about it. Rhoda surmised that Barbara was actually very angry, and her silence was a way of coping with what she could not articulate. For her part, Rhoda, now estranged from Norman, refrained from bringing him up with Barbara, for she knew that anything less than unqualified support of Norman would provoke Barbara, and Rhoda wanted to keep their friendship intact. Not only had Barbara and Norman always been close, but she had sought, according to Barbara Probst Solomon, "self-dramatizing males." Much later, after her divorce from Larry Alson, she proved able to pick men who were not "knockoffs" of her brother, Norman, and to emerge, in Rhoda's view, as her own person.

Later Monday evening, Knox drove Mailer to the hospital, leaving him there to see Adele alone. Mailer then surrendered himself to the police. Dr. Rosenberg briefly interviewed him and issued a report to felony court stating that Mailer was "having an acute paranoid breakdown with delusional thinking and is both homicidal and suicidal. His admission to a hospital is urgently advised." Granted an opportunity to speak for himself, Mailer argued in court that he was sane and that to commit him would destroy his credibility as a writer. Although he spoke articulately, the judge was not persuaded, and Mailer was sent to Bellevue.

In Bellevue, Mailer seemed to Mickey Knox "calm, subdued." They spoke through a screen for about ten minutes, with Mailer describing the conditions there. Knox, now married to Adele's younger sister, Joanne, saw his wife turn from adoration of Mailer to hatred; she could not fathom why he would do such a thing and she refused to have anything more to do with him. Similarly, Adele's mother became quite violent, and Knox supposed she wanted "revenge." Adele's father, Al, on the other hand, surprised Knox. Al still liked Mailer; he was not hostile but sad.

Mailer spent two weeks in Bellevue before he could find a doctor to vouch for his sanity. Adele recovered fully from the stabbing and decided not to press charges against her husband. After changing his plea from not guilty to third-degree assault, Mailer was given probation. Although the couple briefly tried to reconcile, they separated in March 1961.

Mailer has never satisfactorily explained what happened on the night of "the trouble," as his friends came to call it. Norman Podhoretz did not think Mailer had taken leave of his senses. Rather, his friend's extreme behavior had been a reaction to the tense atmosphere in which he lived. Podhoretz opposed the idea of psychiatric treatment even though Mailer would not explain what had happened, saying that for his own protection Podhoretz should not know the details. An analyst who had examined Mailer shortly after the stabbing reported to Larry Alson that Mailer was resistant to treatment: "The defenses Norman had built up were of such intricacy that there was no way to demolish them." In short, he was "doomed."

Diana Trilling thought Mailer "had had a psychotic break" and needed psychiatric help. Nothing in her experience of him had prepared her for this shocking incident, and in spite of Lillian Hellman's warning, she refused to think that it was dangerous to see Mailer alone. Her husband suggested the stabbing had been "a conscious bad act . . . Norman was testing the limits of evil in himself." This is a tempting explanation for a reader of "The White Negro," but Mailer has never owned up to such a motivation, and Diana Trilling had no doubt that he "felt guilty for what he had done. Maybe not guilty enough, but guilty."

This last remark hints at Mailer's aloofness toward his own act. In a curious way, he did not take what he had done personally; it did not alter the way he saw himself. One Mailer acquaintance noticed this when Mailer explained two months later why he had changed his story about Adele falling on broken glass. "After all, I couldn't hide behind a woman's skirt," he concluded. Even confessing to stabbing his wife demanded a manly gesture. He could not admit that he, Norman Mailer, had simply been out of control. Instead he was acting in a "privileged" manner. To an interviewer Mailer confided that "a decade's anger made me do it," implying there was no single explanation. He condemned himself, saying plainly that what he had done was indefensible. He did not make the argument for himself that he was a hipster venting his violence. In fact, he "felt somehow it was phony. . . . It wasn't me."

If Mailer had not done the deed, he would not have to account for it. Chandler Brossard puts it best when he suggests that Mailer "had no central sensibility. He's a kind of intellectual hermit crab, looking for the cast off shell of other animals to throw himself into their house."

Brossard notes that Mailer has a "very usable emptiness," assuming whatever accent fits his mood, sounding one moment like an Englishman and the next as a Texan. This was an "unemployed actor looking for a big role."

Similarly, Adele Morales had been picked to play a certain part in Mailer's life. Midge Decter observes that "he invents a lady character and then marries someone who has to play this role. Adele was cast as the primitive Indian when in fact she was actually a girl from Brooklyn who wanted to be a painter." Many friends noticed the resemblance between Adele and Elena Esposito in *The Deer Park*, who is frustrated when she cannot fulfill Charles Eitel's vision of her. Judy Feiffer thought of Adele as Norman's "creation."

In the short, cryptic poems Mailer began to write after the stabbing and published in 1962 under the title *Deaths for the Ladies (and other Disasters)* he explored the ambiguity of his emotions. What were readers to make of verse that seemed both remorseful and aggressive? Was Mailer simply being true to the ambivalence of his emotions? So it would seem in "Rainy Afternoon with the Wife":

> *So long*
> *as*
> *you*
> *use*
> *a knife*

there's
some
love
left.

Such poems were often written when he was drinking heavily. He would find scraps of paper in his jacket, scribbled lines that he would painstakingly go over with his secretary, Anne Barry, who would retype them. Mailer might spend a whole day poring over the poems and changing no more than their spacing or a word or two. He liked the modesty of his work and regarded his poetic fragments as the embers of his imagination which he was slowly firing together. In his own words, he was "mending."

Immediately after the stabbing, Mailer had gone off by himself, refusing the support of friends and family, dreading the possibility that he might be treated like just another nut case. To regard the stabbing through the jargon of a term like "psychotic break" and to seek the conventional solution—psychiatric care—revolted Mailer. In "Wandering in Prose: For Hemingway," dated November 1960, he began:

That first unmanageable cell
of the cancer which was to
stifle his existence arrived
to him on a morning when by
an extreme act of the will
he chose not to strike his
mother. Since this was
thirtysix hours after he
had stabbed his wife, and
his mother had come at a time
when he wished to see no one
in order to savor the woes
and pawed prides of his soul,
(what a need for leisure
has the criminal heart) his
renunciation of violence
was civilized, too civilized
for his cells which proceeded
to revolt.

Not to hit his mother, and to do the civilized thing, hurt him, for her presence prevented him from exploring the implications of his own violence. What he had done was "criminal," and yet to stifle that criminality before he had the "leisure" to examine it was to inflict a cancer on himself, a cancer (Mailer explained in the poem) that sprang from civilization's tendency to stifle its own instincts in favor of the more orderly "habit." Civilization favored deadened predictable responses over a dangerous spontaneity. If Mailer associated his fears for the extinction of his unique personality with Hemingway, it was because he thought Hemingway had shown how a writer could become his own man.

Except for "The Time of Her Time," Mailer had not been able to create a sustained work of fiction in which self-creation (linked in "The White Negro" with personal violence) emerged as a credible act. Not since Paul Scarr in *A Transit to Narcissus* had Mailer dared to bring a hero to the knife point, to the edge of violence—indeed over that edge—as he had brought himself. His self-dramatizing poems perhaps helped him to work toward a narrative voice that openly addressed this nexus between violence and individuality. Yet there would still have to be a great leap from the philosophizing hipster of "The White Negro" to the invention of a narrator enough like Mailer himself to seem psychologically convincing.

Mailer's stabbing of Adele, his *acte gratuit* (as it came to be regarded in the literary community), actually magnified his mystique. Lionel Abel observed Mailer at *Partisan Review* parties, where the likes of Susan Sontag, Hannah Arendt, and Mary McCarthy paid court to him: "Everybody wanted to *touch* Norman. People would go over and literally touch him." When Abel later described this phenomenon to Alberto Moravia in Rome, Moravia suggested, "Maybe they feel that he's more real than they are. That's why they want to touch him, to hang onto reality."

In "Norman Mailer and the Despair of Defiance" (*The Yale Review*, December 1961) George Alfred Schrader called the stabbing a "*motiveless* destructive act." In his view, Mailer was not mad, he was not compulsive, he was not jealous; rather, he was exercising the defiant despair of the romantic disappointed that the world had not taken the shape of his imagination. Hip had driven Mailer harder and harder to find his own kicks, and like "countless men before him" he had been appalled to discover that the world offered "no self-sustained meaning."

Kierkegaard had written about such "sensuous-erotic" geniuses, Schrader pointed out, and until Mailer conquered the "dread of being responsible for himself," he would not become the "outstanding novelist he so desperately wants but does not yet will to be."

In an extraordinary essay, "The Black Boy Looks at the White Boy" (*Esquire*, May 1961), James Baldwin drew a gallant and profoundly compassionate picture of his literary rival:

> . . . *the fantasy structure the writer builds in order to escape his central responsibility [which is to write] operates not as his fortress, but his prison, and he perishes within it. Or: the structure he has built becomes so stifling, so lonely, so false, and acquires such a violent and dangerous life of its own, that he can break out of it only by bringing the entire structure down. With a great crash, inevitably, and on his own head, and on the heads of those closest to him. It is like smashing the windows one second before one asphyxiates; it is like burning down the house in order, at last, to be free of it. And this, I think, really, to touch upon it lightly, is the key to the events at that monstrous, baffling, and so publicized party.*

Mailer's extreme act, in other words, reflected a predicament that Baldwin had also confronted, that all writers must face when their writing does not go well, or does not go at all. No real politician, Baldwin pointed out, would have assembled such a diverse group of people for a party, and when the gathering got out of control, Mailer may have doubted "perhaps for the first time . . . his ability to deal with such a world, and blindly struck his way out of it." The American writer actually feared experience, Baldwin contended, and that is why he had so "peculiarly difficult and dangerous a time." Baldwin, who shared much of Mailer's feeling even while deploring the philosophy of "The White Negro," knew that few writers had the nerve to hit back at the world as recklessly as Mailer did. Before publishing his piece, Baldwin had consulted Mailer's sister, Barbara. He told her, "I want to show it to you before anyone else. I don't want to betray Norman."

MR. LADY JEANNE

Although Mailer spoke of the stabbing as a mortal wound to his reputation ("I destroyed forever the possibility of being the Jeremiah of our time") it did not take him long to recover or to express other facets of his kaleidoscopic personality. It could be argued that the stabbing of Adele had actually been the final thrust of the Village Norman, the stick-man, for his marriage to Lady Jeanne Campbell in early 1962 more accurately reflected his shift of interest to glamour and position, which had been signaled by "Superman Comes to the Supermarket." In the early 1960s, Mailer wrote what he came to call his "Presidential Papers"—essays in search of a hero, an adventurer who would be able to imbue America once again with a sense of its uniqueness and vitality.

Lady Jeanne, daughter of the Duke of Argyll and granddaughter of the British press baron Lord Beaverbrook (and said to have been the lover of America's media giant Henry Luce), seemed completely different from Adele Morales. Yet she had a competitive spirit, having lasted a full twenty minutes before blinking in a staring match with Mailer at a party, apparently a record time in his experience. He was used to dominating women and Lady Jeanne posed a challenge—independent and feisty and impulsive, knowing after their first meeting that she would "marry him and have his child."

Mailer met Campbell in Provincetown. In the summer of 1961 she was writing columns for the *Evening Standard*. Henry Geldzahler, a friend of Mailer's whom Adele was fond of, accompanied Jeanne on a story about a fat farm near Provincetown and quickly established a rapport with her. He found she had enormous energy and that she was mounting what might be called a campaign to become Mailer's wife.

Many people found Campbell likable, if a bit mystifying. She got calls from everywhere in the world and seemed to fit in no matter the company or the place. Like Mailer, she had an intense curiosity about people and places. One of his friends calls her a "true English eccentric" who could do the twist with great abandon and accommodate the meanest and wildest of his companions.

Roger Donoghue believed that Lady Jeanne helped relieve Mailer of his depression over Adele. She was independent, more in control of herself than Mailer's other women, and in her self-assured way introduced him to a whole new social stratum and set of friends. Yet she was down to earth—even rather comic—like her mother, whom Roger Donoghue saw in action at a party. Jeanne's mother was having a conversation with Jimmy Reardon, "a tough-guy friend" of Donoghue's. When she asked him what he did for a living, Reardon replied, "I'm into meat, I'm a meat purveyor." To which Jeanne's mother responded: "Is your veal tit fed?" All the speechless Reardon could do was nod.

Seymour Krim met Mailer and Lady Jeanne at a party shortly after they were married. "She was not physically quite as sparkling as Adele," Krim observes, "but as far as poise, presence, and general amiability go, I think I liked her. Mailer seemed relaxed with her, and she was somewhat under wraps. She let Norman take center stage." Although Krim was somewhat surprised by the marriage, he points out that Mailer "has always been intrigued—due to the associations of his Harvard days—with upper-crust things. He always reserved the right to be the earthy Jew in relation to it, to have it both ways: admiration and disapprobation. I think they're both parts of his experience."

Larry Alson notes that Mailer's marriage to Campbell is unique in that it was impulsive: "He lived with other wives for a time before marriage. After he found that it was working, he thought it was right to dignify the arrangement. But this was different. If you look at his work, one of his fantasies is nobility." Bea Silverman suggests that a match with Campbell was yet another way of assimilating: "She is the ultimate *shiksa*." Certainly Campbell enhanced Mailer's grand image of himself, for in *Cannibals and Christians* he writes, "what [a man] wants is a marvelous courtesan with social arts."

To others this seemed a very surprising match. Fanny was not pleased with Norman's choice of mate and kept her distance, especially after the reserved reception of a dinner that Fanny cooked for Jeanne's mother, who had come on a visit. Meeting Jeanne's mother was "like touching ice water; you don't stick your hand in it," recalled Fanny, who was not impressed with the "fact of her royalty," and indeed sounded as though she resented it: "Perhaps Norman was impressed with it. But he found it was nothing, it was *poof*."

It seemed important to Mailer that his friends the Rostens meet his new love. "He liked Hedda a lot," Norman Rosten recalls, because "she took him in stride, and he liked her judgments." So he called them to say he would like to bring a lady to meet them. Rosten remembers her as a tall, attractive woman—"a little on the heavy side." She and Mailer made a lively, vivid, intellectual couple interested in books and ideas. After some coffee and tea at the Rosten's Remsen Street apartment, Mailer asked the Rostens what they thought of her. "What could we say?" Rosten remembers. "She seemed all right. We didn't know much about her." Adeline Lubell Naiman, who had stopped seeing Norman after he had hectored her over her alleged dislike of Adele, was surprised to get a visit from him and Lady Jeanne. He admitted that he had been wrong in driving Naiman out of his life. Bringing Campbell for a visit marked the resumption of their friendship.

Norman Podhoretz liked Campbell very much, and she seemed to appreciate him, although he got tired of the fights between her and Mailer. Pete Hamill, on the other hand, enjoyed the couple's "rowdy attraction" to each other. Hamill speculated that Mailer's unpredictability, his ability to act the brilliant man or the Brooklyn hood impressed Campbell.

Stanley Karnow, who worked for Henry Luce at *Time* magazine, was probably one of the few people who had real insight into the Campbell–Mailer match. Having known both men, he was in a position to observe the "remarkable similarity" between them:

> *Luce had a very staccato way of speaking—just the way Norman does. If you closed your eyes, it was very hard to tell the difference between them. It amazed me. . . . Both were very quick, immensely inquisitive—totally different in content but not entirely dissimilar in terms of their hard driving characters.*

A pregnant Lady Jeanne made quite a sight in Provincetown in the summer of 1962. She was a big woman who favored black. To one of Mailer's friends she looked like a "fat nun." Shortly after the birth of Kate Mailer on August 18, 1962, Jean Malaquais was disgusted to see Norman treat Lady Jeanne just as he had his other wives, becoming incensed when he saw Mailer fail to lift a finger during a meal Jeanne had prepared after having just gotten out of the hospital. To Mailer, it was no "big deal." He saw nothing wrong with sitting, talking, and eating while his wife waited on him.

In the fall of 1962 the couple took possession of a brownstone in Brooklyn Heights. Lady Jeanne and the baby took a first-floor garden apartment she had upholstered entirely in flowered fabric. In *An American Dream*, Mailer seems to have it in mind when Rojack speaks of his wife Deborah's apartment as having "the specific density of a jungle conceived by Rousseau."

With Lady Jeanne, Mailer could indulge his highly developed sense of manners: "My Susie doesn't call Jim. Jim calls Susie," he instructed Diana Trilling when she suggested Mailer's daughter might call her son to arrange a meeting. At the same time, Lady Jeanne had "a streak of craziness, of wildness, with no sense of consequences, which only a true aristocrat would have." When a party she and Mailer attended turned into a drunken brawl, she jumped right in, whacking away at everyone with a toilet plunger.

There were periods during his life with Lady Jeanne when Mailer seemed to revert to the manic phases with Adele. At one point, during a brief stay at Hugh Hefner's mansion in Chicago, Roger Donoghue became so upset with Mailer that he phoned Campbell, warning her that she had better protect herself because her husband had "flipped." His friendship with Mailer strained, Donoghue avoided him for a time because he acted like such a "jerk" and embarrassed him in front of his "fight friends." Although he did not "abandon" Mailer, Donoghue found it just too "depressing" to be around him.

In fall of 1962, Mailer hired Anne Barry as his secretary. In 1961, her senior year at Radcliffe, she had taken a course from Erik Erikson, who gave as a final assignment a paper on autobiography. Barry chose to write about *Advertisements for Myself*, producing, in her words, "a galumphing, huge, pretentious, wonderful sophomoric paper, 52 pages long, on Norman Mailer's identity crisis at the age of thirty-nine." For the paper she had written Mailer, who had replied that while he did not usually grant such requests, he would do so in her case because he liked her handwriting.

During spring vacation Barry met Mailer at his sister's Village apartment on Bleeker Street. They adjourned to a bar and had "a lovely time laughing and joking and talking about everything under the sun." By this time, Barry thought it was "the nicest, funniest, most bubbly time I'd ever had. I adored him." Eventually they returned to Barbara's apartment, and Barry remembers Jeanne Campbell was there.

Mailer had suggested at their interview that he might have some typing for her to do and that she should get in touch with him when she returned to New York. Barry remembers coming for an interview at his Brooklyn Heights brownstone just after Kate was born. Campbell had brought her maid, Sadie, to take care of the household. Then Mailer and Barry adjourned to his top-floor studio and were interrupted once by Campbell, who dictated some thank-you notes. Barry thought that Campbell had come up to study her. Mailer asked Barry when she would like to begin. They discussed a salary, and she accepted his offer of fifty dollars a week.

Barry recorded the day of the marriage breakup in her diary: "January 27, 1963: "Jeannie is gone for good. She took off in an aristocratic snit."

It was a stormy marriage, and it lasted less than two years. "At least I can say I went 15 rounds with the best light-heavyweight the British ever sent over," Mailer quipped to interviewer Brock Brower. "We managed . . . to empty a room quicker than any couple in New York," Lady Jeanne told James Atlas. The jocularity in these comments suggests that although they could not get along, there was no deep-seated conflict. He wanted her to take care of his children and to make his breakfast. She liked to sleep late in the morning and loll about in her housecoat. She did no housekeeping, not even bothering to pick up the clothes she would cast off her body. Mailer felt that if he remained with her, he might become "Mr. Lady Jeanne."

If Lady Jeanne furnished in her person a part of the inner architecture of Mailer's soul, she seemed out of place in the layout he designed for his four-story Brooklyn brownstone. It looked out on the East River and New York Harbor, the site of Mikey Lovett's solitary walks in *Barbary Shore*. When Brock Brower came to interview Mailer for an article, he saw a large apartment designed to have a distinctly nautical look, with a brass ship's clock sounding eight bells in the kitchen and a "dismantled engine room telegraph" next to Mailer's bookshelves. The apartment's space had been opened up in the middle. Mailer had designed "a lofty, tenting, glass-and-wood gable that he pushed right out through his room like a small pyramid." The inside had the feel of a ship's forecastle, with many different and difficult approaches to several upper levels: "climbing ropes, boarding nets, trapezes, deck ladders, catwalks and, for those who wish to rest halfway, a rope hammock slung between two beams over the dried-out skeletons of dead sea skates that roll like mobiles in the cross-ventilation below." The living space below had bunks for Mailer's two daughters by Adele when they came to visit, a stereo system, and an observation deck. To enter Mailer's workroom at the top of this pyramidal structure one had to cross a "six-inch-wide plank" requiring a determined "sure-footed" step if one did not grab onto the "handholds along the gable roof." Daring this ascent and journey across the plank represented, in Brower's view, the "psychic right to intrude upon" Mailer's "crow's nest, a solitary eminence that looks out on the world like the eye atop the pyramid in The Great Seal on the dollar bill."

This was an environment that perpetually tested the artist and his confreres. It helped create Mailer's hierarchy of values, his attunement to the elements, but it also acknowledged his domestic arrangements, the ground floor on which he lived his day-to-day life. Brower saw that in this space it was not difficult to sail off in one's imagination, a captain of living quarters built like a vessel. Every movement in this space was like a quest and a testament to Mailer's belief that he had to live what he imagined, that life was a contest, a trial for the soul. Even his concept of a home had to have something heroic about it.

THE PRESIDENTIAL PAPERS

Mailer's collection of his writing since *Advertisements for Myself* read like a medieval romance, a quest for heroes and villains, for the principles of good and evil, that guided the national psyche. Military metaphors abound in his essays as he suggests there can be no creativity without conflict, no great men if they do not risk the absurd. Thus Mailer hails Castro as "the greatest hero since World War II" because with only a handful of men, and on the brink of defeat, his will to triumph eventuated in a revolution.

As in *Advertisements for Myself*, Mailer uses italicized passages to comment upon and to recommend his pieces on politics, foreign policy, the literary life, the theater, and boxing. What is new, however, is his extraordinary conceit that he is serving as President Kennedy's "court wit" and "amateur advisor." In *The Presidential Papers* Mailer offers himself as "the social microcosm—and thus our voluntary scapegoat for weaknesses and corruptions and inadequacies." While this is an extremely dangerous position to take, Midge Decter observes, it can also (depending on the quality of his writing) make him the central figure of his time.

Mailer's coverage of the Patterson–Liston heavyweight title fight (September 25, 1962), the conclusion of *The Presidential Papers*, best demonstrates how he had come to view himself as "the social microcosm." Instead of rooting for Liston, the outlaw, the fighter with a criminal record who strikes Mailer as a "great actor," he sides with the underdog, Patterson, the "negroid white," the favorite of the middle class. For Patterson is the "champion of every lonely adolescent . . . of every protagonist who tried to remain unique in a world whose waters washed apathy and compromise into the pores." Patterson is "the artist" who "could not forgive himself if he gave less than his best chance for perfection." Mailer can feel it: The country wants Patterson to win, and he describes Patterson in terms that virtually fit himself.

Turning the championship fight into myth, Mailer calls Liston Faust, the evil genius who has made a pact with the devils of the Mob. Patterson, on the other hand, is managed by Cus D'Amato, famous for his opposition to organized crime in boxing. Invested in this myth is a vision of boxing as a humanistic discipline, showing "a part of what man is like . . . his ability to create art and artful movement on the edge of death or pain or danger or attack. . . ." By suggesting that boxing has this moral and aesthetic dimension, Mailer augments his own importance and his right to be there to interpret the psychic forces in the ring working for the victory and the defeat of the two boxers.

Mailer attributes Patterson's quick first-round loss to a failure in himself and in the country and speculates that the fighter may have been defeated before he entered the ring, "whipped by the oatmeal of the liberal line" that did not work hard enough to ward off the "Mafia" vortex that had enveloped Liston at ringside. Years later, Mailer admitted that his effort to hold a press conference to explain his idea was "demented," yet at the time his notion of himself as "some sort of center about which all that had been lost must now rally" was not merely a crazy conceit. After all, Mailer identified not merely with Patterson but with all the lonely adolescents, the secret romantics, who had imagined their man would win. A world heavyweight boxing championship had become the vehicle for their fantasies—as it had for Mailer—and heroes could come back from defeat, just like Castro "alone in the jungle, with a dozen men left, seven-eights of his landing party dead, lost, or captured [who had] turned to his followers in the sugar-cane and said, 'The days of the dictatorship are numbered.' "

Patterson and Patterson's followers (Mailer wanted to say at the press conference) had to emulate Castro, who "saw a set of psychic steps which led to victory."

When there was a mixup in the times for his press conference, Mailer had to content himself with interrupting Liston's, badgering the champ and not backing down when they met face to face. Mailer looked like a fool although he managed to elicit a tribute of sorts from Liston, who said of Mailer, "I like this guy." Not exactly a hero's welcome, but enough for a writer beginning to take his own psychic steps toward victory and audacious enough to pose for his book jacket photograph leaning forward in a platform rocker, a favorite of President Kennedy— who would be assassinated before *The Presidential Papers* received its first, mixed reviews.

7.

AN AMERICAN DREAM (1963–1965)

NORMAN MOTHERFUCK MAILER

During the early part of 1963 Mailer was not only struggling over his marriage, he was also meeting new women (over his wife's protests), making a new friend—the light-heavyweight contender Jose Torres—and welcoming into his already hectic and complicated household yet another woman, Jeannie Johnson.

In late October 1962, about a month after the first Patterson–Liston fight, writer Pete Hamill took Mailer to meet Jose Torres at the Gramercy Gym, thinking that it would do Mailer good to see boxing from the inside. To Hamill, Torres seemed an especially good choice because he was his own man and not likely to become one of Mailer's sycophants. When Mailer's secretary, Anne Barry, met Torres, she liked his "sweetness" and "character." He appeared to have more integrity than most of the men who attached themselves to Mailer.

In her diary for February 23, 1963, Barry noted that Jeannie Johnson had moved in. She had come straight from Bellevue after a three-month stay. Mailer took her in, looking very shaky in her "little short skirt and red stockings," as though she were an adopted child. Johnson, quite a prankster, shared with Mailer an oddball sense of humor. She liked to fool around with "funny notes, presents, and with 'hiding things.' " And Mailer seemed to thrive on her "energy and irreverence." She was quite a contrast—the something different he needed from the host of people willing to kowtow to him. Barry never knew whether Johnson actually had an affair with Mailer. Eventually, he introduced Johnson to a friend, Paul Krassner, editor of *The Realist*, and the couple were later married in Brooklyn Heights.

Johnson had arrived just two weeks after Mailer had participated in one of those events that periodically disrupted the decorum of his literary career. On February 6, 1961, at the 92nd Street Young Men's Hebrew Association Poetry Center he read his poems, some of which referred to the stabbing. He warned his audience of seven hundred about the sexuality of his verse; some would find it obscene. After reading a few poems, he asked for a show of hands from people who found them offensive. Although a few hands shot up and were joined by others as he resumed his reading, there were also cheers until the curtain was suddenly brought down on these lines:

> *Dear Kike*
> *I wish you were a dyke.*

Mailer had earlier suggested that his bad poetry would aid his audience's appreciation of good verse, but the management (quoted the next day in *The New York Times*) condemned his "recital of wrong, obscene images and vocabulary which broke the limits of good taste from any point of view."

Such events were poor substitutes for writing a novel—the one thing he always said in his letters to Fig Gwaltney he most wanted to do. At the same time, he had decided that his public persona was an indispensable part of his work as a writer. He sought situations in which he could not know whether an audience would be for or against him, since they gave him an opportunity to learn things about himself and his public he would not otherwise know.

Mailer was becoming the kind of writer who was well known even by people who had not read his books. He was approachable, a conduit for the public mood in ways that were unique. People felt they could say anything to him:

[Roger Donoghue] At the time he'd just separated from Lady Jeanne and was very depressed and the two of us were slumming. We were in P.J.'s [P.J. Clarke's], standing at the bar, when Beverly [Bentley] came by with Jake LaMotta, quite high. We were half bombed ourselves, and I introduced them. Beverly made the crack, "Well, if it isn't Norman Motherfuck Mailer!" and I guess it was love at first sight.

Beverly Bentley, an actress from Florida who had never read Norman Mailer, had come to New York from Florida at the age of seventeen. Discovered by Arthur Godfrey in a Pensacola restaurant where she was working, she became a member of his troupe. Beverly's half-brother, Charlie Brown, remembers that Beverly was always "strong-willed" and the only one of five children to stand up to her father, an army air corpsman. She was "fast" and ambitious and her father could not control her. Her younger brother, Charlie, used to cower at the age of seven when his sister and father fought. Beverly had always wanted to be an actress, a star.

In New York, Beverly, a "little Godfrey," held up signs on television for commercials. Later she found employment as a "hand model" in perfume commercials. Brown remembers that she had "some pretty fancy boyfriends": Orson Bean, Eddie Fisher, Andy Griffith. Then she got on some of the big quiz shows and did small parts in movies. Her most important affair had been with Miles Davis. On one occasion Brown was with Bentley when she spotted Davis and engaged him in a long, intense conversation. She spoke reverently of him, obviously treating him as a genius and empathizing with his "frailities" and fondly reminiscing about the months they had lived together.

Roger Donoghue first met Beverly Bentley in 1956, then a beauty with the perfect kind of smile used in television toothpaste commercials. A regular at P.J. Clarke's, she had been the lead actress in Mike Todd's "Smell-O-Vision" movie, *Scent of Mystery*, had met Ernest Hemingway during its filming in Spain, and had played her first lead on Broadway in *The Heroine*. At thirty-three, no more than a modest success, if that, she hoped to settle down.

To Beverly, Norman seemed quite vulnerable beneath his "tough act," and "quite wonderful in bed" the night of their first meeting. About a week after this sensational introduction, Donoghue called Mailer to invite him to Cafe 72. Mailer said that Beverly had other plans.

"Beverly?" Donoghue replied. "Beverly who?" Beverly Bentley, of course, who did make it to Cafe 72, but who pouted about the change of plans. "What the hell are you doing?" Donoghue asked Mailer. "I'm in love," Mailer replied. "Oh, for Christ's sake," said Donoghue, who could not believe that Mailer could get serious about a woman so soon after Lady Jeanne. To him, it was "*bang*, the next day they're in love." Fay Donoghue was also irritated, especially when Beverly made sure to pick a restaurant where she was well known so that she could "make a fuss and order something a certain way known only to herself and the proprietor." When Fay expressed her pique in front of Mailer, he cautioned her: "Be careful what you say because I'm crazy about her."

Anne Barry's first glimpse of Beverly came one morning. Beverly was sleeping beside Mailer in a corner of the living room next to the kitchen. Barry was surprised. Although Mailer had been "fucking his brains out" since Lady Jeanne had left, he did not usually bring women home with him. Mailer merely said that he really liked Beverly, but Barry's impression is that Beverly took almost immediate possession of the place. Barry's diary records that on March 17, 1963, Beverly moved into Mailer's Brooklyn Heights brownstone. Barry found Beverly "easy." A diary entry for April 1 records that Barry slipped quite naturally into conversation with Beverly while preparing breakfast. To Barry, Beverly "looked corn-fed—you can see it in her pictures, a freshness, an openness that isn't really New York."

On April 18, 1963, Mailer wrote Fig Gwaltney proposing a visit to Arkansas in the middle of May. He would bring with him a Southern girl he was sure the Gwaltneys would like to meet. He mentioned her acting credits and thought she might be familiar to them because of her work in television commercials. They would come for no more than ten days, staying somewhere quiet where he could "get going again on my novel."

It would be September before the Gwaltneys saw the couple. In the meantime, Mailer decided to stage a "benefit" for himself intended to raise money to support himself while he wrote a novel. His performance of himself and his work at Carnegie Hall (May 31, 1963) dismayed his former teacher Robert Gorham Davis. Even supporters like Norman Podhoretz found it "slightly embarrassing" and disconcerting to see a writer act as his own impresario, but such experiences sharpened his willingness to abandon the respect usually accorded to literary eminences. Treated as a notorious personality and not as a revered novelist, many critics deplored the waste of a great talent, yet Mailer saw the advantage of breaking down the barriers between litterateurs and society at large, of cultivating an imagination as an integral part of contemporary life. As Robert Lucid puts it, Mailer did not want to "separate the artist out into a different world from that occupied by the individual in society." He wanted the exposure, not the privilege, of his literary status.

SOME CHILDREN OF THE GODDESS

Angry over the privileged status of certain writers in "Some Children of the Goddess," written in May for July publication in *Esquire*, Mailer termed Styron's new novel, *Set This House on Fire*, "the book of a man whose soul has gotten fat." Mailer treated James Jones more tenderly, characterizing his latest work, *The Thin Red Line*, as "a holding action, a long distance call to the Goddess." Other writers—particularly James Baldwin—were roughed up: *Another Country* was "abominably written." Gore Vidal escaped censure, for he was one of the few writers attacked in an earlier piece, "Evaluations—Quick and Expensive Comments on the Talent in the Room," who had remained friendly with Mailer. In fact, after his release from Bellevue Mailer had visited Vidal to ask his assistance in "reestablishing his reputation with such literary men as Saul Bellow and critic F. W. Dupee." Mailer and Vidal had also agreed not to attack each other in print.

When Styron got advance word of the Mailer attack on him and Jones in *Esquire*, he wrote Jones to say that Mailer "has stooped to an all-time low, even for one who has been flopping around in the gutter as long as Norman." Styron was worried because Mailer had an account of Styron ridiculing Jones during the days the three writers saw each other in Connecticut. It might be true, Styron admitted to Jones, because Styron did not know Jones all that well then and because he was envious of him for having "muscled through with such prodigious energy that second-novel barrier." On the other hand, his wife, Rose, remembered a two-hour argument in the kitchen with Mailer in which she defended Jones before Mailer's "snarls and sneers." This had occurred while "doubtless Adele groped at her crotch." The real point of Styron's letter was to give his analysis of why Mailer had turned so malevolently against himself and Jones. Styron endorsed Rose's speculation that the attack on Jones could be attributed to Mailer's "pent-up homosexuality," Jones "being the cock-object." Styron could not say, but perhaps Mailer liked to "take it up the ass." It now occurred to Styron that Mailer had sent him that accusatory letter five years earlier because of Styron's growing friendship with Jones. Mailer was "insanely jealous" not only of their friendship but of their talent. Styron found it unpleasant to write such a letter but advised Jones that they were dealing with a "lunatic." Styron and Jones remained affectionate friends. Jones did not comment on Styron's analysis, but he did reply with a curt remark on Mailer: "The whole thing of Norman's piece is a sort of tempest teapot hardly worth pissing in to put the fire out."

The vehemence of Styron's response was a measure of just how close this threesome once had been. Mailer had genuinely admired *From Here to Eternity* and believed that Styron's short novel *The Long March* might be the best work yet of his generation. Mailer did worry about how well he could compete with them—especially with Styron, who had already become an ensconced Establishment figure. Mailer later admitted he learned "very grudgingly" from his contemporaries and "hated their talents. I despised and loathed everything about them that was the least bit good. It killed me every time they did something that I couldn't do." For the purpose of his own mythology, which cast him as "psychic outlaw," he was driven to attributing the worst motives to his contemporaries, especially Styron, who he thought compromised his talent by creating "too small a window to look out on the world we have known."

At a 1963 *Esquire* writers' conference in Princeton, New Jersey, Mailer seemed unusually truculent. Calder Willingham observed Styron say "Hi" to a passing Mailer, who "leaned toward him and deliberately bumped him hard with his shoulder as if to say, 'Let's have a fight.' " Styron did not respond. Then Mailer told Willingham in a "quite nasty" way that he did not like Willingham's latest novel, *Eternal Fire*. Willingham recalls that "I casually called him a jerk." Mailer's eyes narrowed and in menacing tones he said: "That's the second time you've called me a jerk. Don't push your luck!" Willingham thought he knew Mailer well enough to use such language and simply told him he had intended no offense. A "surly" Mailer walked away. Later Willingham would take his revenge in the December 1963 *Esquire*, commenting that Mailer's acerbic words about his fellow writers "reeked with the odor of an acute literary illness," and that the real victim of his diatribes was himself, a man cursed to seek "glory and fame" by denigrating others.

NORMAN AND BEVERLY MAILER

One of the consequences of fame was the flood of correspondence. It had such variety it had to be put in different categories. One of Anne Barry's tasks was to keep track of Mailer's correspondence with convicts. Usually they wanted his help with their writing. To one of these types, Raimondo, Barry wrote for a year, having to fend off his periodic proposals. She complained to Mailer and worried about what would happen when Raimondo got out. "Don't worry," Mailer assured her, "he'll never get out." Then he got out. In the fall of 1963 he came to Mailer looking for work, and Mailer obliged by giving Raimondo odd jobs such as window-washing. Mailer left to Barry the task of helping Raimondo with his writing. Then Raimondo forged one of Mailer's checks. Barry had to confront him, and he denied it. Then Mailer took over, but Raimondo made a sudden exit, taking with him Mailer's maid. Barry thought Mailer "more wounded than angry, disappointed." Barry could never figure out why he bothered with such cases, but Mailer insisted on his obligation to do so because his success meant that he should help others.

In the fall of 1963, en route to the second Patterson–Liston fight, Norman and Beverly paid a visit to the Gwaltneys. Ecey introduced Norman and Beverly to their friends as "Norman and Beverly Mailer" and provoked a lecture from him about how Beverly should be intro-duced as Beverly Bentley. It puzzled Ecey. Norman had done just the opposite with Adele, having her wear a wedding ring so everything would seem proper to Ecey's friends.

At this point Beverly seemed content, in Ecey's words, for Norman to have "the spotlight." It would be a different matter, Ecey notes, when she next saw Beverly two years later. "I don't think Beverly was ever passive or starry-eyed. She was always the 'I'm the actress' type, always full of juice with her own ideas," Roger Donoghue observes.

In Las Vegas Norman and Beverly socialized with Harold and Mara Lynn Conrad. According to Harold Conrad, a sports writer and colum-nist, Beverly "fit right in" to the "fight scene, the macho shit. . . . She was tough, and I remember once I grabbed that broad's shoulder, and she was hard, like a fucking rock."

After the fight, Mara (who would later act in three of Mailer's films) and Buddy Rich's wife, Marie, were sitting in the Thunderbird Lounge having drinks when they were accosted by two guys who treated the women as prostitutes. Mara stood up, saw Mailer at the bar, and called for his assistance. Still on probation for stabbing Adele, Mailer refused to get involved. When the men would not let up, Mara chucked her drink at them and started a fight that put Mailer inevitably in the middle of it, although the cops quickly broke it up. Perhaps because Mara had taunted him that night into a confrontation with the men, Mailer (according to Mara) later kicked down the door of some guy bothering him. Her husband had it the other way around, with Mailer slugging the guy after he kicked down Mailer's door.

The next day Mara saw Mailer in the lobby about 5:00 A.M., and he said: "Beverly's out walking someplace." They started out in a car and found her walking toward the desert, "crying her heart out," according to Mara: "She was so unhappy she wanted to die, she was that miserable." Norman confided in Mara, telling her that Beverly was pregnant. They had found out while visiting the Gwaltneys, and neither of them seemed very happy about it. Harold Conrad later learned of a car trip Norman and Beverly took to Death Valley to sort things out. Harold feels that they had not yet adjusted to each other and that Norman was still "suffering from the last few years" over his failures with Adele and Lady Jeanne.

In San Francisco, the next stop after Las Vegas, Mark Linenthal met a "supersober" Mailer. Norman and Beverly had decided to get married. Mailer said he would buckle down to a novel, telling Linenthal in a "straight man-to-man assessment of his life" that he had made a lot of crazy mistakes but he had put it all behind him.

Don Carpenter visited Norman and Beverly during their two-week stay in San Francisco. He remembers Mailer's almost formal protectiveness of Beverly, warning Carpenter (who had too much to drink) that he had no right to call Beverly "baby." Mailer did the cooking, serving cantaloupe with prosciutto, followed by fried steaks. "He's one of those guys who comes on hard, then goes soft and tries to relax you," notes Carpenter.

From San Francisco Beverly called home, announcing that her "ace new boyfriend" was the famous writer Norman Mailer, which made no impression on her half-brother, Charlie Brown, except that he did remember liking the movie of *The Naked and the Dead*. Brown was all set to meet this wealthy New York writer who he pictured driving up in a red Maserati and looking, "at the worst . . . like Steve McQueen." Instead, "this overweight, short, little Jewish guy with a lot of hair and big ears" stepped out of a '61 Falcon convertible. Mailer's "startling blue eyes"—reminiscent of Paul Newman's—were his one redeeming feature. The first evening was "very strange, like a test of who the guy was," Brown recalls. Mailer tried to be amusing, but Brown fixated on the way he talked, waiting to pounce—which he did when Mailer said the word *fuck*. "Shut up!" Brown shouted, telling Mailer he belonged with "the boys," and should not be saying this stuff in front his sister and mother. Mailer ignored him and went on with his story. In half an hour Brown fell "in love with him." As Brown puts it, "The man is very bright, he knows what to do with a fat redneck—leave him the fuck alone."

With Beverly's father, Norman talked about the army, and soon the men were good friends. With Beverly's mother "he was such a charmer. A real winner," Brown adds. The visit lasted two days, and everyone seem bowled over by Mailer's force. The family had known nothing about him before his visit. If Beverly's mother had known about the stabbing, Brown is sure she would have thrown Mailer out of the house.

In December 1963, Mailer flew to Juarez, Mexico, to obtain his divorce decree from Lady Jeanne Campbell "on the grounds of incompatibility." That same month he married Beverly Bentley in the living room of his Brooklyn Heights home. On March 17, 1964—exactly a year after Beverly had moved in—Mailer's first son, Michael Burks, was born. And Norman Mailer had finally begun in earnest on his new novel.

A NEW FICTIONAL PERSONA

Beverly Bentley's entrance into Norman Mailer's life was as quick as Jeanne Campbell's exit. James Baldwin had hinted in his remarks on the stabbing that Mailer was a lonely man. He may also have been a scared man. It had been eight years since he had published a novel. In *Advertisements* he had talked about his ambitious plans for fiction, yet in his Carnegie Hall debacle he had been asked if he had given up the creative life. A fair but a terrible question for a novelist who could not face producing another tepid success like *The Deer Park*. He was still under contract to Walter Minton at Putnam for the big novel he had promised, but the seventy pages or so the publisher had seen came to nought.

The renown of the nonfiction pieces was not enough, no matter how much new ground they seemed to break in the field of journalism. There is no question that Mailer had the discipline to devote himself to the two or three years needed for a novel, and he was hardly devoid of ideas. He could spin off conceits that would happily occupy whole careers for other writers, but he could not be certain that any of his notions would eventuate in a great novel.

Instead, Mailer decided to write a column for *Esquire* in the hope that one of his forays into contemporary culture would yield a subject large enough for a novel. Mailer called his columns "The Big Bite," a genial acknowledgement of his voracious appetite for the phenomena of his time. He speculated on the suicides of Marilyn Monroe and Ernest Hemingway, on the current political scene, and on the careers of his fellow writers. But this time he did not present himself as the Village outlaw. He did not insult or condescend to his readers. Rather he invited them to share in his improvisatory gusto and off-the-cuff philosophizing. Like Hemingway in his later journalism, Mailer adopted a jocular attitude toward his own celebrity. Comfortable with it, he implied it gave him a certain cachet. He could take on any subject, and he became in a way the literary host of *Esquire* magazine.

Mailer was grooming his audience and himself for another one of his literary experiments. In handwritten notes for a Big Bite column announcing his decision to write a serialized novel, he declared: "If you only knew how difficult it is to be a writer, that is, to suffer this fate. Believe me, I absolutely know that if I had 2 or 3 yrs entirely for this novel, like Turgenev, Goncharov, or Tolstoi, I would write something which would be talked about for 100 yrs." He insisted he was not boasting; rather, he knew he had an idea for a novel that was "so splendid" that he did "reverence before it." And yet he had decided to do this novel in eight or nine months in magazine installments. This meant there would be many inconsistencies, verbose passages, and sketchy characters. The true beauty of the novel would not emerge, for "inspiration depends on time." Nevertheless, he was sitting down to write. "Indeed, is it not a torment consciously to raise one's hand against oneself?" he asked.

Mailer did violence to his own perfect conception of a novel because he knew this was the only way it would get done. Too many ideas had already gone begging for want of his ability to execute them. In part, this may have been a failure of will, of a writer who shied away from taking full responsibility for his most promising projects. It was time to abandon grand schemes of multinovel cycles, especially since his need for money was desperate.

Into his fourth marriage and supporting five children, the demand for a large income kept growing. Mailer had become used to having an establishment around him, a secretary and other assistants, servants, and housekeepers. He needed a hundred thousand dollars plus a year—a sum he got as an advance for a novel to be published in hardcover by Dial. A paperback deal with Dell, negotiated by his new agent, Scott Meredith (known for his aggressive pursuit of the highest dollar), assured him of another sizable sum, but stretched over two or three years the advances were still not quite enough, so writing for *Esquire* would fill the financial gap.

Mailer would write his novel as he had written his columns—month by month. As he explained to Fig Gwaltney, a serial would force him to complete work against a deadline. He had "formed the habit, for better or worse, of having my first drafts become the basic body on which the final result was clothed." The serial form would prevent him from indulging in his penchant for third and fourth drafts, for working over a novel too much and not getting it done.

Esquire made much of his daring and theirs. What if Mailer was in "an accident, murdered, jailed?" What if he failed to finish the novel or if he wrote obscene or libelous material? *Esquire* had never serialized a novel as it was being written and wondered who would look more foolish, Mailer or the magazine. Yet the editors were betting on the likelihood that the very urgency of his writing would result in great work.

Both Mailer and the magazine were right. *An American Dream* proved a fine work—albeit a prolix one he would tighten for book publication. More important, the manner in which the book was written helped Mailer achieve his existential aesthetic, which suggested that a style forged out of the contingency of the present would afford the novelist precisely the kind of direct and robust prose he had been desperately seeking since his revisions of *The Deer Park*.

The novel Mailer had in mind would grow out of the voice he had been developing in his columns, a supple first-person patter punctuated with feisty asides and comic exaggerations. The voice would have an Elizabethan baroqueness to it, a metaphorical and metaphysical thrust that represented the novelist at his speculative best. He was through with striving for the elegance of a Fitzgerald. He wanted a prose more pungent than anything one could find in *The Great Gatsby*, his initial model for *The Deer Park*. He hoped for a breakthrough that would be directly based on his own raunchy self.

The first paragraph of the *Esquire* version of *An American Dream* represents the invention of a new fictional persona, consciously drawing on Mailer's public and private selves and for the first time creating a character who can take the full measure of his author's life and times:

> *Everyone of you finds yourself lonely, but you discover your loneliness by living a life which is like the life of everyone else; you are understood perfectly; it is just that nobody wants to listen. Still, you hear of men and women who have a life which proves to be their own; history records their name because they found no place. Ernest Hemingway is the first who comes to mind, and Marilyn Monroe. So too does Patterson, Floyd Patterson, and Liston; Edith Piaf and Dr. Stephen Ward; Christine Jorgensen, Porfirio Rubirosa, Luis Miguel Dominguin. So too do I—to myself at least. For I take from this second species of loneliness a property which is peculiar to us: we believe in coincidences and take our memory from meetings. I know I measure my life by such a rule. I met Jack Kennedy, for instance, in 1946. We were both war heroes and were both Freshmen in Congress. Congressman John Fitzgerald Kennedy, Democrat from Massachusetts, and Congressman Stephen Richards Rojack, Democrat from New York. We even spent part of one night together on a long double date and it promised to be a good night for me. I stole his girl.*

This opening troubled Rust Hills, the fiction editor at *Esquire*. Because of the references to Hemingway, Monroe, Patterson, Liston, and the conversational tone, readers of the magazine might confuse the voice of the narrator with that of Mailer in the Big Bite columns. Hills called Mailer to point out what he apparently thought was an unconscious blunder only to find that Mailer intended an initial confusion on the reader's part between the narrator and Mailer. As Mailer later noted in an interview, "I wanted a man who was very much of my generation and generally of my type." Hills suggested the author detach himself from his character, for the editor did not see what could be gained from confusing Mailer's life with that of his narrator's. This was a novel, wasn't it? Yes, but this was a novel in which Rojack's concerns were to be seen as parallel to Mailer's. Mailer would assess himself through a character who was "more elegant, more witty, more heroic" and physically stronger than himself. "I wanted to create a man who was larger than myself yet somewhat less successful. That way, ideally, his psychic density . . . would be equal to mine—and so I could write from within his head with some comfort."

In the novel's first paragraph Rojack measures himself against Kennedy and against all those great names who have made their lives their own. Rojack's struggle is the same as Mailer's: to invent a unique persona. Jack Kennedy had been Mailer's creation in "Superman Comes to the Supermarket," and Mailer had made himself Kennedy's adviser in *The Presidential Papers.* He had even made Jackie his subject in a commentary on her televised White House tour. Kennedy and Mailer had been in the war, and though Mailer had been no hero, heroism— what it takes to be a man—had always been Mailer's subject. It was not hard for him to conceive of an alter ego who had double-dated with a future president. Why not, then, conceive of a Mailer hero good enough to steal Jack's girl?

Hills was worried. Wouldn't Deborah Caughlin Mangaravidi Kelly (the girl in question who would become Rojack's wife) remind readers of Jackie, especially because of her "Irish & European & Catholic" background? But this is just what Mailer wanted. He had married, after all, Lady Jeanne Campbell, and his ambitions were nothing less than presidential. What better than to create a hero who was a competitor with Kennedy, a contemporary facing the existential dilemmas Mailer had expatiated on in "The White Negro" and "Superman Comes to the Supermarket." Like Mailer, Rojack is a Harvard graduate. Rojack's wartime exploits single him out for public office. Elected to Congress at twenty-six, his early success is reminiscent of the twenty-five-year-old Mailer who quickly became a best-selling and critically acclaimed author. Initially attracted to politics after the war, Rojack marries Deborah, thinking that her father's millions will one day finance his campaign for the presidency. But politics disturbs Rojack; there is too much of a gap between himself and his public appearances. Like Mailer, he feels insecure about himself. Politics makes him feel he is "an actor" with a personality "built upon a void." After one term in the House of Representatives, Rojack follows Mailer's quixotic path by working in Henry Wallace's campaign for president.

Rojack then pursues an academic career, becoming a professor of

existential psychology (Mailer had once considered becoming a psychoanalyst) and a controversial television host of his own program. Author
of one popular book, *The Psychology of the Hangman* (a "psychological
study of styles of execution in different states and nations"), he now
regards himself as the unsuccessful husband of an heiress. If Mailer
considered himself more successful than Rojack, he had briefly faced
the prospect of becoming "Mr. Lady Jeanne," and he had to identify
with Rojack's regret that he has not fulfilled his early promise.

Rojack has "come to the end of a very long street." He has never
recovered from killing four German soldiers—the event that made him a
hero. An acclaimed deed—much like the reception of *The Naked and
the Dead*—stands in the hero's way, blocking his progress and making
him feel inauthentic. The night Rojack kills the Germans is his first look
into the abyss. Instead of filling him with a sense of power, the death
scene actually confirms his feeling of nothingness, as though his own
self has died. He feels used up and violated by his great feat, much as
Mailer felt his life had been emptied of content by his celebrated war
novel.

In *An American Dream* Rojack digs a hole for himself, a grave, a
death scene from which he does not begin to emerge until he kills
Deborah. In combat, he had been able to move with a skill he had never
demonstrated in practice. Indeed, after the war he comes to view himself
not as heroic but simply as part of a larger action: "I did not throw the
grenades on that night on the hill under the moon, *it* threw them and *it*
did a near perfect job." The automatic nature of Rojack's act, similar
to Mailer's feeling that *The Naked and the Dead* wrote itself, immobil-
izes him.

Several elements of Mailer's biography come together in his graphic
depiction of the death scene, elements that had not coalesced in his
earlier fiction, elements he now found the nerve to confront. Rojack
enters the war as a "stiff, overburdened, nervous icy-cold young Second
Lieutenant" reminiscent not only of the aloof Lieutenant Hearn but also
of the young Mailer who had confessed at college that his writing
revealed a certain want of feeling, a lack of sympathetic engagement
with the lives of others. As Rojack describes the soldiers he kills, it is
clear that the presence of death—the gravelike and womblike holes out
of which the Germans surface and to which they return—evokes the
birth trauma and the desire to return to mother. Rojack, like Mailer,
would like to repair to his hole and to renounce the outside world. But

the soldiers keep coming at him, and he becomes gruesomely fascinated with the way they meet their deaths, describing their impact on him in intimate—one might almost say loving—detail. The attraction and repulsion of homoerotic desires reflected in Rojack's depiction of the killings is the result of his fear that he will not behave like a man and his effort to prove that he can act like one. Lack of manhood has been the constant dread of every Mailer protagonist. It is the covert theme that suddenly breaks through to consciousness at the end of "The Time of Her Time"; it is what dogs Paul Scarr in his sadistic beating of the asylum inmates; it is the challenge General Cummings must take up— separating himself from his mother and hardening himself for the world; it is the bane of Mikey Lovett's existence (the fact that Guinevere does not treat him as a mature, adult lover); it is Sergius O'Shaugnessy's plight to be mothered by nuns and Dorothea O'Faye even as he tries to prove his prowess in the bullring. Rojack's confrontation with each German is simultaneously a confrontation with his unconscious motives and with his contradictory selves distorted into a nightmarish, moonlit landscape of war. As he describes his comrades' reactions to his "heroic" feat, he expresses his fear of being defiled, of having his hole entered, of being kissed on the mouth. Each German death has been a frightening revelation of Rojack's and Mailer's entrance into the world; each death makes it harder for this "hero" to fill the void in his life, for each death represents Rojack's fear of contact with others. In the machine-gun hole on his right Rojack points his carbine at

> *a great bloody sweet German face, a healthy, spoiled over spoiled young beauty of a face, mother love all over its making, possessor of that overcurved mouth which only great fat sweet young faggots can have when their rectum is tuned and entertained from adolescence on, came crying, sliding, smiling up over the edge of the hole, "Hello death!,", blood and mud like the herald of sodomy upon his chest, and I pulled the trigger as if I were squeezing the softest breast of the softest pigeon which ever flew, still a woman's breast takes me now and then to the pigeon on that trigger, and the shot cracked like a birch twig across my palm, whap!, and the round went in at the base of his nose and spread and I saw his face sucked in backward upon the gouge of the bullet; he looked suddenly like an old man, toothless, sly, reminiscent of lechery. Then he whimpered "Mutter," one yelp from the first memory of the womb, and down he went into his own blood just in time, timed like the*

interval in a shooting gallery, for the next was up, his hole mate, a hard avenging specter with a pistol in his hand and one arm off, blown off, rectitude like a stringer of saliva across the straight ledge of his lip, the straightest lip I ever saw, German-Protestant rectitude, Whap! *went my carbine and the hole was in his heart and he folded back the long arm with the pistol, back across his chest to cover his new hole, and went down straight and with a clown's deep gloom as if he were sliding down a long thin pipe, and then I turned, feeling something tear in my wound, nice in its pain, a good blood at liberty, and I took on the other two coming out of the other hole, one short, stocky apelike wretch with his back all askew, as if he'd had a false stuffed hump which shrapnel had disgorged beyond his shoulder blade: I fired at him and he went down and I never saw where it hit nor quite saw his face; then the last stood up straight with a bayonet in his hand and invited me to advance. He was bleeding below his belt. Neat and clean was his shirt, level the line of his helmet, and nothing but blood and carnage below the belt. I started to rise. I wanted to charge as if that were our contract, and held, for I could not face his eyes, they now contained all of it, the two grenades, the blood on my thigh, the fat faggot, the ghost with the pistol, the hunch back, the blood, those bloody screams that never sounded, it was all in his eyes; he had eyes I was to see once later in a redneck farmer from a deep road in the Ozarks, eyes of blue, so perfectly blue and mad they go all the way deep into celestial vaults of sky, eyes which go back all the way to God is the way I think I heard it said once in the South, and I faltered before that stare, clear as ice in the moonlight, and hung on one knee, not knowing if I could push my wound, and suddenly it was all gone, the clean presence of* it, *the grace,* it *had deserted me in the instant I hesitated, and now I had no stomach to go. I could charge his bayonet no more. So I fired. And missed. And fired again. And missed. Then he threw his bayonet at me. It did not reach. He was too weak. It struck a stone instead and made a quivering whanging sound like the yowl of a tomcat on the jump. Then it stopped between us. The light was going out in his eye. That light started to collect, to coagulate in the thick jelly which forms on the pupil of a just-dead dog, and he died then, and fell over. Like a noble tree with rotten roots. And the platoon was up around me, shooting a storm into those two holes, and they were cheering, buzzing, kissing my mouth (one of the Italians for certain), pounding my back.*

The vivid memory of this key event in Rojack's life comes to him on a night of the full moon, the lunar phase bringing to mind the moonlit night he had killed the Germans and his obsession with death and the possibilities of rebirth. The emptiness he felt then makes him feel suicidal now, for he is not under attack but must instead acknowledge his defeat of himself. Or as he puts it in gauging the difference between the two nights: "Murder offers the promise of vast relief. It is never unsexual." Certainly the death scene he describes, with its constant emphasis on shooting holes, is a violent version of sexual intercourse with each German taking on the character of a different kind of lover Rojack penetrates and annihilates.

Estranged from Deborah, Rojack has the "itch" to jump from an apartment building, but living with her he has felt "murderous." Not having the strength to "stand alone," he has depended on her, on the solidity of a big, handsome woman who might yet be wooed to support his "secret ambition to return to politics." Deborah has not only the money but the family pedigree, the connections, and the self-assurance that Rojack lacks. Indeed, Deborah supplants his parents, a Jewish father and Protestant mother who are barely mentioned in the novel, and becomes his locus of identity, behaving, in the words of one critic, as "the overpowering, castrating mother." Rojack's mystical belief in woman's psychic powers, in the womb as the source of life "come into human beings from a beyond," gives the haughty Deborah control over his self-image. She reflects what Judith Fetterly calls his biological interpretation of human identity which presumes that "women have the power that derives from a fixed and stable identity, a conviction of existence, an assurance of being on the side of life." Like Mailer, Rojack never has that assurance; on the contrary, both he and his creator must continually establish themselves (and their sense of male sexuality) anew or face extinction. "Masculinity is not something given to you, something you're born with, but something you gain," Mailer remarked in a *Playboy* interview.

Rojack finds in Deborah the withering, demonic dismissal of his manhood that had driven Mailer to knife Adele. In Rojack's murder of Deborah Mailer may have attained a sense of completion denied to him in the stabbing. Deborah has both Lady Jeanne's aristocratic impregnability and Adele's vicious, emasculating tongue. Like Adele and Mailer, Deborah and Rojack have fought each other, with Deborah almost taking off his ear in one battle. When Rojack confesses that he still loves Deborah, she replies: "It must be awful. Because you know I don't love you at all." She dismisses him with such quiet finality that Rojack feels a void open in him. He is "now without center," and in despair he asks Deborah: "Do you know what it's like to look at someone you love and see no love come back?"

When Deborah confesses that there has been a man she loved who did not return her love, Rojack is devastated. Although she has previously claimed to have told him about all her lovers, this one, she insists, was the greatest of all, "far greater" than any man she has described to Rojack. "I tried to make him jealous once and lost him," she confesses. Her malicious remarks strike at Rojack's core, for the implication is that the man was Kennedy, the great man from whom Rojack has always believed he stole Deborah.

Deborah refuses to stop taunting Rojack about his own seductions of women—calling them little girls—and boasts that the very special sexual act he had taught her and supposed she had reserved only for him has become a part of her "famous practice" with others. In retaliation, he strikes her across the face. When she resists him (grabbing for his genitals), he clutches her by the throat and chokes her to death. As in his killing of the Germans, Rojack feels he has been violated—his masculinity undermined—for Deborah has destroyed the basis on which their marriage has existed. Fully capable of murder herself, he feels, Deborah has deliberately tried to deprive him of his reason for living—a particularly vicious act, since she had divined the fact that Rojack had considered killing himself that night.

With Deborah dead, Rojack is on his own, feeling relieved, absolved of his wounds, and refreshed—as though he has taken on new flesh. In this extreme act of rebirth founded on a murder, Mailer projects a hero who finally transcends the dichotomy between Hearn and Cummings, Lovett and Hollingsworth, and O'Shaugnessy and Faye. Rojack is Mailer's first hero to throttle his urge to return to the womb; instead he emerges as his own creation. Rojack, in other words, is the first Mailer narrator who truly invents his own voice, paralleling his author's own quest for a singular style.

Rojack's elation is perverse, but then as Mailer later pointed out in an interview, Rojack is "more corrupt than me." He does not stab a woman with a penknife. Rojack, unlike Mailer, has killed before and looked into the abyss. Mailer had always wanted to destroy his pampered Brooklyn youth, and for his first kill he has Rojack shoot a "healthy, spoiled over spoiled" German boy who goes to his death whimpering for his mother. Rojack's contemptuous yet loving dispatch of this German boy is like Mailer's divided feelings about his earliest self—the tender boy he had kept trying to toughen up. It was hard to let go of his feminine side, of that female breast Rojack imagines himself squeezing as he pulls the trigger on the German boy. Writing *An American Dream*, Mailer had to realize, was like pulling the trigger on himself. Even more troublesome, he had revealed so much in his first chapter that he wondered how he could possibly top himself: "To have your hero kill his wife in the first installment of an eight-part serial is like taking your clothes off in Macy's window. What do you do next?"

BUGGERY

The editors at *Esquire* were excited by the first chapter, which they worked over in October 1963 for publication in January. The scribbled notes of one editor characterized Rojack and the novel: "guy is on pilgrimage thru dilemmas of good & evil . . . while strong—it is also highly moral . . . can defend not just as literature but also moral." This editor was probably responding to the objections of the publisher, Arnold Gingrich—no fan of Mailer's who considered this new work obscene. Harold Hayes, who shepherded the manuscript through the editing process, wrote Gingrich soothing memos, pointing out how "awfully good" everyone had been in "this first handling of Mailer's novel." Rust Hills had done a "fine blue pencil scrutiny" and Mailer had been amenable about Gingrich's suggestions, agreeing to drop his use of the word *fucking*. The editors were extremely careful, marking several passages for questionable taste, occasionally asking Mailer to tone down a word. "We are wondering whether the condescending remarks about JFK (first half) are in the best of taste," Byron Dobell noted on an intraoffice memo. In the end, most passages were not significantly changed.

"The second installment was when the fun started," Hayes later remembered. Mailer had to decide how his hero would react to the murder. Rojack feels liberated, in the state of grace he and Deborah sometimes experienced after making love, and more alive than ever before, with eyes reflecting "the blue of a mirror held between the ocean and sky . . . eyes to equal at last the eyes of that German who stood before me with a bayonet." These are the cold blue piercing eyes of Mailer himself, eyes that express the conceit of a self who believes he can take in all things: "Am I now good? am I evil forever?" Rojack asks himself in exhilaration. When he returns to look at Deborah on the floor, he concludes that she has been "divided by death," willing her grace to him (how else can he account for his elation and composure?) and to herself "every last part" that has "detested" him.

In his state of grace, Rojack is the first Mailer hero to transcend the passive/aggressive syndrome—that predicament of feeling less than manly even while attempting to assert himself. Rojack is now on his own and acutely attuned to the reverberations of his actions, the sounds and the smells, the intimations and tactile sensations of the murder scene:

> I had the sense I had been touched on the shoulder. . . . Something touched me and now pushed me without touch toward the door. Once again I could have been in a magnetic field. . . . And I went with this force.

He is driven not only out the door but into the maid's room; this field of force is, among other things, sexual and is as much connected to his killing of the Germans as it is to his murder of Deborah.

At this point Mailer's writing began to give *Esquire*'s editors trouble, since he intended to graphically describe Rojack's sexual encounter with Deborah's German maid. Not only did Gingrich object to this scene; he wanted to cancel the novel. With so much at stake Hayes and Rust Hills convinced Mailer (who knew he could restore cuts in the hardcover edition) to censor himself. Consequently the connections between death and sex, between the German maid and the German soldiers, between Rojack's desire to love and to murder, were blunted. Mailer had fashioned lurid, sensational prose, brilliantly evocative of Rojack's joy in invading the maid's privacy, of violating another's pleasure:

> The lamp by her bed was on. The windows were closed, the air was close, an oven of burgeonings was that room, and there was the maid, Fraulein Gruta [sic] from Berlin, lying on top of the cover with her pajama pants down, yes there, smack like that, a copy of a magazine in one hand (some flash of nude photographs in color) and her other hand fingering, all five fingers chittering like maggots at her open heat. She was off in that bower of the libido where she was queen.

The fingering and the maggots had to be eliminated in the *Esquire* version, even though they enhanced the scene's voyeuristic quality and also suggested the violation of the grave, evoking those holes out of which Rojack had seen those Germans emerge and the holes he had put into them. Rojack never touches the Germans, even though it is clear— especially in the killing of the first German boy with the "herald of sodomy on his chest"—that sexuality suffuses the killings. In the logic of his own self-redemption, Rojack must penetrate Ruta, thrust to her root, if he is to grapple with the mystery of life and death and sex that has plagued him and all of Mailer's earlier protagonists.

Paul Scarr had wanted to kill the woman to whom he made love and had actually pulled a knife on her, but he was deflected by his own indecision and her refusal to play the victim. Rojack, on the other hand, has given full play to his murderous mood and battled with a mate who is almost his equal in strength. As a result, he breaks through to the questing self Scarr longs to become. Rojack's reaction to Ruta is to join in her sexual play: "I put my five toes where her five fingers had been drawing up on the instant [out of her] a wet spicy wisdom [of all the arts and crafts of getting along in the world.]" Regrettably *Esquire* shortened this passage to "I put my five toes on her," thereby making the scene merely a matter of molestation. For book publication, Mailer restored the bracketed phrases because they do help to show how in the very act of violation his hero is establishing an intimacy with a woman and a connection with the world that Mailer's previous protagonists fail to accomplish. At first Ruta is annoyed, but her fury is checked by the look on Rojack's face—"I suppose I was ready to kill her easy as not." This line is reminiscent of Mailer's comment that *A Transit to Narcissus* presages one of his basic themes: "the whiff of murder just beyond every embrace of love."

Ruta proves responsive to Rojack's sexual attack, to the alley cat in him that knows how to stroke her limbs and thighs before kissing her and how to "lay back like a king lion and let her romp." The jovial, uninhibited exaggeration of this scene is like nothing Mailer had attempted in prose before—except perhaps for "The Time of Her Time." This couple makes a meal of each other, and it is in this very desire to devour, to dig into the roots of things that Rojack overcomes the shame and distaste he felt in killing those Germans, in being so close to the mysteries of life and death. All of those holes become centered in Rojack's fixation on Ruta's body: "I had a desire to pass by the sea and dig the earth, a pure prong of desire believe me that I felt not that often, there was a canny hard-packed evil in that butt, that I knew." Ruta resists his attempt at sodomy, crying *verboten*, but Rojack barrels ahead "to gain an inch and then a crucial quarter inch more. . . ." It is not unlike his murder of Deborah: "I was pushing with my shoulder against an enormous door which would give inch by inch to the effort."

Peter Schwenger points out that Mailer has defended obscenity in his work by claiming "creativity is always next to the *verboten*," as though what is not allowed is precisely what he must have in order to transcend the limits put upon the imagination. The forbidden, Schwenger emphasizes, is what focuses the artist's attention; certainly it is what awakens Rojack's senses.

Rojack calls Ruta a Nazi, triggering in the reader's mind his earlier murder of the Germans just as the crack, crack, crack he hears in Deborah's strangled throat echoes the whap, whap, whap of his rifle gunning down the Germans. In each instance, as Andrew Gordon argues, "Rojack is attempting to eradicate the part of himself that he cannot tolerate . . . the mama's boy . . . the foul, anal homosexual." The mama's boy, in Mailer's view, is "sexually female," Judith Fetterly suggests: "Male homosexuality is not seen as an equal sexual relation between two men but rather as a situation in which one man is used as a woman by another man." Hence the first German Rojack shoots is a homosexual who must be portrayed in terms of Rojack's squeezing of a female breast. In the way he kills the Germans and Deborah, and in the way he takes Ruta, Rojack is overcoming Mailer's anxiety over the "tendency in men to be women" and therefore to lose their distinctive existence.

After her initial resistance, Ruta welcomes Rojack's anal penetration, which culminates in a passage that exquisitely expresses the ambivalence of their lovemaking: "I had one of those splittings of a second where the senses fly out and there in that instant the itch reached into me and drew me out and I jammed up her ass and came as if I'd been flung across the room. She let out a cry of rage. Her coming must have taken a ferocious twist." The explicit references to sodomy were deleted in *Esquire* and sharpened in the book publication, for Mailer was intent on creating a fictional protagonist and alter ego who would genuinely act out his impulses in ways Mailer himself had never quite dared.

In the first draft for *Esquire*, Rojack suggests that "there in that instant the Devil reached to me." In Mailer's Manichean view of things, his hero reflects both good and evil, for God and the Devil are at war for possession of his psyche. At every moment what Rojack does may alter the balance between good and evil in himself and in the world. Good and evil, in other words, are part of the dynamic of human character, part of an economy of action, so that what Rojack does is not merely evil or good; he gives Ruta pain but he also gives her pleasure.

Norman Mailer had been taught by his mother to see only the good in himself, and it had taken him a long time to create a self-portrait that embodied the conflicting good and evil forces of the outside world he knew must be reflected in his own soul if he were to write about life with any honesty and insight. The overwrought quality of *An American Dream* is expressive of an imagination like that of its hero's: It has been fully liberated for the first time.

IT WAS IN THE CARDS, WASN'T IT?

Deciding to write a serialized novel had released new energy and courage in Mailer. Although the pressure of writing a novel against monthly deadlines should have been excruciating, Anne Barry does not remember Mailer being "particularly difficult or wrapped up in himself." He was "tense and stimulated by the writing," and there were "long hours and photo finish sessions"—times when he would have to go to work after a party, but his letters to Gwaltney confirm his excitement and pleasure in taking on this challenge. Indeed, like his main character, he was working himself out of a jam.

As Mailer had done earlier with his poems, he would scribble brief notes about his characters for Barry to type and which he would work up. Mailer encouraged himself to be spontaneous and inventive. This would sometimes cause technical problems that he ingeniously turned to his advantage. For instance, Rojack had thrown Deborah out the window and onto the street, claiming to the police that she had committed suicide. A suspicious detective, Roberts, asks Rojack how Deborah could have bruises on the front of her body when she was found in the street face-up. The question is crucial because dead bodies develop "dependent lividity"—pools of blood that collect in those parts of the body that have been resting against surfaces. Roberts is seeking to demonstrate that Deborah must have been killed before she "jumped" through the window. After stalling for a moment, Rojack replies that he remembers Deborah being placed on a stretcher face-down because of the tremendous wound at the back of her head.

For the first time in his fiction, Mailer is at one with a character who must be as imaginative and as outrageous as himself. Like his author, Rojack is self-inventive—in Leo Bersani's words, feeding on "this sense of constant threat as a kind of substitute for a sense of self." The brilliant passages of dialogue with Detective Roberts constitute those moments in the novel when Rojack seems most alive, for he is pressed to assert a view of himself he finds hard to maintain on his own. Bersani notes how Rojack longs for Roberts's company "much as if that merciless lack of charity which I had come to depend on in Deborah (as a keel to ballast the empty dread of my stomach) was now provided by the detective." Commenting on Rojack's longing for an opposing mate, Bersani wonders "to what extent Mailer's own sense of himself has depended on his ability to provoke attack." It is a keen insight, for Bersani realizes that Rojack, like Mailer, is both attracted to and repulsed by the "outside world":

> *If Rojack responds like an electric coil to multitudinous "invasions" from the outside world, it is because he is pathologically convinced that what he calls his "center" may be stolen from him at any moment.*

What gives Rojack such heart after the murder is his romantic involvement with Cherry, a nightclub singer who is in one of the cars snarled up in the congestion caused by Deborah's fall onto the street. As Mailer later admitted, Cherry is

> *a sentimental conception. . . . She's a shadowy figure. Of course, my cop-out is that she's seen through Rojack's eyes. He's in an incandescent state of huge paranoia and enormous awareness. He's more heroic and more filled with dread than at any point in his life. So she seems like a lighthouse in the fog. What else does one do in such a state but fall madly in love for twenty-four hours and lose the love?*

What Mailer does not confess is that he put so much feeling about the women in his life into one character that she became an impossible ideal doomed to extinction by the forces of a corrupt world represented by Rojack's sinister father-in-law, Barney Oswald Kelly. If Deborah has a pedigree to rival Lady's Jeanne's and a rough tongue to challenge

Adele's, Cherry has Beverly's earthy and homey style. Like Beverly, Cherry knows how to take care of her man, satisfying his hunger with a quick meal after one of their wonderful fucks. Like Beverly, Cherry has been around with some interesting men. Shago Martin, a black singer and former lover whom Rojack beats up, is modeled after Miles Davis, with whom Mailer had an altercation at a party when Davis began playing with Beverly's hair and calling to everyone's mind the fact that Beverly had once been his woman. In other words, Cherry becomes the Mailerian conception of a woman worth fighting for, a woman who intuits her man's deepest feelings, who knows without being told that Rojack has murdered his wife. Cherry is the good Deborah, psychically attuned to her lover and capable of mothering without castrating him. As Judith Fetterly concludes, "Rojack needs from Cherry exactly what he needed from Deborah, and killed her for not providing. His identity and his power are inextricably connected to women. Women are the arbiters of his fate."

Even as Mailer drafted these passages in his novel, Beverly Bentley acted as one of those female ministers of Norman Mailer's fate. She had accepted him with all his baggage and was doing an absolutely extraordinary job running a household, welcoming Mailer's children by his other marriages, and entertaining the vast numbers of friends who came to the Mailers' for dinner and for parties. She appeared to be Fanny Mailer's favorite; she appeared, in short, too good to be true. How could any woman put up with, let alone enjoy, the constant coming and going and the nights out?

Beverly wanted everything to be perfect. She wanted to live the American Dream. Consequently, she was hard on the help. There seemed to be constant hiring and firing of people, with Beverly going into rages when things did not work out. But in its early days the marriage seemed sound, and Beverly and Norman "Motherfuck" Mailer thought they were making it, creating the hip home life and family that Rojack imagines will be his future with Cherry. Beverly knew all about Mailer's other women and thought, in the words of her brother, that she was "tougher than the other ones." While she did this complex balancing act, he was up in his tower in their Brooklyn Heights home doing the dialogue for his novel, saying it aloud, and creating a female paragon who was modeled not only after Beverly but also Carole Stevens, a nightclub singer he had known since 1970 completely devoted to her sometime lover. Eventually Beverly would have misgivings about living this peculiar form of the American Dream, yet the logic of her husband's novel foretold that it could not last, and that Cherry would have to die and the marriage founder on his need for a wife/mother.

An American Dream is a prophetic book in many ways. The title is ironic and hopeful. Rojack by the end of the novel loses Cherry but is off on a westward quest, the quintessential American hero on the road to find his true self. In the figure of Barney Oswald Kelly he has had to defy the threat that makes a mockery of American individualism. With his Mafia connections, his control of politicians and the police, Kelly is a master manipulator. If Rojack has been adept in lying his way out of the murder charge, he has been helped by his powerful father-in-law, who has put out the word for Rojack's release.

The price for Rojack's confrontation scene with Kelly is Cherry's death. Although he senses that he should return to her apartment in Harlem (where he eventually arrives too late to prevent her murder), he knows he must meet the man who pulls the strings of his world, for Kelly is another one of those powerful father figures in Mailer's fiction that his heroes have had to challenge. As Andrew Gordon has noticed, Kelly most resembles General Cummings. Both men have "cold, gray eyes" and "frigid, bitchy wives." They are portrayed as "latent homosexuals" who "tempt and dare the young heroes, Hearn and Rojack." Both Hearn and Rojack are in danger of becoming their superior father figures' women, a danger Mailer makes explicit in *An American Dream* when Kelly proposes a ménage à trois with Rojack and Ruta, who, like Cherry, has been one of Kelly's conquests. To be won to Cummings's or Kelly's side is to be wooed, feminized, and violated. In this light, it is also curious that Mailer should give his father's first name, Barney, to Kelly.

Just as Cummings sends Hearn out on a mission of death, Kelly sets for Rojack the challenge of walking the parapet outside his apartment suite thirty stories above the ground. Allan Wagenheim has pointed out how alike Kelly and Rojack are. They have both desired Deborah because they have taken her to represent the source and the extension of their manhood. Kelly covets Rojack for his nearness to Deborah—she is their incestuous family tie—even as he tries to poke Rojack off the parapet with the umbrella Rojack has appropriated from Shago Martin. Kelly and Rojack have been rivals for the same woman—fighting to ascertain which of them will be her man—just as Rojack and Shago have been rivals and lovers in Rojack's curiously intimate and sexually suggestive assault on Shago, which is provoked by Shago's comment to Rojack: "Up your ass, motherfuck":

> *I took him from behind, my arms around his waist, hefted him in the air, and slammed him to the floor so hard his legs went, and we ended with Shago in a sitting position, and me behind him on my knees, my arms choking the air from his chest as I lifted him up and smashed him down, and lifted him up and smashed him down again. "Let me go, I'll kill you, bugger," he cried out. . . . I got a whiff of his odor which had something of defeat in it, and a smell of full nearness as if we'd been in bed for an hour.*

Rojack must have his Shago as surely as Kelly wants his Rojack. Shago is right. Rojack has been a "bugger" and has wanted it up his ass but instead has given it that way to Ruta and to the other Germans who have tried to invade his hole.

An American Dream is an overdetermined novel with the structure of a dream, obsessively coming back to the hero/dreamer's need to feel intact, to complete himself in the love of woman, and yet to demonstrate he is a man, autonomous and undefiled.

The ecstasy of escape and rebirth Rojack feels at the end of the novel is fated: All dreams perish. He is hardly the victor of Hip that Mailer had once robustly speculated on in "The White Negro." Rojack has certainly achieved, in Allan Wagenheim's words, "an enlarged awareness," but he must opt for "conditional life, life with restraint and compromise. This must be a sad book, indeed, for any of the beat generation who read it knowingly, it represents a sad abdication of the philosopher-King of Hip." Certainly Rojack has a "second chance at independence and manliness" in his trek through Central America, but Mailer, Wagenheim reminds us, "goes to Provincetown."

That Mailer understood the import of his novel is clear in his reaction to John F. Kennedy's assassination. On that November day he was on the phone to Rust Hills at *Esquire*, discussing his novel, which Hills had some difficulty concentrating on, having just heard Kennedy had been shot down in Dallas. It was news to Mailer, who had apparently been working all day without interruption. Hills remembers his surprise at Mailer's reaction: "It was in the cards, wasn't it?" At the time, many people had thought the assassination to be an incredible event; some responded as though their innocence had been destroyed. For Mailer, however, writing about a world that conspires against heroic individuals, about a protagonist who was Kennedy's contemporary and failed rival, whose marriage had been a grim parody of the successful president's, the assassination was an overwhelming affirmation of what he had imagined could happen to a president who had not faced what Rojack calls "the abyss." Mailer must have wondered what had possessed him to write this sentence, which he removed from the book version of *An American Dream*: "I don't think he [Kennedy] ever executed anyone close enough to see their face." Now a whole nation had been caught in a hole. Mailer with his superstitious feeling about names had to be impressed with his naming of the malign Barney Oswald Kelly, an eerie echo of Lee Harvey Oswald.

DOCTOR OF MIRRORS

Michael Burks was six weeks old when Mailer went to Provincetown in April 1964, where he would finish *An American Dream*. Mailer remembers that Beverly was in a "postpartum depression, overly worried about Michael, as most mothers are with their first-born, and I had absolutely no idea of how I was going to end the damned book." Mailer wrote Fig Gwaltney on May 15, 1964, noting that Michael, now two months old, had a head that had "slimmed down from a banana to a lemon." Mailer thought his son looked "three-quarters like Beverly, one-quarter like me. He's got my head, my upper lip, and a nose which gives promise of being just as fat. He looks like a squirrel and he's got a prick on him which makes little girls' eyes open with wonder, carries it in a state of constant erection, as far as I can see. Can you imagine that—a squirrel who's hung?" In June and part of July, Dandy, Betsy, and Susie came to live with their father and his new wife.

That summer Mailer wrote one of his finest political studies, "In the Red Light: A History of the Republican Convention of 1964." Fascinated by the Goldwater supporters, he found merit in the conservative position by structuring his essay around several quotations from Edmund Burke. Never a conventional liberal, Mailer detested Lyndon Johnson and expressed a preference for a Goldwater presidency because it would concentrate new forces of opposition to the status quo.

Between August 1964 and March 1965 Mailer worked on revisions for the book publication of *An American Dream*. He did not fundamentally alter the shape of the novel; instead, he restored some of the censored language, pruned adjectives, and reduced the discursive quality of the prose, beginning with the novel's first paragraph, most of which he eliminated. As a result, Rojack becomes a somewhat less vulnerable character and a little more direct, as in the new abrupt, toughened-up beginning of the novel:

> *I met Jack Kennedy in November, 1946. We were both war heroes, and both of us had just been elected to Congress. We were out one night on a double date and it turned out to be a fair evening for me. I seduced a girl who would have been bored by a diamond as big as the Ritz.*

Gone are the references to Rojack's loneliness, to the struggle to achieve individuality, and to the famous figures who "have a life which proves to be their own." Rojack sounds as though he is already in charge—note the false modesty about the "fair evening" when he was able to seduce "a girl who would have been bored by a diamond as big as the Ritz." Gone also is the statement about stealing Kennedy's girl. In the book version, Kennedy and Rojack start out as equals; Rojack is not straining to make a comparison but takes it for granted.

The result of these changes and others that diminish Rojack's commentary on his youth at Harvard is to downplay the difficulties he has had in growing up and in accepting himself. Excised from the book version is his description of looking at himself in a mirror exploring divided feelings about his "face with its large head, a victim's face at its worst, weak and puffy, and at best . . . strong good rugged features . . . the thin self-doubting face of a young lieutenant fresh out of Harvard." As Hershel Parker observes, the *Esquire* text more clearly emphasizes Rojack's "suppressed doubts about his maturity" and "the consequences of growing up male (or being male and not quite growing up) in an America where suppressing dangerous emotions is a mark of maturity."

The final version of *An American Dream* (Mailer resisted the urging of his editor at Dial to make it a larger book, the great American Novel he had been promising his readers since *Advertisements for Myself*) straddles the question of identity. Rojack is clearly a reflection of Mailer, but the novel is rather like a scene in the *Esquire* text, in which Rojack defines himself as a "Doctor of Mirrors"—seeing images that seem "more impressive than myself" but not quite believing them, not really being sure that he has, in fact, become an adult. Mailer could not bring himself, finally, to believe that he had written even the first draft of the Great American Novel, and yet there were these reflections and intimations of greatness. Mailer had more confidence in himself and consequently Rojack demonstrated less doubt about his capacities in the book version of *An American Dream*.

Writing and revising *An American Dream* had been a creative ordeal, Mailer confided to a friend, the British author Alex Trocchi, in a letter dated January 22, 1965. Mailer's words echo the theme of the book and the feminine fullness and emptiness a writer may feel in composition and its aftermath:

> *I finished a novel a while ago, and its left me a bit on the flat side I fear. These months I care little about the revolution, the past, the future, the emotions—I just want to fill up with a few ideas again. We're like goddam women, Alex, we write novels and suffer post-partum depressions.*

BRUISED BUT UNBOWED

With significant exceptions, the reviews of *An American Dream* when it was published in book form were damning. Reviewers were outraged:

> *Newsweek*: An outpouring of all-consuming ego.
> *New York Review of Books*: . . . willful, recklessly simple, and histrionic.
> *The New Leader*: . . . a dreadful novel . . . pretentious.

The novel had its defenders, particularly Richard Poirier, Joan Didion, Leo Bersani, and John Aldridge. They saw Mailer exercising an essentially romantic talent, pushing his social commentary on America to an extreme in order to reveal the chaos underneath what Didion called "the rationalist establishment."

Mailer was bruised by the reviews but unbowed. John Aldridge, on a visit to Mailer's Brooklyn Heights home in mid-March, 1965, found an impressive scene: the big windows looking out on Manhattan and the Brooklyn Bridge, an energetic space that included "gymnastic ropes and ladders and bars hanging from the roof and reaching down two stories into the living room." Mailer had begun constructing a magnificent model of the city out of Lego blocks, an ideal representation he conceived of as arising out of the "shit" of the present site. Photographs, mementos, cartoons, were strewn about. In addition to members of a jazz group that had played at a party the night before, the household included Beverly, a secretary, and two black maids: "very much a Mailer menage—crowded, busy, vital" Aldridge recalled.

Mailer himself seemed in better form than I had ever seen him, fatter by twenty pounds than five years before but very sharp and intense. He was no longer truculent and defensive as I last remembered him from Connecticut, where for a year we'd been neighbors with houses not far from the Styrons. He seemed to have undergone some obscure, but remarkable inner change. He was putting out enormous psychic energy, reacting to everything, clowning, pacing back and forth, yet clearly a bit tense about our meeting trying to project himself to me.

If *An American Dream* was not the last word on Mailer the novelist, it had come much closer to the ideal, to the big book he had always promised to write, and it had inched him a little closer to the projection of himself on that outside world he had vowed to conquer.

8.

THE ARMIES OF
THE NIGHT
(1965–1968)

HOT DAMN. VIETNAM

By the spring of 1965 the country was heating up in protest over Vietnam. Unlike many liberals who were just beginning to find their way into the opposition, Mailer had already rejected all arguments in favor of American intervention in Vietnam. He was not impressed with the domino theory. What if communism conquered the world? It would collapse of its own weight since it thrived only on an opposition to the status quo. In power, communism was subject to the same strains and stresses of history as any other ideology or form of government.

Mailer contended that America would never have become mired in Vietnam if it had not been for Lyndon Johnson. Mailer believed that there had been a move afoot in the Kennedy administration to quietly pull out of Vietnam and let it go Communist. Johnson had reversed course, Mailer believed, because Johnson thought he could control the war and dominate the social agenda of the country by making the anti-Communist crusade his issue. He could play racial tensions, the sexual revolution—a whole gamut of Great Society concerns—against his war, escalating or de-escalating the action as he desired. Mailer imagined

Johnson reveling in his political discovery: "Hot damn. Vietnam. The President felt like the only stud in a whorehouse on a houseboat."

Mailer's irreverent and outrageous treatment of both Johnson and the liberal and conservative consensus on postwar anti-Communism endeared him to a new generation of student radicals. Some of them, like Jerry Rubin and Abby Hoffman, had read "The White Negro" and were influenced by Mailer's notions of Hip. Rubin proposed to have Mailer speak on a Vietnam Protest Day, May 2, 1965, but confronted considerable opposition from the traditional left because Mailer did not seem politically astute. He did not offer rational arguments, and some were still embarrassed about the stabbing. Mailer lent no prestige to the protest. But when an adamant Rubin threatened to resign as organizer of the event, Mailer was reluctantly included as a speaker.

By no means immediately receptive to Rubin's invitation, Mailer wanted a week to think about it. Rubin enticed him with a vision of speaking before twenty thousand people at an event in Berkeley that would get national coverage and go on for thirty hours. Mailer seemed bemused by the idea: twenty thousand people . . . he had never addressed a crowd like that. In the next week he turned a review of the President's book, *My Hope for America*, into a provocative speech attacking not merely Johnson's war policy but his personality. Mailer treated the war as an extension of the President's monstrous narcissism; the war reflected a politician's concern with his own image, which he had had blown up into two forty-foot-high photographs of himself at the 1964 Democratic convention in Atlantic City. The photographs "spoke of an ego which had the voracity of a beast." Mailer concluded his speech with an oratorical flourish that brought thousands of people to their feet to give him an ovation:

> *Only, listen, Lyndon Johnson, you have gone too far this time. You are a bully with an Air Force, and since you will not call off your Air Force, there are young people who will persecute you back. It is a little thing, but it will hound you. For listen—this is only one of the thousand things they will do. They will print up little pictures of you, Lyndon Johnson, the size of postcards, the size of stamps, and some will glue those pictures to walls and posters and telephone booths and billboards—I do not advise it, I would tell these students not to do it to you, but they will. They will find places to put these pictures. They will want to paste your picture, Lyndon Johnson, on a postcard, and send it to you. Some will*

send it to your advisers. Some will send those pictures to men and women at other schools. These pictures will be sent everywhere. These pictures will be pasted up everywhere, upside down.

Silently, without a word, the photograph of you, Lyndon Johnson, will start appearing everywhere, upside down. Your head will speak out— even to the peasant in Asia—it will say that not all Americans are unaware of your monstrous vanity, overweening piety, and doubtful motive. It will tell them that we trust our President so little, and think so little of him, that we see his picture everywhere upside down.

You, Lyndon Johnson, will see those pictures up everywhere upside down, four inches high and forty feet high, Lyndon Baines Johnson, will be coming up for air everywhere upside down. Everywhere, upside down. Everywhere. Everywhere.

And those little pictures will tell the world what we think of you and your war in Vietnam. Everywhere, upside down. Everywhere, everywhere.

Rubin recalls that "the crowd went crazy. It was the first time anybody had made fun of the President . . . doing this in the theater we'd conspired to create for him." Mailer had "qualitatively changed the event," Rubin concludes, "giving us permission to insult a father figure, indicating it's okay to ridicule the President." Abby Hoffman later suggested that "Mailer also showed how you can focus protest sentiment effectively by aiming not at the decisions but at the gut of those who make them."

The simple repetition of Johnson's name brought the President down to a human, individual level and suggested that his power would be countered by an equal, democratic force shrinking the domination of his ego. *Cannibals and Christians* (1966), a collection of Mailer's short prose since 1960, has an ironic dedication:

to Lyndon B. Johnson
whose name inspired young men to cheer for me in public

This speech had made Mailer feel presidential—and more of a man (no women were cheering him?). Paul Krassner, a friend and publisher of *The Realist*, which reprinted Mailer's speech and a picture of Lyndon Johnson upside down on the magazine's cover, remembers that Mailer was "on cloud nine, flying" after the speech, for "he realized the impact he'd made." Krassner had been emceeing when Mailer had gotten up to speak, and when he finished, "the response began to build rhythmically, getting louder and louder. The cheering was so powerful I just waited." In *The Presidential Papers*, Mailer had the vanity to suppose that his work would be read by Kennedy for guidance. In *Cannibals and Christians*, there is still a trace of that earlier Mailer hoping to catch a president's attention, but now he acted almost like a rival.

THAT EXTRA KILLER INSTINCT

In the summer of 1965, Norman and Beverly rented a house near the water in Provincetown. They had all his kids together, and Adele was also living nearby. His sister, Barbara, visited with her son, Peter, and some of Beverly's friends also dropped in. Other Mailer pals, like Buzz Farbar and Roger Donoghue, also made appearances, and there were countless others—"hangers-on," Anne Barry thought, who gave Mailer the adulation he seemed to crave. Mailer would get angry when Barry tried to raise the subject; he seemed to have no patience for her argument that these people were just a drain on his talent.

Mailer was fiercely loyal to his friends and enjoyed a hearty male comradeship with men such as Farbar. They had met in 1963 at the annual Christmas party given by Rust Hills, fiction editor of *Esquire*. Farbar and Mailer broke up a fight between Hills and another writer, and after sharing a few jokes and taking the measure of each other—something Mailer was prone to do in those days—the two men realized the possibilities of a friendship. Mailer seemed to admire Farbar's build, his Golden Gloves and football playing background—characteristics not usually associated with the Jews Mailer knew. Farbar enjoyed the challenge of being around Mailer, a man who "makes you better." Farbar liked the way Mailer made him "stretch," for Farbar believed he had had a rather easy time of it and had not really tested himself. When Farbar went to CBS Legacy Books in 1964, he and Mailer did a book together about bullfighting. Mailer's fee for the book was only twenty-five hundred dollars, which amounted to a favor to Farbar that Mailer's agent, Scott Meredith, questioned. But Farbar was a friend, Mailer countered, and he had agreed to the small payment. When Farbar became a senior editor at Trident Press (an imprint of Simon & Schuster) he began a campaign to get a million-dollar contract for Mailer. The top management, worried over Mailer's mental stability after the stabbing, insisted to Farbar that Mailer take a physical exam so that they could take an insurance policy out on him. Farbar could not bring himself to tell the truth to Mailer and finally let the matter drop by allowing his friend to believe that the prospect of a million-dollar contract had been no more than a publicity ploy on the publisher's part.

In the summer of 1965 the Gwaltneys visited the Mailers in Brooklyn for dinner at Norman's parents' home. While Norman quizzed his mother about old Jewish customs, Barney went to work on Ecey, saying, "You look just the same, you look wonderful. But Fig, there's something worrying you. You've changed some way." Ecey took Barney's attentions as a way of complimenting her to the detriment of her husband. Norman intervened, but Barney would not let up, provoking Ecey to think: "Here's one little bantam rooster of a man." Barney's behavior was similar to what Ecey had seen of Norman's on previous occasions, and it seemed "ironic" to Ecey that Norman should try to rein in his father when the son was "almost a carbon copy."

Visiting Norman and Beverly that summer in Provincetown, Ecey admired Beverly's cooking. One dinner in particular featured a delicious "striped bass and lobster and a wonderful sauce for the rice of Dijon mustard and butter." Ecey was surprised when Beverly disapproved of her talking with the two black women helping with the dinner. It seemed only common decency to Ecey, and it made her think that Beverly, not having grown up with household help, "didn't know beans" about how to treat them.

Ecey had always noticed how finicky Norman was about cooking—lecturing about using a scraper (his utensil in the army) rather than a knife for carrots and cutting celery on the diagonal, not crosswise. It seemed a bit much to her, since he merely threw leftovers into a wok.

Ecey also noticed that Beverly had become much more assertive. There were several fights. She stayed up late, playing the kazoo, and complained: "Here I am, two months pregnant and playing Bessie Smith records. Here I am thirty-six years old and I don't know what to do." She jumped up and down, her long blond hair flying, and Mailer watched her impassively, "rocking on his feet like a big Indian." Then she attacked: "You treat people worse than niggers in Georgia. You're just a bully! I want a divorce. I want it right now!" To which he replied, "Put it in writin'." He also requested a witness, and she called on Ecey, who actually watched Beverly write a note requesting a divorce.

Ecey found parties at the Mailers' almost incomprehensible. Norman's sister, Barbara, would be there with Al Wasserman, whom she would later marry. On one occasion, Beverly got into a fist fight with one of her guests. Ecey watched Al Wasserman get into a heavy argument, accidently step on someone's foot, mumble a polite pardon me, and immediately return to his "diatribe." After another party, Ecey and Barbara found themselves cleaning up the house, which provoked Barbara to say to Ecey, "Boy, that woman's crazy as a fox. She's got our men, and we're here doing the dishes!"

Jose Torres visited Mailer in Provincetown for the first time in the summer of 1965. He had become light-heavyweight boxing champion of the world on March 30. Mailer had wanted to do everything possible to make sure his friend won the title—including an offer to put up $90,000 to finance a Torres fight. Torres remembers Mailer calling his father and asking him if he could afford to lose that much money. Torres reigned for two years before retiring and turning to writing, a longtime ambition of his first fostered by Pete Hamill and then encouraged by Mailer. Both Hamill and Mailer radicalized Torres and helped him to shed his "colonial mentality." Torres felt Mailer was the only man who could "measure me intellectually and emotionally." And he did not feel patronized. Both Hamill and Mailer "struggled" with him to secure a firm intellectual foundation for his writing career. "We were going to be friends for life," Torres recalls, for he knew that boxing could only be a "temporary" career for him.

In many ways Torres came to feel like a member of the Mailer family. There had been an incident in which Torres had borrowed Mailer's car and run a red light. The police had not believed his story about the borrowed car, and when they phoned Mailer's mother (Mailer was at Madison Square Garden watching a fight), she replied: "My son wouldn't give his car to anyone. The guy has to be lying." Mailer eventually came to the police station to spring Torres. Then he put on his mother, telling her that she might have to be a little careful about Torres, who was one of those Puerto Ricans who are "tough and a little crazy." When Torres met her, he said: "So you're Norman's mother. Do you know what you did the other night? Well, I just wish my own mother would do the same for me!" Relieved and flattered, as well as charmed by Torres's gallantry, she accepted him. When they met he would kiss her and treat her with elaborate courtesy. She preferred men like Torres and got irked when Mailer praised Jean Malaquais as one of his mentors.

According to Torres, Fanny said, "What? How do you compare that old nogoodnik with yourself?"

In the fall of 1965 Mailer had Charlie Brown working on a pet project: a model of the city of the future, built entirely of Lego blocks. Mailer had an aversion to plastic and could not stand the "obscene" sound of the blocks snapping together. So Brown had to do the job, driving the 1961 Falcon with the top down to the Lego factory in New Jersey to pick up thousands of blocks in crates. Beverly hated the sight of them strewn around their Brooklyn apartment. The model took two months to assemble even as people came and went (Mailer's usual assortment of visitors and hangers-on), adding to the confusion. The model rested on a four- by eight-foot sheet of plywood supported by an aluminum frame with five-foot legs. Mailer would come in and out, as would Anne Barry, with sheafs of papers, and give instructions—often arguing with a Provincetown friend, Eldred Mowery, who had, in Charlie Brown's estimation, a much finer "structural sense" than Mailer. Mowery was tactful with Mailer, mildly pointing out flaws in his design that would make the structure topple over. Beverly had no patience for these conferences and would often scream, "I can't stand this shit in my living room." Mailer paid no attention to her, although sometimes they threw things at each other. Mailer was very proud of the model and welcomed the invitation to exhibit it at the Museum of Modern Art. Then he found out there was no way to get it through the doors or windows without making structural alterations in the apartment. He refused to disassemble it, fearing that he would never be able to duplicate the design. Finally, he said to Mowery: "Fuck it. . . . Build a fence around it. Fuck it, that's it. It stays." The model appeared on the cover of *Cannibals and Christians* and to this day it remains in the apartment, taking up about a third of the living room.

Mailer's other major activity in the fall of 1965 was managing boxer Joe Shaw, one of Torres's sparring partners. Shaw had been on the Olympic boxing team with Torres and had shown obvious talent, yet he never seemed able to get the big fights. Mailer decided to assemble a group of friends, including George Plimpton, the cartoonist Charles Addams, and cronies such as Roger Donoghue, Buzz Farbar, and a new addition, Tom Quinn, a stockbroker. Each member of Mailer's "syndicate" put up six hundred dollars to cover the expenses of managing the fighter. Over nearly two years Shaw would show promise, almost win his fights, only to run out of motivation and steam. "If Norman could have given him a bit of his anger or his violent nature, he would have been the champion of the world. But Shaw didn't have that extra killer instinct," Plimpton concluded.

Tom Quinn often wondered why Mailer seemed to enjoy being around boxers so much. "What did we have to offer Norman?" Quinn asks. Well, in spite of Mailer's many accomplishments, there were two things, Quinn figures, he very much wanted to be: Irish, and a fighter. To Quinn, Donoghue seemed especially perfect for Mailer: "totally without pretension—so obvious, so transparent." Quinn knew he could not perform quite the same role in Mailer's life. He did not box with Mailer, realizing that he would either have to best him or be beaten himself, and either way, he did not want to be used by Mailer. But it was different for professionals like Donoghue or Jose Torres, because there was never a question of Mailer's taking a match from them.

WHY ARE WE IN VIETNAM?

For Mailer, the war had an unreal quality. Since he could not take the anti-Communist line seriously and had trouble believing this is what really motivated Johnson's interest in Vietnam, Mailer looked for a psychological explanation. For a *Partisan Review* symposium on the war, Mailer put these questions: Could it be that Johnson sensed the country wanted a war? Was war the "last of the tonics. From Lydia Pinkham to Vietnam in sixty years, or bust"? Was Vietnam a sixties phenomenon, a happening—to use a favorite word of the time? If so, Mailer favored war games in some huge tract of the Amazon. Set the Marines loose there to fight along with

> the Chinks and the Aussies, the Frogs and the Gooks and the Wogs, the Wops and the Russkies, the Yugos, the Israelis, the Hindoos, the Pakistanis . . . with real bullets and real flame throwers, real hot-wire correspondents on the spot, TV with phone-in audience participation, amateur war movie film contests for the soldiers, discotheques, Playboy Clubs, pictures of the corpses for pay TV.

If "little old Vietnam" was "just a happening," a kind of cartoon, then Mailer wondered—addressing himself to "Daddy Warbucks"—why the country could not

*skip all that indiscriminate roast tit and naked lunch, all those bombed-
out civilian ovaries, Mr. J., Mr. L.B.J., Boss Man of Show Biz—I salute
you in your White House Oval; I mean America will shoot all over the
shithouse wall if this jazz goes on, Jim.*

Searching for a new language of politics that would cut through liberal
cant about the war, there was menace, a threat in his prose that suggested
how violent opposition to the war would become.

By the spring of 1966, Mailer was at work on a novel probing the
roots of America's involvement in Vietnam. He began with a chapter on
two Texas boys hunting bear in Alaska based on "a reserve of memories
of Texans I had served with in the 112th Cavalry out of San Antonio."
They would be mean, tough, and rich. The narrator, D. J. (short for disc
jockey), is a parody of Lyndon Johnson, "Mr. J., Mr. L.B.J., Boss Man
of Show Biz," for D.J. announces himself at the beginning of the novel
as the voice of America. D.J. is a creation who pulls the mask off the
public Johnson, the sanctimonious faker who in private, Mailer had
heard, was rather like Broderick Crawford in *All the King's Men:* "roaring, smarting, bellowing, stabbing fingers on advisers' chests, hugging
his daughters, enjoying his food, mean and unforgiving, vindictive,
generous, ebullient, vain, suddenly depressed, then roguish, then overbearing, suddenly modest again only to bellow once more." Mailer's
novel projects a narrator with precisely this kind of verve, scatological
and scurrilous.

D.J.'s initials also stand for Dr. Jekyll, the darker, violent self of D.J.,
of L.B.J., and of America itself. D.J.'s companion is Tex Hyde, the sure-
shooting, obligatory sidekick in this American story of the road. As D.J.
puts it, "Huckleberry Finn is here to set you straight," to reclaim the
raw elements of American life that Johnson, the technological president,
has tried to smooth over. D.J. ventriloquizes many different voices in the
manner of a radio rock personality; the flippant, frenetic beat of his
prose suggests the repetitive rhythms of technology land that heat up the
country's talk.

Mailer's bear hunt, like Faulkner's classic "The Bear," explores the
fundamental quest for an American identity inherent in the conquest of
animals and the environment. Men must prove themselves in the wild
even as they destroy the intimate connections between humankind and
nature. Rusty, D.J.'s father, is "fucked unless he gets that bear, for if he
don't, white men are fucked more and they can take no more." This kind

of racist reasoning leads to Vietnam, to "indiscriminate roast tit and naked lunch."

D.J. is like Mailer's other narrators who have identity problems, doubt their maleness, fear the feminine in themselves, and try to strike out on their own. Mailer's narrators, when they succeed, do so by finding an identity in the roles they play. D.J., however, is unique in playing with the notion of identity itself. Is he, he asks, "a Texas youth or is he a genius of a crippled Spade in Harlem making all this shit up?" Or is D.J. imitating a "high I.Q. Harlem Nigger"? "There is no security in this consciousness," he maintains, since much of what we take to be reality is an American dream, or rather a "dream field," a "part of a circuit" with "you swinging on the inside of the deep mystery."

D.J. brashly appropriates and transforms the styles of others—as Mailer has always done. D.J. commands: "Goose your frequency"—rev up your sensibility, your reception of the totality D.J. imagines.

Like Rojack, D.J. operates on a visceral level, believing that the world is the "shit" human beings make up, and in America such "shit" prevails because of the incredible amount of things used up, turned into waste products. The last words of the novel, "Vietnam, hot damn," spoken by D.J. as he prepares for his tour of duty, recall the words Mailer had attributed to Lyndon Johnson: "Hot damn. Vietnam." D.J., like Johnson, anticipates another frontier to conquer, another territory to light out for, rather than confront the violence within himself. D.J., "Disc Jockey to America" echoes the country's urge to dominate and thereby to damn itself. D.J. and his hunting party have gone after bear with helicopters and in countless ways used their technological superiority to best the environment. They overpower animals with huge guns that rip apart bodies. At the same time, D.J. rejects the corporate, rapacious mentality of his father and in one episode joins Tex in braving the Alaskan wild without weapons and other technological assistance. As a dissenter, D.J. speaks in a minority voice: "Which D.J. white or black would possibly be worse of a genius if Harlem or Dallas is guiding the other, and who knows which?"

All the jive talk keeps the channels of possibility open at the end of *Why Are We in Vietnam?* so that the question of the title has been answered in some ways but is still open-ended, like the identity of the narrator. The reader is left poised between alternative readings, once again in the grip of the shifting, ambiguous reality Mailer has articulated.

INCEST, MAN, FEEDBACK

In Provincetown for the summer of 1966, Sandy Charlebois Thomas asked her landlord if he knew of anyone needing secretarial help. Mailer was suggested (Anne Barry had just taken a job at Dial Press) and Thomas wrote him a note saying she could type 120 words a minute and take shorthand. She also let him know that she had a yellow belt in aikido. Mailer replied in pencil on unlined paper: Yes, he could use someone and he was fascinated with aikido. She should stop by and see him.

When Thomas came over, Stephen (born March 10, 1966) was in a playpen and Mailer was out on his deck in cut-off blue jeans and a sleeveless shirt. He offered Thomas a drink. While they talked he walked a tightrope strung across the deck. He had manuscript pages he would produce every day for her to pick up and type in the afternoon. At work on *Why Are We in Vietnam?*, he asked her not to discuss or to show it to anyone, saying it was a strange book. She should look upon her employment as a "trial period." Each day he handed her fifteen or twenty pages. She never retyped pages. The handwritten pages had a few corrections—usually changes in wording—and he would sometimes ask her if "it sounded all right." He seemed very concerned that it should "read well."

Mailer went through periods in which he wore the same T-shirt and jeans for several days in a row. He had several "raggedy outfits," but even his better clothes seemed in a pretty sorry state to Thomas. Soon she was answering Mailer's "pots of mail," with him directing her as to which ones needed immediate attention and which could wait. A very good typist, she rarely made errors, but when he missed them in proofreading, he would accuse her of deliberately sabotaging his work, typing "the *shit* came into the dock" instead of "the ship came into the dock," and she would have a laugh over it.

Thomas remembers that Mailer had tunafish, rye bread and butter, and sliced tomatoes every day while he was writing. His working hours were totally structured, and this required that only Thomas could eat with him. She also ordered his liquor, although in later years both he and Beverly went on diets—especially during his work periods. It was quite a household, with a full-time young Southern white girl who took care of the kids, a black cook, and a Portuguese cook's helper. The grocery bill could range as high as seven hundred dollars a month, half of it for liquor. Mailer knew how much he spent but proved incapable of saving anything. Having the kids and ex-wives did not seem such a detriment to Thomas, for she believed Mailer's claim that "without the kids he wouldn't work, because essentially he's lazy." It was "passionate" between Norman and Beverly, Thomas recalls, who thought of Beverly as an "injured" person, who could still feel vulnerable over the fact that her former lover Miles Davis had just married.

As Mailer finished *Why Are We in Vietnam?* in the summer of 1966, he returned to labor on his dramatization of *The Deer Park*. What was the point of returning to old work, the product of a very different time? Mailer had an interest in the theater, to be sure, and he believed that "moving from one activity to another can give momentum." Also, Beverly needed an outlet for her frustrated acting ambitions. So the couple established an experimental coffee house/theater, Act IV, in Provincetown. Although meant primarily to be Beverly's project, she found herself enveloped in one of her husband's schemes.

Mailer hoped to explore certain unresolved aspects of both his writing and his life. He wanted both Adele and Beverly to be in the production. This seemed a reckless course to many of his friends, but Mailer could not resist the appropriateness of having Adele as Elena Esposito and Beverly (chafing over the interruption of her acting career) as Lulu Meyers. Beverly had a tendency to identify with Mailer's female characters, screaming at one wild Provincetown party: "If you want to know about it, I'm Cherry. Who do you think Cherry is? Me! *I'm Cherry!*" To some Mailer intimates, it seemed that Adele would do just about anything to remain a part of his life, as though he were the director who had given her her one provocative role.

Buzz Farbar and Mailer did the casting for *The Deer Park*. Mailer liked the way the well-tanned Farbar looked in his white linen suit as he stepped from the plane to Provincetown and decided to cast him as Don Beda, the dapper ladies' man in the play, over the objections of Leo Garin, the director, who did not want a nonprofessional—indeed, someone who by his own admission knew nothing about the theater. Yet Farbar would get good notices for his small role and would be dubbed thereafter "Buzz Cameo." The cast also included consummate professionals such as Rip Torn and Mailer's longtime friend Mickey Knox.

The Deer Park is not a very good play. It is hard to see what sense it would make to an audience that has not read the novel, since it jerks from one brief scene to another, never developing characters and simply lifting dialogue from the novel. Yet Mailer is right to say that the play is "more multi-layered" than the novel. In fact, the play is explicit about certain relationships the novel leaves ambiguous. In the play, Marion Faye makes it clear that he has wanted to seduce both Charles Eitel and Elena Esposito. He is possessive about their lives in the way a child can be about his parents'. Faye is another hipster hero—another Rojack, another Kennedy, another D.J.—who finds his center, his identity, in the connection he can make with people he believes can help him to author an image of himself. When Elena tells Faye he is insane for wanting both her and Eitel, Faye replies:

> Incest is always insane. But that's where the atomic power is buried, little boob. Incest, man, feedback, that's civilization. The mirror. Self-image, you ass, that's sanity, some image you can have of yourself. So bang me, mommy, dig.

Some of D.J.'s jive (he calls nearly everyone an asshole) infects Faye's vocabulary here. D.J. lusts after Tex Hyde who (D.J. imagines) lusts after D.J.'s mother, a sexually mature woman who is akin to Dorothea O'Faye, Marion's mother. Faye has spent years in prison sodomized by convicts, and sodomy (or various forms of being violated from the rear) is never far from Rojack's and D.J.'s minds because they fear, in Andrew Gordon's words, that they will be "feminized"—used as women. Yet sex with mother, incest, yields civilization, Faye maintains, for the boy can have himself, so to speak, in having his mother bang him. Mother is literally where man gets his feedback.

Beverly sensed her husband's vulnerability and went to work on it. She was in her midthirties, anxious about her stalled career, and angry about the way she was becoming a Mailer character. Sometimes the scenes between Norman and Beverly played like re-enactments of *An American Dream*. At a party in Jose Torres's apartment Beverly got drunk. Mailer picked her up and started to help her down the stairs. Torres assumed his friend merely wanted to get his wife out of there, but she started shouting: "He's going to kill me, please come down! He's gonna kill me." Torres remembers that she "fell down the stairs by herself" and afterward sported "a lump like a baseball." They had to take her to the doctor with "a bad contusion."

Torres and his wife, Marie, witnessed a tremendous fight in March 1966 in Provincetown, shortly before the birth of Stephen Mailer. At dinner both Beverly and Norman were drinking heavily and got into a violent argument. Torres had always been impressed that Mailer never cursed in Marie's presence. Beverly's profanity disconcerted him: "You know why you need me? You need my cunt," she told her husband. "Wait a minute," Norman warned Beverly, "I don't want any punches." Beverly complained that he was "hitting her in her private parts." Torres could tell Norman was embarrassed. A white-faced, glaring Mailer declared: "Beverly, 'I'm going to get up and throw you out the window.' " But Beverly continued: "If we keep arguing, I'm gonna hit you in your mother's cunt." Torres had to take a shaking Mailer for a walk to "cool off."

Rojack had thrown Deborah out the window because she had power over his own soul; his only way to survive had been to murder her. Mailer's only way to relieve the tension over his own emasculation was to stab Adele, to open up a hole in her. Beverly knew that the greatest temptation her husband faced was to crawl back into a woman's hole, a temptation he despised because it revealed his dependence.

If Beverly's cruel honesty put strains on the marriage, it may also have proved invaluable to Mailer. When Rip Torn, playing Marian Faye, tried to tell Mailer that the actors were upset about his constant rewriting, Mailer bullied the cast into silence until Beverly spoke up: "You fucking assholes. Rip's the only one who's got any guts. You all put him up to it, and now you're hiding, just the way he said you would." Torn was impressed: "Marvelous. Look, Norman wouldn't have stayed with Beverly all those years if she didn't have certain qualities."

During one fight, when her husband was getting the worst of it, she kept shouting at his opponent: "Don't hit him on the head! Don't hit him on the head!" Beverly, protective and possessive, would not let go of Norman even during his affairs with other women. Charlie Brown remembers that Mailer was "pretty blatant about Carol Stevens." On one occasion, Norman even asked Charlie to keep Carol company because he had to be with Beverly. Brown did not know much about Stevens, a singer who lived in a "dinky" but nice "little place" on the East Side. Carol, as usual, did not reveal her feelings—not even when Brown got drunk and sick. He felt she had no choice about her treatment because she was "totally enamored" of Norman—just as Cherry is of Rojack.

After one particularly gruesome fight, Mailer had a picture taken of himself sporting a black eye, a picture he used for the back cover of *Why Are We in Vietnam?* alongside a more conventional pose, as though to call attention to his Dr. Jekyll and Mr. Hyde sides, to the ruffian and the gentlemen, to the writer who always showed his editor, E. L. Doctorow, "absolute courtesy," who "always had this dream of living a decorous life," treating servants and waiters well and chastising his friends and wives for any rudeness, and who loved charging into a room throwing punches, banging elbows, and butting heads with his pals.

WILD 90

Although the reviews of *The Deer Park* were mixed to negative, the play became a modest hit when it moved from Provincetown to Off-Broadway, running for more than a hundred performances. It is hard to say why a play reduced from four to three hours running time that "cut away all dramatic scaffolding, connective tissue, road signs, guides" should be a success, except that it had, in Mailer's words, "13 wide open characters and a set of one hundred blackouts or quick scenes I called changes, quick as the cuts in a movie, for it seemed right to capture the dislocation of life in Hollywood by a play which played like a movie." Of course, Mailer recognized that the stage changes could not be accomplished as swiftly as cuts in a movie, but he intended to move the theater away from the concept of the well-made play to a sense of the actual grain of experience—its disruptiveness and alogical qualities. Cinematic form intrigued him; it seemed a good way of capturing his open-ended existentialism.

Mailer had been drawn to underground movies, to Andy Warhol's casting his own friends in roles, working without a script so that a story evolved out of the director's suggestions and the personalities of the actors. Although a Warhol film like *The Kitchen* was almost impossible to watch because of its slow scenes, Mailer admired the depiction of real time, the evolution of an aesthetic that countered the speeded-up editing of conventional movies. Directing and starring in a movie would give him an opportunity to work with a new form: "I think I got back to the freshness of it as a kid. I felt the same sort of interest I felt when I was eighteen and starting to write stories. . . . To be corny about it, it was first love," Mailer later commented to an interviewer.

The inspiration for Mailer's first movie, *Wild 90*, derived from late-night carousing in a Village bar with Buzz Farbar and Mickey Knox, the good friends he had put into his production of *The Deer Park*. All three favored the mannerisms of tough Brooklyn hoods as they improvised comic dialogue that Mailer deemed good enough to be filmed. Using his own money (at a cost of about ten dollars a minute), there would be no retakes, no script, and no advance planning for the shoot. Filming quickly on four consecutive nights in March 1967, was supposed to intensify his characters' emotions, putting them in a loft where they have been holed up for three weeks. The Prince (Mailer), Buzz Cameo (Buzz Farbar), and Twenty Years (Mickey Knox) trade insults and obscenities for an interminable ninety minutes, with occasional interruptions by friends and families who visit them.

Mailer wanted to dislocate the predictable, scripted Hollywood plot that lacked real spontaneity. His actors would have to take charge of their roles and motivate each other by supplying their own lines. Mailer recognized that his method meant an enormous amount of repetition in the dialogue that might bore viewers used to well-crafted scenarios, yet in compensation the film would be rooted in character, in the "vanities, bluffs, ego-supports, and downright collapses of front." As in his other work, in *Wild 90* characters struggle to achieve identity, clothing themselves in tough-guy accents and dirty words—as though this is the only way to get at the root of the self. At the heart of the film is Mailer himself, The Prince, who (in Laura Adams's words) is a "pugnacious, preening hoodlum, full of hot air and an inflated sense of self-importance. His accents and his posturings are exaggeratedly self-conscious and at times hilarious." As Mailer later said of his performance, it allowed him to see himself as a "piece of material." In the editing room he had to decide where to "cut myself," a process akin to "getting a psychoanalysis."

As one reviewer puts it, Mailer "hogs the closeups." Pauline Kael called him

> *a growling, grunting, waddling little star, a miniaturized big-brawler, who looks and sounds surprisingly like Victor McLaglen in "The Informer." It must have taken a Harvard man many years of practice to achieve that low-life effect; he didn't acquire it just for the movie. And surely it isn't the Mafia man he pretends to play but Mailer the fantasist who gets punch-drunk from shadowboxing. And it's Mailer, the great lover who, in a scene with his wife, rivals the Burtons at embarrassing*

us. And it's Mailer the professional madman who must assert himself
even with a dog—barking at it until it leaps at him.

Mailer knew *Wild 90* was technically flawed: "In the first 45 minutes
. . . you can't hear what they're saying. . . . It sounds as if *everybody* is
talking through a *jock strap.*" The camera work was sometimes un-
steady, backgrounds were not evenly lighted, focus was a problem, and
scene changes were awkwardly handled. Yet the dynamic between the
three men, the exposure of how such men invent a way of relating to
each other, had captured Mailer's fascination with the "acting" that goes
on all the time in the everyday ordering of personality that does not very
often appear on a movie screen.

BEYOND THE LAW

Not waiting to see what reviewers would make of his first movie, Mailer
almost immediately began work on another, *Beyond the Law*, set in a
police station where detectives are grilling suspects. For the most part,
he again used untrained actors, believing that if he created a situation
intense enough for people who were able "to talk themselves in and out
of trouble," they would produce "extraordinary characterizations" that
more studied professionals rarely achieve. More ambitious than *Wild 90*,
Beyond the Law employed three camera crews to film several interroga-
tions going on in different rooms at the same time and to capture the
manic quality of a police station. But the "first night's shooting was
chaos, and promised disaster," Mailer later recalled in *The Armies of the
Night*. Personality conflicts added to the confusion—as did camera
crews and sound men who had trouble locating the focus of the action.
In a way, however, this is what Mailer wanted: frenzied scenes in which
both the cops and the crooks generated comic and frightening confrontations. At the center of the action is Francis X. Pope (Mailer), a New York
City cop and something of a poet, reflecting Mailer's love of the Irish
who, in his words, have "this great bravura, a style, an elegance." It was
this Irish bluff, this brash willingness to take on the world that Mailer
had admired in *Studs Lonigan*. The Irish had taught him what it meant to
be a character and to have visceral reactions to life. The Irish were the
counter example to his own upbringing, where Jews were trained like
"intellectual machines," learning to dominate every experience with the

mind. *Beyond the Law* created a world where physical reflexes and gut reactions ruled. Mailer wanted to capture on film how far he had removed himself from the "modesty" of his Brooklyn boyhood and youth and how much he cherished the "pride and arrogance and the confidence and the egocentricity he had acquired over the years."

Far superior to *Wild 90*, *Beyond the Law* probes the psychology of the criminal mind and of the minds that must challenge it. The film is obviously linked to Mailer's writings about hipsters and about himself as a "psychic outlaw." Perhaps even more important, making films and the staging of *The Deer Park* gave him a tangible feel for his relationship to his characters. Indeed, as The Prince and Francis X. Pope he had to use his own person to become a kind of character he envied. George Plimpton, who had a role in *Beyond the Law*, thought of the film as a "parlor game." Mailer had to act out, to play his characters as he had done nearly twenty years earlier in Paris, where he and Bea had re-enacted scenes from *The Naked and the Dead*.

D. A. Pennebaker, one of Mailer's cameramen, suggests, Mailer "has the idea he can look at a camera and take it away from the person who's running it, as if he's got the control and is photographing himself. It's like a dream, his own dream." It almost did not matter that most critics would pan both films. He resisted learning how to edit; he was not interested in the technical details; and he was pleased that he had changed the rules by which most films are made. He could watch himself and ask, quite literally, whether he now had a performance that would hold together.

HISTORY AS A NOVEL/THE NOVEL AS HISTORY

Since *Advertisements for Myself* (1959), Mailer had been working toward a conception of his personality he could use to dominate and to unify his work. His nonfiction collections *The Presidential Papers* (1963) and *Cannibals and Christians* (1966) chart the emergence of his persona as the organizing principle of his writing, but these books are not entirely successful because the individual essays vary greatly in quality and do not surpass the best work in *Advertisements*, which is inherently fascinating because it presents, in Mailer's words, the "biography of a style."

With the mixed reception of *An American Dream* and *Why Are We in*

Vietnam? Mailer could not be sure of how far he had advanced his style. If he sometimes thought *An American Dream* was his best novel and that *Why Are We in Vietnam?* had brilliantly stretched his command of the language, his virtuosity had persuaded only a coterie in the literary community, and that was not enough for a writer who wanted to sway his audience in the manner of a great politician.

In fact, Mailer was down on himself. During a lunch with E. L. Doctorow in October 1967, Mailer confessed, "I feel I'm all washed up. I feel I'm out of it now, it's passed me by." An amazed Doctorow tried to "jolly" his friend out of this "very uncharacteristic" mood. This may have been only a moment of weakness. Doctorow took it for an excellent "literary strategy," the ploy of a writer who does his best work when he "feels under pressure, in some way embattled."

Then Mailer got a call from an old friend, Mitchell Goodman, inviting him to participate in a march on the Pentagon (October 21–22, 1967) to protest the Vietnam war. At first a cranky Mailer replied with reasons why he should stay home and write, reviewing all he had already done in his early opposition to the war. Realizing he sounded like a "righteous old toot," Mailer abruptly agreed to join the protest.

The mixed response to Goodman typified Mailer's ambivalence about himself. He had wanted to be at the center of the action, to be in a war, and yet he shied away from combat—his first reaction was often to flinch and then to counterpunch. He took a week to think over Jerry Rubin's invitation to speak at Berkeley, and all through the march on the Pentagon he would calculate the degree to which he would be willing to risk a beating. More than in any event since the Second World War, Mailer felt himself in physical danger. There was no telling how the National Guard would respond to thousands of marchers, and he had a terror of mace and of what it might do to his weak eyes. At the same time, he would be marching as a prominent figure, and he indulged himself in fantasies about the great speeches he would make, ruminating on the possibility that he might actually realize his dream of becoming a great politician and general, motivating and controlling masses of people. The march on the Pentagon was an event, a campaign, a strategy for action and public involvement of a kind that he had not been able to envision since writing *The Naked and the Dead.* Marching alongside Robert Lowell, Dwight Macdonald, Paul Goodman, and other important literary and political figures, Mailer was once again out on patrol, in a united company of distinguished men that forced him to take the measure of himself in the light of history, to relate his private compulsions and his powers as a novelist to the public drama of protest.

Mailer's account in *The Armies of the Night* of his participation in the march on the Pentagon has been corroborated by several eyewitnesses; indeed, many of them have been astounded by his nearly total recall of conversations and of his sure grasp of the ambiance of protest. Perhaps because of his recent experience with film, he had a heightened ability to observe himself and others—even in those moments when he seemed most drunk and out of control. Indeed, the character of the march in *The Armies of the Night*—at once carefully planned by master strategists like Jerry Rubin and Dave Dellinger and yet vulnerable to every vagary of mass confrontations with the authorities and the media—is like a Mailer movie, in which there is no script, improvisation is de rigueur, and yet everything seems "cut" to his "taste." As Mailer describes the fluctuating moods of the demonstrators, the moments when they pull together, when they are in danger of disintegrating into a riot of individual impulses, he comes close to his definition of making a film, which is "a cross between a circus, a military campaign, a nightmare, an orgy, and a high."

Mailer did not go to the march with the clear plan to write a novel of history, although he recognized that he had not written anything worthwhile in many months. Even after the conclusion of the march, he did not begin writing until his agent had secured a twenty-five-thousand-dollar book advance and Willie Morris at *Harper's* agreed to pay ten thousand dollars for a twenty-thousand-word article. Most of what turned out to be the book's first part, "History as a Novel," was written at a fever pitch and on a grueling schedule in Provincetown, where Mailer worked straight through Christmas 1967.

Sandy Charlebois Thomas watched Mailer put in ten- to fourteen-hour days. Willie Morris sat in the kids' bedroom editing while Thomas typed pages that were literally grabbed out of her typewriter. Norman and Beverly continued to fight. A year earlier, there had been "a lot of money around," but now Mailer had to write himself out of a financial jam. *Why Are We in Vietnam?* had not done so well, although he had collected a handsome advance, and he could still count on approximately ten thousand dollars a year from sales of *The Naked and the Dead*. As had Anne Barry, Thomas observed the active involvement of Barney and Cy Rembar in the accounting and investment of Mailer's earnings.

The writing was hard; he had to will himself to do it. Later he realized that his best work often came this way: "writing against great resistance in myself and finishing in great depression. . . . *The Armies of the Night* was written during a towering depression . . . some of the worst weeks in my life. I would come home each night and think it was terrible."

In one month, Mailer wrote ninety thousand words, editing himself and responding to editorial suggestions from Willie Morris, who remembers Mailer's quick and deft responses to suggestions of changes in emphasis or pacing. Morris knew he had a writer working at the top of his form—creating a new genre of fact-based narrative that had the immediacy, power, and sweep of a great historical novel.

The second part of the book, "The Novel as History," was almost an afterthought, Mailer's recognition that he had to balance his view of himself and events with other accounts of the march, other "histories" that readers could compare to his own. Although most readers have found this part of the book less appealing than the comedy/drama of the first part, "The Novel as History" is indispensable, for Mailer is able to display his authority by assessing other sources, probing both their strengths and limitations, demonstrating an impartiality in his scrutiny of both the leftist and the establishment press. Thus Mailer achieves an objective historical voice that complements his third-person treatment of himself in the first part.

The Armies of the Night, published in book form on the twentieth anniversary of the publication of *The Naked and the Dead*, contains, like his war novel, a map—this time not of an Anapopei but of the Pentagon. Both maps are metaphors, however, of campaigns and of armies moved by great conflicting forces of history. In the case of *Armies*, Mailer finds a single character, himself, to embody these conflicting forces. The various titles he gives himself ("the Historian," "the Beast," the "Prince of Bourbon," "the Existentialist," "the Novelist," "the Participant," "the Ruminant," the "nice Jewish boy from Brooklyn") reflect the variety of roles he plays. What is new about *Armies* is the irony and humor with which Mailer treats himself. His use of the third person is canny—at once distancing himself as a writer from the Mailer of the march and yet making himself all the more important as the sensibility upon which events impinge.

Mailer absorbs and distills the march on the Pentagon, embodying both its silly and its serious aspects. There were profoundly dedicated peace activists and there were opportunists using the event for a variety of political purposes; many individuals partook in both the important and the frivolous activities Mailer attended. As philosopher and fool, he is in the best position to understand the sublime and ridiculous qualities of his allies and adversaries. If he is critical of the totalitarian war machine, he is also condemnatory of liberal college professors who adopt an antihuman, technology-based life-style that is part of what they profess to oppose. At the same time, Mailer associates with such people, knows that as individuals they do not neatly fit his generalizations about them, and recognizes he is only one step removed from their way of life. He never forgets, in other words, how deeply implicated he really is in the conditions he deplores.

The author's keen concentration on other characters, particularly on Robert Lowell, keeps his narrative in Part One from becoming too self-absorbed even as it measures Mailer's power as narrator and participant. Lowell is treated as a great poet and a fixture on the American scene. He apparently shares none of Mailer's self-doubt, and he exhibits a moral rectitude that Mailer envies in other Ivy Leaguers such as William Sloane Coffin of Yale. There is a solidity to the poet's identity, which the novelist attributes to his New England ancestry. When Lowell compliments Mailer on being the best journalist in America, the novelist bristles because journalism is not his idea of fine writing, and he replies to a disconcerted Lowell by suggesting that sometimes he thinks of himself as the best writer in America.

Lowell is the epitome of other characters like Dwight Macdonald, Paul Goodman, and Dr. Spock, who seem to feel secure about their place in the march and about their authority as speakers against the status quo. Mailer, on the other hand, is never certain of his powers of persuasion, although his ambition to move people is obviously greater than that of any other character in the book. He worries over slights to his reputation and is vain enough to preen himself on his achievements. He battles for the reader's regard by showing, for example, the defects in Paul Goodman's prose and by demonstrating his ability to appreciate some of Lowell's finest poetic lines.

The theme of *The Armies of the Night* is that history and the interpretation of history go hand in hand. Part Two clearly proves that there is no such thing as "the facts" without someone to give them a meaning. Indeed, the search for meaning is often what creates the facts. Was the march on the Pentagon a significant historical event? Mailer answers in Part Two as both a historian and a novelist.

As historian, he evaluates the evidence. How many people participated in the march? The estimates, from newspaper accounts, differ greatly: from fifty thousand to two hundred fifty thousand people. Mailer allows for bias, on the right and on the left, and usually settles for figures approximately halfway between the counts of reporters and eyewitnesses sympathetic to and hostile toward the march. He takes a similar approach in evaluating reports of brutality and violence, conceding that both sides resorted to physical abuse and presenting a plausible case for reports of police beatings of protestors when the press was not present.

By one measure, Mailer concludes the march was a failure. It did not stop the war; indeed, it may have produced a public reaction against the demonstrators and boosted President Johnson's popularity. On the other hand, the march succeeded in mobilizing masses of people in spite of the government's best efforts to discourage the marchers. As he astutely points out, organizers like Jerry Rubin and Dave Dellinger succeeded in getting the government to negotiate a protest against itself even as it sought every means of disabling it. It is an impressive achievement of *The Armies of the Night* that it maintains a firm balance between "the armies" representing authority and dissent.

Of crucial importance to the book's balance is Mailer's role as novelist and historian. He never forsakes the facts that were available to him or discounts data that do not fit into his view of the march; on the other hand, he shows the limitations of data. Finally, facts cannot tell the story; only the imagination of the novelist can grasp the true significance of the march: It was not a rigidly planned step-by-step revolutionary program. It was a social movement that did not have a final logical goal; it did not rely on either the Marxist or the capitalist understanding of cause and effect. The march was "a new style of revolution— revolution by theater and without a script."

MAIDSTONE

Beverly embarrassed visitors like Willie Morris who witnessed her tirades against her "evil" husband. At other times, she was his sidekick. When the writer Bruce Jay Friedman began messing up Mailer's hair at a Brooklyn Heights party, Mailer gave him a headbutt and said, "Let's go downstairs." Beverly yelled after them: "Fuck 'em, let 'em fight. Let that fucking bastard get killed by Norman." In the meantime, Mailer threw punches at the windows of Friedman's Jaguar. Friedman got out of the car. In the midst of the face-to-face argument Mailer lowered his head and drove it into Friedman's chest. Friedman retaliated with a blow to Mailer's body. Torres stepped in, fearing that the bigger Friedman would beat up Mailer. When Friedman got back into the car, Mailer began punching the windows again, but Friedman drove off. Later Mailer apologized to Torres, for he knew that Torres as a professional could lose his license for getting involved in a fight.

Beverly's love/hate relationship with Mailer—so similar to his marriage with Adele—epitomized in his mind the fate of charismatic figures. Robert Kennedy had been shot in June 1968, confirming Mailer's conviction that heroes had the potential to excite both the best and worst societal forces. Anyone aspiring to public office in order to command the imagination of the country had in store a similar fate. Indeed, Mailer suspected that a future candidate for president might well be a man in the movie business, someone used to projecting himself through the stories he brought to the screen.

Having made himself into a character in *The Armies of the Night*, and having been followed by a documentary film crew during his participation in the march on the Pentagon, it was not much of a stretch for Mailer to think of directing a film about Norman T. Kingsley, a film director making a film even as he considers a campaign for the presidency. Not only did Mailer give his director his own middle name, Mailer also starred as Kingsley and employed former wives, friends, and a few professional actors he had used in *The Deer Park*, *Wild 90*, and *Beyond the Law*. Once again there would be no script and filming would take place over five days, beginning on July 18, at several different estates on Long Island. As for his previous films, Mailer contrived an atmosphere from which the movie would take its mood—in this case, one of characters and plots at cross purposes, of actors not knowing what was expected of them, of drinking and fucking, paranoid reactions, and fighting, of a frenzied political intrigue in which members of Mailer's entourage were in doubt as to his true motivations. At least one cast member was said to be "packing a piece, a real piece with bullets," Mailer later admitted.

New York reporter Sally Beauman found a "shorter and fatter" Mailer than she expected. Wearing a busman's cap out of which his gray curls sprang, Mailer's best feature seemed to be his "brilliant, penetrating" blue eyes and "a bare, impressively hairy chest and back," set off to perfection by a leather motorcyclist's vest. "He's so magnetic," sighed one of his actresses. "It's his eyes. They're beautiful. He seems to know exactly what you're thinking," another answered. James Toback, invited to play an *Esquire* reporter since he was covering the filming for the magazine, noted Mailer's sun-tanned face and warm smile. His face had "magic and power," reported Toback, but his "thin, shapeless legs and swollen girth suggested weakness and age. Look up and he is a hero; look down and he is a clown."

The director sauntered around the grounds, slapping his stomach, clowning around, and reminding Beauman of a "big beery Scoutmaster . . . split[ting] his wide Toby-jug face with its protruding ears from side to side in a colossal and endearing watermelon grin." As the long days of shooting progressed, Beauman noticed that "the bounce and snap ha[d] gone from his walk, yet he seem[ed] taut with tension."

On one occasion there was an explosion. Taunted by one of his actors, Lane Smith, who told Mailer he could take his crew, his camera, and equipment and shove it up his ass, Mailer retaliated with a punch to Smith's jaw that put him out for five or six seconds. It had all happened so fast that when Smith recovered, he asked who had hit him. Mailer said: "I hit you." Smith countered: "You didn't hit me. That was a nigger punch." One of the two black guys nearby hit Smith, who then accused Torres of having knocked him out. Later Mailer paid for Smith's hospital expenses (his jaw had been broken) in exchange for Smith's written agreement that he would not sue Torres.

The ambivalence about Mailer expressed itself in Tim Hickey's Mailer impersonation. Imitating "Mailer's mafia-style walk and voice," Hickey was pelted with paper cups and tin cans by a group of actors who jeered:

> *"You're a little tyrant underneath."*
> *"You're like a man who's had too much love."*
> *"You couldn't make a President; you can't even make movies. You make lousy movies."*
> *"You're a worn-out record, baby."*
> *"All you want to hear is how wonderful you are."*
> *"You never listen to anyone but yourself."*
> *"You're spoiled."*

The word for Mailer's first wife, Bea Silverman, was zaftig. She had an earthy and arousing quality that made Norman the envy of his friends. She was also very amusing and gay, sure of herself and not at all competitive with him—although some members of his family, including Fanny, thought otherwise (Culver Pictures).

Mickey Knox, James Jones, Norman Mailer. In Hollywood, Knox, an actor from Brooklyn, "hit it off immediately" with Mailer, and the two became friends and later collaborators on a screenplay. James Jones came to New York in February 1952 and wrote home saying that Mailer was "a hell of a fine guy" (Harry N. Ransom Humanities Research Center, University of Texas at Austin).

Mailer has said of himself: "It was so difficult for me to arrive at my own style—I didn't start with an identity. I forged an identity through my experience" (UPI/Bettmann Newsphotos).

ABOVE: *Sent to Bellevue after the stabbing, Mailer seemed "calm" and "subdued." He was later able to persuade a doctor to vouch for his sanity and to release him after two weeks of treatment (UPI/Bettmann Newsphotos).*

BELOW: *After the stabbing, Norman and Adele tried a brief reconciliation but in March 1961 they separated. At the time of the stabbing, Adele said: "Things like this don't happen to people like us . . . I can't believe this" (UPI/Bettmann Newsphotos).*

ABOVE: *Mailer called Muhammed Ali "America's greatet ego" and portrayed him as the first twentieth-century hero to dominate the media and the minds of "mass man." Mailer thought that the wit Ali expressed with his body was equal to the exercise of a great intelligence (Wideworld Photos).*

BELOW: *Beverly Bently, Mailer's fourth wife, met him in a bar. She was high and he was half bombed. "Well, if it isn't Norman Motherfuck Mailer!" "I guess it was love at first sight," said Roger Donoghue, one of Mailer's confidants, who introduced Beverly to him (UPI/Bettmann Newsphotos).*

At a fund-raising party for his 1969 mayoral campaign Mailer exclaimed: "I think I'm serious. All day I'm serious. Then I get up in the morning, and I look in the mirror and I say, 'You're not serious.'" His campaign slogan: "No more bullshit" (Wideworld Photos).

Fanny Mailer at her son's fiftieth birthday party. She was never far from her son's concerns. Lady Jeanne Campbell (Mailer's third wife) complained that all they ever did was go to Fanny's for dinner (Wideworld Photos).

Mailer once wrote that Truman Capote was "tart as a grand aunt, but in his way he is a ballsy little guy, and he is the most perfect writer of my generation, he writes the best sentences word for word, rhythm upon rhythm" (UPI/ Bettmann Newsphotos).

In every sense of the word, Norris Church had put herself on Mailer's level; she is the first woman to understand how to model herself, in all the intimate details, on his sense of companionship and marriage (Wideworld Photos).

With the advent of Norris Church, Norman Mailer became part of the New York social scene. Norris admits she likes the "glitter, the back and forth, the small talk." Mailer admits to dabbling in this world; it is an amusement. He finds exotics who appeal to him but there is little at stake, little reason for him to act out or to embarrass his company (UPT/Bettmann Newsphotos).

Mailer balances on a bongo board during a writers' tribute to the fifteenth anniversary of the Big Apple Circus (UPI/Bettmann Newsphotos).

Of course, these attacks were ostensibly against Mailer's character, Kingsley, but as Toback notes, they "struck at the softest part of Mailer's gut." The animosity seemed to go beyond good performances in a movie, and Rip Torn, who helped stage the scene, admitted as much, suggesting it would be more authentic to be candid with Mailer, and it would enhance the movie. Torn confessed that Mailer had heard about the scene and had been "very hurt," but Torn thought the director realized it had been "necessary."

There is no doubt that Mailer had a serious purpose in creating an environment in which assassinations occur, for Norman T. Kingsley announces: "I'm a catalyst. I set loose forces. (*The first of his strengths is candor.*) If I'm not right, then I'll set loose terrible forces." In experimenting with his own person and friends, Mailer was trying to get at the overwrought temper of the times.

There was quite a different sort of tension, however, that Mailer has never acknowledged—at least not in print. Because there was no script, and because several of the actors were not professionals, his cast found it difficult to stay in character. He used ex-wife Lady Jeanne Campbell, for instance, as an English journalist reporting on Kingsley's life—a splendid choice, yet on screen she wavers and loses conviction, apparently amused by playing a character so close to herself. She almost smirks. Similarly, other characters who describe Kingsley sound oddly flat and unconvincing. There is a curious realism to these scenes, for they are utterly devoid of the usual dramatic development given narrative in Hollywood films, but there is little of the actor's skill or intense interest in projecting a sense of character onto the screen. Rip Torn, a profoundly dedicated actor who had appeared in *The Deer Park* and in *Beyond the Law*, was angered by what he took to be Mailer's sham movie.

The best scenes feature Mailer as Kingsley interviewing women for roles in a movie about a male whorehouse. Kingsley is manipulative and even sadistic, finding small flaws in these women and harping on them. He expects them to be completely submissive. Several cast members resented Mailer's swaggering direction and perhaps misunderstood his desire to create a life-threatening scene for Kingsley and for himself, in which the divide between what is real and what is fictional, what constitutes a movie about Norman T. Kingsley and about Norman Mailer, is not easy to separate.

Even before the filming ended, Mailer began to speak clearly in his own voice, having himself filmed addressing his cast. Instead of following the logic of a paranoid violent atmosphere, Mailer shifted (when it seemed no one in the cast would attack Kingsley) to a scene in which *Maidstone* became, less interestingly, a film about making a film that he could not quite bring off. The film of Norman T. Kingsley had not succeeded—as this exchange between Mailer and Torn (playing Kingsley's half-brother) reveals:

> MAILER: *Rip, what were you, ah, what was your attitude toward me?*

> RIP TORN: *Well, I was in constant conflict between you, Norman, as the man, and the character of Kingsley that you're playing.*

One of the actresses admitted she was really "pissed off" when no one had "bumped off" Kingsley, and Mailer's confessed that, in the end, he had not really wanted the assassination to occur. He had scared people for nothing, another actress observed, and the underlying tone of her remarks suggest that many of them had been disappointed by the film's lack of resolution. Mailer thought he had been in control, that even the irresolution of the film had been planned. "You may have some surprises," Torn muttered at what Mailer supposed was the last cinema verité scene in *Maidstone*.

Maidstone replicates the Mailer pattern of veering toward and then away from violence. Having brought himself into proximity with an assassination plot, Mailer retreated into an almost academic lecture on filmmaking. Outraged by the way Mailer had tricked everyone into thinking a film of novel significance was in the offing, Torn refused to accept the ending of *Maidstone* and attacked Mailer during the filming of him with his family the day after the director had declared the movie over. Charging Mailer in an open field, Torn hit him three times with the flat side of a hammer, pulling his blows but doing enough damage to draw blood. Four of Mailer's children—Dandy, Betsy, Michael, and Stephen—were terrified, screaming after Torn's assault on their father. Mailer was furious. Calling Torn a "crazy fool cocksucker" Mailer wrestled him to the ground, biting and nearly tearing off Torn's ear. Calling Mailer "brother" and insisting the film would make no sense without the assassination scene, Torn traded insults with Mailer and yet kept reminding him that this was the story Mailer had planned, that Mailer had even seen him coming with the hammer and had not tried to get away. When Mailer would not acknowledge the justice of Torn's words, Torn called him a "fraud," a charge Mailer later had to countenance, for in the editing room he found that he did not have a movie without the dramatic explosion, the assault not only on Norman T. Kingsley but on Norman Mailer, the half-sincere, half-bogus filmmaker and politician who had to be called to account by a real actor who took his role seriously, as though he were, in Mailer's words, his "true brother." The psychological reality of *Maidstone* was the actors' expectation that Mailer would be attacked, and so Torn "attacked out of all the plots of other actors" and became, Mailer realized, "the presence of the film, the psychological reality that became a literal reality out of the pressure of all the ones which did not."

There is a peculiar integrity to *Maidstone* that is like Mailer's own: It pretends to more than it can deliver. It aspires to effect a whole new way of filmmaking that it cannot bring off. But the film, like so much of Mailer, acknowledges its faults and its incompleteness and somehow makes us feel implicated, "anticipating the formation of plots around us which do not quite form." The fascination of following Mailer is in the anticipation of whether this time he will, in fact, enact himself as we have been led to expect.

9.

KING OF THE HILL (1968–1972)

MIAMI AND THE SIEGE OF CHICAGO

Harvard, June 1968. "I knew the Norman Mailer I had roomed with. And then there was a very different Norman Mailer who became the writer and a still different Norman Mailer who was a sixties radical, a hard drinker, delivering rebellious speeches. Meeting him there at the twenty-fifth reunion," Richard Weinberg recalls, was still another Norman Mailer: "He was very gentlemanly, different from the public Norman Mailer," and somehow settled. "He and Beverly seemed very devoted to each other." Were they on their best behavior? There had been a controversy. His college friend George Goethals wanted him to speak at the reunion, but the "Brahmin types all screamed," Goethals recalls. They were sure Mailer would say something embarrassing: "He'll be dirty, he'll offend the children." When Mailer talked with Goethals about it, Mailer said he felt "fucked over," but Goethals persuaded him to come. Taking a look at the crowd and not really feeling wanted, Mailer decided not to speak.

Mailer had described himself in *Advertisements* as a "quick change artist," a man of many guises. As a result, people were always responding to his last appearance. He was no longer the cocky yet circumspect young author of *The Naked and the Dead*, the "psychic outlaw" of "The White Negro," or the wise fool of *The Armies of the Night*, to mention just a few of his roles. While he would continue to use the development of his persona as the focus of his work in the next five years, *Armies* already gave evidence that he had become tired of himself as a public spectacle. As he would write shortly to James Dickey: "I've seen so much of myself in *Maidstone* that the thought of more of my personality offered to the public holds no great pleasure for me."

Certainly, Mailer's coverage of the political conventions in *Miami and the Siege of Chicago* is subdued in comparison to his flamboyance in *The Armies of the Night*. He refers to himself as "the reporter," and he shies away from the public role he had sought in the march on the Pentagon. His evocation of the steamy, jungle-swamp atmosphere of Miami that is dredged and paved over with modern machinery and alleviated with air conditioning is as provocative as his brilliant dissection of Los Angeles in "Superman Comes to the Supermarket." What Americans do to their places, the sense of a subreality that only Mailer knows how to bring to the surface, gives *Miami and the Siege of Chicago* the same weight as his other important reportage.

Many readers have been surprised and even dismayed at Mailer's sympathy for Richard Nixon, who comes to dominate Miami as Kennedy dominated Los Angeles. While Nixon is not portrayed as a charismatic figure, he earns Mailer's respect for having triumphed over his defeats in 1960 and 1962. Mailer himself is surprised. He has never liked Nixon—in fact he despised him for the Checkers speech and thought of him as not much more than a cheap, manipulative politician. Now, however, Nixon is a survivor. He exudes a competence and confidence and an awareness of how to employ the levers of political power that impress Mailer. For the first time, Mailer exhibits the respect of a professional reporter for the politician he covers, remarking of Nixon: "It was possible he was one of the most disciplined men in America."

Why this turn in Mailer's attitudes? In *The Armies of the Night* he signals his increasing uneasiness with the young; he has more to lose than to gain by being a rebel. In *Miami and the Siege of Chicago*, he is explicit about this: For all his criticism of America, it has treated him well, allowed him to earn his living and to enjoy a status he is loath to give up. If he describes himself in *The Armies of the Night* as a "left conservative" while placing a great deal of the emphasis on his sympathetic relations with radicals, in *Miami and the Siege of Chicago* he empathizes with the conservative Republicans who want to hold onto the very values that have secured them a comfortable place in society. Mailer even admits to finding the demands of black militants tiresome— a shocking admission for the one-time champion of the White Negro. He is moved more by thinking of Richard Nixon as like himself—a family man with daughters, a man who has known how to live with rejection and to maneuver from marginality back to the center of the action. Nixon, like Kennedy, knows how to control environment. Nixon's means are less flashy but perhaps appealing to the middle-aged Mailer for precisely that reason.

Mailer conceived of his white Negro when he was on the periphery— as though he had to find in his circumstances a correlative to his own feelings: "He had lived for a dozen empty hopeless years after the Second World War with bitterness, rage, and potential militancy of a real revolutionary," Mailer admits in *Miami and the Siege of Chicago*, but now he was satisfied with "the pleasures of making his movies, writing his books." The revolution—the march on the Pentagon, the bloody riots in the Chicago streets carried on by students who had been influenced by his writing—had come too late for him. He would make a speech to the dissenting students and offer to lead a group of delegates protesting the nomination of Hubert Humphrey and the police riot in the Chicago streets, but these were gestures and momentary departures from the reporter's professional obligations. Having achieved the quixotic persona of *The Armies of the Night*, he sustains a quieter and beautifully controlled prose in *Miami and the Siege of Chicago*.

The shift in Mailer's style reflected his conviction that he had coped well with his weaknesses. As he puts it in *Miami and the Siege of Chicago*:

> *It seemed to him that he had been afraid all his life, but in recent years, or so it seemed, he had learned how to take a step into his fear, how to take the action which frightened him most ([sic] and so could free him the most). He did not do it always, who could? But he had come to think that the secret to growth was to be brave a little more than one was cowardly, simple as that, indeed why should life not be just so simple that the unlettered and untrained might also have their natural chance?*

This is the philosophy of a Rojack, but expressed in much simpler prose and applicable, Mailer admits, to everyone. All the gorgeous mystique, the densely metaphorical style of "The White Negro" and of *An American Dream* are stripped for this nearly naked admission of what Mailer has learned.

On an everyday level, Mailer had found his equivalent to Rojack's walking the parapet. When writer Don Carpenter visited Mailer in his Brooklyn Heights home, he was struck by his "rope trip," his climbing of a rope he had hung from his living-room ceiling:

> *He also asked me if I wanted to visit his office, which at that time you could only get to by climbing the rope and crossing a two-by-six. I share something with Norman which is absolutely clear in* The Naked and the Dead, *and it was also clear from the office setup; we both have a terrific fear of falling. If I'm in a situation where I could fall, I fall, so I fear heights, and so does Norman. Only his attack on the problem is different from mine. I don't go anywhere where I can fall. He does, and constantly.*

Mailer has often been asked whether his highly metaphorical prose should be taken literally; one answer is that in his own life he has tried to do so while setting reasonable limits on the extravagance of his conceits: He walks no parapet at home.

If Mailer has reveled in imagining a life on the edge, he has also welcomed recognition and the emotional security of family life. He was proud to receive the National Book Award for *The Armies of the Night*. Robert Gutwillig, Mailer's editor at New American Library, remembers the day of the award presentation (March 12, 1968), the scene at a restaurant near Lincoln Center, where Mailer had gathered around him Beverly, his children, and his parents. Fanny had kissed him in congratulation and he was ecstatic. "It was his first prize, and it meant a lot to him, being accepted. I know he has these ambivalent feelings about being anti-establishment, but it was so nice for his family," Gutwillig recalls.

However, the strife with Beverly continued. Sandy Charlebois Thomas remembers that shortly after the making of *Maidstone* in July 1968 she casually mentioned one of the women who had been in the movie: "I just heard she has the clap." Evidently the woman in question was a Mailer mistress, because Beverly immediately turned on Norman and shouted: "You're not bringing that into the house, goddammit!" It was one of the few occasions Thomas can remember Mailer being upset with her, although she tried to explain that she had no idea of their relationship. "It was the first time it dawned on me that he'd probably screwed every woman in the cast." Thomas slunk away as Beverly and Norman "really got into it."

Midge Decter viewed Mailer's penchant for women and children as all of a piece—"making a scenario of his ideas . . . naturally he'd go around knocking up every woman he gets mixed up with. Almost on principle." Of course, this caused him grief and money but then "there is all this life, Mailer with all his progeny and all his women, and he never gives up on any of them." That is what made it interesting for people like Decter who had followed his private life and career. In *Maidstone*, "There they all were—Adele, Jeanne, this one, that one. And clearly there was some other lady he was balling, whoever she was, so by the time I saw the movie I knew well enough to watch and say, 'Oh, that's interesting. Who's that?' "

This was the same Norman Mailer who would invite a friend—in this case fellow writer Don Carpenter—for a family meal. At table: his sister Barbara, Carpenter, Barney and Fanny, Beverly, Charlie Brown and his girlfriend. "In front of his parents Norman was the absolute patriarch, the generous soul for whom every guest is a diamond," Carpenter recalls. One could not ask for a more considerate host, making sure that everyone at the table was comfortable and participating in the conversation. "Aside from being complimented, it was a delight, because Norman didn't feel constrained to be a shit. Ever since, I've always felt that the best kept secret in American literature is what a nice guy Norman Mailer is," Carpenter observes.

In the kitchen Carpenter and Barbara talked "irreligiously about Norman," with Barbara conveying the impression that "we love him, but he's not a god." Outside the home, on the same evening, Carpenter saw an "imperious" Mailer, with Beverly seated beside him, "receiving people." Sandy Charlebois Thomas also remembers Mailer at his best during small dinner parties: "self-critical, charming, funny, thoughtful, and courteous. More times than not he wouldn't be, but he *could* be." With Thomas and other assistants he was rarely rude, but in private with his wives and with others, "he can be either wonderful or a horror show."

THE PROVINCETOWN PLAYERS

In the late 1960s and early 1970s, the Norman Mailer one knew varied from one locale to another, from one kind of situation to another. Even in Provincetown, to which he returned every summer, the impress of his personality differed markedly with the circumstances. Certainly the figure he cut in this small town went through several transformations. Although he had been coming there since the late 1940s, it was in the 1960s that he began to assert himself as a presence, encouraging writers and artists of various kinds not only to summer there but to extend their stays into the winter months. Provincetown had always been a venue for artists, but until the 1960s the year-round residents—the majority of whom were Portugese fisherman, small shopkeepers, and their families—saw the summer influx of outlanders for what it was: a temporary and tolerable, if somewhat exotic, invasion.

As the artists gradually began to extend their stays and to mix with the natives, flaunting their outrageous life-styles and demanding a certain acceptance from the community, they became more of an issue for the local population. To the indigenous Provincetowners, it was as if the artists were asking for some kind of recognition or recompense for the money and the time spent there. Mailer and his friends, concerned that rents were being raised and that they were paying dearly for the privilege of their lengthier stops in town, soon began to involve themselves in local government and real estate. They bought property and subleased it to each other, as the artist Peter Busa did in renting out a small studio to Mailer, who used it as a place to write. Mailer was undoubtedly a draw at the exciting theater, poetry readings, and other events, inspiring a literary sense of community.

To Elizabeth Reis (whose Portugese grandfather came to Province-town before World War I and established himself in the fishing industry) Mailer gave the impression of a "big, broad, hairy man." He resembled the burly Portugese fishermen: "Had he been on my Dad's fishing boat, he would not have been out of place at all." She would hear wild stories about his drinking parties at the end of the Point, but it would not have been a "big deal," Reis suggests: "Provincetown is very much like a little village. He would be taken home by the police. It would not be much of an issue for them." This did not make Mailer a community member, however. "If you are not born there, you are not an insider,"

Reis points out. There would seem to be many levels of acceptance for a man like Mailer, who would be free to indulge in many different life-styles, but it was virtually impossible to penetrate the core of this society. A man like Mailer had a cultural value, an economic value; he could be condoned but not really accepted.

Sandra Kraskin, an artist who lived with Mailer's friend Peter Busa during the late 1960s, saw Mailer several times in Provincetown:

> *What struck me the most about Mailer—I'd heard all these extravagant stories about him—was that he was such a sweet, gentle person. I was twenty-five or twenty-six, from Minneapolis, and I knew little about literature at the time, and he was really interested in what I had to say. He was very personable, yet I had this idea that I was speaking to someone who was a real terror—very disrespectful of women. A lot of that just seemed to be his publicity.*

Mailer was partial to abstract expressionists and from time to time would visit Busa's studio and occasionally buy his work. Kraskin thought Mailer enjoyed helping artists, even though he was not particularly well informed about art.

It was a period of heavy drinking among artists, and Kraskin heard her share of stories about Mailer the wild man, yet at several dinners and on other occasions he never gave evidence of this side of his character—but Kraskin usually saw him during the day. Mailer loved to eat and relished his wine at dinner and apparently partook of the pot that was liberally available. Irving Howe remembers Mailer's conviction that somehow it was all right for him to take drugs, but he was determined that his kids would not.

"Provincetown was honky-tonky in the 1960s," Kraskin adds, "but there were parts of it that were charming." Mailer's house was right on the water. There was nothing "especially elaborate" about the way he lived—"it was more the location, the setting . . . the quality of the light" that seemed to count with him. Mailer liked the local color and found it easy to relax with Provincetowners, and the town got used to him.

Kraskin remembers that Mailer "was always talking about boxing"—using it as an analogy to describe other experiences, and "he was in love with the idea of being involved with the movies." Almost everything

seemed romanticized, and "he loved the romance of Abstract Expres-
sionism, the sea, the harbor." Mailer clung to his visions tenaciously.
Kraskin sees a strong connection between Jackson Pollack's obsession
with Melville, with Ahab and the great male hero, and Mailer's ambitions for himself and his art. "It was the whole sense of inventing a life
. . . and having to go out and do these outrageous things." To Kraskin it
was apparent Mailer always had a sense of his impact on others, on what
his walking into a room would do to them: "He loved that. . . . That was
the actor in him."

It was clear to Kenneth Lynn in Paris in 1947 that Mailer's mother had
had a profound impact on him. In Provincetown in the late 1960s Sandra
Kraskin would hear him praise his mother, saying he had her sewing
machine, which he had turned into a desk, because she was so important
to him, such an inspiration. He was tender and soft-spoken about her.
Kraskin recognized the "chauvinist" in him, but he was "never offensive."

Linked to his chauvinism and his romanticism were his feelings about
nature. "He was so against anything that wasn't natural," says Kraskin,
who recalls a visit he made to Minneapolis: "I had just gotten these new
ski boots and was commenting on this new synthetic material, and oh,
he objected. If it wasn't leather, you shouldn't have it near your skin.
And that seemed to carry over to anything artificial, including birth
control."

To Kraskin it seemed so egocentric—an ostentatious sign of virility—for Mailer to gather around him his wives and his children in his
summers at Provincetown. He liked to talk about his children, and he
seemed "very, very involved with them," but not so that it would
interfere with his work or social life. "On some level he was a very
loving parent but when it was convenient for him."

Mailer enrolled one of his sons, Michael, in the Provincetown Ele-
mentary School. "It was quite a trip," says Elizabeth Reis.

*That was Mailer being folksy. Most people of Mailer's means—even if
they were on the Cape—would have sent their kids to the regional school
which has many more opportunities available. As a girl, I used to dream
of going to the regional school with interesting subjects and real resources. Michael had a hard time. He was a very cosmopolitan kind of
kid dealing with kids who really never made it to Boston. He was*

rebellious . . . facing a very precarious time with his father and his
wives.

Like Kraskin, Reis formed the impression of a parent who was rather lax
about his parental responsibility but a man of his times who did not have
"very much to do" with the actual raising of his progeny. "Beverly and
Mailer were absolutely pips of parents," Reis remarks: "They would
leave a kid with anybody—under the theory that you don't pull him out
of school for this."

Both Adele and Beverly were part of the Provincetown summers and
Kraskin got revealing glimpses of them. Adele had pretensions about
being an artist, and Kraskin's introduction to her was rather startling.
Adele came one day to look at Peter Busa's paintings. Making coffee in
the kitchen, Kraskin happened to look out through the window and
notice that Busa had a rather "funny" look on his face. Adele was
looking at the bursts of color in Busa's paintings, sidling up to him, and
saying things like "You must have good orgasms." Wearing a miniskirt,
then in fashion, a dress cut very short in a simple but striking style,
Adele was "literally trying to seduce him in front of me," says Kraskin,
whom Adele ignored. Busa seemed nonplussed. A handsome man in his
early fifties, a friend of Jackson Pollock and an established artist, Busa
presented a tempting catch. "After a certain point, it would have taken
Peter's participation for it to have gone any further," Kraskin notes, "but
Adele was very open about her invitation." Not knowing Adele well,
Kraskin could not be sure whether she had been serious about the
seduction or whether it was a part of her manner to come on so strongly:
"She was very dramatic and very beautiful." She had a natural quality
and did not use much makeup. Like Irving Howe, Kraskin was more
taken with Adele than with Beverly, who left a less vivid impression.
Beverly looked lovely, but Kraskin found Adele more interesting.

Kraskin was appalled by the permissive way the Mailers were raising
their children, who went around saying "shit this and shit that" and had
little supervision. To Kraskin, Adele seemed a better mother to her kids
than Beverly. Although Beverly did some acting in Provincetown and
was frustrated about her stymied career, she had little specific to say
about it and was not very convincing on the subject. As with Bea, the
more Mailer took center stage, the more Beverly seemed stuck and
overwhelmed by a man who was into so many things.

MAILER FOR MAYOR

On an overcast day in late March 1969, Gloria Steinem, Jimmy Breslin, Peter Maas, and Jack Newfield found themselves enjoying morning coffee together after handing in their copy to Clay Felker, publisher of *New York* magazine. The talk was about the primary campaign for mayor coming up in June. There was no obvious candidate to back, especially in view of their very gloomy assessment of the city. Mario Procaccino, the city controller, seemed determined to run a racist campaign; Congressman James Scheuer spoke as a liberal and yet resorted to the right's rhetoric about law and order; Robert Wagner, the former mayor, was considering a return to office, even though his record showed a conspicuous unwillingness to take on the city's fundamental problems. The best bet, Herman Badillo, the Puerto Rican borough president of the Bronx, was too cautious and prone to "tinkering" with the system rather than "challenging old concepts," as Gloria Steinem later put it.

As morning coffee gave way to early lunch and beer, Jack Newfield proposed a Mailer candidacy. All agreed he had no chance to win, but at least he would be able to shake up the primary and introduce new ideas. Sometimes losing campaigns, like Eugene McCarthy's, changed minds and set a new political agenda. If Mailer could alter the terms of the campaign he would have accomplished as much as could be reasonably expected of him. These writers did not discount the drawbacks. Mailer was controversial; he was a writer, not a professional politician. He was erratic—some would say unstable. He had stabbed his wife and made a fool of himself in public on many occasions. Yet his visionary quality persuaded them that he could, in Steinem's words, "turn this big excessive city on its ear."

As a running mate (for city council president), the group quickly settled on Breslin: "Mailer, the wild-eyed Jewish, Harvard-bred, intellectual-activist; combined with Breslin, the tough street-bred, would-be Irish cop—a perfect coalition for New York." Although Breslin had his qualms about running for public office and wondered why he should take second place on the ticket, he was also intrigued and flattered by the possibilities of doing something about the city's ills he had written about so vividly in his newspaper columns. He hardly knew Mailer, but that did not stop him from leaving the table to call him.

Mailer could not have written a better script for himself. Breslin was his Irish alter ego, the one Mailer had already played as Francis X. Pope in *Beyond the Law*. Breslin had a daily following among the newspaper-reading public that Mailer, the sometime columnist, had sought. Breslin could have been a character out of *Studs Lonigan*, a battling tough of the type Mailer had always envied. It was surely a matter of destiny for these two writers to dominate the city, to give it the imagination that the other candidates so clearly lacked.

Mailer wanted a week to think it over in Provincetown, which suited a wary Breslin, who sensed that his running mate was crazy enough to think he could actually win an election. "You guys got me running with Ezra Pound," Breslin said after a preliminary meeting at Mailer's home. Despite Breslin's concerns, he quickly warmed to a Mailer who laughed at his jokes and seemed to approach the upcoming campaign with humor and humility. What the city really needed, Mailer conceded, was a black mayor, since whites had lost the right to tell blacks how to improve their lives; whites had betrayed blacks too many times for a white candidate to propose solutions to their problems. In the absence of a viable black candidate, Mailer proposed running himself on a platform of power to the neighborhoods. His tack would be to find the funds to allow neighborhoods to govern themselves—which meant policing and educating themselves and establishing community standards of good conduct and citizenship. Mailer considered this a conservative or rightist solution—civic programs would be generated on the local level and people would be directly responsible for the quality of life in their neighborhoods. Federal projects had failed to relieve poor people beset by crime-ridden slums. At the same time, his solution was leftist—public money would be used to help people help themselves. Increased funding would come from the city, with the extra revenue derived from a New York City that would become the fifty-first state. Mailer had figured out that the city produced approximately fourteen billion dollars in revenue for New York state and yet received only three billion in return for support services. With New York City in control of its fiscal and political fate, with two senators and twenty congressmen, he was certain that several billion dollars more could be found to improve the schools, the transportation system, the police force, the polluted environment—virtually every aspect of city life could be enhanced if New Yorkers reclaimed their fortune by making the city a state. While Mailer would run as a Democrat, vowing to make the Democratic political machine hum with his ideas, he would actually seek to unite the best ideas of the right and the left to form a new governing coalition. When Breslin realized that his running mate advocated a whole new context in which to view the city's massive problems, he was with Mailer "all the way."

As Mailer and Breslin soon learned, their biggest obstacle was getting the press to take them seriously. Sporadic media coverage tended to suggest these writers were off on a lark. Mailer's provocative and succinct position papers on air pollution, transportation, housing, statehood for the city, education, city finances, and on crime, narcotics, and the police were largely ignored. His ambivalence about seeking office, his inexperience as a politician, and his inability to control his erratic behavior contributed to the ineffectiveness of his campaign. At a fund-raising party, he exclaimed: "I think I'm serious. All day I'm serious. Then I get up in the morning, and I look in the mirror and I say, 'You're not serious.' "

New York Post columnist James A. Wechsler, who never held a sympathetic thought for Mailer's entrance into the race, skewered him for his appearance on the Johnny Carson show: "This was not the Mailer of local folklore, garrulous, disheveled, rambling, and profane. This was The Candidate, his demeanor sedately and sedatively reminiscent of Robert F. Wagner." Mailer read his own press, and in his heart of hearts knew he should not try to be a conventional candidate. Then he swung to the other end of his personality, swearing at and telling off an audience at the Village Gate, calling them ego-trippers and questioning their interest in his campaign. This ugly performance was featured in *The New York Times*, causing anguish to many of his campaign workers and making Joe Flaherty, his campaign manager, so mad he succeeded in lashing back and demoralizing his candidate:

> *I served up last what had really upset me. "I agree with you," I said when you tell leftists they shouldn't call cops pigs. So where do you get off using that word on your audience?" He looked unbelieving: "Did I say that?" "You called them a bunch of spoiled pigs," I answered. Beverly nodded confirmation. Tears welled up in his eyes, and he turned his head and buried it in the couch. I wished I hadn't pushed that far.*

It was almost as if Mailer had paid himself back for his insipid performance on the Carson show. He had turned in a similar polite and conventional performance on a televised debate—even allowing Wagner

to correct him (erroneously) on the facts. As writer Pete Hamill observed, Mailer had become inauthentic, "like a candidate playing
a candidate." As a result he overreacted, trying to regain his form
by delivering to his Village Gate audience "the ultimate shock"—
challenging them immediately because he doubted he could win them
over. "It's a bit like Floyd Patterson knowing that Sonny Liston was
going to beat him, so instead of bouncing around him for fourteen
rounds he runs right into him," Flaherty suggests.

One of Mailer's biggest conservative supporters, Noel Parmental,
believes the Village Gate crowd had it coming to them. They were, in his
words, "a tacky bunch. Pushy, loudmouthed climbers, and flunkies. . . .
Sleazy and weasely, low-class hustlers, and sycophants." These were the
kind to get themselves invited to the houses of the "beautiful people."
Mailer had met them at countless gatherings where they came to ogle
him but not to contribute to his campaign.

But the evening was reported as an example of Mailer's bizarre public
behavior. At the Village Gate fiasco Mailer lost courage, retreating to
"his worst self," a "fat and sweaty" beast who rejected his audience
before it had a chance to reject him. It also made it virtually impossible
to raise significant amounts of money for the campaign. Mailer ended up
spending a lot of his own money and garnering less than a thousand
dollars from outside sources.

Mailer's later account of the Village Gate debacle cast him as the
"seed of a future Napoleon" castigating his troops. Admitting to a
"demented notion" that he was going to pay for his past sins, his
laziness, by actually winning the election and working hard as mayor,
Mailer took the tack that like a great general he would have to be
"savage with his troops" if he was going to spur them on. "Incredible
speech. And wild. And dumb beyond belief," Mailer confessed, but it
was not without its inner logic.

In spite of the setbacks, Mailer campaigned vigorously, putting in
long days and nights on college campuses, in the streets of all the
boroughs, at various clubs, synagogues, and other organizations. If
elected he expected to give up writing for the duration of his term in
office, since he wanted to put his ideas into action. "If you have certain
ideas, you have to embody them. It's the only thing that people trust," he
told an interviewer. Mailer viewed his politicking as "an adventure
whose end could not be foreseen." By example he hoped to energize his
age: "Alienation is the disease of our time. . . . None of us have any

power. The ideas in our minds have no relation to reality." People had ceded too much to the technocrats: "Remember, the experts, the geniuses of mediocrity, the technicians, have run this city into the ground." It was time that people took ownership of the political process: "Politics is property, and we have none. Washington and Albany own us."

Mailer was usually at his best on the street. When someone responded to one of his eloquent impromptu speeches by suggesting his program was "theoretically attractive . . . visionary and romantic," Mailer replied that he was not offering a "panacea": "The problem would be knotty. Society will still be corrupt," but in "purgatory" rather than "hell." Challenged at a synagogue about giving power to neighborhoods to set up their own schools, police forces, and so on, Mailer responded: "OK. Now let's talk about it. I don't mean ALL power to the neighborhoods, I mean as much as is compatible with the needs of the city."

Two *New York Times* columnists, Russell Baker and Tom Wicker, took Mailer seriously. They saw flaws in his ideas, but he had, in Wicker's words, "dramatize[d] a fundamental issue." The notion of a fifty-first state emphasized that the city needed "a new beginning," a way out of what Wicker called "the fifty historical accidents of the federal system."

Mailer often got the toughest questions from fellow Jews smarting from what they considered the undeserved attacks of certain blacks who rejected the Jewish legacy of social activism and emphasized the racism they found in the ways Jews treated blacks. Jews wanted to know how their rights and neighborhoods could be protected by a decentralized government. Was Mailer really advocating that the blacks police themselves? He was, and his position only confirmed his lack of sympathy for what many Jews wanted. But he never lost his sense of humor. When his yarmulke fell off during his speech in a synagogue, Mailer filled the awkward silence by looking above him and musing, "I hope the Lord has not spoken."

Mailer made a curious speaker, often switching to a Southern accent as if that were the natural language of politics. An irritated Badillo aide once told Flaherty: "Why doesn't your man talk issues and cut out all that Elmer Gantry bullshit?" Mailer's more likely model was Willie Stark, Robert Penn Warren's literary depiction of Huey Long, a politician with a populist streak and an urge to put his big ideas into action. As Mailer told V. S. Naipaul during the campaign, "You are always writing that novel about yourself." Occasionally Mailer injected British undertones, as if to formalize his remarks on the fifty-first state, and project himself, in Joe Flaherty's view, into a "homebred Harold Macmillan." Flaherty liked to watch Mailer address a crowd, getting into a crouch, "the left hand pawing and developing into an effective jab when the tempo of his speech picked up, shifting weight from foot to foot in a wobble like an undecided tenpin." Naipaul treasured Mailer's "abrupt, swift, pithy" replies to questions and the way his tongue flicked against his top teeth, "as though a piece of chewing gum was being hidden away."

Mailer disposed of questions quickly:

> *"Why haven't you gone to Vietnam, Mr. Mailer?"*
> *"I don't want to get killed."*
> *"I was there for two years. I wasn't killed."*
> *"That is a horrible and obscene war. I would have done something. I would have got killed."*

At a meeting on the Lower East Side, Mailer quipped, "I can see you are not a soft Democratic club. Let's have the questions. I can see that the person who asks the first question is going to be in as much trouble as me." The first questioner was skeptical of the idea that any governor of New York would permit the city to become a state. Mailer retorted: "We all know what breaks up an unhappy marriage. It's a smart Jewish lawyer. I submit that I am the smartest Jewish lawyer in town."

Mailer defended the new open admissions policy at The City University of New York. An angry woman shouted at him: "You are asking the kids to pay for it!" After she was shushed by the audience, Mailer offered: "The kids will have the exhilarating existential experience of going to school with black people." Naipaul was surprised to hear applause as Mailer walked "smartly down, arms held out wide, palms open, like a wrestler about to charge." At his next stop in the Village he announced: "Now listen. I'm much more conservative than most of you people here. I'll work for and support your neighborhood, but I don't think I'll approve of it."

At a cocktail party in the Americana Hotel in Manhattan, clutching a bourbon highball, his intense eyes giving off a glint, he appeared to one reporter as the "quintessence of animal energy. The women were coming on strong." The same day in a church basement, hunched over with his "right hand in his pocket and his left jabbing out front like Willie

Pep, Mailer discussed ills and cures." Jane O'Reilly, a reporter who followed the Mailer campaign, was struck by his surprising voice: "Words rumble and bubble and jump out, in a variety of accents; New York, faintly Southern, all g's dropped (as in "Ahm talkin' ") when he is particularly shy."

Mailer seemed to thrive on the exhausting schedule. One reporter covering his campaign noted: "Every day he seemed to be cheerier, happier, and firmer about what he was saying. There was a suspicion that he had been bored before the campaign began." In fact, Mailer had reached an impasse in his work. *The Armies of the Night* had been an epiphany for him, a work in which he finally created the narrator/persona he had sought so long in his fiction, and *Miami and the Siege of Chicago* solidified his command of a reportorial voice that embodied not merely the events of political conventions but of a nation's state of mind. He would win a Pulitzer Prize for *Armies* during the campaign and sign a lucrative contract to cover the moon shot, but he felt no nearer his dream of himself as a novelist, and perhaps this is why he contemplated this sabbatical from writing, even if it meant that as an elected official it might be years before he could again take up his pen.

In an interview with Leticia Kent, Mailer admitted that he was dissatisfied with the writer he had become: "I'm tired of myself as my own laboratory. After all, I've been in that laboratory for twenty years now." Asked whether he feared that campaigning would harm his literary style, Mailer made a revealing statement about why he had entered the race for mayor: Speaking of literary people, he suggested, "There's too much of the hothouse about us all. When you've got a world that's disintegrating around you, if you're a man and you're leading a life that is self-protected to a degree, you really can't feel too agreeable about yourself. So I got over bleating about the loss of my style in a few days. God willing, I'll get it back."

Mailer took James Wechsler's criticism of his campaign very personally. He resented Wechsler's dubbing him and Breslin "The Odd Couple." The phrase had a homosexual ring that provoked Mailer to say, "One doesn't work for one's manhood for forty-six years in order to have it sneered over by a liberal columnist writing in his cubicle." Wechsler and other liberals were isolated from reality—the very suspicion Mailer had of himself, a suspicion he constantly tried to dispel by his daring exploits, his identification with the underclass.

Joe Flaherty puzzled over his candidate's "one-way love affair with street types" who called themselves revolutionaries while drinking up Mailer's liquor, speaking incoherently, and pretending to an understanding of society manifestly belied by their disorganized and incompetent behavior. "If someone had been part of an experience foreign to his own (being black, a convict, a prizefighter), Mailer found in him occult powers bestowed only on the children of the gutters." Gloria Steinem remembers Mailer's defense of a rather brutal "hanger-on" characteristic of the violent types doing the campaign no good. She wondered why Mailer did not get rid of him and seek out thoughtful people who knew how to advise a mayoral candidate? "I'll be devoted to this guy the rest of my life because I once saw him in a fight, he was getting knocked down again and again, and he kept getting up." Steinem feels that Mailer never forgave her for a retort that punctured his illusions: "Norman, anybody who's grown up in a poor neighborhood could tell you he should have stayed down."

Near the end of the campaign, enough money was scraped together to put on a fifteen-minute television broadcast, "Mailer–Breslin Live!" Breslin, now sharing Mailer's mania to win the election, contributed seventeen hundred dollars of his own money to finance his half of the show. The set was simple: There would be blowups of the two candidates taken by their campaign photographer, Richard Frank. Like a Mailer movie, there would be no script, no rehearsal, no notes: "You'll talk for the first seven minutes, and I'll talk for the other eight," Mailer told Breslin. The crew in the studio were tense, not knowing what to expect. CBS had stationed a lawyer in the sound booth prepared to pull the plug at the first word that suggested Mailer would resort to his favorite expletive, *fuck*. When Flaherty arrived at the studio, he observed Breslin fortified with coffee, a cigar, and a note pad and talking to himself. Mailer was exuberant, obviously looking forward to another one of his existential encounters. He was not pleased when the technicians told him it would be better if he did not rise from his chair during the show, and he stepped out to get a drink. In the control booth the debate centered on whether to do a pan of the studio audience, a group of fifty people who were not exactly the standard political gathering. The director was worried about how it would look—the ethnic dress and the Afros—and decided not to do it.

Breslin began with his favorite theme: the tensions between blacks and whites and the fear his opposition had injected into the campaign. He gave his usual aggressive performance but forgot to say his prearranged exit line. The camera in closeup revealed a silent Breslin, and in panic over this dead air the control room switched to Mailer, who suddenly jumped up from his chair, almost knocking his head against the mike boom. As Flaherty recalls, "The booth sounded like a poultry slaughterhouse. Shrieks emitted from every chair: 'Jesus he's up.' " Between switching cameras and the mike boom they barely managed to keep up with the candidate—at one point, however, only the air above the candidates' heads was showing. Mailer prowled the set, making his points with a jabbing left hand and crowning his speech with the announcement that he and Breslin had just received the most important endorsement of the day from Joe Namath, who "is as nutty as we are." Flaherty remembers Breslin, still sitting on the set in the background, burying his head in his hands, "rocking to and fro as if he were sitting shiva," and the director screaming, "What is he doing? Somebody, somebody, tell me what he is doing." Beverly's comment on the evening to Flaherty: "One thing you can say, he wasn't plastic."

In the end, Mailer finished fourth out of five candidates, garnering just over forty-one thousand votes, with Breslin doing slightly better. At one point, a poll had them up as much as a hundred thousand votes, and there was some sentiment that they had peaked too early. It was, in many ways, a noble defeat. Mailer stood by Breslin, a desultory campaigner, often late for his appearances or a no-show. Gloria Steinem was impressed with his kindness and sense of honor. She realized her picture of Mailer did not "square with surly, insulting, paranoid Mailer of occasional parties and the Village Gate." She had no satisfactory explanation, except to suggest that "perhaps we should accept his theory that you pay for everything, that you must be willing to sink down as far as the heights you would learn how to climb."

As Joe Flaherty puts it, when Mailer was "good he was very, very good." He loved to get into the neighborhoods, to swap stories but mostly to listen to what people had on their minds. At a Puerto Rican club on the Lower East Side, he reminisced about the summer he had lived there with Adele, building his own apartment. He had taken real joy in his accomplishment, and he wanted the people of this neighborhood to know that as mayor he would try to give them the same opportunity he had. To be honest, however, he had to point out that the community would have to respect the rights of other people—like the hippies who had recently moved in and who might choose to "make love on top of cars." To Flaherty's surprise, the old Puerto Rican couples "howled and raucously poked each other with their elbows, so that no one in the hall would miss what he had said." Flaherty thought they welcomed Mailer's honesty. He did not "pander to them or ethnically try to shill them." He was telling them what he really thought of the city, and they appreciated his candor. At such moments he was indeed the embodiment of his ideas and of his campaign slogan: "No more bullshit."

OF A FIRE ON THE MOON

Beverly had not shown much enthusiasm for Mailer's mayoral campaign, although Flaherty remembers her getting excited about health issues: "She was always screaming about the air." One day while one of her kids was vomiting, she kept saying, "It's the fucking air! Look at the air outside!" She loyally attended the most important events, but afterward fought with her husband. She had put on weight and continued to worry about her waning career. Sometimes Beverly's public quarreling with her husband seemed itself like an act—an impromptu version of a Tennessee Williams play. "They'd played this game of Big Daddy and Maggie the Cat so many times they weren't aware of it," says Flaherty. Norman, also overweight, seemed just as upset. Seven weeks of a grueling campaign had frayed his nerves.

In the fall, Mailer's absence from home, traveling between Cape Canaveral and Houston covering the moon shot, only made matters worse. Beverly thought the book a bad idea and wanted him to drop it. Beverly told Charlie Brown that besides Carol Stevens, Norman was "fucking" some stewardess. When Beverly took off for Mexico pursuing an affair with a race-car driver, Carol came to Provincetown and even had dinner with Mailer's aunt and uncle, visiting from South Africa. Carol came sporadically to town, yet Mailer seemed unconsoled. "The funny thing about this is that I'm probably going to grow old alone," he confided to Sandy Charlebois Thomas, who had the job of taking care of Michael and Stephen during Beverly's absence.

Mailer confided in Jose Torres about Beverly's affair: "I told her to take a trip with him to find out if she's really in love." To Torres this was "bullshit," and he told Mailer so: It was something that should not be tolerated in a wife. Even if Norman won Beverly back, Torres said he would have nothing to do with her. She could not be trusted: "Norman, we're different. You may feel she's right because you had girlfriends. But with me that doesn't matter."

Barbara Probst Solomon believes that Norman really felt badly about Beverly. For him a marriage had to be "central," and when it failed "your whole universe crumbles." His sister, Barbara, once told Solomon that she thought her brother's trouble was that "he tended to overinvest his wives with what he wanted them to be—in effect he idealized them." Sandy Charlebois Thomas called Norman's relationship with Beverly "one of the great love affairs of the world," and that is why the disintegration of their marriage devastated both of them.

Needing the money but also bothered by his ineffective treatment of the moon shot, Mailer became depressed. He had had misgivings when Willie Morris first proposed that he write about the astronauts for *Harper's*. How could Mailer participate in such an event? After all, he was not going to the moon. Yet the epic quality of the voyage and the big money Scott Meredith was able to obtain for a magazine serial ($100,000) and hardcover and paperback publication ($400,000 each) proved impossible to pass up. With a college degree in aeronautical engineering and the profound feelings about the moon he had put into *An American Dream*, Mailer might just be right for the job.

Of a Fire on the Moon is divided into three parts: "Aquarius," "Apollo," and "The Age of Aquarius." As the titles of the sections suggest, the book begins by introducing its narrator, Norman Mailer, who dubs himself Aquarius because he is born under that astrological sign and because in this period of his life he sees himself as surrendering his personality to a time in history that may redefine human nature and the nature of the world. Mailer suggests that he suffers a loss of ego before the enormity of the moon shot. This is a historic voyage that may mark either a new beginning for the human race or possibly its end depending on how it responds to the new technology. Part II concentrates on the astronauts, on their moon voyage, and on their technological environment at NASA. Here Mailer commits himself to detailed descriptions of the science and engineering of the flight while speculating on how the human psyche has been affected by the rigid demands of a technological environment. Part III (much shorter than the preceding parts) puts the primary focus on the narrator and suggests his need to somehow encompass the moon shot with his own personality, to make it—as he so often says of the astronauts—an "instrument" of his own will.

Mailer's frustration with the people in the space program has to do with their jargon. The astronauts feel uncomfortable when asked about their personal reactions. Being part of a team, part of NASA, means suppressing individuality. As Mailer puts it, "Yes, real Americans always spoke in code. They encapsulated themselves into technological clans." The result, however, is to make the moon shot seem unreal. Surely Mike Collins, the astronaut who had to stay in the spaceship while his colleagues descended in a specially designed vehicle to the moon, must have felt some envy or regret over not going himself. Yet Collins would not allow himself to suggest he might be disappointed.

Unfortunately, the astronauts are circumspect. The complexity of their situation is unprecedented, Mailer supposes, and this accounts for their unwillingness to risk anything like an original or a daring thought. Their press conferences are boring to most of the press, yet Mailer probes for a rather intriguing speculation on the astronauts' dilemma: "Now it was as if they did not know if they were athletes, test pilots, engineers, corporation executives, some new kind of priest, or sheepish American boys caught in a position of outlandish prominence—my God, how did they ever get into this?"

Several astronauts have been test pilots, superb physical specimens ready for the rigors of space travel. Some of them have engineering degrees; some are already administrators. They are treated as heroes, and they are somewhat embarrassed by their publicity. Even on the subject of their own deaths they are silent or they attempt to obfuscate their answers to questions about the danger of their mission. Rather than speaking of their "personal disasters," they employ euphemisms such as *contingency*. This use of language to mask reality disturbs Mailer, who points out that Nazis and Communists have made a similar use of words, resorting to terms like *liquidation* to refer to *mass murder*. As a writer, he fears the damage to the human psyche when "words, like pills, were there to suppress emotional symptoms."

Mailer's forte is to find the contradictions of the moon voyage: the astronauts have been picked for their prowess and virility, yet in space they are "passive bodies." In their preparations for space travel, they have submitted to every kind of hazardous experiment: "They were done to, they were done to like no healthy man alive," he suggests. They eat out of plastic tubes filled with mushed edibles resembling baby food. They are as awkwardly confined in their bulky space suits as trussed-up infants still in diapers. They are protected by every kind of technology, still their voyage could result in their deaths. In this respect, they are simply intensified examples of the technological twentieth century, which contains "huge contradictions . . . profound and accelerating opposites." Technology has made it possible for people to live in the utmost comfort and safety while destroying their environment. This is why, in Mailer's view, the moon shot can be interpreted as forecasting an "exceptional future" and the "real possibility of global destruction."

Although the journey to the moon is an apocalyptic event, Mailer notices that the astronauts refuse to romanticize their roles—as if "technology and the absence of emotion . . . were the only fit mates for the brave." These spacemen are entirely too rational for Mailer's taste, which matches that of the press who keep goading the astronauts to say something heroic or daring.

The space program is a triumph of engineering and science, but it troubles Mailer that the public will take NASA's accomplishments as proof of the superiority of science. Referring to his own education as an engineer, he points out the fallacy of thinking of science as "an exact study with certain knowledge." On the contrary, scientists know relatively little about the structure of the world or about the nature of things. Science can measure nature, but it rarely reveals nature's secrets.

Mailer presses his point by showing how nearly every space flight has suffered by unaccounted-for failures and near-fatalities. And while NASA has employed extraordinary precautions to protect the astronauts, he suggests "some very large chances have been taken" in the space program's quest to make good on President's Kennedy's goal of landing men on the moon by the end of the 1960s. Astronauts have died in a fire on a launch pad; various manned capsules have spilled fuel, failed to fire their rockets properly, and suffered various malfunctions in guidance systems and communications.

Although he sees the flaws in space exploration, Mailer realizes the results of the moon trip may be spectacular. He also wants to honor the efforts of men who, in spite of their bureaucratic talk, are plumbing the mysteries of the universe. Indeed, one of Mailer's aims is to revive a sense of wonder out of which the moon quest has sprung. And characteristically he puts the sense of wonder into a question: "Who was to say it was not the first step back to the stars, first step back to joining that mysterious interior material of the stars, that iron of communion with cosmic origins?" When he verges on the mystical, Mailer checks himself by refusing to make sweeping statements. His prose, like the moon shot, is an exploratory voyage.

Ever on the alert for signs of stress in the highly controlled technicians who guide the moon shot, Mailer notes that their hands are "clammy to the touch." Even in the professionally cool NASA environment, he senses the "aisles of quiet fear," the tension in the men who work on the functions of computers that were "always in as much danger of going awry as society is in danger of some final collapse into crime." Like juvenile delinquents, these men had to check for "sneak circuits" capable of interacting "in ways no one had foreseen."

At almost five hundred printed pages, *Of a Fire on the Moon* is a bloated book. "It is a technical fact that when a writer is working under stress he is apt to write too much," Calder Willingham notes. The best passages in the moon book are descriptive, where Mailer simply allows himself to describe the ascent of Apollo 11 into space, or where his engineering sense stimulates him to provide fascinating insights into how machines are put together. The worst passages are his philosophical flights, where he nags the question of whether the new technology is the harbinger of man's heroic triumph or his destruction of nature. In the end, the moon shot is an event more complex than Mailer can handle and hardly amenable to the good/evil antinomies he would like to force upon it.

THE PRISONER OF SEX

By the spring of 1970, the moon book completed after a hard winter of writing in Provincetown, Mailer departed for Maine for a six-week vacation, taking with him five of his six children: Dandy (thirteen), Betsy (ten), Kate (seven), Michael (six), and Stephen (four). Only Susan (twenty-one), his oldest daughter by Bea, would not be with him, since she had decided to spend her summer in Europe. His children would join him in an effort to see if he could manage "so large a home"—a daunting task that had contributed to dooming his fourth marriage. He would put his career on hold, forsake his personal life and household help, and rely on himself and his children to do the "shopping, cooking, and cleaning." When a "good Maine woman" turned up, familiar with his rented house and adept at all these chores, Mailer's resolution to go it alone was quickly abandoned. Then his sister arrived to help him for two weeks and his "dearest old love," Carol Stevens, came for a visit and ended up staying the summer, for she filled "some critical abyss in the well-concealed hole of his heart." In August she would became pregnant and Mailer felt it necessary to tell Beverly, who declared later, "That was the final split."

Mailer tells this story about himself in the third person at the beginning of *The Prisoner of Sex*, which is, in Robert Solotaroff's words, a "much cleaner work" than the moon book—not only two-thirds shorter but also "consistently genial" and perceptive, particularly when Mailer is writing about literary matters and his idiosyncrasies. He is once again the flawed "hero-creator" of his own life and literature, revealing his inability to meet his highest expectations for himself—in this case as the hero of his domestic life. Although he will try in *The Prisoner of Sex* to see things from the woman's point of view, he will remain infuriatingly male—if not exactly incorrigible, certainly less than eager to give up his masculine prerogatives.

In Maine, Mailer and his mistress (his word for Carol Stevens) "alternated duty days in the kitchen"—a setup that did not displease him when he reflected on the fact that Beverly had rarely been without help in managing the house. But Carol had a much different personality. She had first met Mailer after his breakup with Adele in 1961. Carol sang jazz and the blues in clubs, and at least one of her friends feels that Mailer did not marry her because of her strong career commitment. Yet the dark-haired beauty remained loyal to him throughout his marriages to Lady Jeanne and Beverly. Carol sounded like Cherry in *An American Dream* when she told a friend that she and Mailer had a "true American love story, an historic love affair." She believed that nothing, in the end, could separate them. *The Prisoner of Sex* is dedicated to her. Anne Barry remembers that Carol sang in a "rather sweet, tenuous voice." In Barry's presence, she was quiet, hard to read, and did not seem to have much in common with Mailer's other wives.

Mailer describes his six familial weeks in Maine in glowing, idyllic terms. He loved being the proud father, admiring how well his children did their chores and entertained each other. It made him wonder what it would have been like to be born a woman, but he had no illusion that he had really plumbed the precincts of femininity or motherhood; rather, he had escaped, temporarily, the contemplation of his own ego and could say that "he knew at last what a woman meant when she said her hair smelled of grease."

Into this waking dream of domesticity in Maine intruded a call from a *Time* editor asking for Mailer's thoughts on women's liberation. An interview, even a cover story now, appealed to him. He could plug the release of *Maidstone*, but—wary of *Time*'s tendency to chop up and distort his comments—he demurred. For the past year he had sensed that he was becoming the main target of feminists, even though he professed surprise, asking Gloria Steinem during an Algonquin lunch what women could have against him. "You might try reading your books some day," she replied. Other run-ins (during the mayoral campaign Bella Abzug had told him, "Your views on women are full of shit") and his discovery of Kate Millett's picture on the cover of *Time* goaded him into taking a look at the new literature on women.

Mailer disliked Millett's reductive characterizations of his work (*"An American Dream* is an exercise in how to kill your wife and be happy ever after") but admired the vigor of the new literature, remarking that "a few of the women were writing in no way women had written before." Not until Mailer read the section devoted to him in *Sexual Politics* did he become riled up enough to strike back. Continuing her attack on *An American Dream*, Millett charges that "female sexuality is depersonalized to the point of being a matter of class or a matter of nature." Ruta, the German maid and proletarian, is the stereotypical "guttersnipe" and Deborah a "cruel duchess." Rojack, on the other hand, lords it over all and transcends "any such typology." Somehow, Millett contends, sodomizing Ruta is all right in Mailer's view, for evil "resides in her bowels. . . . Why Ruta has a greater share of it than her master may appear difficult to explain, but many uncanny things are possible with our author," Millett notes sarcastically. She clearly wants to cut Mailer down to size:

> As he settles into patriarchal middle age, Mailer's obsession with ma- chismo brings to mind a certain curio sold in Coney Island and called a Peter Meter; a quaint bit of folk art, stamped out in the shape of a ruler with printed inches and appropriate epithets to equate excellence with size. Mailer operates on this scale on an abstract or metaphoric plane. His characters, male and female, labor under simpler delusions. Guin- evere is indefatigable on the subject of her lover's "whangs"; D.J. is paralyzed with the usual fear that someone else has a bigger one.

Mailer's rebuttal in *The Prisoner of Sex* takes two forms: a keen literary analysis of Millett's other targets (Henry Miller and D. H. Lawrence) that effectively demonstrates how she rips her quotations out of context and virtually rewrites the scenes she describes and a direct attack on "the land of Millett . . . a barren and mediocre terrain, its flora reminiscent of a Ph.D. tract, its roads a narrow argument, and its horizon low." Shrewdly, Mailer does not engage in much special pleading for his work and rarely answers Millett's specific indictment of him. Instead, he concentrates on Lawrence and Miller, treating them as his literary betters who have been trashed by an unworthy mind.

Millett refers in *Sexual Politics* to Mailer's prose as "based on a set of values . . . blatantly and comically chauvinist." He returns the favor in *The Prisoner of Sex* with a denigrating catalogue of epithets. She becomes a "pug-nosed wit," "the perfect gun" of literary analysis, one of the "literary lawyers [who] cannot do criticism, they can only write briefs," the "mouthpiece for a corporate body of ideas," and spreader of the "moralisms of Millett." With a mind "like a flatiron," she has a "squirt bomb at the ready" to attack Henry Miller's prose. Occasionally Mailer gives her her due, referring to "sturdy Millett" and giving her a condescending "pat on the back . . . for collecting such prime questions."

Mailer is at his funniest in jousting with Millett, and he piles up points in showing that the male literary imagination is more subtle and more various than she is willing to admit, but he pales into irrelevance in his mystical flights about the differences between the sexes, in his worries that "lab assistant" Kate would obliterate sexual differences in her harping on technology, on the ways women can control their ability to conceive and deny themselves what he deems to be distinctively feminine characteristics.

Perhaps what gets Mailer into most trouble is his suggestion that "the prime responsibility of a woman is to be on earth enough to find the best mate for herself, and conceive children who will improve the species." In 1986, Mailer remarked that he had meant to go "in and out of this question" and that his statement was speculative, a "maybe," a "51–49" decision. There were other "balancing factors," he conceded. Even in the conjectural mode, however, Mailer's remarks, as Joyce Carol Oates observes in a review of *The Prisoner of Sex*, are "dangerous." He is "shameless in his passion for women," she notes; they become the object of his visionary, poetic, and mystical sensibility, and "dehumanized." Must women necessarily be thought of as ovums, as carriers of the species? Oates asks. What of their character as artists and expressive human beings? Why is Mailer so deterministic, so intent on attaching women's minds to their bodies? Why is it so wrong, Oates wonders, for women to "protest that sexual identity is the least significant aspect of our lives" and that "technology might make our lives less physical and more spiritual"? "We don't know what the *species* is," Oates points out: "A scientific concept? A mystical concept? A word? An identity? An essence?" In short, she objects to the unexamined terms of Mailer's argument.

Oates quarrels with Mailer's effort to compartmentalize women. "The only reality," she asserts, "is personality. Not sex." Like men, women have a multitude of personalities; they are individuals, and she resents the notion that they should be defined by "the mechanisms for reproducing the species." Some of the women writing the new feminist literature are guilty of the same practice, Oates notes, by suggesting there is a single male perspective. Conceptions of "maleness" and "femaleness" are a trap, not a route to liberation.

The birth of Maggie Alexandra to Carol Stevens on March 21, 1971, made Mailer a father for the seventh time. It was his first child by Carol, after having fathered one daughter with Bea, two daughters with Adele, and two sons with Beverly. True to the principles of *The Prisoner of Sex*, Mailer regretted having his infant daughter inoculated against diphtheria. He had been "caught at a weak moment" when his defenses were down. The doctor had prevailed by pointing out that an infant's "discomfort" from the shot would last only "a few hours." To do it later at the age of four or five would probably result in a one- or two-day illness. Mailer had wanted to suggest that perhaps something in the economy of existence dictated that certain people died of diphtheria, but he knew that the doctor would receive such an outrageous remark with "slant eyes." Mailer was troubled because he had permitted his daughter to slip into the "technological chain of being." He did not like the idea of all of those chemicals infesting her body and setting off that precarious cycle of artificial equilibrium and disequilibrium that disturbed him about modern health care. No one could predict the ultimate impact of these substances on the body, Mailer reasoned—although his gut feeling was that each new drug depleted one's ability to recover a natural, healthy

balance. For him, the evil of this kind of technology might be worse than
the diseases it eradicated.

"The Prisoner of Sex," published in the March 1971 issue of *Harper's*,
notched up the debate on women's liberation. More copies of it were sold
than any other in *Harper's* history, and by the end of the month Mailer
had decided to pit himself against his opponents in a public debate at
Town Hall in New York City. Kate Millett had refused to come, for she
was dismayed at how Mailer had made her sensibility the subject of his
book. Germaine Greer, on the other hand, welcomed the opportunity to
best Mailer at his own self-promotional game. Jill Johnson, a radical
feminist and a *Village Voice* columnist, Diana Trilling, and Jackie
Ceballos, president of the National Organization of Women, made up
the panel that Mailer would moderate.

Trilling was alternately amused and irritated by the "half boss-man
and half Old World gallant" role Mailer had taken on for the evening. She
disliked Greer, whom she described as "wearing a floozy kind of fox fur
that trailed over her shoulder to the floor. It was mangy. I expected moths
to fly out of it." Greer had gotten Mailer to pose with a copy of her book,
The Female Eunuch, for the cameras, and the word was out that she would
try to seduce him. Trilling got a kiss from her old friend but felt estranged
from him in the hyped-up atmosphere. Adele and Lady Jeanne were in the
audience, as were a host of New York notables including Arthur Schlesinger, Jr., Jules Feiffer, Susan Sontag, and Elizabeth Hardwick. The
event was filmed, and of course the press was present, but there was not
much of a debate. The speakers took their predictable positions, with
Trilling providing the most incisive criticism of "The Prisoner of Sex."
In Greer's view, Mailer acted like a "carnival barker," at home with his
New York audience and not terribly worried that they would attack much
of what he said; he was still, after all, one of their own. Sandra Kraskin,
now going through her own "ardent feminist phase," reacted in disgust to
the Norman Mailer who "just sat up there and said provocative things.
It wasn't the Norman Mailer I had known at all, and I realized then
that there was no publicity value in just agreeing with and supporting
women. . . . He was being contrary but doing it in a chivalrous way."

Any serious purpose that might have developed during the evening
was destroyed when two of Jill Johnson's lesbian friends jumped up onto
the stage and treated the audience to the sight of "three pretty solid

women embracing with more ardor than aim," as Trilling puts it, "hugging and kissing" and rolling around until they fell off the stage. An angered Mailer started to approach the threesome, bellowing to Johnson that she "get up and act like a lady!" Trilling thought he was about to pull them apart and hissed at him, "Don't touch them!" Instead, he remarked, "You can get as much prick and cunt as you want around the corner on Forty-second Street for two dollars and fifty cents. We don't need it here." Although Susan Sontag berated him for using the word *lady* and he got his share of other barbs, it was amazing how tenderly he was treated by the feminists; they indulged him "as if he were a little boy," Greer remembers.

Greer did not get her chance to seduce Mailer. Instead, she met his parents at a West Village party and admired their simplicity and reserve, noting the pride his mother took in him. Greer felt she had glimpsed a genuine, deep-rooted side of him not visible in his public foolery. "I liked him better for his mother," Greer later wrote in *Esquire*.

In rethinking the debate and "The Prisoner of Sex," it occurred to Greer that Mailer had written so sensitively about D. H. Lawrence because his words about Lawrence could be applied to himself: "locked into the body of a middling male physique, not physically strong, of reasonable good looks, a pleasant to somewhat seedy-looking man, no stud." Greer discovered passage after passage in "The Prisoner of Sex" ostensibly about Lawrence but actually about Mailer himself:

> For his mind was possessed of that intolerable masculine pressure which develops in sons outrageously beloved of their mothers—to be the equal of a woman at twelve or six or any early age which reaches equilibrium between the will of the son and the will of the mother is all but to guarantee the making of a future tyrant, for the sense of where to find one's inner health has been generated by the early years of that equilibrium—its substitute will not be easy to create in maturity. What can then be large enough to serve as proper balance to a man who was equal to a strong woman in emotional confidence at the age of eight? Hitlers develop out of such balance derived from imbalance, and great generals and great novelists (for what is a novelist but a general who sends his troops across fields of paper?).

Greer had struck at the very nerve of Mailer's career: to find an ego outside the home that could be as strong as the one his mother had made for him. His affinity for military metaphors, for the heroic march of fascist generals and soldiers, and for a view of writing and of a writing career as a war stand revealed in his biographical interpretation of Lawrence. In other passages, Mailer makes the identification between himself and Lawrence even stronger: "One senses in his petulance and in the spoiled airs of his impatient disdain . . . a momma's boy, spoiled rotten," who "could not have commanded two infantrymen to follow him, yet he was still a great writer." In Lawrence Mailer saw his infirmities and his hopes for himself, and in his attachment to Henry Miller Mailer saw the graphic representation of his conflicted feelings about sex and maternity. Again, it is Greer, better than anyone else, who recognizes the problem:

> The concept of the worshiped feminine which holds the Prisoner of Sex in thrall is the Omnipotent Mother. To this day Mailer's relationship with his mother is important: when he confesses that he has never been able to live without a woman, it is not just sex and company that he needs but nurture. The near-equal war, a brutal bloody war with wounds growing within and the surgeons collecting the profit from either sex is still the antagonism between the formidable mother and the questing boy child. The goat kicking lust which drove Henry Miller into one woman after another is "man's sense of awe before woman."

No wonder that before the Town Hall debate Greer had announced her desire to carry Mailer "like a wounded child across the wasted world." She had sensed how deeply his need for a woman and his fear of inadequacy were intertwined.

Not surprisingly, *The Prisoner of Sex* received mixed reviews. What bothered Mailer most was not the attack on this particular book but the occasion it provided for a host of writers to draw certain conclusions about his career that capped, in his mind, twenty-five years of distortion. The worst offender was Gore Vidal, a contemporary with whom Mailer had always been on good, if wary, terms. When Vidal learned he could not review *The Prisoner of Sex* for *Harper's* because it had already been assigned, he chose to express his opinion in the July 22, 1971, issue of *The New York Review of Books*:

> There has been from Henry Miller to Norman Mailer to Charles Manson a logical progression. The Miller–Mailer–Manson man, or M3 for

short, has been conditioned to think of women as, at best, breeders of
sons, at worst, objects to be poked, humiliated, killed.

When Mailer read the passage he felt "something blow in his brain." He took it as a deliberate and crude provocation and welcomed the opportunity to appear with Vidal on *The Dick Cavett Show* in December.

In the green room before the show Mailer felt Vidal's "tender and caressing hand on the back of his neck." Vidal had never put a hand on Mailer before, and although Mailer accepted the gesture as friendly, he replied with "an openhanded tap across the cheek." Vidal responded with a slap, surprising Mailer, who flashed a smile, leaned forward with a hand on Vidal's neck and butted him "hard in the head." Vidal said Mailer was crazy. Mailer told him to shut up. "You *are* violent," Vidal countered. "I'll see you on the show," Mailer said as Vidal quickly left the room.

From the start of the program, Mailer was out of control, managing to insult not only Vidal but also fellow guest Janet Flanner and Cavett as well as the studio audience—asking them at one point, "Are you all really truly idiots or is it me?" It was him, the audience assured Mailer. Flailing at Vidal, Mailer failed to get him to read the aggravating passage from *The New York Review*. Vidal temporized, adding qualifiers to what he had originally said and even praising Mailer's writing while regretting the tendency of his work to celebrate violence and demean women. Incredibly, Mailer almost won back the audience—not by the eloquence of his words but by the sheer force of his feeling that he was a misrepresented man. Dropping his specific quarrel with Vidal, he faced the audience directly, frankly admitting his "extraordinary arrogance and loutishness and crudeness," but also pointing out that he had boldly ventured his opinions, declaring himself the literary champ willing to take on all comers. Rather than being challenged in a fair fight he had had to face cowards who kicked him "in the nuts." He was soundly applauded but threw the moment away by standing over a flinching Vidal, snatching the page of *The New York Review* out of his hands, and reading out loud Vidal's passage lumping together Miller, Mailer, and Manson as M3. The show ended in much laughter, with Mailer lamely trying to explain that Rojack "did not simply bugger a woman, he entered her the other way as well and there was a particularly complicated—" "Oh, goodness' sake," an exasperated Janet Flanner remarked, to the vast amusement of the audience.

When it came to a quick retort, Mailer was simply not in Cavett's league:

> MAILER: *Why don't you look at your question sheet and ask a question.*
> CAVETT: *Why don't you fold it five ways and put it where the moon don't shine.*

Cavett had the laughs even as Mailer said to him, "On your word of honor, did you just make that up or have you had it canned for years and were you waiting for the best moment to use it?" To even more laughter, Cavett came back with "I have to tell you a quote from Tolstoy."

It was Mailer's worst evening on television—a medium he has never mastered. Usually his comments are too convoluted or too abrupt as he nervously shifts for some point of vantage. Vidal's accusations were a clever variation on Millett's charges and took hold in an intellectual world swayed by *The New York Review* and entertained by the cute wordplay of Dick Cavett.

After the disaster on the Cavett show, Richard Poirier wrote a perceptive essay noting that (unlike most literary figures) Mailer did not recognize the limits of literature. Vidal knew, Poirier pointed out, that the literary imagination cannot dominate a nonliterary medium like television, which is not "easily hospitable to your impulses to self-expression, your needs to vindicate yourself by elaborated and complex explanations." Vidal and Flanner played by the rules of talk-showdom while Mailer mistakenly thought he could redress an injustice done to him by Vidal in *The New York Review of Books*. Many people in the literary community wondered why Mailer had made such a big deal about a single book review. Why should a writer as important as Mailer seem so shaken? "I found that bewildering and began to wonder if we were not given a public glimpse of some private collapse," Bruce Cook remarked in *The National Observer* (November 4, 1972).

EXISTENTIAL ERRANDS

In spite of accomplishing much solid work since the publication of *The Armies of the Night*, the debacle on the Cavett show revealed Mailer's penchant for presenting himself in public as a goof. He had been fighting a losing battle against events, unable to dominate the political

conventions, the mayor's race, the moon shot, or the dialogue on femi-
nism as he had encompassed the march on the Pentagon. A sure sign of
his literary slough was his decision to cover the presidential conventions of 1972. At the Democratic convention he went around, according to Gary Wills, expressing his fear that he was repeating himself.
The result, *St. George and the Godfather*, is indeed a lackluster
performance—rather dull except for some sharp portraits of George
Wallace, Hubert Humphrey, Henry Kissinger, and Nixon. Mailer favors
Nixon, for it is Mailer's conceit that Nixon's hand can be seen even in the
minutest details of the convention's schedule. But even here not much is
added to the incisive portrait of Nixon in *Miami and the Siege of
Chicago*.

As Mailer admitted in his essay collection for this period, *Existential
Errands* (1972), he kept diverting his desire to begin "a certain big
novel which had been promised for a long time" by having his "immediate say on contemporary matters." He had, then, a "philosophy . . .
being put together in many pieces." *Existential Errands* has few memorable parts and is inferior to his earlier collections. "King of the Hill,"
an account of the first Muhammad Ali–Joe Frazier fight, is the strongest
work, demonstrating a powerful feeling for biography. Calling Ali
"America's greatest ego" Mailer portrays him as the first twentieth-
century hero to dominate the media and the minds of "mass man."
Writing at a time when Ali was hated at least as much as he was loved,
controversial because of his allegiance to Elijah Muhammad and the
Black Muslims and condemned for abandoning his name Cassius Clay,
Mailer emphasizes that the wit Ali expresses with his body is equal to
the exercise of a great intelligence. Ali has refined his moves to make
him "the first psychologist of the body." In his finest descriptive passage, Mailer defines a repertory of Ali's skills parallel to the different
styles Mailer has tried to master as a writer:

> *So Clay punched with a greater variety of mixed intensities than anyone
> around, he played with punches, was tender with them, laid them on as
> delicately as you put a postage stamp on an envelope, then cracked them
> in like a riding crop across your face, stuck a cruel jab like a baseball
> bat held head on into your mouth, next waltzed you in a clinch with a
> tender arm around your neck, winged away out of reach on flying legs,
> dug a hook with the full swing of a baseball bat hard into your ribs,*

hard pokes of a jab into the face, a mocking soft flurry of pillows and
gloves, a mean forearm cutting you off from coming up on him, a cruel
wrestling of your neck in a clinch, then elusive again, gloves snake-
licking your face like a whip.

Having perfected his own boxing style with Jose Torres, Mailer was able
to appreciate just how sly and subtle a boxer Ali had become—fooling,
confusing, frustrating, and wearing down his opponents before he
punched them out. The vividness of Mailer's figures, his switch to the
second person making readers feel what it must have been like to be
punished by Ali and sense that boxing itself can serve as a metaphor for
the ego's mastery of environment, make this single long sentence in
"King of the Hill" an embodiment of what he had tried to tell Cavett's
audience about being "the champ."

Ali had his bad moments—he had been floored by Frazier in the
fifteenth round—but he had finished the fight and Mailer rightly sensed
that Ali would be victorious in the rematch. The boxer and the writer
had extraordinary resilience, and Mailer would yet come back from his
worst performances to give some of his best. He was rather like El Loco,
the Mexican matador who is the subject of an essay on bullfighting in
Existential Errands. Mailer loved to watch him fight:

He was so bad when he was bad that he gave the impression you could
fight a bull yourself and do no worse. So when he was good, you felt as if
you were good too.

Mailer was still seeking a way to elevate personality over technology,
the self over society, reveling in the eccentricities that gave evidence of
originality. He conceded that this is a "romantic self-pitying impractical
approach to the twentieth century's demand for predictable ethics, high
production, dependability of function, and categorization of impulse,"
but he believed in the Latin "allegiance . . . to the genius of the blood."

10.

MARILYN
(1972–1973)

SIZING UP THE OPPOSITION

Now separated from Beverly (it would be several years before they divorced), Mailer spent the summer months of 1972 with Carol Stevens in Vermont. Jose Torres rented a house nearby; he was writing a book on Muhammad Ali, *Sting Like a Bee*. Torres proposed boxing lessons in exchange for editorial assistance. Each day Torres wrote from seven to nine in the morning, boxed with Mailer for an hour before lunch, wrote in the afternoon, and returned to Mailer's house in the evening for discussion of his manuscript. Mailer asked questions but would not tell Torres what to do. Write it the way you say it was Mailer's advice when he and Torres went over passages with problems. Sometimes all Torres got was a curt "This is no good." Torres would have to figure out how to do it better. "Still no good," Mailer would say after another attempt. "That's what I want," a smiling Mailer would finally say when he was pleased. In the end, Torres was enormously grateful: "He was teaching me not how to think or what to think but to think."

In return Torres took enormous pains with his pupil, who "learned fast." Cus D'Amato, Torres's manager and trainer, sometimes watched the two, picking up on things in Mailer's style that Torres might miss. Mailer was "very serious" and would get frustrated, trying combinations against Torres that could not possibly connect, urging Torres: "Jose, c'mon, don't hold back." When Mailer flailed away, Torres would sometimes laugh and say to D'Amato: "Norman comes at you with such feeling." Mailer never seemed embarrassed by his mistakes. "Mostly he would get irritated with himself. He was driving himself, demanding performance," recalls D'Amato, who admired Mailer's willingness to carry fights through to a conclusion even if he did not have the advantage. Mailer did not fear getting marked and willingly absorbed pain. Torres noticed that while he tried to control fear, Mailer tried to block it altogether and dominate it with his ego. His main fault as a fighter, in Torres's estimation, was his tendency to intellectualize, to presume he could control a fight mentally. Fights, in Torres's experience, could not be planned.

Buzz Farbar and his wife visited Norman and Carol that summer in Vermont. Mailer and Farbar boxed, with Jose Torres as the referee. Mailer carefully picked his sparring partners. Either he chose someone so good that he would think it "obscene" to hurt Mailer or a friend who tried to "bring out the best" in them as boxers. Farbar and Mailer had developed a rather tense relationship since the founding of their film production company, Supreme Mix (based on the name of the Hollywood studio in *The Deer Park*, Supreme Pictures), but Torres thought he could trust the much stronger Farbar not to injure Mailer. Torres got "scared" when it became clear that Farbar was trying to knock Mailer out. Mailer had no headgear, but he seemed to be slipping punches well—although Torres was not confident about how much Mailer had learned about boxing and feared that one of Farbar's KO punches might connect. Farbar remembers using a street-fighting style to rough Mailer up, and Mailer retaliated with a tremendous punch to Farbar's head that broke his thumb. While Mailer soaked it in ice, his mother hovered fiercely over Farbar, yelling, "He broke his hand!" The nettled Farbar replied: "How about my head? What do you figure he broke it on?"

Barney Mailer died of cancer in the fall of 1972 after having been ill for about a year. At the funeral, Norman said to Rhoda Lazare Wolf: "Be happy. My father loved a party. Don't feel sad." When Jose Torres, away on a trip to Puerto Rico, asked Norman about Barney, Norman replied that he had died. Torres did not think his friend was too upset, and he

remembers him saying, "He was in no pain, there was no suffering."
Buzz Farbar, whose father died the same year, confided his anguish to
Mailer. Mailer's words held no "cheap comfort." "It's like having a hole
in your tooth," he told Farbar. "It's a pain that can never be filled. Not a
day goes by that you won't think of your father."

Fanny took Barney's death very hard. As Rhoda Lazare Wolf remembers it, "There was a real sadness, and she cried." Fanny's children
knew she had a "real feeling for him." Rhoda suggests that Fanny
always thought of Barney as a "prince, a knight in armor." He still
represented this "fantasy, this dream" that overrode all she had had to
endure. "She loved this man even though very early the dream was
destroyed," Rhoda concludes.

Although Fanny was the power in the family, Barney contributed his
share to its style. He made her feel like a lady, and he shared her sense
that their son was a genius, a hero they would support no matter what.
Although Norman's reaction to Barney's death seemed mild—even
banal—his use of the word *hole* was exactly right, for he was overcome,
once again, by a sense of a void, an emptiness in his life that his dapper
father had always helped to fill. However far Norman traveled, he always
came back to his parents' table, to Brooklyn.

Mailer seemed to grow even closer to his mother, who visited him
often in Stockbridge, Massachusetts, where along with Carol Stevens
and their infant daughter, Maggie Alexandra, he moved in September
1972 to a fifteen-room home on a five-acre estate. He rarely spent time in
his Brooklyn Heights apartment, but the stream of visitors to Stockbridge was steady. According to Anne Barry, Mailer did not like the
Stockbridge house. She remembers that it was quite big: "Upstairs off
the long hallway were lots of rooms that were just cubicles, cookie-
cutter, boxy little rooms. And downstairs there was something painful
about the parlor. Carol had gotten it up with Victorian furniture, little
loveseats and the lady's chair and the gentleman's chair and the rosewood
medallion frames and Victorian 'anti-ques.' It was so stiff no one would
dream of sitting there."

Carol devoted her time to the household but sang in a local cabaret on
Friday nights. At her debut performance a devoted Mailer, ensconced in
a window seat with an excellent view of the stage, was bothered by a pair
of drunks speaking loudly during one of her songs. Leaning into the
nearer one, Mailer asked him to be quiet and was ignored. Obviously
annoyed, he held his peace until the third song, when one of the drunks

cried out: "Is that broad stacked!" Mailer commanded the man to be quiet. "Sex-y!" he yelled. Grabbing the man by the ears, Mailer butted him. The crash of heads was audible, the man moaned, and Mailer turned his attention back to a white-faced Carol, whose voice seemed to have gotten louder as the head-butt victim shouted and pointed at a grey-headed Mailer: "That old man nearly cracked my skull." Mailer got up and pushed away his table, announcing, "I challenge you to a re-butt." At this point Carol stopped singing and two of her friends rushed over to Mailer to stop further fighting. Carol cried and warned Mailer, "If you do this, Norman . . . I'll never forgive you." But Mailer and his adversary went outside and returned as buddies, toasting and embracing each other for having remained on their feet in the re-butt. Mailer had been doing this kind of thing for many years now, he was surrounded in Stockbridge by a battle-hardened entourage that included not only his mother but also ex-wives, a boxer, his children, Carol's twenty-two-year-old son, and numerous others.

In early November 1972, plugging *St. George and the Godfather*, Mailer appeared at the Stony Brook campus of the State University of New York. Bruce Cook got a good look at him coming through a gymnasium door. Mailer had the "developed torso and the rolling bandy-legged gait of a professional boxer . . . the keen quick glance of an intellectual . . . and the assured manner of a celebrity." He seemed comfortable with his different personae, having grown into his roles and, on occasion, relishing his ability to display his conflicting selves. He looked "easy and confident." Reading from a prepared text and "acutely conscious of himself before an audience," he kidded the students and himself "almost mercilessly," and soon had his audience "feeling good" yet wondering what "rude surprise" he had in store for them.

Negative comments on women's liberation turned the students against Mailer. By the end of his talk he had lost half his audience, which simply walked out on him, slamming doors to show their displeasure. Annoyed at this rejection, he still enjoyed the hard give-and-take, hollering at his audience and getting hollered at in return. It was his way of making an impact on students, of getting "nearer to them than I usually do." If they did not agree with him, they were at least "intrigued" with what he had to say.

Not every Mailer appearance in these years resulted in insult and disruption, but it did seem the essence of his style to be combative. He did not see the point of being conciliatory: "The radical movement fell because it lacked radical ideas near the root. . . . Not enough work went into the '60s movement," he told Cook. There was a certain frustration in Mailer as he approached his fiftieth birthday on January 31, 1973, making plans for a huge party at the Four Seasons restaurant in Manhattan. Invitations in purple were sent out to five thousand people. For fifty dollars a couple they would be treated to "an announcement of national importance (major)" on February 5. Shirley MacLaine and Jack Lemmon, Senators Javits and McCarthy, Andy Warhol, and Bernardo Bertolucci were among the honored guests as well as a full complement of the press, including the editors of major newspapers and national magazines, and Mailer's mother, seven children, Lady Jeanne, Adele, and Carol.

Mailer's principal idea for the evening was the "Fifth Estate," a proposal to form a group of citizens who would watch the FBI and CIA and alert the American public to the way these secretive organizations were manipulating opinion and had possibly been involved in the assassinations of John F. Kennedy, Martin Luther King, Jr., and other public figures. It was after 10:00 P.M. when Mailer, drink in hand, got up to address an audience of about five hundred people. He was incoherent, told a dirty joke, drew some boos while some people headed for the doors (with Mailer yelling "Get their names"). It was too late to interest his remaining audience in the notion of "a democratic secret police keeping tabs on Washington's secret police." By 2:30 A.M., the party over, Mailer confessed to a friend: "I blew it. It was a great party and I blew it. I have a demon inside me." At three o'clock he had to fend off an irate gray-haired woman in a "vinyl Eisenhower jacket" who threw her arms around his neck, berating him for not having prepared his speech. "I'm not gonna be your gumshoe," she told him. At three-thirty he was butting heads with boxer Joe Shaw, pretending to be Frazier and Ali. The next day at the Algonquin Hotel he admitted to the press that his speech had been a "disgrace."

There were those like John Leonard, editor of *The New York Times Book Review*, who believed people had come to see Mailer make "a fool of himself, that it was almost willed by the audience, that they wanted him to get drunk—and this was at the time when he certainly had a desperate drinking problem." Some might have felt this man of great daring would pull off an unexpected triumph, but Leonard (echoing Poirier) suspected that Mailer "wills the disaster as often as he wishes it wouldn't occur."

In a curious way, Mailer's performance at the Four Seasons confirmed his conspiracy theory of history, that there was something in the nature of things out to destroy great individuals, great leaders. He had always measured himself against the Kennedys, the Alis, the Hemingways. After he asked his Four Seasons audience if they could hear him and he acknowledged the noise of the people who were still talking, he remarked, "Must size up the opposition." In Mailer's view, the great individual is often, by definition, in conflict with his society. For Mailer to have been embraced by his audience would have caused him to doubt the validity of his ideas. And yet to woo the public, to have the status of a celebrity, had also been his ambition. After the catastrophe of his party, he offered to write for *The New York Times Book Review* an apologetic explanation of the Fifth Estate—as though he could win back the audience he had lost. The piece, titled "The Morning After," did not accept Leonard's criticism of the audience. The fault, Mailer insisted, was "mine." To make the next issue of the *Book Review*, Mailer had to rush his copy to New York City from Stockbridge. He told Leonard the piece would be delivered on Monday morning at 9:00 A.M. (the time the editor said he would be there) by "the person I can trust." As Leonard recalls, on the very hour "this little old woman comes in and says, 'Here's Norman's story. I hope you like it.' I couldn't believe it—it was Norman's mother! The piece wasn't particularly good, but she was so pleased—she was exactly *the* mother, and somehow he needed her. I loved it."

The mother had always refused to see her son as a failure in anything. After the Four Seasons fiasco, a beaming Fanny had remarked to reporters: "I think it's all wonderful. . . . This was the best party for Norman. The second best was his bar mitzvah in 1936."

A NOVEL BIOGRAPHY

Lawrence Schiller had an idea for a book on Marilyn Monroe. He had photographed her in the nude in the weeks before she died, and she had given him world rights to the photographs. In 1971, he had helped put together a collection of six hundred Monroe photographs shown in thirty American cities and five countries. Seeing the commercial possibilities of a publication of these photographs along with a preface by an important writer, Schiller began approaching publishers with the idea.

Robert Markel, editor-in-chief at Grosset & Dunlap, was not very enthusiastic—unless the writer was someone like Norman Mailer. He put in a call to Scott Meredith and was surprised to learn that the agent thought his client would be interested. By November 1972 a deal had been struck: Mailer would receive fifty thousand dollars for a twenty-five thousand-word preface; another fifty thousand dollars would be split among the photographers.

At Mailer's Stockbridge home, where Schiller met Carol, the baby, Maggie, and one of Mailer's sons, Schiller displayed the exhibition of Monroe photographs, spreading them out on the floor, against chairs—wherever Mailer could see the enormous variety of her poses. He told Mailer what he could about his own contacts with Monroe and helped to set up screenings of her movies. From the beginning Mailer felt that her visual images and performances were the most important evidence for an understanding of her life. He was much less concerned, at this point, about what biographers had said—especially since he was only going to write a preface.

Right after signing the contract in November, Mailer had another viewing of the photographs in Markel's office. The editor remembers that "what struck Norman most was how different she looked from one photograph to the next, and he talked a little about chronology and Marilyn's moods." Markel was brought up short when Mailer suddenly said, "What are we gonna do about Bobby Kennedy?" Fred Guiles's biography of Monroe had included the story of a Kennedy (called "the Easterner")–Monroe romance, an appealing idea to Mailer because of his fascination with politics, power, celebrity, and fame. He would soon evolve a portrait of an ambitious woman whose sympathies and yearnings inclined her to an affair with a Kennedy—perhaps both Robert and John.

After a nine-day cruise in the Caribbean with Carol aboard the SS *Statendam*, Mailer returned in early December 1972 to Stockbridge to begin work on *Marilyn*. By early January he had put in a call to Markel to say that he had "completed the first 65,000 of the 25,000 words, and I'm not even up to Arthur Miller yet." Both men laughed, realizing that Mailer had become hooked on his subject and was going to produce a long biographical narrative. Now he had to concern himself more carefully with Guiles's book (the most complete and factually accurate of the biographies) and Maurice Zolotow's earlier but still vivid account. Writing against a tight deadline, Mailer conducted interviews in what he termed "modest depth" with Arthur Miller, Elia Kazan, Eli Wallach, Lee Strasberg, Norman and Hedda Rosten, Ralph Roberts, and others. Mailer knew he could not surpass Guiles in doing original research, but he hoped to present an interpretation, a "hypothesis" that would hold up in the light of future discoveries and assessments of Monroe's life. The Rostens, Mailer's Brooklyn neighbors, were especially helpful. Norman Rosten, an old friend of Arthur Miller and a Monroe confidant, was writing his own reminiscence of her and let Mailer read his manuscript. The two men sometimes met to view her movies, but Rosten was impressed by the fact that Mailer did not try to "pick my brain"— respecting the integrity of a fellow writer's work.

Norman Rosten knew that Norman Mailer had always wanted to meet Marilyn Monroe. In 1958, Rosten had done his best to arrange a meeting, but "it was hard with Miller in the picture. He was suspicious of other men," Rosten recalls. It was Rosten's impression that Monroe knew Mailer's work and probably had read *The Naked and the Dead*, but Mailer had an "image that sort of clashed with Arthur's." To Hedda Rosten, Monroe expressed some reluctance about seeing him, saying: "One writer is enough for me." On the subject of Mailer, Norman Rosten recalls Monroe giggling and shrugging her shoulders as if to imply they might meet one day. At one time, Mailer lived within five miles of the Monroe–Miller home in Connecticut, and she had spent much time in Brooklyn in the Rosten kitchen, where she liked to relax. Envious of Miller and miffed at his lack of access to Monroe, Mailer would comically chafe Rosten—accusing him of favoring Miller and pointing out that he took exception to Rosten's "nasty letters not because I do not deserve them, not because my ego is incapable of accepting them, but because I wonder how often you write nasty letters to the mighty Arthur Miller, known forever in the Jungian archetypes of my unconscious as Marilyn Monroe's Negro mammy."

Mailer's lack of respect for Miller's work and his contempt for Miller's pinched and parsimonious personality come through very clearly in *Marilyn*. Miller was very protective of Monroe and, in Rosten's words:

> *a very proper guy . . . if I danced with Marilyn at a party and maybe held her a little too tight or whispered in her ear, he'd look at me and get a little nervous . . . it's the two Jewish traditions: one, Miller as sobriety; the other, Mailer as rebellion.*

Miller did not want to risk his bride being captivated by Mailer, and Monroe preferred "staying out of the problem," Rosten recalls.

In retrospect, it seems inevitable that Norman Mailer should write about Marilyn Monroe, to respond to the qualities in her that he found in himself and to transform her into one of his characters. Lulu Meyers is partially modeled after Monroe, and he deals with the Hollywood of Monroe's era in *The Deer Park*. She is mentioned at the beginning of the *Esquire* version of *An American Dream* as one of those great historic figures who has made her life her own, and at the end of the novel Cherry, in death, conveys to Rojack Monroe's "hello," establishing an affinity with Mailer's characters that is apparent in scattered references to her throughout his work. She ranks with his other major characters, such as General Cummings in *The Naked and the Dead*. Just as Cummings works to make himself an instrument of his own policy, so Monroe paints herself into the camera lens as an instrument of her own will. To become an instrument of one's own will is a theme and a phrase that is repeated in Mailer's book on the astronauts and in his essays on Kennedy and Ali. Monroe is Napoleonic and yet divided against herself, a Dreiserian character who traverses the continent in quest of her true self.

Much of Mailer's work in film, and his discussions of it in "Some Dirt in the Talk" and "A Course in Film-Making" (both collected in *Existential Errands*), lead directly to his perception of Monroe's disrupted sense of self. In a prophetic line, written before he knew he would undertake a biography of Monroe, Mailer suggests in "A Course in Film-Making" that "the movie star seems to serve some double function: the star feeds memory *and* obsession—one need only think of Marilyn Monroe!" She is, in fact, the quintessential example of how movies can function as mirrors of the soul. Monroe's is the story of identity; she is, Mailer insists in *Marilyn*, the "magnified mirror of ourselves."

Mailer emphasizes Monroe's appropriative tendencies: She took on new names, new husbands, new roles (both on- and off-screen), and new stories, or versions of herself. For Mailer, the biographer is also an appropriator because he makes a story out of someone else's life, projecting himself into those events, and imagining them in the context of everything he knows about that career. Furthermore, he has to confront his own motivations for writing on someone else's life; otherwise, an attempt to remain "neutral" or "objective" deprives the biography of personal energy and commitment and results in a collection of lifeless facts or vivid but unconnected anecdotes.

There is a certain candor in the way Mailer confesses his "secret ambition . . . to steal Marilyn," his vain belief that "no one was so well suited to bring out the best in her." Though his own experiences with a few failed marriages have taught him that "he would have done no better than Miller," Monroe's third husband, Mailer uses his conceit to comment that "the foundation of her art might be to speak to each man as if he were all of male existence available to her." Mailer's biography is one more attempt to "bring out the best in her."

As he explores the crucial incidents in Monroe's life, Mailer envisions himself in a contest: "Set a thief to catch a thief, and put an artist on an artist." As an artist devoted to the process of character creation, Mailer presents Monroe as an artist creating her own career. The raw material of her life—the events that are a kind of prehistory before she fashions her interpretations of them—is elusive, Mailer suggests, as elusive as the person herself whom he never met, the "strange woman whose career so often passed through places where he had lived at the same time."

That the biographer and his subject never meet will "prove a recurrent wound in the writing," Mailer admits; yet his admission carries some authority, for it exemplifies his awareness of the nature of biography: The biographer and his subject often do not meet; and were they to do so, they would probably not agree on the significance of the life in question. Mailer's ambition, then, is to investigate the elusiveness of his subject and the ambiguities of his own work as a biographer by viewing both in terms of his creative role as a novelist.

At every point in his novel biography Mailer takes pains to show how he had made up his narrative. At the same time, he demonstrates that the creation of his fiction is simultaneously growing out of the fiction that Monroe created out of her complex reality. Mailer is constantly mindful of his paradoxical closeness to and distance from Monroe. He has been able to identify with her in an intense but provisional way, but he emphasizes that there is still much which has eluded him and much that has confused all of her biographers.

"Has Mailer created a Myth of Marilyn in order to fall in love with it? Or did that Marilyn already exist?" Ingrid Bengis asks these astute questions in her *Ms.* review of the biography. She recognizes that there are no easy answers because, as Monroe said in her last recorded interview, "You're always running into peoples' unconscious." This is, in fact, Mailer's point: Monroe was quite aware of her impact on the public and knew that it was projecting into her its own feelings. But to know this about herself suggests that Monroe was capable of absorbing and reciprocating the feelings the public had for her. Anyone who has read Monroe's last interview and carefully studied her movies realizes that Mailer is on very solid ground indeed.

Mailer supposes that because Monroe was plagued by the absence of a clear identity she struggled to find the "close fit of a role." She is missing a parent (the identity of the father is never clearly established) and grows up in a family with a history of insanity (her mother is eventually committed to a mental institution). She feels, like many of Mailer's male protagonists, orphaned. The ambition to become an actress, to discover a script that can be used to put one's imprint upon existence, seems wild and uncontrollable in her. Certainly Mailer provides ample evidence of both her ambition and her Napoleonic desire to have everyone submit to the part she preferred them to play in her life story. Over and over again she rejects those people (like her acting coach Natasha Lytess and her husbands Joe DiMaggio and Arthur Miller) who fail to follow her script.

Mailer presumes that Monroe's creation of dramatic and sordid details in her life—such as her rape at the age of seven and long hours of child labor in an orphanage—compensate for the dullness and emptiness of her early years. Most of the horrific incidents she relates reveal a psychic rather than physical reality; that is, she felt her personality was violated and voided in an apathetic and torpid environment. There was no call for others to pay attention to her. Thus her stories are a form of getting recognition, a way of shocking others into a complete absorption in her experience.

At nineteen, photographed in a wartime factory where she is spray-painting airplanes, Monroe finds "the first focus of her life, and it is in a camera lens." Several of her professional colleagues point out that she deliberately studied those photographs, in which she was able to produce a sense of romantic mystery within herself. In her later years, Mailer remarks, she became an expert in the application of makeup and developed a sense of how to paint herself into the camera lens. At the same time, trite "films strip her of existence . . . leave her empty, livid, and insomniac" because her roles are lightweight and provide no opportunity to find what Mailer calls her "true self."

As a way of finding her true talent—which is to say her true self—she studies with drama coaches and peruses anatomy books in order to maneuver herself into the best of physical positions before a camera. But the code of commercial production, the rigorous shooting schedules, turn her tasks of self-improvement into self-indulgent displays at the studio, in which she comes into conflict with her directors and fellow actors. She tries to escape the phoniness of stereotyped roles, but every superficial part she plays is a negative evaluation of her talents and career. As Mailer points out, such "an actor can only squander energy in a bad role—he cannot be reimbursed by discovering new sides of himself as he plays the role."

Monroe's film scripts are "simpler in their surface than [her] life"; they put her in the grip of silly plots at the very time she is trying to be serious about her life; where she strives for originality, her films aim at cliché. Mailer understands how restricted Monroe felt because his own attempt to make movies without scripts had as its objective the liberation of actors' identities from literary blueprints.

In Arthur Miller, Monroe hoped to find "a character in whom one can rest one's identity." Mailer suggests that Miller's play *Death of a Salesman* appealed to her because it held that "every moment of existence went into sustaining one's identity, and the moment one weakened, it was over." Miller was the ideal figure, the playwright who supplied roles, the man who unlike her previous two husbands could satisfy her desire for intellectual development and could fill "the lonely summit of her mind."

By the time she comes to make *The Misfits*—the movie her husband had meticulously planned as a vehicle for her talent—Monroe's love for Miller is lost and her sense of herself is very shaky indeed. Mailer charges that Miller has written a lie, that Marilyn was "as lovely and vulnerable as Roslyn Taber," the character she plays in the film. Since she had to work in daily collaboration with a man she had grown to detest, did Marilyn feel she was acting a lie off the screen as well as on? Never has she been forced to view her own life so closely on a movie set, Mailer suggests.

Slowly recovering from her breakdown on the set of *The Misfits* and her divorce from Miller, Monroe perks up with a new interest in her life: The Kennedys and a whole new world of politics opens up for her. The Kennedys represent Monroe's new ambition, her hope that she can attain some kind of "historical eminence," so that she will be "grander than she has known." She leaves the set of her movie *Something's Got to Give*, which has been troubled by her frequent absences, to sing "Happy Birthday" to JFK in Madison Square Garden. Then she propels herself into the center of world attention by her nude bathing scene: "Never does she look more in command of herself than in the photograph by Larry Schiller that shows her with one leg hooked over the edge of the pool and the devil of the orphanage in her eye."

Yet Monroe is fired from *Something's Got to Give* and spends the last summer of her life in the care of two doctors, an internist and a psychiatrist, brooding over her dismissal and devising future plans. Mailer takes the time to develop this period—so near the end of her life—in order to set down the basic rhythm (or lack of one) in her life:

> *She is triumphant and crushed. She is a female Napoleon but only for one pride. The other soul, more timid than ever, is a virus ridden orphanage mouse. . . . It is why so many of her affections are replaced by hate. Few are the activities she can perform where both of her selves can participate. . . . [She] is in the psychological midnight of being unable to know if she really wished to end the filming, or simply miscalculated what stress the studio could bear.*

The passage shifts between opposites; her existence, from its very beginning, has been bifurcated, possessed of a "double root."

In one of the best passages of prose he has ever written Mailer sums up the logic and counter-logic of Monroe's life:

> *No force from outside, nor any pain, has finally proved stronger than her power to weigh down upon herself. If she has possibly been strangled once [by her grandmother], then suffocated again in the life of the orphanage, lived to be stifled by the studio and choked by the rages of marriage, she has kept in reaction a total control over her life, which is perhaps to say that she chooses to be in control of her death, and out there somewhere in the attraction of that eternity she has heard singing in her ears from childhood, she takes the leap to leave the pain of one deadened soul for the hope of life in another, she says goodbye to that world she conquered and could not use. We will never know if that is how she went. She could just as easily have blundered past the last border, blubbering in the last corner of her heart, and no voice she knew to reply. She came to us in all her mother's doubt, and leaves in mystery.*

Mailer is quite aware, of course, that he is plotting Monroe's life in this passage. He is looking for a consistent pattern that synthesizes the contradictions of her career. In his search for pattern he is simultaneously working as a biographer and novelist; he underlines speculation in his use of such qualifiers as *if*, *possibly*, *perhaps*, and *we will never know*. As he says earlier in his book, he is offering a *possible* Marilyn Monroe. At the same time, as a novelist he has written himself into the divisions of her life, imitating in his prose style the contradictions in her character. His long analytical passages tend to split in two, offering alternatives Monroe herself always seems posed between. Her motivations in the last days and hours of her life may have appeared as ambiguous to her as they do to her biographer. Mailer's final characterization of Monroe as a "fatherless child" echoes her own sense of incompleteness. In one of her last interviews she is reported to have said: "To put it bluntly, I seem to have a whole superstructure and no foundation."

SOMETHING HAS BEEN WITHHELD FROM NORMAN MAILER

The importance of Mailer's achievement in *Marilyn* was not recognized. Even before the publication date it was in trouble. On June 22, 1973, Hodder & Stoughton, the British publishers of *Marilyn*, announced it would delay the release of the book because of charges that Mailer had plagiarized from Guiles's and Zolotow's biographies. On July 13, *60 Minutes* broadcast a Mike Wallace interview with Mailer centering on the book's last chapter, which probed the possibility that her involvement with Bobby Kennedy had led to her murder. Wallace then cut to an interview with Monroe's housekeeper, Eunice Murray, denying anyone could have visited Monroe on her last night. Mailer then made the mistake of asking Wallace whether he thought *Marilyn* was a good biography:

> *I've got to say no . . . because you acknowledge that you have taken most of your chronological material from a couple of other people, and you don't know if it's accurate or not. And in the crucial last chapter you have failed to do the necessary research that would have made it a good biography.*

Mailer did himself further damage by candidly admitting that he thought the book was "important enough to get out there half finished rather than not to get into at all." This left him open for Wallace's devastating conclusion: "The best criticism of the book we've heard so far is Norman Mailer's own: It got out there half finished."

On July 18, Mailer held a press conference to report on his investigation of Monroe's death (the results of which would appear in a chapter added to the paperback edition of *Marilyn*). He found much fault with the autopsy report but came nowhere near offering a persuasive explanation of who might have murdered her. He rejected the idea that the Kennedys were involved. Even if she had become an embarrassment to the family and had threatened to expose them, they would have taken it in stride, suggesting it was a "grievous and tragic situation, a lovely, talented, and highly disturbed woman with fantasies. It was her career rather than theirs which would have suffered most. The Kennedys were skilled in handling scandal," Mailer concluded.

On July 16, Christopher Lehmann-Haupt questioned in *The New York Times* book review the book's status as biography, calling it a "self-contained mythology that is impregnable to argument." Two days later, in a press conference at the Algonquin, Mailer denied the charges of plagiarism but was challenged about his murder theory. At this point, his biography was clearly something to be scoffed at. Pauline Kael, on the front page of *The New York Times Book Review* (July 22, 1973), pointed out yet another unworthy aspect of the biography—Mailer's envy of Arthur Miller. Summing up Mailer's career, Kael noted that he

> *has made us more aware than we may want to be of his titles and campaigns, his aspiration to be more than a writer, to conquer the media and be monarch of American arts—a straight Jean Cocteau who'd meet anybody at high noon. . . . Something has been withheld from Norman Mailer: his crown lacks a few jewels, a star. He has never triumphed in the theater, never been looked up to as a Jewish Lincoln, and never been married to a famous movie queen—a sex symbol . . . Mailer's waddle and crouch may look like a put-on but he means it when he butts heads.* Marilyn *is his whammy to Arthur Miller. . . . Miller and Mailer try for the same things: he's catching Miller's hand in the gentile cookie jar.*

Although *Marilyn* received some excellent reviews, in the public mind it came to be regarded as a rush job, a rip-off, and another example of Mailer's overweening ego.

It was impossible to explain on television—as Mailer had tried to do with Wallace—that he had never intended to write a biography, that the finished product was interpretative and not primarily meant as a work of original research, or that the themes of Monroe's life related very deeply to his own. Truth to tell, it was a commercial book, but then all Mailer's books were commercial in the sense that he hoped to profit from them. Facing a deadline, with a commitment to the Book-of-the-Month Club for summer publication of the biography, and with other financial obligations that made it imperative to publish sooner rather than later, the charges of plagiarism were quickly settled. Larger-than-usual per- missions fees were paid to Guiles and Zolotow, and Mailer included handsome acknowledgments of their work in his book. He did not alter in any significant way the passages that were allegedly plagiarized, and a close study of Guiles and Zolotow shows that he relied heavily on the information in their books while developing a style and point of view entirely his own.

Another year or more would not have substantially changed Mailer's reading of Monroe's personality, although he would certainly have added details—particularly concerning her death and her connection with the Kennedys. But as a "hypothesis" of a "possible" Marilyn Monroe, the biography still stands as a significant achievement in American letters with which biographers must reckon.

11.

THE EXECUTIONER'S SONG (1974–1979)

KNOWING A WOMAN

In the summer of 1974 Mailer took Carol Stevens and several of his children to Maine. Once again he tried to get a novel going, although he was plagued by the necessity to accept journalistic assignments that helped pay his enormous expenses—alimony, child support, household staff, and literary assistants. Separated from Mailer, Beverly seemed to tolerate the liaison with Carol—perhaps because Mailer gave no sign that he wanted to marry her.

Confiding in Buzz Farbar, Mailer said he felt no "bitterness" about his marriages. It seemed to him that he had gained as much as he had lost from each one. His experience had taught him about the different phases he had to go through in "knowing a woman." First came living with her. This was not the same thing as marriage. Indeed, it had been only through marriage that he had learned the most important things about his women. Then the appearance of children had altered how he looked at his wives. Divorce, for Mailer, represented another phase—a kind of finality to what he could learn about a woman. He likened these various phases to a "culture going through major transformations." The fact of children is what made marital breakups so enormously painful to him. The children had originated in his cherished conception of marriage; they were the embodiment of his union with a woman, and a divorce meant not only injuring the child but doing damage to that wonderful vision of what the marriage could become. Mailer was also perfectly willing to concede that he had failed himself; not having been able to live up to his own "code," he found it "hard to maintain any self-respect." He had given himself completely to each marriage and discounted the possibility that he could love two women simultaneously. He could bed two women "at once," but that was not the same as having a loving conception of them.

Mailer seemed to have few illusions about his lovemaking, admitting to Farbar: "Anybody who knows anything about women can recognize that the pleasure we assume we are giving to them can be a little less, in most cases, than we assumed." He did not put much stock in being a sexual athlete, noting that it was not so much a man's skill at sex that was important as it was the woman's feeling about him. Mailer had had his share of successes and failures at sex, but scorekeeping made no sense, and he dreaded the thought of a woman reporting on one of his "worse nights." At the age of fifty, promiscuity did not appeal to him. A decade earlier he had told Mike Wallace on a television interview show that he believed in "joyful promiscuity," and Adele had walked out of the room when she saw the interview, calling her husband a "son of a bitch." Now Mailer feared making love to a strange woman and dying in bed. In the past, he could not seem to stay away from women who were good lays. It gave him a sense of power. And he had to admit that sometimes "you need a fuck the way you need a shit." But now he felt guilty about using a woman's body that way. It made him depressed to think of fucking a woman without any real feeling for her, without committing an important part of himself. It would influence his karma, that belief of his that what one did in one life would be rewarded or punished in another.

Farbar admired Mailer for getting on so well with three of his four ex-wives. It seemed so civilized of Mailer to have kept them as friends. For Mailer, it meant acknowledging the love he had felt for these women, who he believed had also loved him. Although the marriages had failed for different reasons, he had shared with his ex-wives a desire to honor unions that had brought forth children. Above all, the suffering of the children should be mitigated. And in some ways, it was actually easier to be friends with ex-wives, since "sexual vanity" was no longer a factor.

He could look back on a marriage with some respect and regret, saying: "Yes, we were pretty good together, but not good enough." He could be content with that judgment and even relish precisely those aspects of an ex-wife that had attracted him to her in the first place, for the hassles of marriage were now over; the stakes were now much lower. Mailer had almost what he might call a tender feeling for his ex-wives.

Carol Stevens had become used to living a part of each year with Mailer and his children. The very things that bothered Beverly—his rushing off to cover conventions, the moon shot, and prize fights while she was tied down with the children—were not so much of a problem for Carol, who continued with her own career. In the early fall of 1974, he left her once again to cover the George Foreman–Muhammad Ali world championship fight in Kinshasa, Zaire.

THE FIGHT

The Fight may well be the most enjoyable book Norman Mailer will ever write. It contains all of the virtues and none of the vices of his best work. As in *Miami and the Siege of Chicago*, there is his superb traveler's evocation of environment:

> *If there were charms to Kinshasa, where to find them? The center of town had all the panache of an inland Florida city of seventy or eighty thousand people who somehow missed their boom—a few big buildings looked at a great many little ones. But Kinshasa did not have eighty thousand people. It had a million, and it ran for forty miles around a bend of the Congo, now, yes, the Zaire. It was no more agreeable than passing through forty miles of truck traffic and car-stained suburbs around Camden or Biloxi.*

Zaire is the domain of the dictator Mobutu, whose control of the fight is like his control of the country: total. Describing the political setting for the heavyweight championship bout, Mailer's command of his metaphors and sources is perfect:

> *Like a snake around a stick, the name of Mobutu is intertwined in Zaire with the revolutionary ideal. "A fight between two Blacks in a Black nation, organized by Blacks and seen by the whole world, that is a*

victory for Mobutism." So says one of the government's green and yellow signs on the highway from Nsele to the capital, Kinshasa.

Unlike *Of a Fire on the Moon*, Mailer does not have to make up his mind about his material, to digress in long, tortured passages about the "psychology of machines." Foreman and Ali are not white astronauts with technocratic vocabularies. The fighters live on a more elemental plane of magic. It is a world Mailer first explored in "Ten Thousand Words a Minute," in which he thought that his own behavior could somehow alter the outcome of the Patterson–Liston fight.

Everything had fallen into place for Mailer's trip to Africa when he discovered in a New York City bookshop a work on Bantu philosophy, which develops a cosmic and porous sense of identity akin to Mailer's own:

> *Men or women were more than the parts of themselves, which is to say more than the result of their heredity and experience. A man was not only what he contained, not only his desires, his memory, and his personality, but also the forces that came to inhabit him at any moment from all things living and dead. So a man was not only himself, but the karma of all the generations past that still lived in him, not only a human with his own psyche but a part of the resonance sympathetic or unsympathetic, of every root and thing (and witch) about him.*

Karma had been an operative word in *Marilyn*, in which Mailer speculated that parts of her behavior were the result of just those past and present forces that Bantu philosophy invokes. Before leaving for Africa, Mailer had begun what would become his Egyptian novel, the summa of his belief that human beings were the products of every force, every life, that had ever existed.

The speculativeness of *Marilyn* which critics tend to dismiss as Mailer's imposition on Monroe's life is not a problem in *The Fight*, where the African atmosphere is heavy with the portentousness of violence and death. Foreman seems so awesome, so vicious in the ring, that even his supporters fear he will kill Ali. It does not seem at all foolish that Mailer and George Plimpton briefly consider indulging in some African magic to aid Ali. Superstition is the stuff of boxing. Boxers and their handlers and their fans do seem to create forces that make Mailer's own mysticism acceptable. Like Rojack, Mailer must test

himself, must master his own fears even as he roots for Ali's conquest
over what Mailer assumes to be Ali's dread of Foreman's invincible
savagery. So Mailer must overcome his fear of vertigo in daring a seven-
story fall by swinging around a partition separating his balcony from the
one next door. It is not much of a physical feat, he confesses, but it is like
crossing an ideological barrier: He will not know how to deal with the
other side of things, and he will not be able to imagine how Ali can beat
Foreman, if he does not go through his own heroic rituals. Like all fans,
he thinks he can influence the game.

All the same, Mailer is a minor character here, referring to himself as
"the interviewer," and taking up the modest tone of a man fed up with
his ego, evincing a self-critical—even comical and mellow—style. The
set piece of *The Fight*, in which Mailer goes jogging with Ali, captures a
newfound attitude about himself that also sums up why he has always
been so competitive. Proud that he has been able to force his middle-
aged, out-of-shape body to run almost two miles with the fighter, Mailer
is walking through a forest "dark as Africa is ever supposed to be,"
admiring (in admittedly clichéd terms) "the clarity of the stars! The size
of the bowl of heaven!" when he is brought up short by a "lion roar." In
his ears it sounds cosmic—like "an unfolding wave of wrath across the
sky and through the fields." Where is the lion? he wonders. All alone, he
imagines the lion running him down, taking him silently. Mailer then
interrupts the moment to recall a day of sailing in Provincetown harbor
when a "frolicsome" whale passed him by. Suppose the whale had
swallowed him? Mailer speculates. Even at the time he felt "singularly
cool," thinking it was a "perfect way to go," securing his place in
American literature—"(see Croft on the mountain in *The Naked and the
Dead*) with Ahab's Moby Dick," he adds. Back in Africa, Mailer thinks
it is "Hemingway's own lion waiting down all these years for the flesh of
Ernest until an appropriate substitute had at last arrived." As a coda to
this aggrandizing passage Mailer appends, "They laughed at Ali's villa
when he told them about the roar. He had forgotten Nsele had a zoo and
lions might as well be in it." It has all been Mailer's fantasy, which he is
quite willing to puncture in a single neat sentence.

In *The Fight* Mailer manages to write of himself in a succinct,
amusing vein, dispatching his own conceits and yet richly enjoying the
process of originating them. His is an imagination that has grown in
proximity to whales and lions and made the most of his adventures while
vouchsafing that those very adventures are an invention much like the

fabrication of the persona that had begun to emerge in *Advertisements for Myself.* Indeed, from the start of his second year at Harvard, Mailer conceived of having a career that was literary, that would have the mythic dimensions of the career of a Malraux, a Hemingway. The immensity of Africa is for Mailer a literary immensity.

The Fight is 229 book pages, yet Mailer's description of the bout takes up less than thirty pages near the end of the book. It is not, however, a padded performance, for he wants to immerse his readers in the mood of a championship event, in Ali's apparently phlegmatic preparations and Foreman's awesome workouts. Ali seems to do everything wrong. Mailer is shocked to observe a listless Ali who seldom spars with any energy and who jogs at such a slow pace that even Mailer can keep up with him. Ali puts most of his energy into talking, haranguing reporters about his greatness and abusing Foreman for having fought so many nobodies. Foreman, on the other hand, is quiet and dignified, a man of enormous strength who can apparently throw knockout punches round after round without tiring. Foreman's people think Ali may have two advantages: He can dance away from danger and his hands are faster than their fighter's. But Foreman has been working on dominating the ring and driving Ali into a corner where he will be trapped in Foreman's merciless barrage of punches. Ali, past his prime, will tire. He will not be able to run forever. Suspense builds and Mailer puzzles over whether Ali really thinks he can win. No one makes much of the fact that Ali weighs nearly as much as Foreman or that he has almost a two-inch reach advantage.

In the ring, Ali surprises everyone. In the first round he stuns Foreman with sharp left- and *right*-hand leads to the face. A right-hand lead is a particularly daring and dangerous attack, Mailer points out, since it usually leaves a boxer open to instant retaliation. Foreman's reaction, however, is anger. He bulls ahead and does not try to pick apart Ali's offense, to anticipate the right hand by throwing one of his own. He expects to overpower Ali. But Ali, it turns out, is just as strong as Foreman, and reacts to Foreman's rushes by grabbing him roughly by the back of the neck and clinching so that Foreman's punching power is neutralized. Eventually Foreman does succeed in backing Ali into a corner. Unlike most boxers, Ali stays there and does not try to fight his way out, protecting himself instead by raising his forearms so that between his gloves and elbows he has most of his face and upper body covered, exposing only his belly. It suddenly becomes apparent that virtually all of Ali's training has centered on his disciplining himself to take Foreman's punishing blows, to live with the pain, to block as much of it as possible, to distribute and therefore diminish the force of the wrenching punches by having the slackened ropes absorb and cushion the battering. Just before the fight, Mailer has signaled Ali's strategy without commenting upon it:

> *Angelo Dundee [Ali's trainer] went methodically from ring post to ring post and there in full view of ringside and the stadium just as methodically loosened each of the four turnbuckles on each post which held the tension of each of the four ropes, and did it with a spoke and a wrench he must have put in his little carrying bag back at Nsele and transported on the bus and carried from the dressing room to the ring. And when the ropes were slack to his taste, loose enough for his fighter to lean way back, he left the ring and returned to the corner. Nobody had paid any particular attention to him.*

There it is: Ali will not dance; he will lounge on the ropes, taking the edge off Foreman's punches by reducing the vertical angle of his body while giving himself a rest at the same time. Foreman will have to do all the work, with Ali occasionally bouncing off the ropes to score punches on Foreman's head. It will be all the leverage Ali needs.

What Ali has learned to do is pace himself, and Mailer has done something similar in his literary strategy for *The Fight*. By the time he is ready to describe the bout itself, there is an air of anticipation, of dread, and of sheer wonder at Ali's genius. He has completely psyched out his opponent against enormous odds. In one of the most moving moments of the book, there is just a hint of how much Ali has concealed from everyone—including his retinue—and how much he needs bolstering. He has had a brief quarrel with Bundini, one of his confidants. Ali has rejected Bundini's choice of a robe for his impending appearance in the stadium, and in retaliation Bundini refuses to speak to Ali:

> *"Say, Bundini, we gonna dance?" he asked. Bundini would not reply.*
> *"I said, are we going to dance?"*
> *Silence.*
> *"Drew, why don't you speak to me?" Ali said in a big voice as if exaggeration were the best means to take Bundini out of his mood.*

"Bundini, ain't we going to dance?" he asked again, and in a droll tender voice, added, "You know I can't dance without Bundini."

"You turned down my robe," Bundini said in his deepest, huskiest and most emotional voice.

"Oh man," said Ali, "I'm the Champ. You got to allow me to do something on my own. You got to give me the right to pick my robe or how will I ever be Champ again? You going to tell me what to eat? You going to tell me how to go? Bundini, I am blue. I never seen a time like this when you *don't cheer me up."*

Bundini fought it, but a smile began to tickle his lips.

"Bundini, are we going to dance?" asked Ali.

"All night long," said Bundini.

"Yes, we're going to dance," said Ali, "we're going to dance and dance."

The dialogue dances, a literary equivalent of Ali's own metaphorical style; Ali has always considered himself a poet inside and outside the ring and does not literally dance but rather puts a set of moves on Foreman that utterly flusters him. When Broadus, a Foreman representative sent to observe Ali's preparations for the bout, answers Ali by saying Foreman "don't dance," he is unwittingly admitting the flaw in Foreman's attack: He lacks the play and the nuance of Ali's style.

The match between Ali and Mailer is so perfect that Mailer does not even have to comment upon it in *The Fight*. They are both aging champs with self-reflexive styles designed to triumph over their faults and weaknesses. Both men enter their bouts and books under a cloud; it is not clear whether they can pull off another win. Ali does take a terrific pounding from Foreman, but in the moment that Foreman succumbs to punched-out weariness and the disorientation caused by Ali's harrying blows to his head, it is apparent in Mailer's prose how Ali has been able to take Foreman apart:

Then a big projectile exactly the size of a fist in a glove drove into the middle of Foreman's mind, the best punch of the startled night, the blow Ali saved for a career. Foreman's arms flew out to the side like a man with a parachute jumping out of a plane, and in this doubled-over position he tried to wander out to the center of the ring. All the while his eyes were on Ali and he looked up with no anger as if Ali, indeed, was

*the man he knew best in the world and would see him on his dying day.
Vertigo took George Foreman and revolved him. Still bowing from the
waist in this uncomprehending position, eyes on Muhammad Ali all the
way, he started to tumble and topple and fall even as he did not wish to
go down. His mind was held with magnets high as his championship and
his body was seeking the ground. He went over like a six-foot sixty-year-
old butler who has just heard tragic news, yes, fell over all of a long
collapsing two seconds, down came the Champion in sections and Ali
revolved with him in a close circle, hand primed to hit him one more
time, and never the need, a wholly intimate escort to the floor.*

The first sentence catches Foreman in all his surprise: He has been
unprepared for this jolt. It seems to come out of nowhere, a startling
blow Mailer does not identify as Ali's until the second half of the
sentence. (Foreman would later say a fighter never anticipates the shot
that will knock him out.) For Ali it is a psychic blow, Mailer implies,
saved up for his greatest moment of need, since nothing less than a
knockout will prove he was destined to best Foreman. Deprived of his
senses, Foreman acts like a man bailing out. Mailer's picture of him,
focused on Ali, calls to mind the words Ali said to Foreman at the
beginning of the bout, words—Ali claimed—that would destroy his
opponent's concentration: "You have heard of me since you were young.
You've been following me since you were a little boy. Now, you must
meet me, your master!" Foreman's fall is an epic moment, a champion is
brought down to earth, but rather than overloading the scene with tragic
significance, Mailer turns to comedy. All along Foreman has been
portrayed as a rather stiff personality, old-fashioned, even stodgy. As
incongruous as it seems, yes, he does have the rather correct air of an old
butler. Something in the rhythm of Mailer's last sentence on the knockout conveys Ali's reaction as though it were being filmed in slow motion.
Foreman has been known for punching his opponents even as they are
going down from a knockout. Mailer says Ali "revolved" around Foreman, thus choosing a word that just slightly prolongs the instant, the two
seconds it takes Foreman to come apart, the two seconds it takes Mailer
to speak of Ali's providing Foreman with "a wholly intimate escort to
the floor." The whole thing sounds poetic, and it is meant to be, for Ali
has become a part of Mailer's literary sensibility.

George Foreman was a special challenge for Muhammad Ali, who
had to regain his title and prove he was still the greatest. In Mailer's

mind, it was also *the* fight of his literary life. As George Plimpton recalls:

> *In Africa I had never seen Mailer in such a relaxed mood and at ease with himself, which always meant that he was splendid company. I remember being slightly surprised because he had spoken of the country as Hemingway's territory, which was going to require him to be on his mettle.*

THE DISCOVERY OF NORRIS CHURCH

In March 1975, about three months after returning from Africa, Mailer headed south to see the Gwaltneys and to deliver a lecture at Loyola University in New Orleans. Both Fig and Ecey taught at Arkansas Polytechnic College and prevailed on Mailer to visit a few classes and meet faculty members. The Gwaltneys had not seen him in years, and he wrote ahead to say that he had gained thirty pounds and had changed his drinking habits, preferring rum and tonic now to bourbon, which was "too rich" for his fifty-two-year-old blood. Ecey heard about Carol Stevens when Mailer put in a call to her after he had arrived, assuring her that he was on his best behavior. He turned the phone over to Ecey, who also told Carol that he had become so well behaved he was boring. That afternoon he met Barbara Norris, aka Norris Church.

It happened during a party for Mailer. Ecey got a call from Barbara Norris, a Russellville High School art teacher who had illustrated one of Fig's books. "Could I crash?" she wanted to know. When Norris walked into the Gwaltney home, Mailer was sitting by a window. In the intense sunlight his white hair seemed to glow like a halo. Spotting her, he smiled and got up to speak. Norris has often told what her first meeting with Mailer was like:

> *I walked in and had on blue jeans and a shirt tied at the waist and tall wedgie shoes, and I was about six feet two. Well, Norman is five feet eight. I walked up and said, "How are you, Mr. Mailer?" and he turned around and walked out of the room.*

Norris's beauty, Mailer would later confess, had overpowered him. Speechless, he could not bear to look at her any longer and had to get away.

Mailer asked Fig to invite Norris to dinner. The Gwaltneys could see he was smitten. Soon Mailer knew all about her: She was from Atkins, Arkansas, a town of two thousand. She had been reared as a Baptist, her father worked at a Job Corps Center, and her mother ran a beauty salon. She was an only child and like Mailer had grown up being told "I was loved, I was told I was beautiful, and everything my parents could do for me they did within their means." In high school she had shown a preference for art—especially the work of Hopper and Wyeth—and once drove to Little Rock (about sixty miles from her home) to get a look at a Wyeth painting. "We stood there for hours," she later recalled, exclaiming, "look at the way he did this, and look at the way he did that!" She enjoyed getting on her bike and riding from one end of town to another, playing in the creek, and eating peanut butter sandwiches. Later, she would take trips to the mountains, to the Ozark Folk Center, where she would pose people in chairs and do five-minute portraits for five dollars.

Norris had worked in a pickle factory and married the first boy she had dated, Larry. She had divorced him after his troubled return from Vietnam and now lived with her three-year-old son, Matthew. Norris had read *Marilyn* but really did not know much about Mailer's reputation. She was twenty-six and not particularly literary. That suited Mailer fine. He wanted her to like him, not his notoriety.

Norris had to sense, however, that Mailer was something special, and she was known for her ambitiousness and independence—there had been some controversy over her wearing jeans to the high school art classes she taught and she had dated Bill Clinton, who would later become governor of Arkansas. Norris confided to Ecey that she had rather enjoyed "the fuss" her principal had made over her clothing. In Norris, Mailer would find a woman who handled public confrontations with aplomb. For her part, she found him good company: "charming, funny, and witty—and very sexy. He has this way of talking to you that makes you feel like no one else in the room." As Norris puts it:

> He was giving me a pretty heavy line about how beautiful I was, just on and on and on. I was pretty used to that, so I quipped, "Well, it's a wonderful line, Mr. Mailer, but, then, I've always bought a good line if it's well presented."

They spent most of the night together. He gave her "a thick silver ring, the metal molded around its pale blue stone." Mailer had to leave the next day but gave her a post-office-box address in Stockbridge. He told her about Carol Stevens, but Norris made no secret of her interest in him—even telling him about the local modeling she had done. Mailer wrote a "sweet, wonderful inscription" in her copy of *Marilyn*, and a few days later she wrote him a "funny note" and enclosed some of her modeling photographs. She had no idea how things might work out for her, but she was obviously prepared for an invitation. As she told Peter Manso, "I wanted him to remember me." He sent her a crate filled with his collected works. She "read them all at once. It was a really dumb thing to do. I was just overwhelmed," she later confessed to Marie Brenner.

After the spring trip to Arkansas and his return to Stockbridge, Mailer told Jose Torres about the new woman in his life. He showed Torres a picture of Norris. "I think Carol knows because she found this," said Mailer, referring to the picture. Torres says another of Mailer's girlfriends was pressuring him to marry her. "Give me six months," he had replied before he met Norris.

Soon Mailer returned to Arkansas, spending three days with Norris in a Little Rock hotel, staying in bed most of the time, taking a few outings to places like the Marriott to watch politicians going to it at lunch, and absorbing the local color. Mailer came to see Norris as his soulmate: They shared the same birthday, January 31. Although separated by twenty-six years, they had been born one minute apart. Mailer, Norris remembers, made nothing of his fame. While he made no promises, she sensed they would soon be living together. "I knew he had at least four steady girlfriends, so from the beginning there was no lying."

Norris accompanied Mailer on a trip to Chicago to tout *The Fight*. Her very proper Baptist parents were upset about the affair, and she suspected that the Gwaltneys, especially Fig, thought she was out of her depth, but Norris felt comfortable, accepting Mailer's invitation to see him in New York and to consult with his friends about modeling. Amy Greene, wife of Milton Greene, the photographer who had also been Marilyn Monroe's business partner, assured Norris she had a real shot at a career in New York if she lost twenty pounds. She went back to Arkansas for the summer of 1975 and "starved" herself, reaching her goal of one hundred seventeen by the end of July.

In the meantime, Mailer had Carol Stevens to think about. They had not lived together full-time. His pattern had been to divide his time between Stockbridge and New York, with summers in Bar Harbor, Maine, where he could concentrate on his children. A *People* magazine

reporter visited Mailer's summer home and saw his kids wandering in
and out of the kitchen:

> *an attractive, disparate group who look like a gathering of the brightest*
> *of the neighborhood children: here two dark Mediterranean beauties*
> *[Dandy and Betsy], there two handsome Nordic boys [Michael and*
> *Stephen], another lovely girl [Kate] of medium coloring and finally a*
> *dazzling little blue-eyed girl [Maggie] who bears no resemblance to the*
> *others.*

Mailer might take off for a day to write in a motel room, but he would be
back, bursting through the kitchen door attired in his summer fashion:
"a T-shirt, cut-off jeans and ratty sneakers." Carol seemed down-to-
earth and sensible. The reporter thought she looked like "the classic
gypsy wench," even though she was a refugee from Philadelphia's Main
Line. At her orders, Mailer put on a clean shirt for dinner.

Around his children Mailer appeared to be the perfect Fred MacMur-
ray father—patient and affectionate, spending a good half hour after
dinner checking their camping gear and putting them to bed. Then he
retired to the den with a bottle of rum and a bucket of ice, telling the
reporter: "I don't drink nearly as much as I used to. I just can't do it
anymore and keep up with the writing. I'll have a couple of drinks in the
evening, but after six or seven drinks you're into booze and even if your
mind stays clear you don't do anything else." He wrote at the rate of
about fifteen hundred words a day and fought his waistline with a round
of pushups and leg lifts in the morning.

According to Norris, by the end of August 1975 Mailer had decided
in her favor. She could imagine how hard this new development was on
Carol. It wasn't exactly easy for Norris either, but as she says, "Me, I
knew I wasn't going back to Arkansas."

Norris painted as well as modeled, and New York City seemed
extremely glamorous to a young woman who had not traveled out of the
state of Arkansas before she met Mailer. She liked the attention and was
unabashed about the pleasure she took in seeing her picture in the paper.
As she says, with Norman there were "no conditions, no promises."
Their relationship "just evolved." His one injunction: "Don't bring any
of your Arkansas polyester clothes."

Norris had calculated the risks: "Suppose in five years he's tired of
me? I'll already have made my own friends and I'd be all right. I'll

survive," she told Ecey. Mailer's family took to Norris quickly. Norris liked Barbara. She knew that brother and sister were close, but it came as a shock to see how much they resembled each other. Fanny got Norris an apartment in her building and spent considerable time with her in the fall of 1975 when she first moved to New York. While Mailer was in Maine with Carol, Norris and Fanny would have lunch or dinner together and walk on the Promenade in Brooklyn Heights. Norris remembers her as being "really agile in those days, and we became very close." Fanny had never confided in Carol, and Norris felt that Fanny enjoyed this new friendship with a young woman so different in age and background from her sisters. When Mailer told Fanny about his feelings for Norris, Fanny apparently had her doubts and asked Norris not to accompany her son on a trip to Manila, where he would be working on a screenplay for Sergio Leone that was eventually rejected. "Darling, I want you not to go," she said, but Norris was firm, and Fanny admired her determination, saying later: "She was easy to be with, and, like Norman, she has a very honest personality. She's unique, very different from Norman's other wives. She has character. She knows when to overlook things and she doesn't fight and scream." (Fanny probably had in mind her son's quirks. He forbade Norris, for example, to wear perfume. Ecey Gwaltney found this out when Norris offered her a bottle of Charlie. "Once we were going out and I'd put on some cologne, and he made me come back and take a bath," Norris told Ecey.)

During her first year in New York, Norris got to know many of Mailer's friends, including Harold and Mara Lynn Conrad, on whom Mailer decided to play a trick. They were such a "hip" couple that Mailer wanted to see whether he could put them on. For her appearance, Norris bought a "very low-cut, sexy red dress and a cheap blond wig" from A & S (a New York City department store), and wore heavy makeup. "This is Cinnamon Brown from Waco, Texas, and she wants to be a porny star," Mailer said, introducing Norris to his friends. Mailer remarked he did not approve of this career move, but Norris insisted: "That's what I want to do. I can make a lot of money." Then Mailer started shouting that she would never be successful because she did not have "any tits." Norris's rejoinder: "Oh, tits, what're tits? I got a terrific pussy." The Conrads were uncertain as to how to respond, although Mara took Mailer aside and counseled him to "let the kid do it. She's cute, she's terrific, she might be a big star. If that's what she wants, keep out of it." During this tête-à-tête Norris retired to the bathroom, got rid of the wig, toned down her makeup, and emerged in a classic high-necked black dress from Saks. "Who are you?" Mara asked. "I'd like to introduce myself. I'm Barbara Norris," said Norris while Mailer rolled on the floor enjoying his jest.

A photograph of Norman and Norris, taken in the fall of 1976, is emblematic of their relationship: He stands facing forward, his hands on his hips, his short-sleeve shirt open at the neck revealing his hairy chest, his feet spread apart and firmly planted on the ground. He looks straight ahead, his features in tense focus, and the space is his, with Norris leaning against his left side, her left arm and hand draped on his shoulder, her hair covered in a scarf, her neckline plunging in a blouse tied up to reveal her midriff, and her knees bent to reduce her height. She hangs there on him, sexy in very tight-fitting jeans, her head angled toward her left and tilted downward slightly. She is poised yet casual in this display of herself. In every sense of the word, she has put herself on Mailer's level; she is the first woman to understand how to model herself, in all the intimate details, on his sense of companionship and marriage.

By December 1975 Norris's painting and modeling career was well under way. She signed herself "Norris," and Mailer introduced her at parties that way. "Norris what?" people wanted to know. At Mailer's suggestion she decided to call herself Norris Church. That month they visited Arkansas to see the Gwaltneys and to pick up her son, Matthew, whom she had left with her parents. A suspicious Fig cautioned Mailer not to get involved with this young, ambitious woman. "They all thought I was just using him," Norris believes. With her parents Mailer behaved like the perfect gentleman, arriving in a conservative tweed suit, worrying about whether he was presentable, and assuring them that Norris had her own apartment in New York—an important, if dissembling representation to religious parents who were concerned about their daughter living in sin. Ecey had coached Mailer to speak slowly so that he could be understood and was surprised to learn everything had gone smoothly. How could Norris's parents reconcile themselves to an illicit relationship? "They had to," replied Norris, who knew how much her parents loved their only child: Opposition meant giving up their daughter. The name Norman Mailer meant nothing to them. "I gather her father went out and bought a book about the Jews, because he'd never met a Jew before. He's a nice guy and was probably eager to win Norman's good wishes," Ecey recalls.

After Christmas 1975, Mailer told Carol about Norris and his new life. From now on he and Norris would be a couple and marry as soon as he obtained his divorce from Beverly. Mara Lynn Conrad suggests that Norris became "everything he thinks a woman should be. She's very feminine, soft, affectionate. She's ambitious but not in an unpleasant way, and she's willing to work for whatever she wants. And on top of this she loves *Norman* first, she genuinely loves him as a man."

There is a calm and inner confidence about Norris that even casual acquaintances can spot. John Aldridge, who has seen Mailer off and on after their brief time living near each other in the 1950s, has noticed that Norris never seems at a loss. She handles Mailer without seeming manipulative or pushy. The air of competition so palpable in his dealings with previous wives is absent.

With the advent of Norris Church, Norman Mailer became part of the New York social scene in a way he had never been before, going to dinner parties with Pat Lawford, Jan Cushing Olympitis (a celebrated New York hostess), the agent Morton Janklow, TV producer Mark Goodson, and the de la Rentas. Norris admits that much of this was of her doing. She likes the "glitter, the back and forth, the small talk," their "moving and doing." Mailer's controversial history meant little to his new friends, who found him "mellow" and "gentlemanly" in Norris's presence. Jan Cushing Olympitis remarks that Mailer is dabbling in this world; it is an amusement; he finds exotics who appeal to him but there is little at stake, little reason for him to act out or to embarrass his company. "He's on the outside looking into this zoo of animals," Olympitis concludes. Similarly, Pete Hamill thinks that Mailer treats such parties as "sheer entertainment." And for such entertainment he regards Norris as superior to the other women Mailer has courted and married.

Arthur Schlesinger, Jr., a frequent dinner companion of Mailer's, describes the change that occurred with Norris this way:

> *Before, Norman was like a bomb that might explode at any moment. He had so many facets of possible development that he moved off in all sorts of directions. But as you grow older, you begin to realize more and more what works for you and what doesn't, and you begin to see what roles are really comfortable as against those you assume, and after a while aren't, for better or worse, working. I think that's all that's happened. He's settled into himself and simplified his life by realizing these aren't right for him.*

If Schlesinger is right, Norris benefited immensely from good timing, from catching Mailer at the precise moment when settling down had an overwhelming appeal. While ambitious herself, Norris allowed her husband to help show the way in New York, to feel a part of her career without having to "carry" Norris or confront the nagging that finally made Beverly such a bore for him. Then, too, Mailer has allowed himself to be adopted by others above him in social class. He attributes their interest in him to his role as "maverick." So long as he is perceived to be a kind of outlaw, he will be of interest to these people. If he becomes too docile, too observant of their rule, he is sure "they will become bored with me, and then, boom, I'm out." The danger for himself, he admits, is taking this social game seriously.

GENIUS AND LUST

During the summer of 1975, while Norris moved in, Barney Rosset, then publisher of Grove Press, approached Mailer to do a commentary on the writings of Henry Miller, a natural subject for Mailer, who had often expressed his admiration for the Brooklyn-reared Miller and had already published pieces on him in *The Prisoner of Sex* and *The American Review*. Studying Miller for three months as the anthology was put together provided Mailer with a way to measure his own talent: "Genius may depend on the ability to find a route between irreconcilables in oneself." In Miller's case, the irreconcilables were his father, a "finely dressed German tradesman," and his mother, "a strong dour intolerant German woman." Beginning with the Cummings–Hearn conflict in *The Naked and the Dead*, Mailer had taken a Manichean view of the universe, seeing things in terms of their opposites, as he must have done in his own household, observing his brisk, ambitious mother and his immaculate and ineffectual father. Like Miller, Mailer knew his manners, but he also knew what it had cost him in rudeness and roughness to become a writer. Indeed, he associated becoming a writer and achieving his own voice with violence, with a rejection of the passive father in favor of the aggressive mother.

Mailer locates Miller's literary force in his unabashed efforts to dominate women, for they are the locus of power. Speaking more nearly for himself than for Miller, Mailer claims Miller's lust actually expresses

man's sense of awe before woman, his dread of her position one step
closer to eternity. . . . So do men destroy every quality in a woman
which will give her the powers of a male, for she is in their eyes already
armed with the power that she brought them forth, and that is a power
beyond measure—the earliest etchings of memory go back to that
woman between whose legs they were conceived, nurtured, and near
strangled in the hours of birth.

For Mailer, if not for Miller, the very act of writing may be associated
with the desire to get out, to throw off the limbs that simultaneously
seem to hold him back and propel him into the world, so that he can
become his own creation. Yet he is attracted to his root in woman and
aware of how inauthentic his efforts to be autonomous can make him
feel. Mailer argues that Miller left Brooklyn for the world, for Paris
specifically, to remake himself only to find he could not escape self-
doubt: "That self-acquired Brooklyn culture, that sense of himself as an
imposter (am I the greatest writer alive, or do not even know how to
construct a novel?), his prodigious competitiveness, had to take on all
forms, all manners, even all vices of avant-garde writing."

Much of the commentary in *Genius and Lust* is disguised autobiography—true enough for Miller, but even more accurate on Mailer
himself. Take the discussion of Miller's obsession with June, his second
wife. With her "burning dark eyes . . . huntress profile . . . bizarre,
fantastic, nervous" feverish nature she might as well be Adele. June has
a "false ego"—she postures in "whirlpools of feeling," poses sensually
and is "heavy with experience. Her role alone preoccupies her. She
invents drama in which she always stars. . . . She is an actress every
moment." Mailer takes the words from Anais Nin but the passage might
as well be Mailer's, for he uses it to evoke a place for June in Miller's life
that matches Adele's in his own. Both second marriages last seven years
and are "as emotional as blood." According to Mailer, Miller is "a
faithful and tortured young writer helplessly in love with a voluptuous
woman whose maddening lack of center leads him into an awareness
of his own lack of identity." With June, Miller discovers there is
no "geological fundament in the psyche that we can call identity."
So he has to "re-create himself each morning. Soon, he realizes he
has been doing it all his life." This is the grand theme of *Marilyn*,

of most of Mailer's writing: the search for identity, the fear that it is
not to be had.

There is no better explanation for Mailer's own erratic behavior than
his analysis of Miller's narcissism:

> What characterizes narcissism is the fundamental relation. It is with
> oneself. That same dialectic of love and hate that mates feel for one
> another is experienced within the self. . . . Like animals are each half of
> themselves and forever scrutinizing the other.

This seems literally true for Mailer, who has been partial to including
self-interviews in his collections of journalism and criticism and to
inventing interviewer voices so he can talk to himself. He and Adele
were, to use Mailer's term, narcissists resonating for each other. They
acted out roles for each other, watched each other perform, and nearly
destroyed each other at that moment when Mailer stabbed her. The
gossip in Provincetown after the party had been that Adele had threatened Mailer with a knife and in his efforts to take it away he had
inadvertently stabbed her. The truth of the gossip is that husband and
wife egged each other on.

Norris contributed heavily to calming Mailer: It is significant that he
had her do the drawing of Miller for the cover of *Genius and Lust*. With
Norris beside him, he found it easier take the retrospective tone, to note
that "in those seven years with June, Miller was shaping the talent with
which he would go out into the world." At the moment of writing that
sentence, Mailer might well have had in mind *Advertisements For Myself*, written right in the heart of his years with Adele. Certainly he made
Miller into his kind of writer and was closing a circle for himself in
suggesting Miller knew that "a writer of the largest dimension can alter
the nerves and marrow of a nation."

THE ANCIENT MARINER

"He was excited about Carter's theological convictions. He wanted to
hear more about them," writes Mailer about himself in his September
26, 1976, *New York Times Magazine* piece "In Search of Carter." After
the honest industry of his mayoral campaign, Mailer had found new
respect for the dogged sincerity of a man like Jimmy Carter, and he was

intrigued by a politician who seemed to combine religious principles with a canny drive to win public office. Yet in spite of his intense interest, Mailer made a mess of his interview with the presidential candidate. Admitting that Carter had very little of the dramatic in his character and realizing that he would get no more than the candidate's polite but cautious attention, Mailer flailed about in his own theories about reincarnation and karma. Carter believed in this life and the judgment to come, and Mailer felt foolish in trying to draw him out with notions about "a powerful God who was at war with other opposed visions in the universe." Referring to his embarrassment in the third person, he concluded: "Mailer did too much of the talking."

Mailer's failure to take Carter's measure was reminiscent of his disengagement from the astronauts. Indeed, he referred to Carter as "another variety of spaceman—he had that silvery reserve only the most confident astronauts ever showed." It was painfully apparent, in Susan S. McDonald's words, that Mailer had an "Ancient Mariner compulsion" to tell Carter about his life and a "need to be as real and consequential to Carter as Carter [was] to him." The Carter interview represented the basic flaw in the Mailer project to imagine America in his image. If he could fail so badly with Carter, the man of the hour, Mailer would have to reconstitute his literary career on an entirely new basis.

A TRUE LIFE NOVEL

November 11, 1976. Lawrence Schiller picked up a newspaper and read about Gary Gilmore, scheduled to be the first man executed in America in ten years. Gilmore had refused to file an appeal; in fact, he was insisting that the state of Utah carry out his death sentence as soon as possible. Adept at putting together book and movie projects, Schiller sensed that Gilmore could be the biggest story he had ever worked on. He immediately set about interviewing the principals in the case and obtaining exclusive rights to the story. When Schiller read the letters of Nicole Baker, Gilmore's lover, he knew he had a potential best-seller and thought of Mailer to write it. Gilmore had killed two men right after his breakup with Nicole. Gilmore spoke of the two murders he had committed as a way of venting his rage, of "opening a valve" to release the tension. Schiller thought of Mailer's stabbing of Adele. Gilmore, with his belief in karma and reincarnation and his violence, was a natural subject for Mailer.

On January 17, 1977, Mailer picked up a paper to read that Gilmore had been executed by a firing squad. The publicity surrounding this event had been enormous, and Mailer sensed that Gilmore "embodied many of the themes I've been living with all my life long." The true-life characters in *The Executioner's Song* confirmed much of what Mailer had imagined in *An American Dream*. When Gary Gilmore first meets Nicole Baker, for example, he exclaims, "I know you," and proceeds to suggest that he and Nicole have known each other in "another time." Not only does Nicole respond instantaneously to Gary just as Cherry does to Rojack, but the psychic bond between them is palpable; they can practically read each other's minds. Gary is certain that he and Nicole will meet in death and that they are soulmates; after his death she senses his presence in a scene reminiscent of Rojack's telephone call to Cherry after she is murdered. Like Rojack slinging his mental darts at people in a nightclub, Gilmore claims, "You can control people with your mind" and gets into staring matches to establish his dominance.

Like Mailer and so many of his characters, Gilmore is "an actor putting on one mask, taking it off, putting on another for a new voice." He even uses a Texas accent to tell certain stories. In *Marilyn*, Mailer is bemused with the occult coincidence of names. In *The Executioner's Song*, Gilmore impresses his cellmate, Gibbs, by pointing out that their last names begin with "GI," they both have girlfriends with a daughter whose name begins with an S and a son whose name begins with a J, and both girlfriends have a mother whose first name is Kathryne.

In January 1977 Mailer did not think in terms of a book until he watched Schiller on the evening news. Schiller seemed moved by his involvement in the story. But Schiller had a problem. His collaboration with Mailer on *Marilyn* had been stormy; they had fought about the design of the book and related issues, and Mailer was wary of further collaboration—although he and Schiller had later worked together briefly when Mailer combined an essay on graffiti with a collection of photographs. How could Schiller get Mailer's attention? Mailer had finally buckled down to writing the great novel he had promised for years and would not be diverted from it except for quick essay assignments that brought in sorely needed income. Schiller's solution was to keep sending Mailer material in batches—interviews and letters and other items that demonstrated just how rich a vein Schiller had opened.

Then he sent Mailer the interview he had done with Gilmore for *Play-boy*. Mailer admitted it was the best interview he had ever read and suggested it might form the basis of a two-character Off-Broadway play he would like to direct. "You can, but first you have to write the book," Schiller replied. Then he made his pitch by telling Mailer about Nicole: "Look, I've got this girl out here in Malibu. She's gonna be the key, the other half of the book. I want to bring her to New York so you can meet her."

Mailer and Nicole had lunch at Trader Vic's. Schiller had primed her by giving her a copy of *Marilyn* to read. Mailer asked her if she played chess. Schiller had just bought her a set, and she retired with Mailer to her hotel room for a game. A half-hour later Mailer and Schiller took a walk down Fifth Avenue. Mailer said: "You're right. There's a book there."

But what kind of book? Schiller knew Mailer would be taking a risk. There were people who said the project was "beneath him," a "trashy *National Enquirer* story," to use Schiller's words, who realized that his involvement with Mailer would hardly be viewed as the writer's "road back to the Nobel Prize for literature." Since *The Armies of the Night* there had been some decline in his reputation. "In the trade he was being characterized as someone who wrote essays as an excuse for serious literature," Schiller discovered when at least one publisher insisted on a guarantee that Mailer would write a narrative and not merely a collection of his thoughts.

Critics had faulted *Marilyn* for its inadequate research and felt Mailer had somehow forced himself on his material. This time Schiller inundated Mailer with dozens of recorded interviews and thousands of pages of transcripts. Each interview was itself a biography, a searching probe of the source's family background, way of life, and surroundings. As Schiller later put it, he would circle and circle around his subjects, filling in the context of their lives, before getting to the areas he was really interested in. It relaxed him and his subjects and helped them to forget the tape recorder.

Mailer began work on *The Executioner's Song* in May 1977. He felt overwhelmed: "I spent the first six months wandering around in bewilderment trying to put people and events together. I really had to work it out. Try encountering a hundred names at once. It's like looking at the laid-out pieces of a clock."

How to order this massive amount of material and be true to the

myriad voices that made up Gilmore's story? Mailer made one false
start. He thought he needed "some ironic framework" and hit upon the
idea of creating a middle-aged, recently divorced screenwriter, a "big,
ungainly man" miserable in Paris with two big suitcases full of the
Gilmore interviews who had been told by a director (someone like
Francis Ford Coppola) to write a treatment that would tell everything
known about Gilmore. The screenwriter's letters to the director would
discuss not only how the Gilmore story was shaping up but also how
Mailer (who would be identified as writing a book on Gilmore) was
dealing with the material. Through this fictional character Mailer
thought he could comment on and control the action of his book.
Fortunately, he abandoned this approach, for Mailer knew it would add
several hundred pages to a long book and that it "would probably violate
the material. . . . It would have been like putting ribbons on a prize
bull."

Instead, Mailer would "move through everybody's head." Used to
writing in the first person, this return to a third-person, objective voice
troubled him: "Make no pretty bones about it. I was paralyzed for a
month. I just couldn't do it. Finally I thought, 'Well, you're going to
have to make the jump.' To this day I feel uneasy about it. I feel I've
violated the fundamental integrity of the novel." It troubled him not to
exercise a single, commanding narrative voice—as though he were
depriving himself of that hard-won ego invention he had spoken of so
brilliantly in *Advertisements for Myself.*

Overcoming "10,000 habits—intimate habits—" Mailer had to resist his penchant for trying to improve upon the "strong and simple"
material that had been handed to him. There would be no asides, no
"little essay" or direct address to the reader. (He would eventually write
such a piece on capital punishment in the February 8, 1981, issue of
Parade.) In a "claustrophobic room with its single high window,"
Mailer learned what it was like to live in a space that is "physically too
small for you," making his connection with Gilmore, oppressed with
the feeling that "slowly the best things in you are being cut out. Stifled
and dying." Thus Mailer came to believe that he knew his subject "as
well as I know some of my ex-wives." The self-reflexive approach, he
realized, was "ridiculous. You just have to bite the bullet. You have to be
brave enough to write this book without putting yourself in it at all," he
told himself. He was to find a better way of showing how his novel had
been shaped by including Schiller as a character in the narrative.

By June 1977, Mailer had reviewed over nine thousand pages of transcript and had taken his first trip to Utah, visiting Gilmore's and Nicole's house to absorb the atmosphere, to touch it, smell it, soak it up, Schiller observes, "like a sponge." From May to December Mailer made another six trips to Utah—as well as one to Marion, Illinois, where Gilmore had been imprisoned. Schiller and Mailer would sometimes form a team for interviews looking like "two detectives on the fat side." Mailer dressed casually. In old Levis or corduroys, he came across as a man at ease with himself. Even his notoriously rapid speech slowed down. He did not use a tape recorder and took only sporadic notes, which made Schiller edgy, but to Mailer the evidence had already been collected; now he had to immerse himself in the environment. Mailer respected Schiller's "passion for verification," remembering that after one interview Schiller had pounded the steering wheel of his car and exclaimed, "She's lying, she's goddam lying!" Schiller worried that Mailer was getting too close to some of his sources, like Gilmore's uncle Vern and cousin Brenda. But Mailer wanted more than facts he could embroider, he wanted focal characters; he wanted to see things as they did, so that he could get inside his material and readers could feel as if they were *there*. He did not want merely to describe Vern's reactions to Gilmore; he wanted the reactions themselves on the page, stripped of commentary and of the transitions from one moment to the next that a narrator might ordinarily supply. Instead, readers would be confronted with blocks of experience and margins—white spaces between the words—that suggest everything that is unsaid, everything that makes life suspenseful in ways fiction rarely reveals:

> *Gary started hitting on the beer in the refrigerator. Vern didn't have to be told Gary had been through a few already.*
> *"Gary," Vern said, "are you going to shape up, or am I going to have to knock you on your ass?"*
>
> *"What are you going to do?" asked Gary.*
> *"I'm going to have to do it."*
> *"Aren't you afraid of me?" Gary asked.*
> *"No," said Vern, "why should I be?" In his gentlest voice, he said, "I can whip you."*
>
> *Gary's face lit up as if for the first time he felt like they wanted him in this house.*

> *"Aren't you afraid?" he asked again.*
> *"No," said Vern, "I'm not. I hope that doesn't sound crazy."*
> *They both began to laugh.*

The only speculation, the only intrusion, in this scene is the *as if* in the description of Gilmore's reaction, an *as if* arising out of more than one hundred interviews. Mailer added about fifty to the sixty Schiller had done on his own, comparing them with the help of his secretary, Judith McNally, and his research assistant, Jere Herzenberg, in order to determine "what probably did occur in a given situation."

In the course of researching the book Mailer evolved a style that reflected his desire to be absolutely faithful to the integrity of the experience he was recording. When Schiller saw the first fifteen or twenty pages of *The Executioner's Song* he was startled at the absence of Mailer's "voice." He remembers Mailer looking straight at him and admitting that he had "so much material, so much fact" that he did not have to rely on his own ego. Much later, to Kenneth C. Doves, Mailer explained how the book had become a turning point in his career:

> *Before I got started I thought I could write an essay about why certain people choose to die rather than live and about the liberal concept that human life is immensely valuable. But when I finished, I had created something I think bears some relationship to the complexity of life. When you realize how complex things are, you lose your desire to editorialize.*

Mailer found he could not explain Gilmore and that it was "more interesting not to." Guided by the words of the witnesses, he used "very little invention" because the interviews were so detailed.

Mailer began to think of *The Executioner's Song* as a great social novel and to realize he was coming "full circle" back to *The Naked and the Dead*, with a plot and characters practically ready-made. Indeed, the rich material helped to correct his tendency to "focus upon the main character and not see the secondary cast and how important they are." Now he could deal with whole panorama of society: Gilmore's family and friends, the prisons, the criminal justice system, Gilmore's victims and their families, Schiller and the account of how the press helped create the story, the state of Utah and the Mormons who figured centrally in Gilmore's upbringing and crimes.

The idea of writing a panoramic social novel seized Mailer's imagination just at the time he had concluded, "I've sort of used up my audience, and I thought, well, I want another audience. I want those people who think I'm difficult to read." He saw the 1970s as a time when people had become "tremendously fed up with personality." The seventies, he admitted to Kenneth Davis, had been "too much for me. They appall me the way the '50s appalled me. Only then, I was full of youthful fight." To Davis, Mailer seemed almost weary and wistful when he added, with a laugh: "I used to hate America for what it was doing to all of us. Now I hate all of us for what we're doing to America." Although he went through the "literary bends" at the start, he wanted to show that he could write in "simple sentences" and create great literature. To write of Gilmore against the huge background of his society also deflected a criticism Mailer had anticipated: "They're going to say there's something swinish about glorifying a two-time killer and a bad man." Mailer persisted in seeing Gilmore as a "another major American protagonist" who encompassed "a deep contradiction in this country and lives his life in the crack of that contradiction," a man who was "malignant at his worst and heroic at his best" with enormous desire for "revenge upon the American system."

The composition of *The Executioner's Song* took fifteen months— about the same amount of time it took to write *The Naked and the Dead*. When Mailer hired Jere Herzenberg (a musicologist and journalist) after the Thanksgiving holiday of 1977, he was well launched into drafting the book. She had just arrived in New York City from San Francisco and was looking for a job to tide her over during a break in her doctoral work. Herzenberg had heard from a friend in Mayor Edward Koch's office that Mailer needed a researcher/editor, and she managed to get an interview at his Brooklyn apartment.

Herzenberg was impressed with the loft. It had windows all the way across the front that overlooked the harbor and gave a breathtaking view of Manhattan. To the left of the windows was a wall of bookcases well stocked with books. The squared-off living room had a Provincetown look, with old New England velvet couches. The dining room had a simple table with the kitchen and bathroom behind it. Rope stairs led to a series of bunks for his kids. Another rope went to the very top of the rafters, where Mailer had his office that could be reached only by walking a plank. It felt like being on a ship; everything had a weatherbeaten look to it without seeming too studied or pretentious.

Mailer's previous assistant had had a background in sociology, and he

asked why a musicologist who wrote opera criticism would want to
work on a book on crime. "I need money and want to go back to San
Francisco," she replied. He started to laugh, then he looked down at her
résumé and saw that their birthdays were on the same day. "So we tried
it, and it worked beautifully," Herzenberg recalls. Soon it seemed as if
writer and researcher could read each other's minds.

The researcher before Herzenberg had not been very good. Now
Mailer required someone to research right behind him, chapter by
chapter, as he drafted the book. Herzenberg would take Larry Schiller's
research and build a chapter up. Mailer would say, "Okay, this chapter is
going to be about the night of the two murders. Tell me everything every
character was doing." If Herzenberg found gaps, she would reinterview
people and confer with Schiller until all of Mailer's questions were
answered. She remembers that he was "meticulous on this book. If you
put a fact down, you had to say what interview, what page, and you had
to have it right behind the outline, footnoted."

Herzenberg worked on huge pieces of graph paper making outlines
for Mailer's inspection. If a chapter outline and research were complete,
it would be reduced to an $8^1/_2$-by-11 booklet with the graph-paper
outline on the front and photocopies of the research inserted inside to
make the story of the chapter. The booklets contained chronologies,
chapter sketches, and biographies. Herzenberg arranged material in
blocks. Sometimes a block was a day, sometimes a month, sometimes a
year. And around each block, condensing or expanding, Mailer would
write his narrative. "I created what he wanted, and he wrote on top of
it," Herzenberg recalls.

Mailer always seemed to know what he was doing. Herzenberg was
awed by his total command of the material:

> There wasn't a day he didn't know what chapter to focus on. He knew the
> book was going to be called The Executioner's Song. He knew he was
> going to make it in the voice of the people of Utah. So he dictated just
> about everything into a tape recorder to get the accent and the rhythm
> down. I would go over the transcriptions of the tape checking for
> grammar and punctuation, and then he would edit the transcripts.

Day after day Herzenberg sat at home in front of her huge Bose speakers
listening to Mailer dictate and driving her boyfriend nuts. Mailer was
perfecting a new narrative voice aimed at embodying the lives of

his characters: "And Gary said to Brenda . . . And Brenda said to Gary . . ."—Herzenberg still carries the cadence of Mailer's words as she describes how deliberate his method became. Even his silences had their equivalent on the page, the gaps between paragraphs expressing, in Herzenberg's estimation, "the white plains of Utah." The open flat plains, the drawl of Mailer's voice was his effort to articulate the feeling of another country, another people. To Herzenberg the whole book came to sound like a song.

Mailer had prodigious work habits, retiring to his room for the afternoon and emerging with forty or fifty pages—sometimes a chapter an afternoon. His mood was steady. Herzenberg had been a little scared about working for him because she had heard about his volatile behavior, yet she found that "he was a doll, actually." He was very happy living with Norris. "Calm, sweet, and fatherly"—even "shy and gentle"—is the way Herzenberg remembers him: "He was terrific." She felt he needed to have a strong family around him. And Norris was amiable and nurturing during a period when New York was still very new to her. Herzenberg could tell that Norris and Mailer had a "great relationship. They really clicked." Fanny and Mailer's kids were around and a few friends would drop in. Jose Torres would come over, and sometimes he and Mailer sparred, although Torres often expressed his fear of hitting him in the head and knocking out America's greatest literary genius. Nothing got in the way of Mailer's professional timetable, however, and he always remained focused on the book. Herzenberg, in the apartment almost every day, rarely saw Mailer depart from his rigorous schedule. "Occasionally he would go to a party, but his eye was on the line."

Mailer was very much the family man—even sharing the same housekeeper with his mother. Herzenberg recalls that

> at lunchtime we would break, and he would cook these enormous lunches in his wok. He used to say that when he was in the army he would cook, and that one day he made lemon meringue pie for nine hundred soldiers. He loved whipping up meals for the whole household in no time at all. It was sort of his therapy to cook.

During meals they would discuss the book. Everyone spoke, mulling over, for example, Nicole's part in the story. Mailer, overweight and supposedly on a diet, liked to stash his candy bars in his study behind some books. Occasionally Herzenberg would see him sneak a snack when he thought no one was looking, but there was no drinking: "Nothing," she emphasizes.

The other sides of Mailer—particularly the celebrity and public personality—were not much in view, but Herzenberg got a glimpse of how he saw himself when she invited him to go see the King Tut exhibit at the Metropolitan Museum of Art. Mailer started to laugh and said, "You have to understand that I'm famous, and I don't have to see King Tut with crowds of people. I can go see King Tut all by himself. It's one of the privileges of fame." Everyone laughed. "He was actually so unpretentious," Herzenberg recalls, "that you forgot, in fact, who he was." He was amused at this aspect of his life and would say to her, "I've never known what it's like to be ordinary because, you have to remember, I became a household name at the age of twenty-five. At times, I think it happened to me when I was too young."

BIOGRAPHY IN A NEW KEY

Book One of *The Executioner's Song*, "Western Voices," begins with Gilmore's release from prison nine months before he commits two murders. His cousin Brenda has persuaded his future parole officer that thirteen years in jail are enough. "I think it's time Gary came home." Brenda suggests that there is a compassionate and secure place for Gilmore where he won't get into trouble. Yet, of course, she is worried about his adjustment to the world outside prison. She is unsure of his responses and anxious to see what kind of man he is. On his release from prison he seems affable and affectionate: He slips easily into conversation with Brenda and her husband, but as they drive home Mailer inserts a single sentence: "The first silence came in"; it is just part of the normal rhythm, a momentary break before the conversation is resumed. Mailer's mention of the silence nevertheless marks the difficulties of communication, especially the trouble Gilmore has in absorbing and responding to the messages of others.

For example, there is a conversation between Gilmore and his boss, Spencer McGrath, in which McGrath (who has repeatedly helped Gilmore with pay advances and tried to ease the ex-convict into a normal work routine) presses Gilmore about the driver's license he promised to get after McGrath had helped him purchase a car:

Before leaving work that night Spencer asked if he had gotten his license. Gary said that Oregon still hadn't sent it over. Something about how they couldn't find the license. The story was one darn thing after another.

Spencer said that since they couldn't locate the old one, Gary ought to sign up for the driver's training course.
Gary said, "That test is for kids. I'm a grown man and it's beneath me."

Spencer tried to get him over this. "The law," he said, "is for everybody. They're not singling you out." He tried to explain. "If I were in some state and didn't have a driver's license, they would make me take it too. Do you think you're better than I am?
"Excuse me," said Gary at last. "I've got to call Nicole." As he walked off, he said, "Real good advice. Thanks, Spencer, for the good advice." Quick to get away.

The spaces between paragraphs indicate Mailer has structured this scene in three parts, each centering on an exchange between McGrath and Gilmore. The three parts also provide a paradigm of Gilmore's characteristic behavior and are an excellent example of Mailer's subtle narrative arrangements in the book.

After so many years in prison it is second nature for Gilmore to make up a story that excuses his negligence. That he should make getting a driver's license an issue of male pride is also typical, for he does think he is better than other people. He is quick to take offense, and even quicker to condescend or ridicule those he believes are beneath him. No doubt he has had to listen to too much "good advice," and so he won't stand to listen to any more of it from Spencer McGrath. In spite of a high IQ Gilmore is immature, even childlike, in his anger that the world does not recognize his needs. Conversely, he seems only dimly aware of life outside himself, and so it has always been easy for him to violate the rights of others, and even easier to wrap his life around his girlfriend, Nicole, whom he can powerfully manipulate. Except for Nicole, Gilmore is always quick to get away from the responsibility of dealing with others.

Thus this three-part episode is a miniature model of the countless situations in which Gilmore fails to register other points of view.

Although Mailer never makes such an explicit judgment of Gilmore, the book's discrete paragraphs—built of thousands of details—converge in an awesome totality that shows how Gilmore evades so much of the world that attaches to him.

A great deal of the book is dialogue or paraphrase of dialogue enhancing the dramatic clash of details and conflicting points of view. With no privileged retrospective narrator to unify the disparate, the patterns we perceive depend on our ability to piece together the discrete.

Gilmore's murder of Max Jensen starkly documents the gulf that governs so much of human behavior in *The Executioner's Song*:

> *Gary walked around the corner from where the truck was parked and went into a Sinclair service station. There was only one man present, the attendant. He was a pleasant-looking serious young man with broad jaws and broad shoulders. He had a clean straight part in his hair. His jawbones were slightly farther apart than his ears. On the chest of his overalls was pinned a nameplate. MAX JENSEN. He asked, "Can I help you?"*
>
> *Gilmore brought out the .22 Browning Automatic and told Jensen to empty his pockets. So soon as Gilmore had pocketed the cash, he picked up the coin changer in his free hand and said, "Go to the bathroom." Right after they passed through the bathroom door, Gilmore said: "Get down." The floor was clean. Jensen must have cleaned it in the last fifteen minutes. He was trying to smile as he lay down on the floor. Gilmore said, "Put your arms under your body." Jensen got into position with his hands under his stomach. He was still trying to smile.*
>
> *It was a bathroom with green tiles that came to the height of your chest, and tan-painted walls. The floor, six feet by eight feet, was laid in dull gray tiles. A rack for paper towels on the wall had Towl Saver printed on it. The toilet had a split seat. An overhead light was in the wall.*
>
> *Gilmore brought the Automatic to Jensen's head. "This one is for me," he said, and fired.*
>
> *"This one is for Nicole," he said, and fired again. The body reacted each time.*
>
> *He stood up. There was a lot of blood. It spread across the floor at a surprising rate. Some of it got onto the bottom of his pants.*

> *He walked out of the rest room with the bills in his pocket, and the*
> *coin changer in his hand, walked by the Coke machine and the phone on*
> *the wall, walked out of this real clean gas station.*

Max Jensen is unable to make a clean connection with his murderer. He tries to smile and maintain his well-ordered and neat world, but his blood spreads across the floor as Gilmore walks out of "this real clean gas station." Gilmore, frustrated and depressed for many days over his breakup with Nicole, has found an outlet for his madness.

Other than explaining the murder as Gilmore's "rage at how life had ruined his chances," no reason is given for the murder. Gilmore himself said: "I was always capable of murder . . . I can become totally devoid of feelings for others, unemotional." David Lodge suggests that "the uncomfortable idea that Gilmore compels us to contemplate is that there may be such a thing as innate evil, which can be neither explained nor expelled by conditioning." Gilmore never gives a precise cause for the murder; nothing about him or his background can mitigate the brutality of his act; and he emphasizes throughout the last months of his life that he cannot excuse the murder by pleading insanity. Jensen's death scene allows us no sympathy for Gilmore; he shows no hesitation, no doubts; and he is oblivious to Jensen's friendliness. As nearly as possible after the fact, Mailer lets the scene present itself, so that we witness the nothingness in between the moments Gilmore and Jensen act and speak. No human transaction takes place in the gas station, so Gilmore is able simply to walk out of it, the evil of his act just as simply stressed by the station's cleanliness and by his clean-living victim.

Reading such sparely created scenes tempt one to comb through the details in search of the pertinent clue that will point to the meaning of Gilmore's story. But Joan Didion seems right in saying "the very subject of *The Executioner's Song* is that vast emptiness at the center of the Western experience, a nihilism antithetical not only to literature but to most other forms of human endeavor, a dread so close to zero that human voices fade out, trail off, like skywriting." Mailer has chosen to make a literature that is articulately mute, almost muzzled in its restrained revelations of actions such as Gilmore's, which remain voiceless, dumb, and frighteningly uncommunicative:

> *"Why'd you do it, Gary?" Nielson asked again quietly.*
> *"I don't know," Gary said.*

"Are you sure?"
"I'm not going to talk about that," Gilmore said. He shook his head
delicately, and looked at Nielson, and said, "I can't keep up with life."

Gilmore's perceptions, like the way he shakes his head in this scene with
the detective who extracts his confession, are often delicate and direct.
He had a fine intelligence, yet neither he nor anyone else can do much
more than show how he "can't keep up with life."

The second half of *The Executioner's Song*, "Eastern Voices," shows
how Mailer recovered enough material to write a narrative of Gilmore's
life and of the characters who made up that life. One character, Lawrence Schiller, dominates the action as a conniving producer and a
recorder of history who becomes "part of the story." As David Lodge
shrewdly observes:

> *Schiller performs the role that Mailer himself, ironically distanced by a*
> *third-person narration, performs in his earlier books of reportage: not*
> *merely a reflector of events, but a consciousness in which the ethics and*
> *pragmatics of the writing process itself are laid bare.*

Much of the integrity of *The Executioner's Song*, as Mailer acknowledges in his Afterword, is attributable to Schiller's revelations of both
his successes and failures in bringing Gilmore's story to light. And by
choosing to expose his source so nakedly Mailer opens up—as he does
brilliantly in his other works—the whole problem of biography.

Gilmore is not always cooperative with his biographer; he refuses to
answer certain questions about his family life, his relationship with
Nicole, and about the murders. Schiller realizes that Gilmore is in
charge of telling his own story and is careful to supply only those parts
that allow him some space apart from the searching questions and the
media attention. When Schiller accuses Gilmore of not remembering
the truth of his early childhood, Gilmore replies: "Do you remember the
truth of *your* early childhood, Larry?" In a way, this is Gilmore's
profoundest reaction to the publicity and the prying that threatens to
overwhelm the way in which he wants to take his life. Such moments
prompt Schiller to wonder whether "he was qualified, at bottom, to
know Gary Gilmore." Perhaps it is such moments that provoke Mailer in
his Afterword to confess, "The story is as accurate as one can make it.

This does not mean it has come a great deal closer to the truth than the recollections of the witnesses."

Schiller is alert to Gilmore's manipulative maneuvers just as Gilmore is alert to Schiller's. "Sometimes you sound like you're telling a story you've told many times before," Schiller tells Gilmore, as if "you wanted to charm the reader the lover, the observer in a very practical, calculating way." Similarly, Schiller is suspicious of his collaborator, the writer Barry Farrell, who uses the interviews to direct Gilmore's story into a form Gilmore himself may not have intended: "Barry tended to shape his questions upon conclusions he'd already made."

The second half of *The Executioner's Song*, then, raises the disturbing question of authenticity. Diane Johnson, for example, wonders which are the "true parts." She suggests that "the author of a true-life novel tries to have it both ways—to improve the dull, invent the spicy parts, leave out the inconvenient things, and not be held accountable for veracity or completeness . . . the text is mined with Mailerisms when you look closely." She cites a few examples; and others can be added, such as Mailer quoting the thoughts of Gilmore's arthritic mother and then adding his poetic commentary: " 'Oh, Gary,' whispered the child that never ceased to live in the remains of her operations and twisted joints, 'Oh, Gary, how could you!' " Or the scene in which Bessie is moved by her recollections of the past: "Her heart turned over, as if a great wheel had revolved. She felt a tear drop, pure as sorrow itself." The descriptive words, at least, are Mailer's invention.

Johnson pursues questions of veracity the book itself recognizes and explores. Even in the first half of the work the carefully controlled paragraphs, neatly set off from each other, imply that *every* moment, every scene, has been contrived for the design it makes upon the page. Each paragraph is tantamount to a block of research. In his Afterword, Mailer (perhaps too briefly) indicates his principles of selection and invention. The residual ambiguities in the text are the ambiguities that survive in all works of interpretation. Mailer knows that another writer would have looked at the Gilmore story differently.

Thus "Western Voices" and "Eastern Voices" dramatize the dialectical tension between documentary form and narrative invention. Of course the truth of some parts of the book are questionable. That is why it is a "true life novel." In true life memories are fallible, and the way people present themselves is an amalgam of fiction and fact. Gilmore was aware of this ambiguity, but he wouldn't talk about it. If there was to be a narrative that attempted a whole view of his life, then that narrative had to be researched and re-created by a writer willing to take on and explore the nebulous boundaries, the nexus between fiction and fact.

The Executioner's Song is for Mailer biography in a new key, since he attends as never before to the integrity of individual lives without quickly elevating those lives into symbolic significance. At the same time, the continuity of Mailer's concerns is apparent in his ambitious desire to show that true life must be mediated through the imaginative power of a singular intelligence.

12.

ANCIENT EVENINGS (1979–1982)

THE FOURTH MRS. MAILER FIGHTS HER FINAL MARRIAGE BATTLE

On February 26, 1979, Beverly—still legally married to Norman Mailer—went public with her grievances. ONCE NORMAN MAILER'S CONQUEST, THE FOURTH MRS. MAILER FIGHTS HER FINAL MARRIAGE BATTLE was the headline of a *People* magazine article. She was suing for custody of her sons, Michael and Stephen, requesting $52,000 a year in alimony plus child support, and their $135,000 home in Provincetown. Mailer denied that she had been promised the house and claimed he could not meet her financial demands since he owed at least $100,000 in back taxes. Beverly was not impressed: "Listen, he said he was broke when I met him, and it's the same story now. Norman is a corporation. He's screaming poverty, but he makes $347,000 a year." She acknowledged her share of mistakes and the tenderness she once felt for him but charged that "he argued and beat on me all day, and then wanted to go to bed at night. He wanted to fight me." What really ruined the marriage, however, was his womanizing: "When I was pregnant he had an airline stewardess. Three days after bringing home our baby, he began an affair." Beverly admitted that she had retaliated with her own affair in Provincetown and that "Norman's ego was shattered because I'd done it in *his* town." When he brought home one of his girlfriends, Beverly attacked her, admitting, "I may have hit her, but she invaded my nest. Anyway she was a karate expert. I had a black eye. Norman watched, and when it was all over he said, 'Wouldn't it be funny if she got the house?'"

Sandy Charlebois Thomas later disputed Beverly's claim to the house: "The number of things that Beverly didn't know, though, it's pretty incredible." According to Thomas, Mailer had said to Beverly when they separated that the house was hers if she took responsibility for it, and that included paying the bills—which she did not do. Ownership of the house had always been in his name.

Norris took this public embarrassment calmly—in part because Mailer had leveled with her about his tangled relationships with women and in part because Beverly's descriptions of Mailer simply did not accord with the man Norris knew. After Barney's death Norris had assumed management of day-to-day household expenses and taken a direct interest in Mailer's financial affairs. She knew how much he was worth. She knew how much he was spending in child support and alimony and how much he could afford. In short, she had a mastery of the household and of Mailer's career that none of his previous women came near to attaining. Norris knew, for example, that Mailer was supporting Carol Stevens at the same level as Beverly and yet Stevens had no complaints. In spite of his large income, there were times when he was strapped for money, when he had to send his daughter Maggie (by Carol Stevens) to public school because he could not afford to send both Maggie and Matthew (Norris's son by her first marriage) to private school. And Norris had been deeply impressed that in spite of obligations to his other children, Mailer had immediately taken a responsibility for Matthew that was equal to what he felt for his other children. Hard, shrewd, and canny, Norris could sympathize with Mailer's other women, but she was not about to share Beverly's self-pity or to view herself as Mailer's victim.

Mailer made no great claims for having changed as a person. What was different, however, was the way Norris treated him. Of course, he still found other women attractive and would sometimes give them the eye. Norris seemed to have a sixth sense about such things, for

Mailer remembered an incident in which she had asked him about what he had been doing around three o'clock. In fact, at about that time he had noticed a desirable woman while he was crossing the street. It seemed to amuse and almost comfort him that she was so "tuned into" him.

Beverly and Norris could agree on only one point: Beverly's statement that Mailer was a good father. Yet Beverly wanted custody because "I won't let the boys grow up like him—to treat women the way he does." She also had a warning for Norris: "Norris says, 'I want to be famous,' and I guess she is. But she'll get hers. Norman tells you stories about his other wives to make you feel sorry for him. All his ladies do for a while. And then he tramples them."

Beverly's predictions did not hold true for Norris, for Mailer's ideas about sex and about women had evolved over the years. He would say in a 1981 interview that he no longer felt that he could dominate sex, although he claimed to have gotten a bad back from trying to do so in too many beds as a young man. There had been extraordinary experiences in whorehouses and combative relationships with several women that, in some respects, had proved a healthy way of testing what he knew about himself and his ideas, but in the end such affairs had become dreadful and had worn him out.

Mailer's view of sex was romantic. Next to Henry Miller's accounts of "riproaring sex," Mailer felt like a "nice Nelly," a maiden aunt, turning his erotic passages into highly metaphorical scenes that reminded at least one critic of medieval romances. Almost twenty years earlier at the Edinburgh Festival, Rebecca West had observed that beside Henry Miller, Mailer looked like a "wholesome farm-boy." There was, indeed, something forced in Mailer's writing about sex, an allegory of himself that never really got down to the act itself. In its way, his feeling about sex was as veiled as his mother's diffident description of the plot of *Romeo and Juliet*: "Well, I think they kind of liked each other." Mailer confessed that in his family, one simply did not have a vocabulary for talking about "personal relationships."

When one of Mailer's daughters spoke about losing her virginity he was alarmed that she might do so just to have the experience. He wanted something more passionate from her—a feeling that she just had to lose it because she couldn't control herself with an overwhelming attractive guy. He suspected that she did not take his advice.

OF WOMEN AND THEIR ELEGANCE

The reviews of *The Executioner's Song* in the fall of 1979 were some of the best of Mailer's career:

> *At long last, Mailer has used his immense narrative powers, a true gift of the gods, the way they are meant to be used: to tell a story that is not about himself.* —Walter Karp, Esquire

> *This is the best thing Mailer has done in years, and considering the good books he has given us that's saying a lot.* —John Garvey, Commonweal

> *This is an absolutely astonishing book.* —Joan Didion, The New York Times Book Review

Critics still debated whether or not he had delivered a genuine work of fiction. Instead of thoroughbred novels, he had produced hybrids: "history as a novel" and "the novel as history," a "novel biography," a "true life novel," and with *Of Women and Their Elegance*, published just one year after *The Executioner's Song*, an "imaginary memoir" of Marilyn Monroe. Indeed, his movement from *Marilyn* to *Of Women and Their Elegance* constituted a pattern exemplary of his effort to treat fiction and fact as doubles of each other.

Fact and fiction, in Mailer's mind, are reciprocal; one completes the other: "I was never satisfied with the first book, *Marilyn*. I felt that it had an awful lot to say *about* her but that she never necessarily emerged, she was never a presence. So I wanted to try and do her from the inside—see if I could." In *Marilyn*, Mailer hovers around Monroe like Rojack circles around Cherry without, finally, navigating by her lights. He presents Monroe's concerns without coming to a full sense of how she situated herself in them. The novel part of the biography consists of guesswork that is frequently inspired but inconclusive. Mailer the biographer hesitates on the threshold of her consciousness, "out of respect for the intricacies of her mind." If he dares more with *Of Women and Their Elegance*, it is because "I believe I know more about her now."

At times, there is a flatness in the prose as if Mailer has tired of providing a continuous narrative for a person who, in life, often jumped much more quickly from one subject to another than the transitions on the page would indicate. Too many distracting, irrelevant photographs mar the text. The best passages manage to convey a life brilliantly imagined and documented:

> *When I sat down at the mirror, I would see the commencement of little lines. In years to come they would be wrinkles, and that would make me pour a drop of foundation right on the glass table. I like the feel of the oil on the glass under my fingers. Then I rubbed it in. Now, my thoughts would start. It was like an orchestra tuning up. Stories would begin to go through my head, that is, memories of things that had happened to me. As they did, they began happening again. I couldn't turn off such thoughts any better than you can switch off a projector if you don't know where to find the switch. I mean, you could stop it with your bare hand. So I guess I could have gotten up from the mirror, but I didn't. I kept looking at all the memories of my life including the dirty memories and the really filthy ones. Sometimes a tear would come out of my eye, and run mascara down my face like a knife opening a cut. Something very sad in me would begin to bleed.*

Mailer summons a tactile Monroe, one who likes "the feel of the oil on the glass under my fingers." The lines of her experience lead naturally to the wounds of her remembering.

It would be misleading to imply that the imaginary memoir is an improvement on the biography. On the contrary, it is a strangely univocal book about a multiple personality containing intermittent powerful scenes that evoke a woman's way of creating herself. The remarkable tensions of *Marilyn* that pit a relentlessly interpretative mind against an elusive subject are missing from *Of Women and Their Elegance*. But taken together, each book does complement and, in a way, complete the other. Mailer is often his own toughest judge, and he has said of *Of Women and Their Elegance*:

> *I confess I wanted to do a book where I wasn't stretching. It was a big stretch on* The Executioner's Song, *and my book about Egypt is a huge stretch, so huge that I walk around winded most of the time in relation to it. And I thought, "I want a little vacation." And it may be that the book suffers from that.*

Of Women and Their Elegance received some good reviews, but it was generally dismissed as exploitative. Did Mailer *have* to do another book

on Monroe? critics wondered with some asperity. Moreover, the novel
was swamped in the wake of the tremendously favorable reviews of *The
Executioner's Song*, which rivaled his success with *The Armies of the
Night* and *The Naked and the Dead* and won him a Pulitzer Prize.

MERRY MARRIAGE-GO-ROUND

In November 1980, Norman Mailer made headlines: IN A MERRY
MARRIAGE-GO-ROUND, NORMAN MAILER PLANS A DOUBLE WEDDING, TO
WIVES FIVE AND SIX. Mailer planned to marry Carol Stevens to "legiti-
mize" nine-year-old Maggie and to "honor" the years he lived with her.
He then would initiate a quick divorce in order to marry Norris, thus
recognizing their union and legitimizing John Buffalo, his two-and-
a-half-year-old son by Norris. Norris told columnist Liz Smith that she
found it all "a bit disconcerting," but she supported Mailer's decision:
"I understand why he feels he must do this." Later she confessed to
another worry: What if Carol decided she liked being married to Mailer
and balked at a divorce? Beverly continued to claim that she was not
divorced from Mailer: "It's still in litigation. So how can he get married
even once?" But Beverly's declarations did not deter Mailer, who told
Liz Smith that it was important that all eight of his children be
legitimate—"every last one of the little buggers." Consulted by *People*
magazine, Letitia Baldrige, author of the revised *Amy Vanderbilt Complete Book of Etiquette*, advised that no gifts be sent to celebrate either
marriage, since "it's not a formal type of ritual." The marriage–
divorce–marriage went ahead as scheduled, Beverly's objections notwithstanding.

THE *FRISSON* OF A ROLE

"I was fascinated by Norman Mailer as a writer and as a person,"
explained Milos Forman, who cast the writer in a cameo role as Stanford
White in the film adaptation of E. L. Doctorow's *Ragtime* (released in
December 1981). "There are certain similarities, culturally and socially,
between him and Stanford White, and an aura of accomplishment in
art and social life. Then I found out he had an ambition to perform."
With Norris beside him in a nonspeaking part, Mailer swaggered onto

the scene in a curly gray wig and stick-on mustache, impersonating the famous architect who is shown in the film being shot in the head by Harry K. Thaw, the outraged husband of Evelyn Nesbit, White's mistress.

Stanford White had been entertained in the highest circles of society and Mailer, having recently adorned the tables of the wealthy with Norris as his consort, had looked forward to this appearance, for which he lost a considerable amount of the bulk he had been carrying around his middle for several years. His scene had to be shot over and over again so that the director could capture from every conceivable angle the impact of the bullet on White's head as he fell to the floor. It was the antithesis of Mailer's filmmaking in the 1960s, which emphasized spontaneity, not production values.

The day Mailer's scene was shot came shortly after the murder of John Lennon. By then, Mailer

> dreaded doing it. I hadn't thought it through when I took on the part. I didn't realize that when you get killed in a movie you get it in close up. Charges detonate on your skull and on your back. The killing of John Lennon altered everything. I no longer took my own movie death seriously, I had the shock of a real death going through my system. Like fifty million other people I cared about Lennon; my own concerns were put into proportion. I had to do something tricky physically: Be shot, slump to my right, knock over a Champagne bucket, without braining Norris or decapitating myself, and do a little twist as I fell. There was a man under the table controlling a pipe full of blood, which came up my leg and ended at my ear. The gun fired and the charges went off, time slowed as it always does when there is violence; it took forever to get going. I remember thinking, "Get moving you dummy," and then I began jerking, my head flew to the left, to the right, I fell to the table, clawed the Champagne bucket, it flew in the air, and hit me on the head. I did my twist and there I am on the floor and Norris is screaming and the extras are surrounding me, and I feel content. I can feel the pool of artificial blood spreading under me, and there's a "CUT!" There is something compelling about experiences you don't control.

That Mailer should submit to the sheer tedium of filming the scene suggests how important it was for him to get on screen in a major motion picture that millions of people would see. He wanted to be Stanford

White in the same way he wanted to be an Irish prizefighter or a
Southern sheriff—for the *frisson* of a role. Some reviewers thought
Mailer was not playing White but merely himself. "I'm a good Ameri-
can boy: I want to be in the movies," quipped Mailer.

IN THE BELLY OF THE BEAST

By the time Jack Henry Abbott was released from prison on June 5,
1981, he and Mailer had been corresponding for four years. Abbott had
first written Mailer when he heard Mailer was working on *The Executioner's Song*. In his midthirties, Abbott had spent most of his adult life
in prison, including penitentiaries in Utah and in Marion, Illinois,
where Gilmore had done his time. Abbott knew of no writers who really
understood the prison system; even convicts needed at least a ten-year
stretch to comprehend its complexity. Unlike most correspondents who
asked Mailer to read their work or wrote to praise or criticize his books,
Abbott apparently expected nothing. He offered, rather, to provide
background material on the conditions Gilmore confronted in prison.
Mailer was impressed with Abbott's style: "intense, direct, unadorned,
and detached—an unusual combination." Mailer realized he "did not
know much about violence in prisons," admitted as much to Abbott, and
found himself within two weeks engaged in a "thoroughgoing correspondence."

Abbott seemed an original to Mailer, providing him with an unvar-
nished prose and a point of view different from Gilmore's letters to
Nicole, from other prison literature, and from interviews Schiller and
Mailer had conducted. Gilmore was a romantic and a mystic and not
interested in the prison experience per se. Abbott, on the other hand,
struck Mailer as having doped out the system, taking both an empirical
and political approach to the penitentiary that would yield an invaluable
inside picture of convict life.

Soon Mailer began to see possibilities in Abbott's prose, to suspect he
had in hand a budding writer who had faced the challenges Mailer
himself had sought. Abbott portrayed himself as an unreconstructed
rebel who would not be bowed by the "devastating nature of civilized
violence" in the penal system. In his letters he presented an unrelieved
report of institutional brutality: Guards were pigs who beat prisoners at
will; courts did virtually nothing to protect prisoners' rights. The whole

organization of prisons was designed to deprive convicts of their humanity:

> *The Shah of Iran will chop off your hands, but he will not (because he cannot) take your soul from you. In America, for example, if its prisons hold the slightest authority over you, it both can and will destroy you—it can and will take your soul.*

The vehemence of Abbott's expressions, literally underlined in nearly every page of his prose, delineates a view of a repressive society that Mailer had held in "The White Negro," a trace of which showed up in his introduction to *In the Belly of the Beast*, an edited collection of Abbott's prison letters:

> *There is a paradox at the core of penology, and from it derives the thousand ills and afflictions of the prison system. It is that not only the worst of the young are sent to prison, but the best—that is, the proudest, the bravest, the most daring, the most enterprising, and the most undefeated of the poor.*

Certainly this is how Abbott dramatized himself: a man who refused to be broken by the system, who spent years in solitary rather than adopt the meek appearance and behavior expected of him.

In one letter to Mailer, Abbott described an incident that was typical of the way he had been treated. He was taken from the Atlanta Federal Penitentiary to the Butner, North Carolina, Federal Correctional Institution for "psychological experimentation." He had been "falsely accused of involvement in an almost-fatal knife assault on a prison guard." At Butner an inmate informed on Abbott, claiming that he was planning an escape. Taken by "about twenty guards and other employees" to a glassed-in observation cell where it was "impossible to see or be heard by anyone but the prison staff," he was stripped of his clothing and forced to lie down on a "steel slab on iron legs bolted to the floor." His ankles were chained to two corners of this "bed," and his wrists were chained over his head to the other two corners, putting him in a "complete spread eagle position." To relieve himself he had to twist his body over on one side so that his penis could point in the general direction of a drain in the concrete floor. The next day he was beaten and choked by guards. Because of a report by a "medical technician" that the nerves in

Abbott's arms were dying, he was released from his bed of torture (by now his eyes were blackened and he was covered with bruises), dressed in nylon coveralls, handcuffed, and put in leg irons in the "regular segregation section." With only one hand "chained to the iron crossbar at the head of the bed," Abbott found he could stand. "It was at that time that I began writing *you*, in the hole," Abbott recalled for Mailer. The plain but sharp repetitiveness of Abbott's prose (the image of the one-handed writer in chains), his pointed singling out of Mailer worked its effect. Mailer was hooked.

Jere Herzenberg remembers how moved Mailer was by Abbott's letters, as he had been moved by Gilmore's. Mailer was "very upset about Gilmore and felt he had not been given a chance, and he empathized with Abbott who was playing him like a violin." Abbott would send letters complaining he had no one to get him jeans or shoes and would Mailer get him those things? Mailer would say to Herzenberg, "Could you go get jeans and a shirt for Abbott?" Herzenberg would refuse: "No, I'm not going to do it. You want to get the shirt and jeans? You get the shirt and the jeans! I'm not going to goddam do it." To which Mailer would reply, "All you have to say is no." Herzenberg distrusted the letters and said to Mailer:

> *"My God, this guy is violent. They've had him in isolation for years and years. Why do you think they have him in isolation?" And he used to say, "Oh, come on," you're just a bourgeois capitalist. . . ." And I'd say, "Please. . . ." It was the one thing we irritated each other on.*

Mailer's other assistant, Judith McNally, went through Abbott's prose with a fine editorial pencil, giving Abbott the chance Mailer felt Gilmore never got. To this day, Herzenberg's voice aches with frustration over Mailer's gullibility: "I used to explain to him. These people have been psychotics since they've been kids. They don't change. Once they've crossed the line, they've crossed it."

> [*Rollyson*] Why do you think he couldn't see that? I mean, there must be something personal to Mailer, because he has identified with people like this in his fiction, and then here it happens to him in real life.
>
> [*Herzenberg*] It's the Jewish boy taken by these tough types.

Herzenberg had had another writer friend also "taken by a convict." Convicts like Abbott, she suggests, are the "absolute antithesis of a Jewish mama's boy. These street guys are everything writers like Mailer are raised not to be. I think, in a sense, it's a very deep rebellion, a very deep rebellion." Except for the Abbott episode, Herzenberg had felt very close to Mailer, to his shy and reclusive side and his need to have strong family around him. The aggressive antisocial Mailer was not what "he had been spelled out to be," Herzenberg concludes.

Mailer, who had seen his career in literature as an opportunity to reinvent himself over and over, saw in Abbott the makings of a "new writer of the largest stature among us." Anticipating Abbott's release from prison, Mailer had written, "It is certainly the time for him to get out"—notwithstanding the fact that Abbott had murdered ("in combat") a fellow convict, had a record of assaults, admitted his immaturity ("At thirty-seven I am barely a precocious child. My passions are those of a boy"), accepted no personal responsibility for his long prison record, and told Mailer, "No one, not even you . . . has ever held out a hand to help me to be a better man. No one." Abbott confessed that "I'm tenuous, shy, introspective, and suspicious of everyone." On the eve of his release, he declared, "My vision of life outside of prison has become a fading dream. . . . I cannot imagine how I can be happy in American society." It was, in fact, "the most unjust and oppressive country in the whole world." Yet he wanted his freedom and ended his book of prison letters with a plea for his right to "find my life again and see and do things other people do."

Mailer accorded moral merit to the literary excellence of Abbott's writing. He was uneasy, to be sure, noting in his introduction to *In the Belly of the Beast* that "Abbott looks to understand the world, he would dominate the world with his mind, yet in all his adult life he has spent six weeks in the world. He knows prison like the ferryman knows the crossing to Hades. But the world Abbott knows only through books." That world, moreover, was the world of Marxist dialectics. Abbott the ideologue made Mailer uncomfortable: "I am much more impressed by the literary measure of Abbott's writings on prison than by his overall analyses of foreign affairs and revolution." Here Mailer made his fatal mistake, for Abbott excused his own presence in prison by adopting a militantly Communist position. He saw himself as a political prisoner: "I have never accepted that I did this to myself. I have never been

successfully indoctrinated with that belief. That is the only reason I have
been in prison this long." The only reason? If the consequences of his
actions were not so deadly, Abbott's refusal to accept any responsibility
for himself would be comic. It is telling that he observes in an aside that
"I keep waiting for the years to give me a sense of humor, but so far that
has evaded me completely." Everything that happens to Jack Abbott in
In the Belly of the Beast is filtered through a narcissism greater than that
Mailer has diagnosed in himself and others.

Abbott remembers Mailer visiting him in prison after the publication
of *The Executioner's Song*. Having brought a signed copy of the book, a
quiet, nervous Mailer gazed at Abbott during a gap in their conversation.
Out of the silence Abbott caught a glimpse of a deeply compassionate
man who was saddened by Abbott's plight. Mailer arranged for the
publication of an excerpt from Abbott's letters in the June 11, 1981,
issue of *The New York Review of Books*.

Erroll McDonald, a young black editor at Random House, found the
letters intriguing and visited Abbott to discuss their publication as a
book. McDonald was appalled by Abbott's sexism and racism, having
read an Abbott letter to Robert Silvers, editor of *The New York Review of
Books*, referring to women as "niggers." McDonald had no doubt about
Abbott's talent; however, he was more troubled by the "hints of weakness and vulnerability" in the letters.

McDonald, Mailer, and other writers sent letters to Abbott's parole
board testifying to his talent and to his ability to make a living as a
writer. Indeed, Mailer promised Abbott a job as his editorial assistant.
The April 8, 1981, hearing of the Utah Board of Pardons focused on
Abbott's record of violence. In 1964, a prison doctor had described
Abbott as "extremely angry" with a "longstanding thought disorder."
Another report the next year stated he had "never developed the ability
to interact socially with others." He was in a "paranoid state" and
"capable of sudden violence." Examinations in 1969, 1971, 1973, and
1975—sometimes filed after violent episodes—found Abbott, in the
words of Dr. Steven Shelton of the Menninger Clinic in Topeka, Kansas,
"a potentially dangerous man" with a "hair-trigger temper." In his 1973
report, Dr. Shelton concluded: "One gets the impression of a very
explosive person whose hostility and aggressions are barely controlled
and lie on the surface ready to erupt." On April 2, 1981—less than a
week before his hearing—Abbott was tested by Dr. A. L. Carlisle, a

prison psychologist, who reported that Abbott was "angry and hostile about his captivity" but that "his hopes were up and he had a lot of plans." Interviewed later by *The New York Times*, Dr. Carlisle commented: "It wasn't a report saying the guy looks really good and is ready to go out, and it wasn't a report saying he looks like he's going to go out and be violent. The biggest problem in psychological testing is predicting who will be violent." Captain Thomas Bona, director of the maximum-security unit in Abbott's Utah prison, sent a report to the Board of Pardons that opposed Abbott's release and later told a *New York Times* reporter: "I thought, and so did my lieutenant and the social worker, that Mr. Abbott was a dangerous individual who should be given a rehearing in two years. I had known him when he was in Utah before, and I didn't see a changed man. His attitude, his demeanor indicated psychosis."

Thomas R. Harrison, chairman of the Board of Pardons, opened the hearing with the statement that Abbott's case was "probably one of the most fascinating" ones he had ever considered. Impressed with Abbott's letters of support, Harrison still had qualms about Abbott's "extremely violent temper, explosive at times, that leads you to do things that really work against your own interests very much." Harrison knew that putting Abbott on the street was very risky, that "there are going to be disappointments; there are going to be people who rub you the wrong way; there are going to be people who make you angry. And it's of great concern to the board how you're going to react to this situation."

Abbott responded that he had "grown up in a cage," no one had "given a damn" for him since he was a child, and he had had to "fight" his way "through all that." His anger was "rational," however; it had helped him survive; he was no "maniac." When asked by Harrison about his "potential for hurting somebody," Abbott quickly replied, "No, no. There won't be nothing like that."

Mailer met Abbott at the airport in New York on the day of his release and took him home with him. It was after 1:00 A.M. Norris and his children were asleep, and he and Abbott spent about an hour on his terrace talking. Then Abbott took a cab to the Lower East Side halfway house to begin his reentry into society. With everything shut up for the night, he had to spend his first hours staring out the window waiting for daylight. It was depressing—the dust and the soot and the pervasive smell of garbage, winos and addicts staggering on the street, collapsing

in the gutters, and hallucinating. Abbott felt he was among the walking
dead. He witnessed a stabbing and the firebombing of a car. Soon he was
carrying a knife.

For relief, Abbott could run uptown, see his editor at Random House
or Bob Silvers at *The New York Review*, and confer with Mailer in
Brooklyn, but he was told he would have to stick it out at the halfway
house, for by the time the papers for a transfer came through he would
be finished with this trial period in his life anyway.

Jay McInerney was sitting in McDonald's office one day when Abbott
"stormed in." He seemed completely disoriented—not knowing where
to purchase things or how to cope with people who did not understand
his behavior. He had gone into a hardware store for toothpaste and been
laughed at. He did not know what to do with his rage. After Abbott left,
McDonald (who had grown up in Bedford-Stuyvesant) looked at
McInerney and said: "He's not going to make it, man." McInerney
realized that "Erroll was the only person in this enterprise who had the
street smarts to understand what Abbott was going through."

Norris's immediate reaction to Abbott's release from prison was negative. "You wrote the book about Gilmore—didn't you learn anything?
It's not gonna work, these guys don't change," she told her husband. She
did not want Abbott in the house or around her children. But Mailer
coaxed her into inviting him to dinner—just "once," and then she would
not have to deal with him again. What she saw surprised her. "He was
very sweet, very touching, because he was nervous and almost like a
little boy." Neatly dressed and well groomed in a suit that resembled one
of Mailer's—"a three piece navy pinstripe"—with his "little round
glasses" and meek appearance he hardly seemed like a threatening
criminal. Norris's three-year-old son, John Buffalo, took Abbott by the
hand and said, "Let me show you my room." A grinning Abbott seemed
nonplussed but agreeable to following this little boy around the house.
Norris admits to being "totally taken" with Abbott after this meeting.

Ecey Gwaltney remembers a dinner she attended shortly after Abbott's release. There he sat next to Norris, her son, Matthew, and Dandy
(Mailer's daughter by Adele), now twenty-four and working as a painter
and art teacher. They talked about the possibility of Abbott spending
time at the MacDowell Colony as soon as he was allowed to leave
the city.

Norris did not lose her perspective on Abbott. She sensed the deep
anger he tried to control by taking long walks. Little things could set him

off—momentarily misplacing his shoes or having his suit stolen. He talked of tracking down the culprit and killing him. As with Gilmore, the day-to-day business of life—getting his clothes cleaned, buying toiletries, ordering food in a restaurant—frustrated him. Perhaps by way of compensation, he told Norris very "Gilmoresque stories" about stabbings and other gruesome events in prison. She felt he was boasting, and she questioned his credibility.

Others saw only the nasty, brutal side of Abbott, the convict-ideologue who ranted about fascist America and stared people down with his "cobra eyes." Author Dotson Rader remarked: "I've seen killers twice in my life, and he's the third." Jerzy Kosinski, who had written the parole board on Abbott's behalf and was invited to a dinner party in his honor, remembers his misgivings: "How could we disregard the twenty-five years of prison, his past which was still his present, and talk about his forthcoming best-sellership, his weekend career as a writer?" Abbott himself may have sensed the unreality of his position and that he had, with Mailer's help, turned his life into a "romantic fiction." As Carl Bailey shrewdly observed, "What kind of respectable con would want to live a life of wine and cheese parties, hobnobbing with literary lights?"

Mailer remained loyal to Abbott, but he was disturbed to learn in a letter from another prisoner that Abbott had snitched on inmates to get out of prison. Abbott denied it, saying he had informed only on some of the lawyers representing the prisoners.

Mailer tried to get Abbott to think beyond his day-to-day life in the city, which he detested. He had Abbott visit him in Provincetown and made plans for Abbott to join him in Maine. Abbott kept tensing up, calling up Norris and saying, "I'm gonna blow, I can't stand this." He could not tolerate the rude behavior in the city. New York was "like that," Norris pointed out to him, as she tried to cope with "all the imagined insults" he reported to her. It was bad with Abbott, but neither Norris nor Mailer viewed his situation as an emergency.

Objectively, Abbott's circumstances did not seem so dire. However unpleasant he found the Lower East Side, it was a considerable improvement over the prison life he had described in his letters, and he had an impressive support group to get him through the rough spots. But Abbott could no more be objective about the Lower East Side than he could be about prison. Once again events, the system, were conspiring against him.

Just six weeks after Abbott had been released from prison, he stabbed and fatally wounded Richard Adan, a twenty-two-year-old Cuban-American actor, dancer, and playwright working in the Binibon Restaurant at Second Avenue and Fifth Street. This is how Abbott later described the murder: At about 3:00 A.M. he and two girls went to the Binibon to get something to eat. They started to order and Adan, who had given them the menus, put his hand on Abbott's shoulder and said, "I don't take orders," while pointing at another waiter. As Abbott and his friends were eating, Adan supposedly looked at Abbott and remarked, "What are you looking at?" Abbott remembers trying to ignore him, but Adan began to approach him, so Abbott got up, walked over to him, and asked, "Have I done something to you?" Adan answered "No, no," and Abbott asked, "Then what did you say that for?" Adan replied "Say what?" and continued with "What's wrong with you?" Disturbed by Adan's "talking loud," Abbott turned and offered: "Look, if you really got a problem, let's talk about it someplace besides the middle of the floor." Adan responded by suggesting they go outside. Abbott thought *"He's really coming on. He's really too aggressive."* As Abbott asked another waiter for someplace he and Adan could settle things, Adan allegedly taunted and mimicked him, muttering something about "how the customers aren't sanitary" and reached "behind the counter" to put something in his pocket. He acted, in Abbott's words, "like he's got a knife in his pocket." After Adan and Abbott walked out into a dark street with "broken bottles and garbage all over the place," Abbott got nervous—anticipating that Adan was going to dive at him with a knife. Abbott remembers Adan being about ten feet away from him when Abbott pulled out his knife, holding it up so Adan could see it. "Now stay where you are," he shouted at Adan. Abbott started to say, "Now don't come any closer" when Adan tried to jump him. "There's no question in my mind that he came right at me," Abbott later told Peter Manso. Abbott was still yelling at Adan when Adan "stopped dead at the end of that knife" and said, "You didn't have to kill me." Adan died so fast his eyes didn't close. Later, an eyewitness at Abbott's trial described how Abbott had "reached around from behind Richard Adan and expertly plunged a knife into his heart." The stabbing was a "terrific blow" that still rang in the witness's ears. The wound was so deep that nearly all of Adan's blood pumped out into a "pool going from the body across the sidewalk to the curb and out into the gutter."

In fact, Abbott later realized to his great chagrin, Adan had no knife and only meant to escort him to the alley to urinate since customers were not allowed (for insurance reasons) to go through the kitchen to use the restroom. As Detective William Majeski later discovered, Adan "never carried a weapon, never drank heavily, didn't use narcotics, not even marijuana. He was the type of person who always interceded when other people were having problems, and he certainly didn't belong in that neighborhood and he didn't belong in that job." Adan worked there to support himself. He had just come back from Spain, acted in a series on public television, and was looking forward to a performance of his play about the Lower East Side scheduled to be performed the next season by the LaMama experimental theater.

A few hours after the stabbing, *The New York Times Book Review* appeared on newsstands hailing *In the Belly of the Beast* as "awesome, brilliant, perversely ingenuous," and with an impact that was "indelible." A skeptical *People* magazine doubted Abbott's "claims that he endured brutal beatings and months of starvation diets that reduced him to eating protein-rich roaches," noted that he had minimized the extent of his crimes, exaggerated his height (from five seven to six feet), and pointing out that Mailer was wrong about Abbott's being the only prisoner to escape from maximum security in the Utah State Penitentiary.

Six hours after the stabbing Abbott showed up at Jean Malaquais's house for brunch. Seeing nothing amiss except for the fact that Abbott seemed "extremely subdued," Malaquais was shocked later in the day to learn from Detective Majeski about the murder. Majeski then called a stunned Mailer in Provincetown. A few days later, in an Italian restaurant on Forty-fifth street in Manhattan, a tense Mailer had dinner with Majeski. Mailer kept fidgeting, moving around his utensils and plates, speaking rapidly and in a pitch slightly higher than usual and shifting between different accents. Majeski was not surprised, for he had spoken to one of the detectives who had investigated Mailer's stabbing of his wife. Majeski saw what had happened: Mailer had failed to "make a separation between the man's literary ability and his personality, his capabilities outside the literary realm. Abbott's whole personality was based on the premise of prison society."

By September 23 Abbott had been apprehended and sent back to New York City from New Orleans. Mailer was relieved that he had not been killed. Abbott was interviewed by Majeski, who had read *In the Belly of the Beast* several times. A well-written book, he thought, but "bullshit."

Abbott's accounts of prison were "vastly exaggerated," Majeski told him, and surprisingly Abbott gave him no argument. At his trial, Abbott would testify that many of the incidents in the book were "fictionalized."

Mailer wanted to help Abbott, but Norris was extremely hostile. She became very angry when Mailer decided to testify at the trial. She wanted him to stay completely out of it, and she wanted Abbott put away forever, arguing with his attorney over his plans to plead not guilty and to secure Abbott's release in six months into Mailer's custody. Abbott's feelings about Mailer were mixed; some days he wanted to see him, other days he did not. Mailer stayed away but spoke with Abbott on the phone, insisting at one point that Abbott stop lying to himself and admit he had "killed a decent guy" and acted as a snitch at Marion. However hard Mailer was on Abbott, he could not abandon him—especially after a call from Abbott, who said he felt "fated," a remark that provoked Mailer into telling Abbott about his stabbing of Adele: "He said that he'd felt that compulsion of fate when he'd stabbed a woman, even while he was doing it—that it was irreversible, the logic of events," Abbott later told Peter Manso.

No matter what the cost to himself, it would have been out of character for Mailer to desert Abbott. As Buzz Farbar observes: "Norman has to follow through what he's started. He's always done that. He'll see it through to the end, and even if he knows that each step is going to get worse and worse, he'll go to the last step. It's his morality. It's in Rojack in *An American Dream*, walking the parapet right to the end, even though he doesn't have to."

By the time Mailer testified in court, he was under tremendous pressure. Detective Majeski had watched him waiting, not knowing whether Abbott's lawyer would call on him after all. Mailer's appearance on the stand was quite brief. He described how he had come to know Abbott and helped him after his release from prison. If Mailer had been psyching himself up for the ordeal of a tough cross-examination, he was sorely disappointed. When the district attorney announced he had no questions for Mailer, Majeski noted that the "expression on Norman's face was priceless, a combination of surprise and relief—but also a little disappointment, I think."

Instead of a lawyer ripping Mailer apart, it would have to be the press. On January 18, 1982, Mailer walked out of court at 4:30 P.M. a frustrated man who had agreed earlier in the day to meet reporters after his testimony. With microphones thrust forward the hostile questions came rapidly and Mailer retreated into the corner of a back room, trying to fend off what Paul Montgomery of *The New York Times* has called "the worst New York press gang bang I'd ever seen." Mailer rocked back and forth on his feet like a fighter against the ropes, switching to a mean-sounding Southern accent. He emphasized Abbott's sensitivities as an artist and hoped he would not get the "maximum sentence." He declared:

> *It's too easy for people to say they ought to put this guy in jail and throw away the key. Jack Abbott didn't benefit from this. The only people who have gotten anything out of this whole mess are the ones who are calling for more law and order, and more law and order means moving this country toward a fascist state.*

These loaded words angered reporters. It was not enough for Mailer to bellow: "If you want my blood, you can't have it—but you can have my psychic blood if you want it. It's obviously something Abbott's friends are going to have to live with for the rest of their lives."

To his concern that a long prison sentence would destroy Abbott and threaten his chances as a writer, a reporter shouted: "What about the retribution of the family?" Mailer replied that "the family of the victim doesn't have the right to demand blood atonement of a criminal." In his most inflammatory statement, Mailer vowed, "I'm willing to gamble with a portion of society to save this man's talent." *New York Post* reporter Mike Pearl asked him "who he was willing to see sacrificed. Waiters? Cubans?" Now Mailer lost his temper and challenged the reporters: "What are you all feeling so righteous about, may I ask?" Yes, Mailer admitted he had been badly mistaken about Abbott's ability to cope with freedom. When Cynthia Fagen of *The New York Post* asked him if his faith in Abbott was shaken, he replied: "If it hadn't shaken my belief, I'd be a little nuts." Then he turned on her and exclaimed, "Look at the hate in your eyes!" Then Thomas Hanrahan of the *Post* yelled, "You don't want to answer her questions, so you attack her. And I believe in law and order, and I don't think Abbott should get off so he can kill somebody else. And I'm not a Nazi. You are full of shit." Mailer shouted back: "*You* are full of shit. Fuck off. No more questions." End of press conference.

Mailer realized afterward that he had allowed the press to manipulate him, and he was disappointed that he had not handled himself better. But why should he have expected better treatment? As Thomas Hanrahan put it later, Mailer seemed callous:

> *Instead of starting off by saying, "I'm really upset about the death of this kid," it seemed all I was hearing about was Jack Abbott and his problems. I wasn't hearing anything about the poor bastard who'd been cut up, and to me this was just a typical cheap street murder that there was nothing glorious or interesting about it. . . . It was a matter of style, really, and that night when I thought about it I realized he must've been loaded for bear, because he'd really set himself up.*

Norris, who had been at Mailer's side during the press conference, was shocked. Hardly a nervous person, she felt close to a breakdown. She had never seen Mailer act like this before. She thought: "My God, this is the Norman of twenty years ago." In tears over the stories that appeared in the next few days, she contemplated taking the kids and leaving for Arkansas, but she stayed, realizing she could not leave him to "face it by himself."

When Jose Torres read about the press conference, he called Mailer's home. When Norris answered, Torres asked her: "What the hell is wrong with Norman?" Torres was hearing the angry words of Hispanics who could not understand a writer who showed so little interest in and sympathy for Adan.

In this time of trial, Mailer had support from unlikely sources: a kind, sympathetic letter from Diana Trilling, a public defense from William Styron, who felt Mailer had been shabbily treated in the press. It was the beginning of renewed relations between these estranged rivals. Styron, like many other writers, had had his own experience with trying to rehabilitate a criminal. As Michiko Kakutani pointed out in a *New York Times Book Review* front-page article (September 20, 1981), "the 'ordinary' criminal who espouses a radical mode of thought, after all, has long exerted a certain hold on the literary imagination." Kakutani cited the writings of Jean Genêt and the efforts of Sartre and others to elevate Genêt to sainthood.

Kakutani shrewdly notes that Abbott, a prodigiously well-read man, could not have failed to see how he might almost have been invented by Norman Mailer:

Like Lieutenant Hearn in "The Naked and the Dead," Mr. Abbott asserted his own identity in the face of an arbitrary system of officially regulated morality; like Sergius O'Shaugnessy in "The Deer Park," he was self-educated and self-made; like Stephen Rojack in "An American Dream," he had killed without apology.

If Abbott played Mailer like a violin, it was because Mailer had taught him how to use the instrument. The Abbott of the prison book was as much an invention of literature as Norman Mailer was. Paul Ray Sheffield, who served time with Abbott, suggests that *In the Belly of the Beast*

is essentially a false literature which deliberately creates a misrepresentation of reality. Where Abbott's primary concern should have been reporting and interpreting the true reality of his experiences, he chose an ego-starved kind of martyrdom whereby he intentionally deceived his readers through over-dramatized suffering (of very questionable proportions), a great amount of fabrication, and a high degree of mendacity.

Sheffield denies Abbott's claim that no one helped him. Both convicts and guards tried to keep him out of trouble. Far from being a young tough, Sheffield remembers him as being "young and pretty" and bothered by inmates who tried to "hit on" him to have sex. In some cases where Abbott's grim account is fairly accurate, Sheffield reports that the events happened to other inmates, not Abbott. "Abbott wanted to be one of us but he wasn't a fighter," Sheffield notes. To prove himself, Abbott decided to murder a snitch in an incident he refers to briefly in *In the Belly of the Beast* and Sheffield characterizes quite differently:

Abbott came out of the mess-hall with a large vegetable knife concealed in a folded magazine or newspaper. He headed down the corridor for A block. The tier-runner was leaning up against the wall in the corridor in front of A block talking to another "ding" [a nobody]. In front of God, and "guards," and everybody, Abbott slides up next to the runner and plunges the shank into his gut. By the time he got through it was a mess—a pretty amateurish job. The guy didn't even die. He died almost three weeks later of pneumonia brought about by complications of surgery. So much for "killing in combat!"

Everyone Sheffield knew "thought Abbott an idiot for killing that guy, and we told him so." Disputing not merely specific incidents but the whole tenor of Abbott's book, Sheffield points out:

> *If Abbott were as "bad" and as much "trouble" to prison administra-*
> *tions as he would like people to believe, they would have killed him a*
> *long time ago. . . . I have found the prison guard to be as much a victim*
> *of a brutalizing system as the prisoner. Out of humaneness I have seen*
> *guards "walk the extra mile" to look after some prisoner's comfort—an*
> *extra blanket when he's cold, a sandwich when he's hungry. I could*
> *name a thousand incidents of kindness I've seen expressed by guard to*
> *convict. I could also name acts of meanness, but not nearly as*
> *many. . . . But in the prison hierarchy it is people from the rank of*
> *captain on up who set policy. This is where the cruelty of prison systems*
> *is spawned: at the top, not with the guards.*

Everything Abbott did was "advertised," Sheffield emphasizes, and "Abbott was just being what Mailer wanted him to be." *In the Belly of the Beast*, it turns out, is an advertisement for the self in its most maniacal form.

Convicted of first-degree manslaughter, Abbott is serving a fifteen years-to-life sentence.

THE PRACTICE AND PHILOSOPHY OF MAGIC

On the same day Mailer had his disastrous run-in with the press about Jack Abbott, he was scheduled to read at 8:00 P.M. from his novel in progress at the 92nd St. YMHA in Manhattan. Twenty-one years earlier, he had addressed a similar crowd in the same auditorium. Then on trial for stabbing Adele, he had obliged the public's taste for controversy by reading obscene poems that provoked the management to bring down the curtain halfway through. Dressed now in the same dark three-piece suit he had worn in his court appearance for Abbott, he seemed remarkably at ease detailing the difficulties of writing *Ancient Evenings*. He had interrupted the writing of the novel several times to publish other books, and it was not like *The Executioner's Song*, which seemed to write itself. "If I had passed away before the final fifty pages, I could have turned it over to any of my contemporaries without a backward look, even Gore

Vidal," he claimed by way of showing how at ease he was now with his public feuds and notoriety. The audience laughed. Mailer said he did not know how, but he was sure his detractors would find a way to call his Egyptian novel a "piece of journalism."

Even in the question-and-answer session, Mailer kept cool. To one query about his obsession with the "sadism of the battlefield" (he had just read an impressive account of the Battle of Kadesh replete with gore and guts and human mutilation) he replied by quoting in Latin *Nihil humanum mihi alienum est*. Since nothing human was alien to him he did not want to divert his imagination from those periods in history that were too easily dismissed as "barbaric." Another questioner bluntly asked him about the Abbott press conference. "I fear I lost my temper," he admitted. Without any apparent sign of rancor he added: "Reporters are the most self-righteous bastards I've ever encountered in my life" and was rewarded with a resounding round of applause. George Plimpton was there and remembered that Mailer was

> *so* good, *and you saw the great depth of the man—the studying, the focus, the discipline, the concern, the artist. I've always liked him, but when he's wearing his spectacles and is concerned about his craft there's no effrontery, none of those geysers; there's something very vulnerable and touching about him too.*

After all, Mailer was reflecting on a novel that had taken him more than ten years to write and that by his own estimation was his most ambitious work. The idea for the novel had come even earlier, during the period in which he had put together *Advertisements for Myself.* Around 1964, Walter Minton, Mailer's publisher at Putnam, had seen a part of what was supposed to be a big novel. Its starting point had not been Egypt, but the plains of Poland or Russia. According to Minton, "It literally began with what was the essence of Norman Mailer—with a gene, a sperm in the testicles of an ancestor." Mailer remembers it somewhat differently:

> *The 50 pages Walter saw were from a novel that starts in a hospital in a small town in New Jersey. A child is being born.* Ancient Evenings *did, in fact, have its beginning of all beginnings as the saga of the Mailer family back in Russia with my grandfather as I imagined him; the 50-page manuscript went from Long Branch, New Jersey, back to Russia.*

Mailer studied Hebrew for a year, trying to absorb his grandfather's culture, but he eventually abandoned this approach after reading Isaac Bashevis Singer and concluding there was "absolutely no need for my book."

Mailer admitted that his ambition to write a big novel that somehow prefaced his age, told its prehistory, so to speak, was born of a crisis in confidence. Still searching for a way to write a panoramic, picaresque novel, Mailer thought to imitate the method of André Schwarz-Bart's *The Last of the Just* by telescoping centuries of history chapter by chapter. As he later told Marie Brenner:

> *I'd read a chapter of H. G. Wells on ancient Egypt, and I was kind of taken with it, and my idea was I would start in Egypt and then go on to the Greeks and the Romans and acquire all that classical culture and have a marvelous time, taking it right up to the present.*

After six months of work, he realized he would never get out of Egypt. He read close to a hundred books on the country, aiming at as much fidelity to his sources as he could manage, and setting his novel during the nineteenth and twentieth dynasties (1290–1100 B.C.). Intrigued by the tremendous gaps in scholarly knowledge and rather pleased that he could make up a plot of his own while remaining faithful to what was known, Mailer came to see that this would have to be his big book— actually a better way of attaining his large ambition than attempting to write an "all-encompassing novel about America." "It can't be done," he confided to an interviewer. One writer would have to "learn about many different occupations" and places and would lose the respect of sophisticated readers who were bound to know more about certain areas and subjects than the novelist. In *Ancient Evenings* he could create a "consciousness that's so different from our own that we read it in wonder as if we were reading about Martians." The author of *An American Dream* and *Why Are We in Vietnam?* wanted nothing less than to discover the sources of his imaginative power, the emanation of the psyche from "a single mind," a psyche capable of entering other minds, and overpowering the sense of alienation that has been the modern experience and the subject for so many of its writers.

Beginning with the first sentence—"Crude thoughts and fierce forces are my state"—*Ancient Evenings* embarks on a style that is new to Mailer and to his readers accustomed to an active voice transforming

everything it articulates. The novel's first narrator-protagonist, the *ka*
(spiritual emanation) of Menenhetet II, is undergoing the process of
rebirth. The first book of the novel is awesome and quite wonderful in its
depiction of a consciousness trying to differentiate itself from all that
surrounds it. The narrator of the first book, who struggles to remember
his past life, is the direct ancestor of that unnamed narrator in "Advertisements for Myself on the Way Out," which Mailer presented in
Advertisements for Myself as a fragment of the great eight-part cycle of
novels he never completed. In *Ancient Evenings*, Mailer finally solves
the problem of showing how to give birth to a narrative voice.

   After the first book, much of the novel is narrated by Menenhetet I,
the great-grandfather of Menenhetet II. Menenhetet I is the great ancestor who has been able to live four lives by learning how to ejaculate into
a woman at the very moment of his death, thereby conceiving himself
anew in a lover who becomes his mother. Menenhetet I, who aspires in
his first life to supplant his Pharaoh as ruler of Egypt and dies in the act
of impregnating the Pharaoh's queen, is the ultimate Mailer protagonist
and a surrogate of the great rabbi ancestor linked in Mailer's family
history to himself, Norman King. Menenhetet I carries Mailer's conception of himself and of the hero in his fiction to the farthest extreme: He is
a man of many ages, the self-invented avatar of Menenhetet II's quest for
distinction. Menenhetet I has been a warrior and high priest, a scholar
and man of action, a great lover of queens and a farmer of peasant
origin, beginning his career in a station no higher than Mailer's own
family. He has the physical prowess Mailer has always coveted. Menenhetet I teaches the Pharaoh's charioteers how to control their vehicles
with the reins tied around their waists, so that each chariot can carry two
archers into battle and gain the advantage against enemies who use one
of two men in their chariots as drivers. In his fourth life Menenhetet I
would like to be the vizier of Ramses IX (Ptah-nem-hotep), as Mailer
would have liked to be John F. Kennedy's adviser in *The Presidential
Papers*. But Menenhetet I, in the act of telling his four life histories to
Ramses IX, reveals an overweening ambition and fatal attraction to
magical practices (including the repulsive eating of bat dung) that
disqualifies him for the role of Pharaonic confidant—much as Mailer's
own bizarre theories and actions (he contends in *Cannibals and Christians* that human excrement contains all of those rich elements that the
human body rejects) relegate him to a marginal position among the rich
and powerful.

Menehetet I relates the story of his four lives on the Night of the Pig (when it is permissible to speak frankly of all things in the Pharaoh's presence) in a family setting reminiscent of the Mailer home. Menenhetet II observes Nef-khep-aukhem, his weak, fastidious father, Overseer of the Pharaoh's cosmetic box, and Hathfertiti, his beautiful but businesslike mother. Menenhetet II identifies with the Pharaoh as his true father, as Mailer's other fictional heroes identify with the strongest males. At six years of age, the precocious Menenhetet II is the fictional alter ego of Norman King being prepared for a great future. The unrepressed life Mailer dreamed of, the one that was so much greater than the safe domesticity of his Brooklyn home, finally appears in ancient Egypt, where the writer's deepest fears and greatest triumphs can be literally worked out, where Menenhetet I, a favorite in his first life of Ramses II, is sodomized by the Pharaoh—shafted with the divine phallus that both humiliates and ennobles him. In short, this is a world where men can be fucked by fame with all the rewards and pains that such prominence entails.

What Mailer could not express in a novel about his family roots in Russia he articulates in an Egyptian novel, where Judeo-Christian taboos do not exist, where men can partake of each other's strength through anal intercourse, and where Menenhetet I can discharge his bitterness and disappointment by forcing Menenhetet II to perform fellatio on him. As Joseph Wenke suggests, *Ancient Evenings* makes clear that "the problem of identity may be solved only by rediscovering one's connection to the mythic heritage of one's previous life. And, as in much of Mailer's work, the possibility of making a life-sustaining connection with one's heritage depends upon establishing a relationship with a father figure."

If men literally penetrate each other in ancient Egypt, Mailer says it is because he is "exploring power relationships among males, the way they seek and exercise power in relationship to each other." As he told an interviewer, the Egyptians were a "tactile, sensitive, visceral people." To Bruce Weber, he explained, "It's a world of dominance . . . where you find your place literally by whom you're doing it to." Mailer's Egyptians gain knowledge and power over one another through the penetration of every orifice, and in *Ancient Evenings* he is determined to explore every route, physical and metaphorical, to human identity. As he put it in a *People* magazine interview:

In Egypt, given the Nile flooding its banks and turning villages into islands in the river, with detritus everywhere, animals living in the houses, everyone huddled together, one knows that it was an incredibly fecal place. . . . It's no secret that Freud gave us a firm set of connections between anality and power . . . and what I learned about Egypt seemed a kind of confirmation.

In *Ancient Evenings* the prose is driven by what Menehetet II calls "the long slow current of my great-grandfather's mind," and that mind is the receptacle for "what any of us might wish to put within it." Coming from Mailer's previous work, one has to learn to read him anew, and not all readers have been willing to grant him the luxury of this novel's style. On the one hand, it is embedded in the lush details of ancient Egypt, in the rhythms of an alien time that eventually become almost as familiar as our own. On the other hand, even sympathetic readers have noted a numbing sameness in the prose that suggests the author has striven too hard for unity, for the merging of the opposites that create so much exciting tension in *The Naked and the Dead, The Armies of the Night*, and *The Executioner's Song. Ancient Evenings* is Norman Mailer at his neatest, with the loose ends of his philosophy and his prose knit together rather impressively. Nevertheless, it seems static and a little too thoroughly thought out; absent from it is the rough-edged stimulation of a writer on the make, best when he is suggestive rather than explicit, when he is promising to complete the circle and join the halves without ever quite doing so.

13.

TOUGH GUYS DON'T DANCE (1983–1987)

PAPA MAILER

In contrast to the raucous party for his fiftieth, celebration of Mailer's sixtieth birthday on January 31, 1983, was a private affair. He and Norris had a quiet dinner at a restaurant. A few nights later Pat Kennedy Lawford arranged a dinner for him with several dozen guests, an event indicative of his growing appetite for high society.

Mailer planned a kind of semiretirement to "cultivate my own garden." As he told Michiko Kakutani in *The New York Times Book Review* (June 6, 1982), he was forsaking the position of "embattled artist" (his term) for one of "alchemical artist. Art as magic rather than art as war."

For the first time in many years, Mailer's finances were in order. He had paid off his back taxes by selling off parts of the Brooklyn brownstone as well as his house in Provincetown. The enormous success of *The Executioner's Song* had helped him pay off other debts, and a renegotiated $1.4-million-dollar contract with Little, Brown assured him an income of $30,000 a month, which covered the $325,000 a year he needed to support himself, his ex-wives, and his eight children. To supplement his income he would continue to take occasional journalistic assignments so long as they did not involve major commitments of his time. His main concern now was delivery of the three novels (in addition to *Ancient Evenings*) that were part of his million-dollar contract.

As part of the buildup for the appearance of *Ancient Evenings*, Mailer allowed *Time* to report on the five days he spent with students at the University of Pennsylvania. He was surprised at their docile, even respectful reception, and offered to pay five dollars for the most insulting question. There were no takers. Instead of getting the business in a class taught by a feminist, she served him coffee. Expecting to be booed at a lecture for pressing one of his more obnoxious theories he got no more than sour looks for his claim that "homosexuals want to become heterosexual. . . . If you're homosexual, you might have to ask yourself what God thinks of you."

Wary of the reviews of *Ancient Evenings*, which would appear in the spring of 1983, Mailer took the offensive, granting several interviews that tried to put the novel and his career in perspective. One of Mailer's largest fears, naturally, was that the reviews would focus on him, not on his novel. It was essential to Mailer that he seem somehow to rise above his past to meet himself on the heights as the august author of *Ancient Evenings*.

Mailer also wanted it known he had patched things up with William Styron. They had met in Paris during a conference on "Culture and Development" sponsored by François Mitterand. They did not discuss the past or refer to Styron's disparagement of Adele. As Mailer told Barry Leeds a few years later, he and Styron and James Jones had all taken each other very seriously and were part of a "very self-conscious generation" who believed they had been handed the roles of "young major novelists." Feelings ran high when they had to force their still-undeveloped talents to meet such great expectations.

In these interviews Mailer did his best to diffuse the hostility he had fomented in his youth. About *Ancient Evenings* he took a mellow, philosophical, almost resigned position:

> *Look, either it's a very good book or it's not. If it's a very good book, well, fine. If it isn't, well, that will be disappointing, but I'm probably not going to know for a few years anyway. I think there will be people who will think it is a great book; I think there will be people who will say it's a preposterous book.*

Absent from the interviews was the apocalyptic, go-for-broke, mood of *Advertisements for Myself* and the truculent defensiveness he had sometimes shown when he anticipated attacks on his life and work. He expected reviewers to accuse him of having "a Pharaoh complex" and to mention the Abbott affair and the stabbing of Adele.

About the stabbing, Mailer remarked: "If any of us does something like that, people just don't look at them in quite the same way." It was a good turn of phrase, "any of us," for it kept the extremity of his deed within the community even as he admitted that he sometimes rued his status as "odd man out."

A year after the Abbott trial, Mailer still received hate mail and "some fairly serious threats." People stopped him on the street demanding his response to the Abbott case. In one instance, Mailer asked if his interrogator had read Abbott's book: "Yeah, yeah, he sure had his head together in the book—that's what I can't understand." Mailer liked this reply and stressed to Marie Brenner that he thought Abbott would be all right when he got out of prison because he had "such a command of the states of emotion." Why Mailer should think a prose style was some kind of proof of character is puzzling and does indeed seem naive. Because Abbott had helped him, he felt he should help Abbott to get out, although Mailer professed surprise at Abbott's quick release: "I thought it would be a year or two, if at all. It was his bad luck that he got out so quickly." Mailer could not bring himself to admit the enormity of his mistake and told Brenner he still corresponded with Abbott. It would not be easy for Abbott to continue writing, Mailer noted, but writing looked to be his only salvation.

Not in a mood for regrets, Mailer admitted to a certain amount of "youthful arrogance," but that attitude masked a secret need to feel accepted, to make America love him. It was the "cry of the immigrant heart." Acknowledging that his period as "psychic outlaw" had sabotaged his standing, he did not renege on it: "It takes a toll if you don't do anything, too. As many people die from an excess of timidity as from bravery. Nobody ever measures that." Yet he had to agree there were other ways—just as good—of creating a career and had come around to appreciating Updike's "great wisdom as a writer. He sets his marks properly. He just improves from book to book. On the one hand, there is nothing wild about him, and on the other there is nothing overcalculating. He has a natural sense of progression." A younger Mailer, keen to edge past his contemporaries, could never have made such a remark.

Mailer did everything possible to assure himself a good press by inviting reporters into his Brooklyn home and allowing them to tag along with him on the street as people recognized him and spoke to him as if he were a friend. Mailer compared his status to that of "a small-town politician, able to confer minor favors on the local populace." He had lived so long in the neighborhood that he had become one of the familiar, approachable sights.

Very much the fond father, Mailer delighted in showing pictures of his eight children by his five previous marriages. His daughters by Adele, Dandy and Betsy, told Paul Gray of *Time* that they had seen no sign of the public, irascible Mailer. He had always been quite gentle with them. Robert Lucid (professor of English at the University of Pennsylvania, Mailer confidant and authorized biographer) vouched for Mailer's "great success as a father. With all eight of them, you'd think he'd have a disaffected child somewhere, but he doesn't."

If Mailer had often been nettled by the press's inability to read his moods, to distinguish between his serious and comic moments, and to see the shifting complexity of his attitudes, he had to be pleased by Gray's vignette of the author turning sixty and speaking as a family man:

> *"You don't have the strength to push people around any more." At this moment, Michael Mailer, 19, handsome and muscular [and a proficient amateur boxer], is heard moving about in a nearby room. Mailer leans forward in his chair and lowers his voice conspiratorially: "I used to be able to* look *at that kid and he'd cower."*
>
> *The moment is quintessential Mailer, combining swagger, a touch of menace, self-mockery and high good humor. Such charm in close quarters could overwhelm a roomful of enemies. How could anyone not wish this impish iconoclast happiness, prosperity, long life, enough success to make him happy and enough failure to keep him on his toes?*

Gray's acute response speaks volumes about the collective temper of the press as it has swung from adulation to ridicule, sometimes embracing Mailer's highest opinion of himself, sometimes spurning his pretensions.

Gray was impressed with the calm atmosphere at Mailer's home, full of banter and "mutual affection," with Mailer's grown-up children dropping by for "visits of unpredictable length" when they were in the neighborhood. They seemed to have little difficulty in relating to him as a father and a famous writer. A year later Michael would tell an interviewer that, sure, "There's been domestic conflict over the years but no deep strife. My father gets into bad moods sometimes, but it's usually because someone has eaten what he wanted in the refrigerator or he got a bad review."

Mailer's child with Norris, John Buffalo, was now four years old. "Like me, he's both stubborn and proud," Mailer commented to Marie Brenner. When John Buffalo refused to eat dinner, declaring he hated pot roast, Mailer sent him to his room. "He'll stay in his room all night to show us we can't win," Mailer explained.

Mailer's normal work routine was two three-hour shifts four days a week and one shift on Saturdays, in a room he rented down the block. He needed a small space where he would not be interrupted. In bare surroundings he confronted his work, not wanting to get too comfortable or to surround himself with the trappings of fame. He was unwilling to show people this private place, considering such a visit "bad luck" and definitely a threat to his creativity.

In his much-written-about nautical-looking apartment, with its "slanting skylights" and "dizzying straight-up views" in a room three stories high with a hammock "slung across a chasm," Mailer gave evidence of his adventurous and varied life. Pictures of himself and his friends and many of Norris's paintings filled the apartment. On one wall a visitor was treated to one of her abstracts, on others to a campaign button with the slogan "I'd sleep better if Mailer were mayor," and photographs of Mailer boxing, in a brooding mood, or in a sociable pose dressed in evening clothes with Norris at his side.

Cathleen Medwick found Norris an easy interview: ("Not too quickly familiar. Cautious, then close. A strong, proud, cool, intimate woman with topaz eyes") and quite a contrast to Weber's depiction of Mailer: "He resembles a well-made snowman. His hair is gray, going white; he has a bowl-like torso and a round face that widens to smile." Medwick was quite taken with Norris's "bold, sunstruck" work, which had been exhibited in a Soho gallery. The bright colors, the "fleshy" and "sociable" people seemed to reflect her forthright personality and sense of humor. She had proved a good match for Mailer, holding her own with the likes of dinner guests like John Simon, the acerbic movie critic who once tried to correct her grammar. "You're at my house, eating my food, sitting on my right, and you dare to correct my use of a word?" she told him. Norris was the practical one and perfectly capable of instructing her husband in the facts of life: "He calls me 'bottom line Barbara'—you know, what's the bottom line on this, let's get to the heart of this.' " Mailer wanted her to read poetry every day, but she had no interest in it. Well, Medwick observed to her, "Norman could be accused of having too *much* poetry." Norris liked that line and laughed, " 'Yes, that's it! Too much poetry! I'm the one who's always dragging his balloon back down.' "

To Marie Brenner, Norris praised her husband's neatness and sense of order. He was not the kind of man a woman had to pick up after. She had learned to read his moods and routines, to allow him some time to himself after a work session before she spoke to him about her day and her concerns. While having her own careers as model, actress, and painter, she felt none of the competitiveness or jealousy that had marred Mailer's earlier marriages. Mickey Knox, one of Mailer's oldest friends, suggested that Norris combined all of the elements that Mailer had sought in his previous wives. She was "the one woman who had everything: beauty, grace, intelligence, talent, and a very strong will." They enjoyed going to dinner parties and spent about three nights a week out. Mailer compared it to "finding a new sport," seeing how he could get along with new dinner partners and not knowing how an evening might turn out. Occasionally the obstreperous Mailer with his old hangups would put in an appearance at these social gatherings: "It's nice to meet you, Mr. Sinatra. I've hated you for 40 years because I've always thought you could always get any girl that you ever wanted." Mailer thought it was good for the novelist in him to get out and meet people.

Mailer spoke with Paul Gray in tones that suggested a certain resignation about his own place in American literature, frankly admitting he had not attained the stature of a Hemingway, the "clear influence" on his generation. "I don't think my work has inspired any writer, not the way Hemingway inspired me." In his kitchen, Mailer had pasted a collage of himself and Hemingway. A very round, gray, and bearded Hemingway stood beneath a moosehead, and below this picture Mailer had appended a photograph of himself at twenty-five, ultra thin with a kinky pompadour and large ears—a portrait of the artist flush with the success of *The Naked and the Dead.* "Look at that picture," Mailer said to Gray, "God, how thin I was. Isn't it strange, I've grown into Hemingway's body. I think he was 60 in that photograph, too. How strange, how damn strange." Perhaps not so strange—considering that Mailer had been looking all his life for such a role to grow into: Papa Mailer.

THERE IS SO MUCH I WOULD TEACH

The reception of *Ancient Evenings* turned out to be just about what Mailer had expected. Some reviews were highly respectful and laudatory, others were mixed, and several were downright damning. Judging by the titles of the reviews alone, it was immediately apparent whether the author or his work would get the most attention: "Norman in Egypt," "Mailer Hits Bottom," "A Chthonic Novel," "Excess Without End," "Tales from Beyond the Tomb." Some newspapers and periodicals could not resist making bad puns: "The Naked and the Mummified," "Ra, Ka, Bah Humbug."

If there had been a prize for the most damaging and funny review, it probably would have gone to *Harper's* for "Enter the Mummy," subtitled: "Norman Mailer gets his Egyptian novel out of his system." James Wolcott's dismissal of *Ancient Evenings* was topped by an illustration of Mailer dressed in the regalia of a Pharaoh, standing in the cleavage of huge human buttocks serving up a platter of turds, with the pyramids behind him in the distance sloping downward to the left as though dwarfed by his obsession with excrement. Like other reviewers, Wolcott noticed that "in his hardiest moments" Menenhetet I "bears a canny [sic] resemblance to his creator and true master" and quoted a passage from the novel describing Menenhetet I's hair, which "showed the silver of a virile maturity while the lines on his face had not yet become a myriad of wrinkles, terraces, and webs, but exhibited, instead, that look of character supported by triumph which comes to powerful men when they are sixty and still strong."

Anticipating that the autobiographical aspect of the novel would be noted, Mailer told Marie Brenner: "You must realize that when I started the book I wasn't even 50 yet. Sixty seemed to me a great distance away. It never occurred to me to consider myself remotely like him. He was ancient. He was 60." For Mailer, the style and the subject matter were a departure: "I don't recognize myself in this book," he told Bruce Weber.

Unsympathetic reviewers saw the sexual dynamics of it as simply "bugger-the-loser," failing to note that both winners and losers are buggered, a reflection of Mailer's passive/aggressive personality and an extension of his own quest both to express and to transcend the influence of his literary father just as surely as Menenhetet I both loves and plans to usurp Ramses II as Pharaoh. That Menenhetet I fails to live up to his ultimate ambition and is himself murdered in the act of penetrating the Pharaoh's wife is Mailer's sad and mortified recognition of his inability to fulfill his highest aspirations. Like Mailer, Menenhetet I is born of a mother who believes her son has been destined by the gods for greatness; the Egyptian son becomes a priest in one of his lives; the Jewish son in the later phases of his career absorbs himself in magic.

Mailer's romantic, irrational, anti-Enlightenment, anti-Judeo/Christian view, his metaphysics not of the mind but of the belly, in which the passage of shit through the anus can express as much about human character as do the words that issue through the mouth has appalled a large part of his audience. Seeing the resemblance between Menenhetet I and Mailer, Edmund Fuller quotes a speech from the Egyptian character that articulates Mailer's anguished frustration: "I have done many things of which pious people—and those who are less than pious—would not approve. But in the public mind, two foul suppers [of bat shit, which contains magical properties] equal all the rest. It is a great pity. There is so much I would teach."

In one of the most provocative reviews of *Ancient Evenings*, Leslie Fiedler contended that Mailer had deliberately inverted

> the myth of exodus—in which he is able to project once again his lifelong fantasy of becoming the "Golden Goy." His surrogate, Menenhetet, rises by his own wit and courage to sit at the right hand of a king who is also a god and makes it into the bed of his wife. The Egypt, moreover, in which Menenhetet becomes rich and famous is an Egypt in which Moses is demoted to the status of a second-rate magician, who slips across the border under cover of night with a handful of fellow slaves, but never challenges either Pharaoh or his Gods. A world, that is to say, out of which Judaism never emerges triumphant, so that in its alternate future Sam Slovoda [Mailer's passive surrogate in "The Man Who Studied Yoga"] will never be born.

Like Menenhetet I, Mailer has found a way to father himself. The novel itself—the idea of writing novels—has been his great adventure, his way of detaching himself from the world he grew up in. In a very telling characterization of *Ancient Evenings'* style, Walter Clemons marvels at the "Homeric sweep, the cynical ribaldry of the crack-voiced Egyptian elder, and a kind of boy's book-of-wonders naivete." There it is: The boy/man, who keeps a heroic watch on himself and on his characters,

who at the age of seven wrote a three hundred-page story that sent his
characters to Mars, who at sixty projected *Ancient Evenings* as part of a
trilogy, the second part of which would about "a spaceship in the future,
maybe two or three centuries from now," to be followed by the third part
set in the present—all forming a complicated universe of his own
devising hardly less difficult to accomplish than the eight-part cycle of
novels he projected in *Advertisements for Myself.* It was to be his own
myth, all connected up, and the metaphor for it would again have to be
sexual:

> So that they will all truly be three parts of the same novel, but in the way
> a tree might have three trunks growing out of a common root. Or, like the
> mythical phallus of Osiris which presented itself with three prongs.

COMPROMISED BY SO MANY ACTS

Even Mailer's staunchest supporters viewed *Ancient Evenings* as prob-
lematic and cautioned readers about the dull passages, the unintentional
humor of a style intended to capture the formality of court speech, and
the "badly mixed imagery." James Wolcott complained: "Ease of expression doesn't exist in this novel; the conventions of the historical epic
truss Mailer like mummy bandages, allowing him to take only a wee
step at a time." Walter Clemons, a great admirer of *Ancient Evenings*,
had to admit that in one of Mailer's "purple flourishes . . . the dread
specter of Cecil B. DeMille rose before me." Only George Stade un-
equivocally called the novel "a new and permanent contribution to the
possibilities of fiction and our communal efforts at self-discovery."

Ancient Evenings was officially published on April 25, 1983, and less
than a month later it had climbed to number 6 on *The New York Times*
best-seller list and would remain there for several months. Evidently the
controversial reception of the novel, the readership Mailer had cultivated in decades of promoting his books, and the recent appearance of
the first biography of him by Hilary Mills all helped generate sales.
Warner Books paid $501,000 for the paperback rights.

Mailer was now approaching a financial position that might make it
possible for him to devote himself almost exclusively to fiction. Although he had published seven books with Little, Brown, he had begun
to doubt the wisdom of staying with a firm that had first shown *Ancient*

Evenings to paperback houses in advance of its publication date and had been able to obtain an offer no higher than $130,000. In the summer of 1983, Scott Meredith began negotiating with Random House a nine-year, four-novel, four-million-dollar contract that would in all likelihood cover the balance of Mailer's career.

Mailer owed Little, Brown one more novel and needed the steady monthly income it had been supplying. To leave Little, Brown abruptly would mean returning the advance already paid him for a novel he had not written and then drawing immediately on Random House against an advance for another novel he had yet to produce. To dig himself out of this dilemma, Mailer resolved to write a novel in two months and deliver it to Little, Brown by September 30, 1983, thus triggering his new contract with Random House.

Having already spent several fruitless months trying to get a new work of fiction underway, Mailer tried a new tack: writing according to a formula. He had "always wanted to write a detective story with a hero a little braver—just a little—than thee or me," Mailer told an interviewer. Usually the hero in detective fiction expressed the "strong side" people presume "they might have had." Mailer resolved to test the viability of the genre by creating a detective hero of only "average bravery" and see whether he would "attract and interest the reader." As in his selection of Rojack as the narrator of *An American Dream*, Mailer decided the quickest way to get the new novel done was by casting it in the first person and choosing a personality who was "not at all me in any real way, but was near enough so that his style wouldn't seem false to me. In other words, I wouldn't have to stretch for a style." In fact, he created a fellow middle-aged writer, someone who could have read Mailer and who would find Mailer's sensibility within "the dome of his aesthetic purview."

Mailer decided to use an incident in his own life, when he almost became the victim of a government attempt at entrapment. In December 1982, his old friend Buzz Farbar, recently arrested for buying a fake kilogram of cocaine from a federal agent, invited him to lunch. Mailer knew nothing about Farbar's fix or that he had been offered a deal. He would not go to jail if at a taped lunch he could get Mailer to talk about his involvement in the Richard Stratton case. Mailer had known Stratton in Provincetown, drank and boxed with him, and talked with him about writing. Stratton, working on a novel titled "Drug War," had come under the investigation of the Drug Enforcement Agency compiling evidence that he had imported hashish in private planes. Mailer was suspected of having invested in the Stratton operation. The lunch did Farbar no good, since after his repeated attempts to discuss the Stratton case, an annoyed Mailer—speaking in his best imitation of a hood— barked: "Look, I don't have anything to do with any of these guys, and I don't want to hear nothing about it." To use the phrase Mailer chose for the title of his new novel, he was a tough guy who did not want to dance.

The idea that he could be set up intrigued Mailer—as did the probability that his name had been "bandied about in drug circles." How would he or someone like him have reacted if his name had been used to set up a drug deal or he were implicated in something worse—say a murder?

At first it does not dawn on Mailer's surrogate hero, Tim Madden, that he has been set up. Like Mikey Lovett in *Barbary Shore*, Madden is an amnesiac: He cannot remember what happened the night before, and he cannot account for the large amount of blood on his car seat. Although he is clearly kin to Stephen Rojack, Madden is more like Mailer himself—a faltering writer of fiction who is at least as tentative as he is tough. Like the Mailer of *Advertisements for Myself*, Madden questions his talent even as he tries to promote and to cultivate it. He worries over a timid tendency of his character which he connects with his defeat in the only Golden Gloves bout he ever fought. More or less kept by his prized wife, the wealthy Patty Lareine, he cannot write when she deserts him.

As her name suggests, Lareine has been Madden's imperious queen, and he seems at a loss when he is not in the service of his "medieval lady." At the same time, he has clearly chafed under her rule, for he regrets having broken his code of male self-sufficiency. As a result, the couple's marriage has been turbulent, and in its later stages they seem most alike in their murderous inclinations. The novel begins with Madden wondering if the severed head he discovers in his marijuana hideaway is the result of a drunken evening's debauchery with another woman (Jessica Pond) which turned violent when Patty Lareine returned home.

The characters in *Tough Guys Don't Dance* relate to each other as in an Arthurian romance. Madden discovers that his wife has had another lover, the deputy police chief, Alvin Luther Regency, a powerfully built, maniacal rival who is part of the plot to set up Madden (who has already served a short term for possession of cocaine). Complicating matters further for Madden is the lurking presence of his envious former schoolmate, Meeks Wardly Hilby III, who was once married to Patty Lareine and from whom Madden stole her. If Madden can make sense of the two murders (he discovers a second severed head in his hideaway), he can also begin to put his life back together—including his failed relationship with Madeleine Falco, his witty tough counterpart who left him when he took up with Patty Lareine and who now finds herself mired in a bad marriage to the dangerous Regency.

The first two sentences of the novel emphasize the somber setting of winter in Provincetown for the waste of a life that Madden will redeem only by recovering the courage to accept his human vulnerability: "At dawn, if it was low tide on the flats, I would awaken to the chatter of gulls. On a bad morning, I used to feel as if I had died and the birds were feeding on my heart." He remains throughout his story perilously poised between life and death and in desperate need of a new code by which he can be reborn. For he has reservations about the seemingly simple-minded macho injunction by which his father has lived. In pondering the anecdote to which the remark "Tough guys don't dance" refers, Madden comments:

> Surely my father had meant something finer than that you held your ground when there was trouble, something finer that doubtless he could not or would not express, but it was there, his code. It could be no less than a vow. Did I miss some elusive principle on which his philosophy must crystallize?

Madden never does offer a definition of his father's remark, but given the behavior of both father and son, the key to what Madden calls his koan, "Tough guys don't dance" has to do not so much with toughing things out (which implies a kind of static defense of what one already is) but with recognizing the elusiveness of principles and perceptions that inevitably change in the course of time. Madden's father, Doughy, admits that, in some ways, he has not been as tough as his son supposes, and thereby Doughy gains toward the end of the novel an impressively supple strength on which his son—always somewhat abashed by his father's macho superiority—can rely. In other words, Doughy, who faces the prospect of his own death by cancer, is willing to shatter the stereotype of toughness in which his son has invested so heavily.

Readers who prefer a genre with taut, spare plots and prose may bristle at the complications of Mailer's syntax and philosophizing. Evil has many sources that are not easily linked up in the satisfying way of most murder mysteries. The two heads and bodies (Patty Lareine's and Jessica Pond's) buried in different locations are indicative of the splits in the human psyche that Mailer has pursued in much of his writing. Or as Tim Madden has it: "We live with not one soul but two" that are often as unequal as two badly matched horses. Usually Mailer is able to finesse the shifts between the novel's ideas and events, and his delineation of characters through clipped dialogue is convincing, but sometimes his transitions and asides are awkward and forced ("This is no exposition of dualities, but . . ."). At such times his narrative flags, because he has tried to do too much, to integrate characters, ideas, and plot simultaneously in a single narrative voice.

What is never in question, however, is Mailer's evocation of setting. Provincetown, past and present, is vividly portrayed through the novel in tantalizing vignettes. Each digression into Provincetown history is meant to give a concrete context for the narrator's divided soul. His house—Patty Lareine's house, he reminds himself—is built out of the very stuff of "whoretown" or "Hell-Town" that thrived in the days of whaling:

> Half of our holding of sills, studs, joists, walls, and roof has been ferried over from Hell-Town more than a century ago, and thereby made us a most material part of that vanished place. . . . Provincetown, then, was just far enough away to be able to keep up the Yankee proprieties of widows' walks and white churches. What an intermingling of the spirits, therefore, when the whaling ended and the shacks in Hell-Town were floated over to us.

Tough Guys Don't Dance is about the intermingling of spirits, about Jessica Ponds's doubling for Patty Lareine, about Alvin Luther Regency's two names for himself, and about each character's counterpart or alter ego. Fortified by the strong presence of Provincetown as a place and as a paradigm of history, a paradigm of division between perversity and propriety, Mailer is able to create his characters and plot with considerable, if occult, persuasiveness.

As the novel's title suggests, there is a sportive and amusingly combative tilt to Mailer's writing. Other titles—*Dead Men Don't Wear Plaid* and *Real Men Don't Eat Quiche*—come to mind. Apparently, the author is willing to have a little fun with the macho attitudes he has been attacked for espousing. Reviewers have seldom been willing to praise Mailer for his playfulness and to appreciate that, for him, even ideas he is deadly serious about have their comic side. Even at his most intellectual Mailer is rarely ponderous because he has the saving grace to puncture or to back away from his more inflated notions. This is surely one reason why he appends the definitions of comedy and tragedy to the end of his narrative. The humor of these definitions—they are so close in meaning to each other that their juxtaposition makes for irony—as does Madden's final remark after Madeleine shoots her husband and goes off to Key West with Madden: "All my present stability of mind rests on the firm foundation of a mortal crime." The difference between surviving and perishing—as between comedy and tragedy—is perilously slim, and Madden knows he can never count himself safely sane.

Tough Guys Don't Dance, for all its ruminations on telepathy and the occult, is a more relaxed and measured performance than Mailer's earlier novels. Tim Madden, approaching forty, is older than Mailer's earlier erstwhile authors, Mikey Lovett and Sergius O'Shaugnessy, and more willing to settle for the incompleteness of character and for the promise of security his writing may never fulfill: "I am so compromised by so many acts that I must try to write my way out of the internal prison of my nerves, my guilts and my deep rooted spiritual debts." Such words suggest a writer of considerable experience, a writer of middle age still capable of reaching his prime—a writer similar to Norman Mailer himself.

THE HAZARDS AND SOURCES OF WRITING

In the interval between finishing *Tough Guys* in the fall of 1983 and its appearance in the next fall publishing season, Mailer took on a number of miscellaneous assignments as the idea for another novel slowly began to take shape. Two trips, one to cover the British elections and the other to visit the Soviet Union, resulted in very slight articles in which he had to concede his ignorance and rely on brief, superficial impressions. Knowing so little about these cultures, Mailer was loath to practice his usual speculative style, yet in settling for being a responsible reporter he had less to offer by way of insight. And in an article on Jacqueline Onassis, he was content to repeat himself, to go over the ground of his work in *The Presidential Papers*, pointing out that as First Lady she

brought together the "schizophrenic halves of our nations. . . . The
Hollywood dream life and the superhighways of technology came closer
for a little while."

Mailer gave a much more moving performance at the University of
Michigan in the spring of 1984. In "The Hazards and Sources of
Writing," an address for the prestigious Hopwood Writing Awards, he
spoke soberly and somewhat sadly about his own experience, giving his
audience an intimate sense of what it felt like to write year after year—
the early success, "the bruises left by comments on his works," the
ruggedness all writers have to develop if they are to create a body of
work. Dressed very smartly in a dark three-piece suit, delivering his talk
in his usual staccato, slightly off-balance way of attacking a sentence, as
if he could not quite find himself in the rhythms of his own style, Mailer
was utterly serious, almost mournful in speaking of "Those failures of
life, those flashes of old fiascos, [that] wait like ghosts in the huge house
of the empty middle-aged self." In describing the actual process of
writing, Mailer was down-to-earth: "It is in the calm depression of a
good judge that one's scribblings move best over the page." Here was the
voice of the consummate professional, never for a moment daring a
lyrical phrase that might misguide young writers, who would have to
demonstrate not only talent but stamina: "It is difficult to keep up one's
literary standards through the long slogging reaches in the middle of a
book."

Summarizing his career, identifying both the wild, impulsive strain
and the measured, calculated routine of his own writing days, Mailer
characteristically left his audience poised between alternatives: "We
may be sturdy literary engineers full of sound literary practice or, as
equally, unwitting agents for forces beyond our comprehension."

PRESIDENT MAILER

On July 11, 1984, Norman Mailer was elected to the presidency of the
American chapter of PEN (Poets, Playwrights, Editors, Essayists, and
Novelists), an international organization with over eighty affiliates
around the world. On taking office he declared:

> There is something audacious in the very conception of PEN and in the
> idea on which it was founded: that writers can speak to one another

*across the world, more quickly than can governments, and that they can
create bridges of comprehension between nations.*

Never an organization man, even when it came to writers, this was a
surprising development that provoked much initial skepticism. Why
would such a maverick want the job? And would he devote time to it?
At the beginning of his term, Mailer was presented with the task of
organizing the 48th international congress that would be hosted by the
PEN American Center in January 1986. The congress's theme would be
the imagination of the writer and of the state. A statement written by
Donald Barthelme and Richard Howard noted that these two imaginations "are in radical conflict all over the world, and that such conflict is
the most important issue facing the writer in the 1980s." It was the kind
of grandiose topic that would engage Mailer's energies, for it asked the
kinds of questions he had explored in many of his books:

*Is there a connection between the private dream and the public dream?
Having created a community, what does the writer do with it? How does
the state imagine? How does the writer seize the attention of government? What is the conflict between a writer's national consciousness
and his international consciousness?*

"My first act as president was to cluck over it in approval," Mailer told
Publisher's Weekly in February 1985 when plans for the congress were
announced publicly.

As president of such a distinguished organization, Mailer would have
a forum and a way of dealing with the Establishment that had to be
appealing to the psychic outlaw who had already confessed to a secret
need for acceptance. More than 250 participants from eighty-five PEN
centers around the world would be invited, in addition to thirty-five
guests of honor, and about 800 members from the United States. "People will have to learn all those foreign names and begin taking writers as
seriously as generals," Mailer predicted to Madalynne Reuter. He
thought that organizing an international congress would be harder work
than writing books. "But after you turn 60, you have to take up church
work. I must say this is an interesting form of it," he told Reuter.

Mailer remained very much in the public eye in the mid-1980s—not
only because of his work in PEN but because of the appearance of Peter
Manso's oral biography of him in the spring of 1985, following quickly

the reviews of *Tough Guys Don't Dance* in the autumn of 1984. In fact, Mailer had reached a saturation point. He knew people were tired of hearing of him: "I'm bored with myself," he told interviewer Garry Abrams.

With few exceptions, the mixed reviews of *Tough Guys Don't Dance* had tended to suggest that it offered nothing new. In *The Nation*, Earl Rovit expressed the feelings of many readers: "There's not much point in beating up on *Tough Guys Don't Dance*. In fact, both Justice and Mercy might agree that the proper response to this casual fling of self-indulgence masquerading as a roman noir should be indifference."

From *The Deer Park* to *Ancient Evenings*, in Mailer's obsession with Monroe, the Kennedys, and various prizefighters, the issue was always the same, Rovit noted: "Someone is in danger of plummeting from a high place." It was not the ascent to the top that intrigued Mailer but "the fear of impending fall and the accompanying rush which quickens a man trying to survive." Mailer had been trying to get this rush ever since the great success of *The Naked and the Dead*, and his incessant activity was all of a piece with his quest to "keep from falling from that position of early eminence."

> *It is as though Mailer had decided that his 1948 transformation from writer to celebrity was, in some arcane way, magical. In order to sustain the transformation (what fairy tale prince could bear a return to froghood?) he must force himself into more and more risks.*

Rovit spoke for many in his skepticism about the value of Mailer's work.

Mailer's best reviews were not for his writing but for his accomplishments as PEN president, for he had managed to organize and to find the funding for the first international congress in the United States in twenty years. Edwin McDowell reported that it might be "the largest gathering ever of foreign writers on American shores," and a PEN board member commented: "We had been talking for three or four years about hosting that congress but we never knew where to raise the money. But Norman knew what to do and how to do it." Other countries had hosted congresses with government support. The American PEN chapter knew it could not obtain public money, and it was Mailer's idea for PEN to sponsor in the fall of 1985 eight literary evenings with sixteen major authors. The price of the tickets for this Broadway series would be a thousand dollars. A smashing success, with appearances by Saul Bellow, Eudora Welty, John Irving, Susan Sontag, Joan Didion, Tom Wolfe, Arthur Miller, Woody Allen, John Updike, Kurt Vonnegut, William Styron, and George Plimpton, Mailer had the eight-hundred-thousand-dollar budget in hand for the congress. He had even been able to coax Gore Vidal into participating in an evening with him on Broadway, although the event itself (according to several accounts) turned into a bore when it became apparent that they were not willing to engage in "the literary slugfest that had been hinted at."

Mailer had also persuaded the Shubert Organization to donate both the Booth and the Royale theaters for the writers' series and then got Donald Trump to bestow free of charge two hundred rooms and six suites at his luxurious St. Moritz Hotel. "We want to behave in the European style to which the members are accustomed," President Mailer announced. Karen Kennerly, executive director of PEN, remarked that "Norman almost solely spearheaded the fund-raising effort. The work he has put into this, and into the PEN presidency overall, has been incredible." A gracious Mailer, in turn, praised his "good, intelligent, hardworking" staff and the executive board, while Gay Talese affirmed that Mailer "has been the most effective president in my memory." Of all things, Mailer was praised for his "statesmanship." He had run into some trouble for acting on a suggestion from John Kenneth Gailbraith (then president of the American Academy and Institute of Arts and Letters) to invite George Shultz, Secretary of State, to the congress. President Mailer had not consulted the executive board, but as one PEN member put it, Mailer "was most apologetic and the charm just exuded from that gray-haired eminence. He had a way of apologizing yet doing what he wanted to do, without incurring the displeasure of the critics."

On January 10, 1986, two days before the congress began, *The New York Times* reported that several members of the PEN board of directors were criticizing the decision to invite Shultz as the welcoming speaker. No one had called for a withdrawal of the invitation, but Galway Kinnell (Mailer's predecessor as president) had sent Mailer a letter stating his opposition to having a "high official of the government participating in an international writers' meeting." The Shultz invitation was particularly galling to some PEN members because of their hostility to the Reagan administration. E. L. Doctorow went so far as to say that PEN had "betrayed its charter" as a nonpolitical organization, that the invitation put PEN "at the feet of the most ideologically right-wing administration this country has yet seen." Kurt Vonnegut, on the other hand, surprised some of his fellow writers by noting "it was an honor for the organization to have the Secretary of State present, and that the invitation did not mean an endorsement of American foreign policy." John Updike, not a PEN member but a participant on one of the congress's panels, expressed sympathy for Doctorow's position and admitted that "perhaps the invitation wasn't such a hot idea," but since Shultz had been invited it seemed only right to "give the Secretary of State the courtesy of listening to him."

Five minutes before Shultz arrived at the New York Public Library on January 12 to address the congress, a group of writers delivered into Mailer's hands a letter to the Secretary of State suggesting his appearance was "inappropriate." Signed by Susan Sontag (a PEN vice president), E. L. Doctorow, John Irving, and sixty-two other writers, the letter pointed out that the Reagan administration "supports governments that silence, imprison, even torture their citizens for their beliefs. Under your leadership the State Department has, in the past, excluded many writers from the United States using the McCarran–Walter Act."

Most of the writers from abroad were not aware that Shultz would speak until they arrived at the congress, and the general membership had received no announcement. Many writers had difficulty getting into the congress for Shultz's speech and were offended by "bullying guards who blocked the doors and admitted a trickle of journalists and whichever 'guests of honor' could push their way to the front." Mario Vargas Llosa observed, "There are Nobel Prize winners standing in the street wondering what is going on here." West German writer Günter Grass declared: "I don't feel comfortable traveling from Europe to New York and the first thing I get is a lecture about freedom and literature" from Mr. Schultz.

Seven hundred writers jammed into the South Reading Room on the evening of January 12, with one mezzanine "lined with a battery of TV cameras and the other patrolled by a Secret Service man." It made some writers feel "out of place in their own home." Shortly after the session began (an hour late), Per Wastberg, international PEN president, provoked applause and shouts of support when he appealed to Shultz to abolish the McCarran–Walter Act. Mailer had shown the protest letter to Shultz when he arrived, but he angered his fellow writers by not reading it aloud before the Secretary of State's speech. Grace Paley stood up and called from the floor: "Norman, we would like to have our letter read. Norman, please read the letter." Soon other voices joined hers, but Mailer refused to acknowledge the protestors.

Mailer began his keynote address by admitting that he had accepted the PEN presidency eighteen months earlier because he hoped he would be "enough of a figurehead to draw attention to PEN's affairs. This unspoken understanding was agreeable to me. I had always wanted to be president of something." At first he had been dismayed to discover he would have to be a "hardworking figurehead, a contradiction in terms, an oxymoron." He had dutifully carried out PEN's mission to foster the "collegiality of writers everywhere," to rescue them when they were in trouble, to protest their imprisonment and torture, to appeal to the conscience of tyrants who sometimes could be swayed by the power of the word, to support writers in need of financial assistance, to run programs for handicapped writers, to conduct writing workshops in prisons, and to offer prizes to writers, editors, and publishers. But what had really motivated him was "the theme of this conference." He conceded that many writers had attacked the idea that the state had an imagination. George Steiner had pronounced the notion "almost meaningless" and "vacant." Consider, however, the Third Reich, Mailer countered. Surely "it did possess an active imagination, a most debased, horrible, paranoid, and catastrophic imagination, but still it was a state that drew its strength from the intoxication of perceiving itself as a protagonist on the world scale." Like individuals, the two great states of the modern world, the United States and the Soviet Union, were in search of their identities, and writers could not hope to understand "the evils of the state and its possible services to us until we shift the style of our thought, take a venture into the absurd, and commence to look at the state with the understanding and the intimacy we might bring to pondering the nature of a complex individual."

In introducing the Secretary of State, Mailer acknowledged the "*division d'opinion*" but said his audience would be surprised at Shultz's liberal attitude toward the McCarran–Walter act, which Mailer had briefly discussed with him after delivering the protest letter. He informed the audience that no one from abroad had been denied admission to attend the congress. According to Maria Margaronis and Elizabeth Pochoda, Mailer acted in an "overbearing and authoritarian manner (now more Oxonian than in the days of his Southern sheriff impersonations)" as though it were a "state occasion." He apologized to Shultz for the "silly bad manners exhibited tonight," against "a representative of a government, no matter how far right, who recognizes the importance of the writer." He seemed especially angry with the "puritanical leftists" in the audience.

When Shultz rose to speak, only two members of the audience, both members of the press, left. Although there was some sporadic heckling, he received a polite reception and provoked laughter when he remarked that he looked upon Mailer's invitation to speak "as another shining example of that charitable spirit for which New York literary circles have long been famous." Many in the audience termed Shultz's performance "adroit and even disarming" and felt that it "touched on several of the themes that speakers would elaborate on during the week." The secretary assured the audience that "America is proud to have you here. Diversity, debate, contrast, argumentativeness are what we as a people thrive on." He was applauded when he pledged that "We will never deny physical access to anyone because of the beliefs he or she may espouse." Sensitive to the difference between the state's demand for order and the writer's creation of "an imaginative order of his own," Shultz pointed out that a distinction had to be made between governments that silenced and killed writers and governments, such as the United States, "where writers can speak, write and publish without political hindrance." It was mistaken to think that "creativity forged in the crucible of totalitarianism is greater than that in politically free but culturally commercialized societies." There were some boos and hisses when he concluded that "we have more in common than you think. . . . Don't be surprised by the fact that Ronald Reagan and I are on your side."

At a press conference after Shultz's speech, Mailer said he had been "baffled by the disturbance" and had not heard the protests. He regretted he had not recognized Paley. They were "old comrades" who had joined hands and faced jail together in the 1960s, but even if he had understood, he might not have responded to her: "I didn't invite Secretary Shultz here in order to be insulted, to be, uh, pussywhipped." To a reporter he explained: "The letter was certain to get lots of publicity. I just felt since I'm conducting the meeting which has a certain form to it, I didn't like the way that form was being overturned." He pointed out that board members like Susan Sontag had had two months to "do something about" the Shultz invitation, and he charged that some PEN members were out to "sabotage this evening." In frustration, he concluded that it was irksome to be put in the role of a "literary bureaucrat, a commissar who would keep others from speaking."

Rhoda Koenig of *New York* magazine observed Mailer at a party after the Shultz speech joking with a couple of reporters, telling them the bruise under his right eye was from "sparring," and advising one of them not to ask "general questions." Koenig introduced herself to Mailer just after he offered his example of a specific question: "What do you think of Susan Sontag's remark that Norman Mailer is a mean-spirited dog?" Mailer was surprised that Koenig was "much better-looking" than he had imagined: "When I read your review of *Ancient Evenings*, I thought you'd be desperately ugly." Koenig replied: "Mr. Mailer. That's exactly what I had predicted you would say." He objected to her presentation of herself as "some kind of high priestess breathing flames down my neck." Still, he complimented her on her style and "with the beginning of a twinkle," he said, "I won't have any more respect for you if you don't get our conversation right."

During one of the next day's panels Nadine Gordimer spoke for many writers when she contended that the state had no imagination; the imagination could not be a collective product but was always "private and individual." The writer was alienated from the state precisely because "it is always certain it is right." And it was the inevitable function of the state to get writers to reinforce "the type of consciousness it imposes on its citizens, not the discovery of the actual conditions of life beneath it, which may give the lie to it." That evening at a cocktail party at *The New York Times*, a "boisterous but terrifically genial" Mailer seemed to relish the controversy. The rumor was his presidency was part of his campaign for the Nobel Prize. PEN members were split—some thought his organization of the congress had been a "tremendous achievement"; others accused him of "vulgar grandstanding."

By the third day of the congress, a new issue arose: the underrepresentation of women. As Miriam Schneir put it, "we women" had begun discussing it privately—"at first in absolute amazement and perplexity—a kind of stunned feeling of what *year* it was. We just didn't want to believe it." Betty Friedan, speaking for an informal caucus of women, asked Mailer why there were so few women on the panels. Mailer laughed and said, "Who's counting?" In fact, Schneir's count was two women among twenty-four panelists on Monday, six women among twenty-eight panelists on Tuesday, and three of four panels composed solely of men on Wednesday. Altogether only twenty out of 140 panelists were women. Less than two hours later, a group of about a hundred women banded together and voted for a statement demanding time at a plenary session the next afternoon (Friday). "If they will not give our representatives room on the platform, we bodily will take that platform," declared Friedan to cheers and applause.

The protest had been slow to develop because the women had deep respect for PEN and for their male colleagues. "The men are friends of ours and they even believe in social justice," Friedan pointed out. But women like Schneir were shocked when Kurt Vonnegut, a writer deemed especially sympathetic to the cause, had declared that "had he been in Mailer's position he would have invited substantially the same panelists." Evidently the organizers of the conference did not realize, in Friedan's words, "how this looks to us and to the world." On Friday, "the entire front section of the conference room was occupied by women . . . in a militant, angry mood," Schneir reported. After hearing the protests of Margaret Atwood, Grace Paley, and others, Mailer took the microphone and defended himself: "Now, that may be terribly unpleasant to a lot of you, but there are countries in the world where there are no good women writers." He then read a list of twenty-four distinguished women writers who had been invited but who were unable to attend the congress. Moreover, he informed them that twelve women were among the twenty-eight PEN members who had selected the panelists. "There were six months to register a complaint and you choose the week of the congress," he concluded.

Although several women publicly praised Mailer for his work on the congress, the protesters were not placated and remarked on the conspicuous absence of people of color. They were joined by Salman Rushdie, who noted "as the only writer present from India or Pakistan he too was part of an underrepresented" minority, and Nadine Gordimer said that "for me, the feminist cause is part of the cause of fighting for human rights for everybody, irrespective of sex." It was requested that for the next international congress, in Hamburg, women be included in "decision-making roles."

To the press, Mailer cited the factors that had led to the charges of underrepresentation:

> Since the formulation of the panels is reasonably intellectual, there are not that many women, like Susan Sontag, who were intellectuals first, poets and novelists second. More men are intellectuals first, so there was a certain natural tendency to pick more men than women.

In defense of his comment to Friedan about not counting women, Mailer said:

> *There was a time when the civil-rights movement was trying to dispense with tokenism, and all the rest of it, and insisted on quotas— construction jobs and so forth. This was for something fundamental, the right to make a better living.*
>
> *But here, what's being asked for is symbolic, women on panels. That's not a way of saying that I think women are incapable of high discussion, it's just that, given specific circumstances, the lack of many women writers is disproportionate on the panels.*

Many women had walked out on Mailer when he remarked, "We invited the best writers that we could get. We didn't want a congress that would establish a political point at the cost of considerable mediocrity. You're all middle-class women, and the standard for the middle class is obligatory excellence." His parting shot: "You can leave with the surrogate literary pope's blessing. Thank you for your *courtesy.*"

Another account of this volatile meeting suggests Mailer had also tried to be conciliatory, saying he was sorry the women were "upset." One of them replied they were not upset, they were "insulted." When he tried to shift the focus back to the congress's theme, a woman shouted: "You cut us off for this boring speech of yours!" A peeved Mailer stuck by his rights as chair but called for a vote to determine whether or not he should remain in that position. With the votes in his overwhelming favor, he went on to criticize the manners of the women and to suggest that "the reason that conservatism is thriving . . . is because of the belief that the left is going to wipe out everything."

A week after the end of the congress, Mailer sat down with Walter Goodman of *The New York Times* to conduct a "PEN postmortem." He thought that the theme of the congress was a "great mistake," but he dismissed some of his critics as "catatonic leftists" and felt he owed the women no apologies. Although there had been many lively exchanges, the very intellectuality of the theme stymied writers, Mailer believed. It was a topic better suited to philosophers, he now realized. He was angry with Susan Sontag. Why hadn't she just picked up a phone earlier and spoken with him about her complaints? And the reaction to Shultz suggested to Mailer that the left was as "tight in their mental

habits as right-wing reactionaries." In his view, "the more clout we have
with the State Department, the more effective we are." PEN itself was
not a sexist organization, said Mailer, pointing out that six of eight
permanent committees were headed by women and three of the American group's six vice presidents were women. He bore some hard feelings
toward E. L. Doctorow and other PEN members who had done little
work for the congress but felt free to criticize it, but then he seemed to let
go of the particulars of controversy in observing: "How can you have
a literary conference without friendships and feuds being formed out
of it?"

Like so many other Mailer enterprises, the PEN congress had become
emblematic of the man. Immediately after the congress, Walter Goodman had written an article suggesting that "at first, many Mailer
watchers thought they were seeing a new Norman Mailer," shedding his
combative image and cozying up to the Establishment, but by the
conference's last session he seemed like the same old Norman, intent on
"provoking a roomful of already indignant women." In *The Nation*,
Alexander Cockburn had no doubts: "Norman Mailer made an ass of
himself." This was nothing new to report, but in the past "there was
occasionally a largeness to his antics and to his words and thoughts that
made one forgive, and at least in my case, sometimes to admire him."
Cockburn thought that "the last decade has made him considerably
more mean-spirited," and he was especially offended by Mailer's
charge that elements of the left had become the "avatars of entropy."
The next thing, Cockburn predicted, Mailer would begin sounding like
the neoconservatives and would line himself up with Saul Bellow. "Too
many dinners on the Upper East Side, I fear," Cockburn surmised.

In the same issue of *The Nation*, Maria Margaronis and Elizabeth
Pochoda leveled a similar charge. There was a time when Mailer, the
radical, would have approved of Grace Paley's "bad manners," when he
would have recognized that her making a scene, of misbehaving in
public, was the only way to counter the authority of the Establishment,
of a power structure that hid behind its good manners. Margaronis and
Pochoda claimed that Mailer had lost sight of himself in his "flirtation
with pomp and circumstance, White House style," and they were especially effective in presenting the image of him behaving like "a dowager
who's afraid she's given a crummy party, turned sour and imperious."

These critics were hitting only one side of Mailer, who had termed himself in *The Armies of the Night* a "left conservative" as a way of encapsulating his contradictions. If Mailer had thought of himself as a "psychic outlaw" and written favorably about the White Negro and ridiculed William Styron for his Establishment literary career, he had also fawned over John F. Kennedy in "Superman Comes to the Super-market," confessed to a sneaking liking for Richard Nixon in *Miami and the Siege of Chicago*, and had confused himself in *Of a Fire on the Moon* in not knowing whether to go left or right in his assessment of the astronauts. If his fiction swayed in the direction of liberal dissenters like Lieutenant Hearn, it also veered toward reactionaries like General Cummings. This is the Mailer who freely announced in his PEN keynote address that he had always wanted to be "a president of something." Mailer has been saying for more than forty years that like so many of his characters he embodies the contradictions of his country. This was never clearer than in his performance at the PEN congress.

ONE OF THE AGING MALE BEAUTIES

Of course there had been changes in Norman Mailer. He drank in moderation now after having gone through a year-and-a-half of complete sobriety. The prospect of hangovers deterred him from self-indulgence. He avoided trouble and even dared to say he was happily married and thought of himself as one of the "aging male beauties," no longer thrilled to see a picture of himself in the newspaper because there were "no good photographs any longer."

There were signs that Mailer had come to terms with himself and his affairs. Marriage and family had always been important to him, but only with Norris had he been faithful to his vision of the family man. He was enormously proud of his children. Lawrence Shaw, a friend of Kate Mailer's, remembers once asking Mailer: "Did you ever worry that one of your kids would blackmail you?" Mailer gave Shaw a surprised, perplexed look. Shaw continued with an example: "Look, Dad, if you don't give me thus and such, I'll just do something to embarrass you." Mailer slapped his thigh and laughed, saying, "They wouldn't dare because I could outembarrass any of them." Shaw then heard some fond stories about the family—particularly about Fanny Mailer. Shaw had met her once. Her health was failing and she had trouble following conversations, often repeating herself. Shaw vaguely remembers a "really filthy joke" Mailer told in front of one of his daughters. Shaw saw that he was a family man, yes, but very much his own man as well.

Over the years there had been changes in the Brooklyn Heights fifth-floor apartment. Shaw remembers a large living room lined with books and family photographs facing the bay. Mailer's city sculpture still sat in its appointed place. There were two bedrooms, and a guest room on the fourth floor. Matthew (Norris's son) and John Buffalo shared one of the bedrooms. Shaw met six-year-old John Buffalo, who thought nothing of approaching visitors to the Mailer home, taking them in hand to show them his room and acting with a degree of self-possession that is associated with prodigies. A few years later, on a visit to the Mailer home, Norman Rosten would observe John Buffalo "picking up four-letter words right after papa." They had a very jolly time, and Norman mentioned that his son had written a poem about money. "Yeah, this kid sees what the world is like." It was a "charming poem about a penny," Rosten recalls.

An excellent mimic himself, Shaw was struck by Mailer's shifting speech patterns, by the way he would lurch between Texan and Irish accents, expanding his chest as he talked. A small man, he obviously wanted to make himself bigger. Shaw had the impression of someone who had worked diligently on himself as a great actor perfects his instrument, honing a voice and a presence that could not be ignored. One could almost score Mailer's dialogue—so full of different inflections—like a musical composition or choreograph the way his body moved. Even sitting, he was something of a boxer in the way he shifted his weight and switched arguments like a dancing, feinting fighter. After his cameo role in *Ragtime*, Mailer told interviewer Andrea Chambers that he would "like to play some kind of godfather . . . Jewish or Italian. I think I could do it. Ask any of my kids."

Shaw had become friendly with Kate Mailer in the autumn of 1984, later casting her in an independent film he was making. He saw in her some of her father's traits: not only an attraction to acting but her precision with words. He was shooting a silent movie, but in her scenes Kate talked. "If I had put a tape recorder on, it would be perfectly scripted dialogue," Shaw claims. Later he saw her give a thrilling performance at the Actors Studio as Marilyn Monroe in Mailer's play *Strawhead*.

THE LUNCH CLUB

In Brooklyn Heights Mailer, Norman Rosten, and David Levine (the brilliant painter and cartoonist) have formed what Rosten fondly calls The Lunch Club. They like to eat (when their work schedules permit it) at a Greek restaurant. Over the years Rosten has playfully observed "the other Norman's" movements, which seem coordinated with "certain psychic impulses. If he walks with a springy step, he may be dodging an ominous thought; a slouch may indicate oncoming paranoia. Time has slackened him a bit. *L'enfant terrible* is showing signs of *le tigre doux.*" Yet it would be unwise, Rosten warns, to "misjudge his present quietude: the volcano has some jolts left for the surrounding countryside. His scars are honorable and well earned."

When Levine is absent from the club, the two Normans are fond of concocting "lots of halfass dialogue probably worth a fortune," according to Rosten. He attributes the success of the threesome to the fact that they concede to the other Norman as "king novelist of the hill and terror of the streets," and Levine's artistry is no threat to the two Normans, although Rosten has watched Mailer pen a self-portrait entitled "Norman Mailer getting a brain wave while listening to Norman Rosten," a work of art Rosten vows to one day "put up for auction with a floor of $250,000, though we'd consider less."

The stuff of their lunches is gossip as much as it is food, and Mailer is low-key on the subject of sex—perhaps because he has "high-key lady Norris" at home, Rosten speculates. Rosten, the impecunious poet, listens ("fascinated and bored") to Levine worry over his "subsidiary rights" and Mailer moan over the complications of his contracts. Levine, the neighborhood wit, Mailer—lately the devoted family man, and Rosten, poet laureate of Brooklyn, discuss food, money, and sex—in that order. "Not quite the stardust stuff of *People* magazine," Rosten notes wryly. They consider opening the club to women. "Toil and trouble," Mailer mumbles. "Tabled until the next meeting," pipes the "wise Levine." "You're cowards," Rosten concludes.

At another meeting at a Chinese restaurant overlooking Montague Street, the two Normans discourse on the women passing by, "the emphasis more on beauty and grace than carnality," emphasizes Rosten. Although married only once, Rosten agrees with Mailer that having an "eye for women" is comparable to a "cosmic perspective." Did Rosten, married so long to one woman, know something that Mailer did not? Or was it Rosten's wife who knew it? Mailer wanted to know. Neither had an answer. They split the check, "as befits any two Normans."

On another day Rosten is out walking. He is peeved over a radio spot, a public service announcement he has contributed but is now tired of hearing and cannot seem to get it off the air. A man walking a dog approaches and turns out to be the other Norman. "Don't you know it's against the law to walk your dog on the promenade," Rosten begins belligerently. "Yeah, but city people like to sidestep shit," says Mailer, grinning. "Anyway breaking the law is an urban necessity," he adds for good measure. Rosten detects a "smudge" near Mailer's eye. "It shows, heh?" remarks Mailer. "I could say I ran into a doorknob but how can I lie before the poet laureate? A critic lady took a swipe at me and didn't miss." Mailer chuckles. "I tell you, kid, the last frontier isn't space, it's women, and that should keep the writers busy for centuries, or until sex is passé which it is now almost." Asking Rosten why he appears so glum Mailer is told: "I'd like to kill a certain critic." Mailer nods. "That's what your agent is for," he points out. "I asked her but she refused," rejoins Rosten. Mailer is sympathetic: "My man Scott would do it for a client. Never too late to switch." Then the dog barks, and Mailer says, "Come on, you little fucker." Patting the dog, he is off on a light trot.

MY AFRICA

In May 1985, at the Cannes film festival, Menahem Golan, chairman of the Cannon Group, was negotiating with Jean-Luc Godard to direct a contemporary version of *King Lear*. Godard would do it, provided Golan could get the writer the director wanted: Norman Mailer. Producer Tom Luddy, who knew Mailer and who had worked with Godard, was dispatched to interest the author in the project. A wary Mailer realized he would have "thirty thousand Shakespeareans out to slaughter me," not to mention the fact that Godard was notorious for ignoring the scripts written for him. Luddy knew, however, that Mailer wanted to make a film of *Tough Guys Don't Dance* and worked a deal so that Mailer would write a screenplay for Godard and get the opportunity to write and direct a film of his novel. As Mailer had suspected, there was no meeting of minds with Godard, who abandoned Mailer's screenplay—a "mad farce," Mailer calls it, featuring Lear as a Mafioso, Don Learo, who repudiates his daughter for disloyalty.

Having fulfilled his commitment to the Godard project, Mailer looked forward to directing his first mainstream film with a modest five-million-dollar budget. Thinking of the director as a kind of "executive," Mailer welcomed the opportunity to make the countless practical decisions of the filmmaking business. To journalist Karen Jaehne he claimed to have a "practical nature." Determined to bring the picture in on schedule and within budget, he hoped to earn a reputation as an "average-to-good" director known for his reliability, and (Mailer laughed) as a "guy you can trust with the money!" He wanted to make more movies. As in his role as President Mailer, he relished the feeling of being in charge: "The managerial aspect of directing this operation is much like the military. Think of it as NATO exercises because not much destruction can come of it," he told Jaehne. An agile Mailer, obviously enjoying himself, bounded onto the set, all bundled up in his large parka, his vigorous white hair hidden by a thick fisherman's cap, and bounced around like "the Michelin man." He spoke of his need for a change. As a director, he felt:

One's living free in the world in a funny way. It's like being in combat. Things happen every day as you inch forward from place to place. It's marvelous because it's combat without blood. We'll have a rout now, then we'll stop and eat, clean up the crumbs, and take the next hill.

Novel writing is so visionary in contrast, so obsessive. You love the novel, you hate it. The novel nags at you, accuses you, reminds you what you haven't done for its life. Terribly personal, like a mate, I repeat, a wife. It's total and sometimes has nothing to do with anything else in reality but it has to claim you. It's confining in the same way marriage is confining. All the sides of yourself that don't fit the other person can't be used. I know. I've been doing it for 40 years.

The Cannon Group had agreed to accept Mailer as director only if he had help from professionals like John Bailey, credited as "visual consultant," and several other old hands who had worked for Francis Ford Coppola and on other major motion pictures. Mailer was content with this arrangement—indeed, eager to make a film that would be much more conventional than his experiments in the 1960s, which he had no desire to repeat. At a showing of *Maidstone* in early 1984, he had told

Nan Robertson that "years ago I thought it was a good and important film that people didn't understand. Now I think it's a terribly flawed and imperfect movie that's really interesting for people who are obsessed by film. The production is an interesting idea, made by a man who didn't know how to make movies."

In writing a novel, he enjoyed delving into the depths of his characters; in directing a film, he liked to "tighten the surface till your work resonates." In terms of the sound, the editing, the sets, Mailer wanted a technically correct movie—if still "out of category," more concerned with the "style of people's relationships" than with plot or character development. He called it a "comedy of manners" and anticipated that "some will slam it as absurd, because it doesn't add up to anything at all."

Mailer used his visual consultant well, realizing that he had to get the look of Provincetown right if he was going to probe the "style of people's relationships." Shot in Provincetown in the quiet, lonely, half-deserted months of October, November, and December, Mailer aimed at capturing Tim Madden's forlorn frame of mind, his isolation—bereft not only of Patty Lareine but of his sense of himself in this dry, barren, windy landscape. Lareine's sensuous, vulgar flamboyance is felt everywhere in the house, in what Karen Jaehne calls

> a maddening mixture of apricot, pink, peach—a medley of intrauterine colors, topped off as one ascends the stairs by a gigantic conch shell of vaginal dentata. Feathers, fluff, and a white baby grand on a lime-green oriental carpet downstairs, while in the upstairs bedroom, white chintz flounces and 19th century porcelain bath fixtures figure in a feminist scheme to asphyxiate reason.

It is a "war between the sexes recapitulated in the decor," observes Jaehne, who quotes Mailer's set designer, Armin Ganz: "Norman is about as clear in his visual imagery as a director can possibly be."

Although Mailer got fine performances from his excellent cast, including Ryan O'Neal and Isabella Rossellini, there seemed to be little rapport between him and the actors. Francis Fisher, playing "the other blond," Jessica Pond, was outspoken:

> I think Norman hates women. Not because of anything personal. He's gawd-awful nice to me, but look at what I'm doing in this movie: I go

down on two guys, get fucked on a jeep, and get my head chopped off.
Norman Mailer hates women. People ought to know.

To Jaehne, Mailer insisted, "I like women." They were intriguing, but he sometimes got frustrated in trying to figure them out, especially in these times when women's roles were changing. He was uncomfortable pursuing the subject. "Talking about women is dangerous, especially to a woman," he told Jaehne.

Ryan O'Neal, a sometime Mailer sparring partner at the Gramercy Park Gym and a surprisingly good choice to play Tim Madden, found himself mediating between the director and the actors, for Mailer had a tendency to be overbearing, to shout "Stop that," cutting off an actor in midspeech rather than cultivating and nurturing a performance. He would not follow O'Neal's advice to take an actor aside and to handle him gingerly. Mailer seemed to have no idea, or did not care to acknowledge, how easily actors could be embarrassed or humiliated. Offended by his director's rather abrupt style, Lawrence Tierney, playing Madden's gruff but intensely loyal father, told Mailer: "You're supposed to ask the actor if he's ready." "I will," said Mailer, who saw himself as a "benign director," although almost in the same breath he called himself a "policeman" who had to "rein in" the actors' instincts so that they did not "detour the movie." As one of the cast put it, "Actors are confused by his methods. He knows what he wants but doesn't know how to get it." He had his moments, however. When Debra Sandlund, a devout Christian, kept covering her breasts with a sheet in the bedroom scenes, Mailer gently suggested: "Debra, I'm not trying to see you. But Patty wouldn't pull the sheet up over her like that."

It was an exhausting but exhilarating experience for Mailer to direct a film, to be on call twelve hours a day, when most of his life had been spent in three- or four-hour writing shifts. His deep enjoyment of this change of routine was apparent to a *Time* reporter who described Mailer as "a cross between a Roman senator and a retired longshoreman as he hobnobs with the crew, rehearses the cast and then stands back to watch the action, his eyes twinkling." Part of the pleasure was the opportunity to shoot the interior scenes in his own Provincetown home, redecorated to reflect Patty Lareine's garish tastes. And Mailer was just steps away from the Provincetown pubs where he could take a reporter across the street, peer in at the "real life revelers" and "roar with proprietary delight. 'That's classic Provincetown.'"

In an "expansive" mood during much of the filmmaking, Mailer referred to his directorial assignment as "my Africa," comparing it to Hemingway's testing of himself: "When you get older, you've settled most of the questions of the ego. You know which part is good to keep and which part to scuttle. The only thing left to find out is if certain ideas of yourself are true or not." On the last day of shooting Mailer felt he had found out. Hoarse, exhausted but jubilant, he declared: "We finished on time—actually a day-and-a-half ahead of schedule, and we're *under budget!*"

TOUGH GUYS SHOULDN'T DIRECT

Upon its release in the fall of 1987, *Tough Guys Don't Dance* was greeted with considerable contempt. Film critic David Ansen reported that audiences at Cannes responded to a showing with "derisive laughter." Mailer countered that the movie was meant to be "a kind of self-parody." Ansen conceded this could be so, that "it *is* possible to have some campy, degenerate fun here." Nevertheless, "Tough guys shouldn't direct."

The problem was consistency of tone. Without the valuable resource of a narrator—a reader could accept the baroque, outrageous scenes of the novel because they were of a piece with Madden's eccentric style— the dialogue of the film seemed foolish or simply impoverished. For example, when Madden reads Madeleine Falco's note explaining that her husband, Alvin Luther Regency, is having an affair with Patty Lareine, an anguished Madden shouts out, "Oh God, Oh Man, Oh God" several times as the camera whirls around the Provincetown sand dunes in a 360-degree arc in imitation of his disorientation. The words seem so ludicrous that at least one critic said O'Neal had been given the worst line in any motion picture that year.

Mailer had begun the picture determined not to use a voice-over narrator, suggesting to Dinita Smith that "narration in a film is a confession of weakness," an inability on the part of the screenwriter to fully dramatize characters and scenes. Yet in the end he had been obliged to use O'Neal's voice to help establish the continuity of certain scenes without noticeably helping his audience to identify with him.

Other critics echoed Ansen:

An easy film to laugh at, but that is to deny how much genuine if loopy fun it is to watch. There's a singular mind behind this work, but it's refracted through a foreign substance—film. —Vincent Canby

Mailer isn't enough of a moviemaker to draw us into the story on a primitive level: we're not caught up in the hero's fear that he may be a murderer, and so we're outside the movie from first to last.
—Pauline Kael

. . . it's difficult to distinguish the intentionally straight-faced from the would-be parody. In short this is a motley display—albeit a flamboyantly entertaining one.—Joy Gould Boyum

Tough Guys *manages to combine enough melodrama and suspense to raise it above embarrassing-hoot level. . . . But I won't lie to you: much of this movie is fruitier than last Christmas' uneaten dessert.*
—Richard Gehr

Mailer thought that even if his film were reviewed as a disaster, it would not damage his literary reputation. But in a way it did. Some of the feature articles on him carried the implication that he was through as a writer. The Abbott controversy, the mixed reviews of *Ancient Evenings* and *Tough Guys Don't Dance*, the negative publicity over his PEN presidency, the dismissive reviews of his film all combined to convey a picture of a played-out talent. Some reviewers seemed just plain tired of Norman Mailer. In *Mademoiselle*, Ron Rosenbaum spoke the mind of many when he concluded: "Somehow the movie, even more than the book, reveals what a caricature Mailer has become."

14.

"HARLOT'S GHOST" (1987–)

"A HARLOT HIGH AND LOW"

When Mailer began his directorial stint in the fall of 1986 he had drafted approximately four hundred pages of a new novel titled *Harlot's Ghost*. By the end of 1989 he was projecting that the manuscript might be as long as twenty-five hundred typewritten pages. Publication had been announced for January 1991. He was hard at work in the summer of 1990, hoping that in July he could finish the novel he had promised his publisher. He was quite secretive about the book—not wanting to hex a work in progress—even though he published a brief excerpt from it in the July 1988 issue of *Esquire*. *Harlot's Ghost* was rumored to be a spy novel having to do with the CIA—long one of Mailer's obsessions.

In the August 16, 1976, issue of *New York* magazine, Mailer published a long article, "A Harlot High and Low," the title of which came from an English translation of a Balzac novel, *Splendeurs et misères des courtisanes*. As an epigraph he used a statement from his mentor Jean Malaquais: "There are no answers. There are only questions." Mailer began by pointing out that Balzac's book was "concerned as much with secret police as with the prostitutes who passed through its pages, but then whores and political agents made a fair association for Balzac." What did whores and political agents have in common? They were both actors, role players, pretending to be what they were not. The harlot acted "*as if* she loved you, and that was a more mysterious proposition than one would think, for it is always mysterious to play a role. It is equal in a sense to living under cover." For different clients, harlots can play different roles, and the assumed roles may become the most intense moments of their lives, more real than anything else to them. Mailer implied that this is what had happened to the CIA; it had become consumed by its undercover roles; it had infiltrated every aspect of American life so that its ultimate roots were now untraceable. The CIA had become the country in some fundamental, weird way that Mailer knew he could not prove; he could only imagine the complex truth as a novelist turned essayist. To say that the CIA had this kind of subversive, mysterious hold on American life was tantamount, in Mailer's mind, to showing how novelists had lost their grip on the country's identity. Or as he put it at the end of the essay: "What a crazy country we inhabit. What a harlot. What a brute. She squashes sausage out of the minds of novelists on their hotfooted way to a real good plot."

In the forty years since *The Naked and the Dead* Mailer had been searching for a way to write the great panoramic American novel. He had abandoned the eight-cycle scheme of Sergius O'Shaungnessy novels; he had discarded the trilogy begun with *Ancient Evenings.* America had seemed too complex for any single novelist—no matter how mature—to take on. With *The Naked and the Dead*, Mailer had exploded his naive notion that he could supply answers, and most of his work beginning with *Barbary Shore* had been filled with questions and musings as he tried to plumb American society. In *The Naked and the Dead*, he had been young enough to believe he could get at the essence of an institution like the army. In *Harlot's Ghost*, a much-chastened novelist would, in a sense, do just the opposite. He would hope to write a great novel by demonstrating through the institution of the CIA that America's raison d'être had become, in a sense, one big plot, a conspiracy that only a novelist could hope to gauge if not to comprehend.

In "A Harlot High and Low" the CIA stands for the obliteration of history, for it is an organization in which "facts are wiped out by artifacts; proof enters the logic of counterproof and we are in the dream; matter breathes next to anti-matter." This is the Watergate world of "scenarios," a factoidal world as far-reaching and devastating to the

imagination of the real as the phantasmagorical world of Hollywood that
had shredded Monroe's identity in *Marilyn*. Given the broad, ambiguous
mandate to collect "intelligence" and tracking the CIA's enormous
growth in terms of its personnel, its connections with different government departments and with private companies, Mailer suggested: "No
vein, therefore, of American business or culture was independent of
Intelligence—not finance, media, economic production, labor–management relations, cinema, statistical theory, fringe groups, Olympic
teams. There was no natural end to topics the CIA could legitimately
interest itself in."

Because the CIA depended on secrecy to develop its contacts and
because it put a premium on the exclusivity of its information, it had no
organization chart: "No one would be certain finally who belonged and
who did not." Even the director, for his own protection, did not know for
certain about all the cells, the "enclaves," that operated within the
organization. Try tracing the CIA's use of funds—a futile enterprise,
Mailer suggested. There were compartments within compartments—
set up like Chinese boxes: "It is novelistically intoxicating to contemplate the pyramiding of wealth which must have gone on in some
enclaves of the CIA."

In such an Alice-in-Wonderland world it seemed probable to Mailer
that certain CIA agents would find the boundaries of their identities
clouded. Given the plots and counterplots, double agents and moles—
not to mention the proliferation of scenarios, what truth is there for
an agent to believe? How can he know for certain the Agency has not
had a part in the assassinations of the 1960s? Mailer asked. "Where is
the root of identity in that kind of man?" Mailer supposes that in such
a mysterious situation the personality divides—like the two halves of
the brain, a lobe, so to speak, for each plot and counterplot, for the
various shifts of identity and cover stories required of agents. The CIA
itself becomes a "mammoth of shuffled identities."

Covering much of the convoluted history of the 1960s and early
1970s, "A Harlot High and Low" seeks to build a case for mystery,
for showing that the country's history may indeed be unknowable,
with the novelist's task now to show various routes into the maze, the
smoke, and the mirrors, to at least size up the dimensions of the enigma.
One of Mailer's few footnoted articles (it also contains a bibliography), "A Harlot High and Low" is a paradoxical Balzacian achieve-

ment, an informed foray into a society that the novelist fears he cannot fathom.

The excerpt from *Harlot's Ghost* in *Esquire* is brief but evocative of Mailer's usual themes: Written—as is his wont—in the first person, it is the record of an initiation, the quest for a father, the test of a young man's courage. The narrator, Harry Hubbard, is the product of St. Matthew's, a Catholic private school, who describes his encounter with Hugh Tremont Montague, a mysterious, legendary figure at St. Matthew's, a teacher of English and Divine Studies, a mountaineer and rock climber. Montague takes Harry (with his father's blessing) on a terrifying rock-climbing trip, representing (in Harry's view) "the objective correlative of Virtue, which is to say, the meeting of Truth and Courage." The trip is of inordinate importance to the teenage Harry, who is obsessed with becoming a man, having already suffered the attentions of an assistant chaplain who has "*glommed*" onto his penis with his "tight, unhappy lips" and observed the humiliation of a small boy who has been regularly buggered by his schoolmates.

The rock-climbing scenes are some of the best writing Mailer has ever done, evolving naturally out of Harry's fear and his desire to please his surrogate father. The whole passage of identity from childhood to adolescence to adulthood is conveyed in Harry's remembrance of what it was like out on the rocks:

> To put one's heels on a ledge and lean backward into space, holding only to a rope, is equal to the wail one hears in childhood on falling out of bed. One discovers that the voice is one's own. My first few steps, feet pressed flat against the vertical rock, were as clumsy as if my legs were concrete posts.

Scraping and bruising himself on the rocks, determined to find his own way up the climbs Montague has staked out for him, Harry has to keep conquering his fear, the little boy in himself, the physical coward who never quite feels he has made it:

> There is no psychological transaction more compelling. I think one is raising at such times all the ships lost in childhood from loss of courage, yes, hoisting them up from the sea bottom of oneself. I felt as if all the great fears that weighed me down had begun their ascent to the

surface—I was being delivered from the graveyard of lost hope. But
what a chancy operation it was! Each time I failed to complete a climb,
the fear I was hoping to free was not consumed but turned corrupt, and I
was left wholly rotten within.

This is the familiar universe of Norman Mailer, in which identity is
always a thing in motion, always subject to the possibilities of enlarging
and lessening itself.

Hugh Tremont Montague, it turns out, is a former member of the
OSS, the precursor of the CIA. After Harry has proved himself on the
rocks, Montague requests that when they are alone, Harry call him
Harlot, "the name a few of my associates know." It is the name for a
quintessential role player, a man of many identities, with as many lives
as Menenhetet.

THE MAD BUTLER

Like Faulkner, like Hemingway, like most major writers, Mailer has
found it harder and harder as he ages not to give way to certain mannerisms, tricks of style, and habits of thinking. It is easy to make fun of
him—this fat man in his safari shirts whose terrain is not Africa but the
Brooklyn Heights Promenade. When he involved himself in the Salman
Rushdie furor, it was not surprising to find him the target of a Guy
Trebey *Village Voice* piece that pictured Mailer at a support meeting
waddling up "amid an orgasm of strobe. Neckless and rumpy, today he's
playing the breezy patriarch." Trebey found Mailer unprepared to address the subject: "It's standard-issue Late Mailer, strafing the room
with ideas. Some may be sound, but the audience is hard-pressed to
notice, so riveting is the image of Mailer shooting himself in the foot.
Mailer's Vegas lounge act seems flabby for anyone A-listed for a Nobel."
Mailer praised the power of words, the need to defend literature while
castigating the cowardly bookstore chains for withdrawing *The Satanic
Verses* from the shelves—although it was about what could be expected
from merchants who sold books as if they were soup cans and hired
clerks who would not know a serious author like Bellow or Mailer if he
walked into a chain store. He got his biggest reaction when he referred to
Tom Wolfe, never one of his favorites, as someone a clerk might recognize because he was "the fastest selling can of soup around." Trebey

reported that there was "a giant insuck of breath in consideration of Wolfe's feelings." It seemed so gratuitous, especially with Wolfe in the room. Mailer's words were later published in *Writer's Digest* and seemed, as usual, more reasoned than the press accounts, although rather offensive in his expressed willingness to offer himself and to encourage others to offer themselves for the hit list he imagined would be made up of those who defend literature. Surely he knew there was no real danger in making an offer that would not even be noticed by those who made Rushdie a marked man.

Interviews with Mailer for the last fifteen years have spoken of his "mellowing," a term he has alternately accepted and rejected. No longer interested in being the center of public controversy, Mailer bridles at what he sees as cheap shots at his past. In a letter to Lewis Allen, the co-producer of *Tru*, a play based on a recent biography of Truman Capote, Mailer complained about a line in the first act spoken by Capote at a time when he was concerned about the controversial publication of an excerpt from his novel *Answered Prayers*. On the phone to his lecture agent's secretary, Capote says, "Listen, hon, when Irene gets back in, ask her when Norman Mailer stabbed his wife, how much his fee went up." Mailer called the line "kind of crass" and charged, "There's no use hiding behind Truman. It's an ugly line designed to cater to rich out-of-town yahoos." The play's author, he contended, "is not averse to getting a 10-second hype on my name and my bad deeds." And the play's author, Jay Preston Allen, certainly knew that "one's fee doesn't go up, not for the worst things in one's life." The playwright's reply—as reported by Glenn Collins in *The New York Times*—was obviously designed to put Mailer in his place. It also revealed how futile it was for him at this late date to try to diffuse such uses of his biography:

> *A pretty poor show, kid, for someone who for over three decades has assiduously worked at creating the very public image of a provocateur, a tough guy who takes on all comers, a mythic brawler. But when a small shot comes your way, you toss your curls and sob "foul."*

There was something bitchy in Mailer's complaint, the reaction of a grande dame gone testy over the bad manners of a lesser literary light.

If Mailer has a final contribution to make, it will have to be in the novel. His essays, since the weak piece on Jimmy Carter in 1976, have been undistinguished and have gone over old ground—like "Cosmic

Ventures: A Meditation on God at War" in the December 1989 issue of
Esquire, although his article in the March 1991 *Vanity Fair* on the
controversial novel *American Psycho* represents a recovery of his literary form.

Approaching the age of seventy, he is, at 195 pounds, very heavy but
handsome, reminding some interviewers of Spencer Tracy. As he told
Carole Mallory in a recent interview, he does not mind his heaviness:
"I'm not tall, only 5′ 7″, that lacks bulk. I like walking around as if I
were a big man." He still loves good parties and the social scene. He is
rather baffled by the changing roles of men and women over these past
twenty years. In some respects he seems wistful, for the world has come
a long way from the one he thought he knew how to conquer in his
younger years. He sometimes sounds like a relic—as in this confession
to Mallory:

> *I once made love to a girl six minutes after I met her. I was at the end of a
> dance and I took her across the street into some bushes. I was so proud
> of that. Now the sex wasn't all that good. But I was so proud of it. It gave
> my ego the equivalent of political standing. Very few men could do that,
> I thought, and I was proud of myself.*

One of his regrets is that he and Elizabeth Taylor "never got together."

With his distrust of modern medicine, attraction to magic, and theories about how people contract and ward off cancer, his view of his last
years and of how he will approach his death would be curious to know.
"It's silly to talk about how you're going to end," Mailer said in response
to Mallory's query. "You might just get your prayer answered." So he is
superstitious about his own death and figures on no more than another
ten years, if that, to write.

Although both his father and mother are dead, Mailer remains tied to
Brooklyn. He still has not written about his life there or about his
Jewishness, yet it remains (in Norman Rosten's words) "the nest, the
place where you want to be if there is a crisis." It is a where he can be the
hero of the neighborhood, observed on his winter walks, the subject of
concerned gossip and affection: "I saw Norman walking. He looked
tired. He looked pale." In recent years he has suffered from gout and has
had to hobble around on crutches. Rosten and Mailer have breakfasted
many times over the years in the Promenade Restaurant in Brooklyn
Heights. Over the long haul of this last novel, Rosten has seen him

downhearted, exhausted by the effort, and worried about the relevance of a CIA novel and political theme that may have become outmoded by recent developments in Eastern Europe and the consequent shift away from the paranoid, conspiratorial atmosphere of the Cold War years.

In discussing other writers, Mailer has always seemed to have himself in mind—not merely so that he can size himself up against the competition but so that he can project his career forward. He is the great failure of American literature, and he is the first to realize that the phrase confers on him high honor. Writing about Henry Miller and about the "paradoxes of a great artist," Mailer observes: "For it is impossible to talk of a great artist without speaking of failure. The greater they are, the more they do not fulfill their own idea of themselves. Dostoyevsky failed to write The Life of a Great Sinner, and Tolstoy never brought a religious metamorphosis to man." It was Henry Adams who characterized his whole life as a failure in his autobiography—the accents of which are so clearly assimilated into *The Armies of the Night.*

A former editor of *The New York Times Book Review*, told about this biography of Mailer, responded rather portentously: "After those last two novels, he better come up with something good, or he's finished." In nearly every decade of Mailer's career, someone has said something like this; sometimes it has been Mailer himself. Norman Rosten takes exception to this attitude: "You never write off a good writer—he might have a knock-out punch waiting, and I hope he does."

What other American writer approaching seventy is still being asked to prove himself and has actually abetted the question? "I didn't start with an identity. I forged an identity through my experience," Mailer told Hilary Mills shortly after the publication of *The Executioner's Song.* For four decades, each new work of his has been greeted with great anticipation and skepticism. This has gone on so long that there will be no end to it until there is an end to Mailer, this Menenhetet who has reveled in his many lives: "People think they've found a way of dismissing me, but, like the mad butler—I'll be back serving the meal."

TO BE CONTINUED

February 25, 1991. Mailer is making his third appearance in thirty years at the Poetry Center of the Ninety-Second St. Y. Tickets to his lecture have been sold out for days, and a line of about twenty-five hopefuls without tickets has formed, speculating that there will be enough no-shows to make room for them in a large auditorium that must seat close to a thousand. Like me, some of the hopefuls have known about Mailer's appearance for months and yet have not bothered to get tickets. At the last minute, some sense of urgency has seized them, and they are now eager to get in as they watch a seemingly endless stream of ticket holders. I grab a ticket from a guy who comes along and charges me fifteen dollars for a twelve-dollar ticket.

It is a grand auditorium, paneled in dark wood, and inscribed at the top with the names of Brahms, Bach, Beethoven, Lincoln, Washington, David, Moses, Isaiah, Jefferson, Shakespeare, Dante, Goethe, Maimonodes. A bank of eighteen theater lights shine down on the podium, and several other banks in the balcony flood the stage with light. The audience is impossible to describe: all ages, all types. Flushed with happiness at being there, I turn to the elderly woman next to me and blurt out: "I'm writing Mailer's biography." She smiles and says, "These events are often disappointing. Arthur Miller, ugh. He came and read his stuff and walked off. So boring." To a biographer, of course, the boring part doesn't matter. To be there is the thing.

Mailer does not disappoint. After Robert Lucid's gracious introduction, he walks out on stage, a barrel of a man dressed in an unbuttoned double-breasted blazer and matching pants, looking the part of an aging but vigorous white-haired literary lion. His hands clutch the podium as he first turns one side, then the other side of his body to the audience, always catching us at an angle, almost never remaining for long in a full frontal pose, as if he were a boxer protecting at least half of himself from damage. Occasionally a hand will slip into a pocket, and it will be a good hour before he seems truly comfortable with us.

Mailer's voice is interesting. It sometimes has the rough, guttural edge of someone whose throat is dry; sometimes it is fluid and mellow. One can't be sure if the raspy quality is affected, natural, or now such a part of the persona that it is second nature to him. No sign of Southern or Irish accents—just his Brooklyn/Harvard amalgamation.

After so many years in public, Mailer has a standard routine—the one he first developed in *Advertisements for Myself*: disarmament of his audience. He begins by apologizing for the passages he will read from *Harlot's Ghost*. It is not a novel with easily extractable set pieces, he tells us. It is a novel of "touches" which gradually accumulate to make his point, a comedy of manners that will make us smile but not laugh out loud. In fact, he advises us, "You might want to make a bet on whether there are five laughs in this evening's reading."

He tells a joke—to relax us, to relax him, to get the laughs he may not get with his novel. It's about two mangy buffaloes in a draw in North Dakota. Mailer takes his time describing the setting and the immaculately dressed cowboy, decked out in black and silver, who rides up to the buffaloes, looks them over, makes critical comments on their sorry appearance, and rides away. One buffalo turns to the other and says, "I guess we just heard our first discouraging word." A hearty laugh from the audience. "It's the only clean joke I know," Mailer responds.

Always the first critic of his work, Mailer continues preparing his audience: In the first reading, "We're all going to have to work a little bit." It is a selection from Hugh ("Harlot") Montague's Thursday lecture to new CIA recruits. Taking as an example the items found in a renegade CIA agent's pockets, Montague constructs an exercise on evidence. What scenario can be derived from these fragments? he asks his men. His brightest pupil correctly answers none, and Montague cautions them not to be seduced by the "auto-intoxication" of their work, finding significance in things that actually have no meaning. Montague continues with a lesson on recruiting agents in "satellite countries." He emphasizes the importance of paying foreign agents: "Money confirms the virtue of the vice." A foreign agent should be worked like a "good farm animal. Don't make him gallop." Developing a new agent is like developing a new identity, concludes Montague as he leads his neophytes through the intricacies of agent recruitment.

After reading several pages Mailer is breathing a little heavily and has a slight whistle in his nose. He calls for questions. The audience is impressed with his knowledge of the CIA. Where did he get it? Mailer confesses that it has been very exciting to think of himself as a CIA agent. In fact, if he had grown up in a different time and in a different family, he thinks he would have been an agent—like Harry Hubbard, his protagonist in the novel. Although he does not say so, Mailer is obviously attracted to the role of an espionage agent and the moral ambiguities inherent in the enterprise of gathering intelligence. A connoisseur of books on the CIA, many of which came out while he wrote the novel, Mailer welcomed the challenge of using his imagination to fill in the gaps of what he did not know.

The second long passage Mailer reads puts him back into the arena of

Ancient Evenings and much of his other work, for the central scene is Harry Hubbard's confrontation with Dix Butler, a physically powerful agent Harry admires. Still a virgin at twenty-three (the setting is Berlin in 1956), Harry is shocked by Dix's plea to sodomize him. Dix is contemptuous of Harry's virginity and innocence, suggesting that many agents are homosexuals. Dix's logic: Homosexuals lead a double life, agents lead a double life; ergo, many agents are homosexuals. Dix tells Harry that to be a good agent, "You have to be able to turn yourself inside out," experience, in other words, homo- and heterosexuality. Harry's "asshole is tight," remarks Dix, who advises him, "Taking it up the ass is the next thing to yoga."

The audience laughs on this line, but Mailer pays no notice as he slips into a Southern accent for Dix's dialogue. The question of tone, as in *Ancient Evenings*, is troubling. I suspect Mailer means the line to be taken seriously while at the same time making Dix a little comical, since no character in an espionage novel can be a privileged authority or know the truth of things. In Berlin in 1956, Mailer explains to the audience, there were several different intelligence organizations working at cross purposes. The situation was a mess politically, and it serves as a good metaphor for the personal mess, the identity conflicts of his characters.

Until Dix reveals his desire for Harry, he has been known as a womanizer—"before the word was invented," Mailer adds. Even after a frightened Harry refuses to sodomize Dix, he admits to himself that he loves Dix, who holds the power of a father over him. Mailer's obsessions about how to father oneself and the split psychopathic personality of the modern hero continue to bedevil his work. How revealing that his identification is with the CIA, with Harry Hubbard, and with the fiction he has been driven to make up about other lives he has longed to make his own.

In the second question-and-answer period, the audience virtually ignores the reading, evidently not knowing what to make of it or how to discuss it. They leave in good humor. I overhear someone say: "I liked the first passage better. But thirteen hundred pages [Mailer announced this as the length of the novel], I don't know if I want to read that much." Mailer himself had joked about his gargantuan work, which he said was really only half the novel: "Anyone who reads thirteen hundred pages won't care if it has an end." The last page would be marked "to be continued."

AFTERWORD

I first became interested in Norman Mailer in the summer of 1969 after reading *The Armies of the Night*. I remember finishing the book late at night. Flushed with enthusiasm, I wrote five hundred words calling him the last romantic. In graduate school I continued to read him, knowing that someday I would write a book about his work. It would not have occurred to me then to write a biography, even though I was fascinated with the way his personality intersected with history. A graduate student who thought more about literature than about lives, I had it in mind to teach a course on "History as a Novel, the Novel as History" at The New School for Social Research. I would explore the phenomenon of what was then termed the "nonfiction novel." Insufficient enrollment prevented me from teaching the course, but whenever I had the opportunity I included Mailer in my teaching at other schools.

The appearance of *Marilyn* crystallized my interest in Mailer and in biography. I was intrigued with the way he used his own personality and showed how Monroe evolved out of the literature—the previous biographies—of her life. In the next fifteen years, I reviewed his work as it came out and wrote several essays on his career while also producing my own biographies of Marilyn Monroe, Lillian Hellman, and Martha

Gellhorn. I also began a book on Mailer (a work of literary criticism), which I abandoned at the start of my Hellman biography.

When I decided to return to the Mailer manuscript, I realized I could not complete it without making it a full-fledged biography. Mailer, of all writers, has made his personality an issue, and his impact upon me has been profound—often dictating my choice of subjects and my approach to biography.

What kind of biography would I write? I had reviewed Hilary Mills's biography. It was a competent survey of Mailer's life, a well-organized marshaling of the facts, and a useful compendium of opinion. Mills had interviewed Mailer for *The Saturday Review* but he had not cooperated with her on the biography. She had been able, however, to interview many of his close friends, who provided important insights into his life. She was not a literary critic, and she did not probe his work or explore its connections with his life.

Less than two years after Mills's biography appeared, Peter Manso published his oral history of Mailer's life and times. Although he and Mailer had had a falling out, during the time his book was in preparation he had been an insider—involved not only in Mailer's mayoral campaign but also part owner of a piece of Mailer property in Provincetown. Manso interviewed most of the people Mills had questioned as well as several members of Mailer's family. Mailer and his mother spoke for the biography. Out of this rich tape-recorded archive Manso crafted a chronological account of Mailer's career. The virtue in this approach is that you hear the individual voices of the witnesses and not the biographer's third-person summary. The flaw in Manso's method is that there is no integrative narrative point of view. Like Mills, there is no significant coming to terms with Mailer's work. Both biographers ignore the archival sources: the letters and manuscripts scattered in various libraries throughout the country.

It seemed to me that a very different biography could be written, almost carved out of Mills's and Manso's labors. One could compare the stories in both books, take a much closer look at Mailer's writing than they had, and conduct additional interviews where that seemed necessary to provide new insight or corroboration. This had been the tack I had taken in my biography of Monroe and the one Mailer himself had adopted in *Marilyn*.

I had one other key decision to make: Should I contact Mailer? I had written him twice while working on Monroe, hoping that he would add his endorsement of the book to the one I had already received from Gloria Steinem. He replied quite courteously, saying he hoped he would find the time to read it—although he had stacks of books from friends who hoped he would write blurbs for them. I did not hear from him again. A few years later I wrote him asking for an interview about Lillian Hellman, and he replied with a charming little note declining to speak with me because he thought he might someday write about her himself.

So I was fairly certain that if I wrote to him again, I would get another polite reply and a rejection. After all, he had an authorized biographer, Robert Lucid whom I had met once after having given a paper on Mailer at a Modern Language Association meeting, and he had complimented me on my treatment of *Marilyn* and of *Of Women and Their Elegance*. I wanted Mailer to know I was writing a biography of him, so I wrote to Lucid about my plans and suggested that we might meet and talk things over.

I have had previous encounters with authorized biographers. William Abrahams had written me that he was Hellman's "one and *only* authorized biographer" and flatly refused to allow me to see Hellman's papers at the University of Texas. Lucid, on the other hand, was extremely cordial and thought he could arrange for me to see certain items in Mailer's vast archive housed in Manhattan. About a year later, when I wrote him asking to see the items we had discussed, I did not receive a reply.

Even before I met Lucid, I had resolved to contact Mailer only after I had finished a draft of my biography. I thought it more likely that he would speak with me if he knew my book was going to press. Just as important, however, was my feeling that I should write the biography and have a whole vision of the man before I met him. If I did not meet him, it would be a disappointment but not a disaster, for I did not believe I had to meet him to write about him any more than I would have to meet Shakespeare in order to write his biography. Indeed, the way a biographer knows his or her subject and the way we know our contemporaries are two entirely different things.

In the late spring of 1990, I wrote to Mailer. With his usual courtesy he replied, explaining that he was trying to finish a draft of his novel by the end of July. He could not hope to see me until late summer or early fall, and perhaps it would be too late for me then. He did not promise an interview. Instead he asked me to send him a copy of my Hellman biography and pointedly said he wanted to see where my sympathies lay.

In August I wrote him again, and a month later received a call from his assistant, Judith McNally, apologizing for the delay in replying to my letter. They had misplaced my first letter and were not sure whose biography I was writing. Oh, I said, well . . . actually . . . a biography of Mailer. There was a brief pause. "You know he has an authorized biographer?" Yes, I said, in fact I've spoken with him. McNally assured me she would be in touch with me soon.

I did not hear again from Judith McNally. Instead, I received a letter from Russell Galen, a vice president of the Scott Meredith Agency, replying to my request to quote from several of Mailer's works. Galen noted that the agency routinely granted such permission to scholars, but in the case of a biography he felt they needed to see a copy of my manuscript. He would not ask me to change a line of it, but the agency did not want to grant permission to quote if they did not approve of the biography. I thought his position was outrageous, and I wrote him (with a copy to Mailer) to say so. It seemed to me that notwithstanding his statement that he had no desire to alter my work, he was in fact exerting pressure on me to submit an acceptable manuscript—whatever he might deem that to be. Quite a correspondence ensued about the First Amendment and unauthorized biographies. Although Galen promised to reconsider his position, the final determination of the agency was that I would not be granted permission to quote if I did not submit my manuscript for their inspection. This I refused to do.

Then I heard from Norman Mailer. He wrote to say that he had been busy editing *Harlot's Ghost* and had not paid attention to his correspondence. He could not recall ever having refused permission to quote from his work. If I would send him a list of the passages quoted, he would grant permission. I sent him the list. I also asked him, for the third time, for an interview.

I never did get the interview, but Scott Meredith sent a letter of permission to quote from Mailer's work, adding that Mailer had specifically requested I be charged the smallest possible fee.

SOURCE NOTES

Consult the bibliography for full citations of the publications referred to in this section by the author's last name, or by last name and short title if there is more than one work by the same author. At the beginning of each chapter I have cited my principal sources, including interviews, which are then followed by citations of works I have quoted or paraphrased.

The Shits Are Killing Us

Interviews: Max Lerner, William Styron

xvii   Hopelessly down the tubes: Author's interview with William Styron.
xvii   God, I wish . . . : Author's interview with William Styron.
xviii Since it reveals . . . : Lindner, *Must You Conform?*, 175–76.
 xix   with the desire . . . : Mailer, *Advertisements*, 2–3.
 xix   fuck it . . . : the same, 2.
 xix   started going . . . : Manso, 179.
  xx   He and Bob . . . : the same.
  xx   Lindner was almost alone. . . : Mailer, *Advertisements*, 270.
  xx   And it is this sensitivity . . . : the same.
 xxi   his charm . . . : the same, 269.
 xxi   Robert Lindner's death . . . : the same, 271.
 xxi   the shits are killing us: the same, 3.
 xxi   Now, in the writing of our days . . . : the same.

1. The Education of a Novelist (1923–1943)

Interviews: Stanley Karnow, Harry Levin, Kenneth Lynn, Richard Sisson, Richard Weinberg.
Brenner; Gordon, 55–65; Lennon, *Conversations*, 9, 47, 78–80, 188–89, 308–17; Mailer, *Pieces and Pontifications*, 1–5, 13, 18, 33, 110, 125; *The Short Stories of Norman Mailer*, 9–13, 113–34; Manso, 11–73; Mills, 38–72; Poirier, 17–21; Sokolov, 84–88; Wenke, 11–12; Suess, 1–83.

 1   Rabbis were *schnorrers*: Manso, 13.
 2   excitable; flare up: the same.
 2   an impoverished figure . . . some funny way: Brenner, 36.

3 It was the army . . . : Manso, 206.

3 Norman was perfect . . . : the same, 15.

4 Mrs. Mailer . . . : the same, 16.

4 cheap *goyim*: the same.

4 furrowed brow . . . afraid of her: the same, 23.

4 mad about Barbara . . . genius: the same, 24.

5 a big fat Irishwoman: the same, 19.

5 Here, write something: the same, 21.

5 fostered . . . insisted on: the same, 18.

6 avoid the overtime . . . stepped in: the same, 23.

6 had a way of driving my father . . . : Brenner, 37.

6 hardly a number-one temple . . . : the same.

6 middle-class pretensions . . . good enough for her: the same.

7 I am not a typical Jew . . . : the same.

7 premature expert: Mailer, *Pieces and Pontifications*, 33.

8 Sex had enormous fascination . . . : the same, 13.

8 projectile-shaped breasts . . . : the same, 110–11.

9 big brother: Manso, 33.

9 He encouraged me . . . : the same, 33.

9 Norman was always trying . . . : the same, 34.

9 shy youngster . . . : Suess, 25.

9 odyssey . . . : the same, 17.

10 physical coward: Mailer, *Advertisements*, 6.

10 glowingly. . . go far: Manso, 37

10 Ability to enter Harvard: Suess, 31.

10 the brain: the same, 38.

10 It's as if Norman . . . : the same, 37.

11 trousers with orange stripes: the same, 43.

11 You've got to be eighteen: Lennon, *Conversations*, 314.

11 crusty old man . . . : the same, 311.

11 never occurred to us . . . : the same, 310.

12 broad-minded breakthrough: Author's interview with Harry Levin.

12 day to day . . . one was Jewish: Manso, 39.

12 I don't think . . . : the same.

12 as a place where . . . the same, 40.

12 suffered . . . accepted: the same, 179.

12 a little Brooklyn boy . . . fitted in: Mills, 64.

12 always the youngest . . . : the same, 68–69.

13 lavishly decorated . . . Kaufer suggests: Suess, 37–38.

14 Fuck, shit, piss: Mills, 56.

14 Norman would delight . . . : the same.

14 dirty-little-boy: Manso, 45.

14 almost anyone else . . . : Author's interview with Harry Levin.

14 one notch: Lennon, *Conversations*, 189.

14 changed his life: "The Books That Made Writers," *The New York Times Book Review*, November 25, 1979, 7.

15 a hero in his own mind: Farrell, 182.

15 This business of inspiration . . . : Mills, 70.

15 We both graduated . . . Norman Mailer: Manso, 46.

15 Norman Kingsley Mailer . . . : the same.

15 a love for literature . . . a writer herself: the same.

16 novice in the Golden Gloves: Mills, 48.

16 stuffy junior . . . : Suess, 50.

16 five mystical chambers . . . : Mailer, *Pieces and Pontifications*, 2.

16 visual structure of a sentence . . . : Manso, 52.

17 delicate . . . Meissen figurine . . . : Suess, 55–56.

17 the quiet grays . . . : the same, 52.

17 It was like an anthropologist . . . : the same.

18 bully and a lout: the same, 81.

18 a little ashamed . . . : Lennon, *Conversations*, 311.

19 He used to say . . . : Suess, 60.

19 reads like the early work: Mailer, *Advertisements*, 52.

19 I'd go out in the field . . . : Mailer, *The Short Fiction*, 129.

19 cluster of themes . . . : Gordon, 56.

20 gray, failed man: Manso, 64.

20 Our father . . . huge debts: the same.

20 crazy . . . really existed: the same, 65.

21 very black, oiled, wavy hair . . . : the same, 55.

21 discover what the world's all about: the same, 56.

21 sleeping out in the open grass . . . : the same, 56–57.

21 parents who thought . . . : Mills, 54.

21 very bad novel: Lennon, *Conversations*, 79.

21 absolutely insupportable . . . mother love: Mailer, *Armies*, 153.

22 easily the best writer . . . : Suess, 62.

22 "Four Pamphlets for Jesus" . . . : the same, 70.

22 cold . . . : the same, 72.

22 In Brooklyn . . . : Manso, 57.

23 something big and impressive . . . : the same, 61.

23 slum child: the same, 63.

23 kind of hovered . . . : Mills, 65.

24 baby: Manso, 61.

24 had an honest and good relationship: Mills, 68.

24 preoccupation with sexuality . . . extreme: Suess, 72.

24 Have you ever been so tired . . . : the same, 73.

24 muscular and wiry . . . : the same, 54.

24 Nice to know a *percocious* writer . . . : the same, 74.

25 cleaning bed pans . . . : Mills, 70.

25 a war had begun . . . : George James, "Noted and Not-So-Noted Relive Pearl Harbor Day," *The New York Times*, December 6, 1988.

26 He turned it into an attack . . . : Author's interview with Harry Levin.

26 We were going through . . . : Mailer, *The Short Fiction*, 233.

26 progressive-liberal . . . : Mailer, *Advertisements*, 10.

27 a hero . . . : the same, 9.

27 To die in terms . . . : Mailer, *The Short Fiction*, 77.

27 Certainly in my years . . . : Lennon, *Conversations*, 317.

28 Malraux says . . . : Mailer, *The Short Fiction*, 50.

28 another Malraux: Mailer, *Advertisements*, 11.

28 threatening future lightly . . . : Suess, 83.

2. The Naked and the Dead (1943–1948)

Interviews: Stanley Karnaw, Harry Levin, Norman Rosten, Richard Sisson, Richard Weinberg.
Bufithis, 15–29; Gordon, 55–72; Lennon, *Conversations*, 80–88, 97, 101, 190; Mailer, *Advertisements*, 70–71; *Pieces and Pontifications*, 97–105, 147, 152, 160; *A Transit to Narcissus*, Manso, 74–121; Merrill, 25–42; Mills, 73–102; Suess, 83–140; Wenke, 24–41.

29 feel a certain magnitude . . . : Mailer, *A Transit to Narcissus*, 13–14.

29 first coming to grips. . . : the same, viii.

30 good son of the middle class . . . : the same.

30 Kind of heroic figure. . . : Author's interview with Stanley Karnow.

30 lugubrious weight. . . not going to war: Mailer, *A Transit to Narcissus*, viii.

31 My mother and my father . . . : Mailer, *Pieces and Pontifications*, 152.

31 big brother and hero . . . shadow: Manso, 96.

31 His need was action . . . : Mailer, *A Transit to Narcissus*, 334.

32 almost mystic fear . . . : the same, 426.

32 deep fear and attraction to brutality: the same, 459.

32 The day was very gray . . . : the same, 659.

32 exist in nakedness: the same, 684.

33 People . . . : the same, Appendix F, 226–27.

33 Never is there a novel . . . : the same, ix.

34 the nearness of violence . . . : the same, x.

34 I was ready to think . . . : Lennon, *Conversations*, 97.

34 melted before [Scarr] . . . : Mailer, *A Transit to Narcissus*, Appendix F, 227.

34 very embarrassed . . . marvelous: Mills, 75.

34 her little genius: the same.
35 *fait accompli* . . . : Manso, 98.
35 the Rock of the Ages: the same.
35 an arrogant, nasty young man . . . : Lennon, *Conversations*, 3.
35 looked like a skeleton . . . : Mills, 76.
36 there wasn't anything . . . : Lennon, *Conversations*, 3.
36 testing the system: Manso, 80.
36 fucked up completely . . . : the same, 84.
36 We can't all be poets: Mills, 78.
37 general's eye view: Lennon, *Conversations*, 10.
37 I was brought up . . . : the same, 11.
38 looking a bit like high school seniors . . . : Suess, 115.
38 He became aware again . . . : Mailer, *Advertisements*, 102.
38 a modest young man: the same, 70.
38 little to offer . . . : the same.
38 the book of a young engineer: Lennon, *Conversations*, 84.
39 wonderful brother: Manso, 108.
39 subdued: the same, 109.
39 quiet, serious girl: the same, 96.
39 disappointment . . . competition: the same, 100.
39 bright, capable woman . . . different direction: the same, 59.
40 world's worst housekeeper . . . : the same, 117.
40 fat and rather noisy . . . dances behind: the same, 110.
40 first real woman: the same, 100.
40 fuck piss cock . . . : Suess, 118.
40 Nobody could sleep on the night . . . : Manso, 105.
41 Hey, I've got to hang onto you . . . : Author's interview with Norman Rosten.
41 They used to scowl at each other . . . their work: the same.
41 Let's go and see him . . . : the same.
42 virtues & vices . . . : Suess, 121.
43 Far in the distance . . . : Mailer, *The Naked and the Dead*, 348.
43 wealthier . . . good reviews now: Mailer to Amussen, May 10, 1948, Alderman Library, University of Virginia.
43 nearly all his afternoons . . . : Mailer, *The Naked and the Dead*, 65.
43 of old furniture . . . : the same, 267.
44 deep significance . . . unmoved: the same, 269.
44 Okay . . . : Author's interview with Harry Levin.
44 He has lived in a vacuum . . . : Mailer, *The Naked and the Dead*, 269.
45 A half hour later . . . : the same, 469.
45 The fall . . . : the same, 443.
45 The general sitting alone . . . : Bufithis, 20–21.
46 narrow emotional range: Gordon, 69.

47   grunts and curses . . . Jew Radical: Suess, 121.
47   The chances are . . . : Lennon, *Conversations*, 4.
47   scary: Mills, 84.
47   certain kindness . . . caustic: Manso, 89, 93.
47   juice: Suess, 127.
48   We were all living . . . no kidding quality: Author's interview with Stanley Karnow.
48   a little less stuck . . . : Mills, 95.
48   apolegetic . . . vulgar: Manso, 110.
49   there were a whole bunch of us . . . fuck-all about anything else: Author's interview with Kenneth Lynn.
50   Boy Scout . . . : Suess, 133.
50   the veins in his forehead . . . : Mailer, *Pieces and Pontifications*, 100.
50   eager, touching, romantic . . . : Manso, 113.
50   waste a postcard . . . fresh and lovely: Norman Mailer to Norman Rosten, 1948; courtesy of Norman Rosten.
51   inner voice: Author's interview with Norman Rosten.
51   Southern son of a bitch: Manso, 114.
51   Tough shit . . . : the same, 116.
51   how close they were . . . spoiled boy: the same, 115–17.
51   Everything she said . . . her ownership of Norman: the same, 96.
52   welcoming . . . : the same, 111–12.
52   sisterliness: the same, 110.
52   getting too enjoyable . . . in August: Mailer to Amussen, May 10, 1948, Alderman Library, University of Virginia.
52   the greatest book . . . : Manso, 119.
52   particularly precarious mountain pass . . . : Mills, 101–102.
52   You're going back to America . . . paled visibly: Manso, 120.
53   a bit of an imposter: Mailer, *Pieces and Pontifications*, 160.
53   My life seemed . . . : Mailer, *Advertisements*, 71.
53   Success had been . . . : the same, 72.

3. Barbary Shore (1948–1951)

Interviews: Irving Howe, Stanley Karnow; Norman Rosten.
Gordon, 73–86; Gutman, 29–43; Leeds, 53–103; Lennon, *Conversations*, 5–8, 12–13, 15, 19, 81–82, 84–87, 90, 317; Mailer, *Advertisements*, 72–73; *Pieces and Pontifications*, 123, 147, 159–60, 165, 180; Manso, 122–60; Mills, 103–26; Stark, 403–8; Suess, 140–202.

54   sinister: Suess, 140.
54   Norman was always living out . . . : Mills, 104.

55 new and fresh: the same, 103.

55 faded tan sports shirt . . . : the same, 105.

55 it was still possible . . . : Lennon, *Conversations*, 8–9.

55 unreal: Mailer, *Pieces and Pontifications*, 147.

55 a movie queen . . . : Lennon, *Conversations*, 12–13.

55 goading . . . : Manso, 127.

56 scary . . . hurts. . . . : the same, 126.

56 somehow both vulgar and innocent . . . : Suess, 146.

56 devilish and healthy: the same, 147.

56 negative: Lennon, *Conversations*, 5.

56 collective action: the same.

57 Italy is pretty bad . . . : the same, 6.

57 ugliest city in the world: Suess, 148.

57 hit it off immediately . . . socks over your calf: Manso, 130–31.

57 Norman was very full of himself . . . full of spirit: Confidential interview.

58 white-faced: Author's interview with Irving Howe.

58 I have come here . . . : Mills, 113.

58 probably a phony: Manso, 136.

59 opinionated . . . : the same, 129.

59 very smart in his limited way: Author's interview with Irving Howe.

59 the last hurrah . . . : the same.

59 Then there occurred . . . : the same.

59 I wasn't altogether sure . . . : Mailer, *Pieces and Pontifications*, 180.

60 Second-novel panic: Lennon, *Conversations*, 81.

60 The army was the only milieu . . . : the same, 15.

60 village literary teas: Suess, 163.

61 radiant prime . . . : Manso, 137.

61 very quiet and sylvan . . . : the same, 176.

61 beautiful pregnancy . . . : the same.

61 horse of a Belgian Police dog . . . : Norman Mailer to Norman Rosten, 1949; courtesy of Norman Rosten.

61 I've been running . . . : Manso, 145, 148.

61 Susan is cute . . . : the same, 147.

61 pinching all the girls . . . : the same, 147–48.

62 timid and sweet: the same, 144–45.

62 experimental, tricky: the same.

62 dummy books . . . : the same, 138.

62 There'th not enough hearth: the same, 147.

62 stank . . . : Lennon, *Conversations*, 19.

62 Norman, get a haircut . . . : Manso, 143.

62 It will amount to no more . . . : the same.

62 *the* American success story . . . : the same, 141.

63 all our local bourgeois mothers . . . : Suess, 154.

63 You wouldn't stand a chance . . . : Manso, 145–46.

63 inordinately . . . : Lennon, *Conversations*, 317.

63 brilliant . . . creative control: Manso, 146.

63 much more macho . . . : Mailer, *Pieces and Pontifications*, 123.

63 a premature Women's Liberationist . . . : Mailer, the same.

64 a little intimidated . . . served in Hollywood: Manso, 149.

64 It wasn't like . . . : Mills, 121.

64 literal terror: Lennon, *Conversations*, 81.

64 for the first time . . . : the same, 82.

64 How do you. . . no good in bed: Manso, 152.

65 little Susan crawling . . . : Mills, 123.

65 chip on her shoulder . . . no question: the same, 153.

65 absolutely miserable: the same, 123.

65 despondent . . . gloomy: Manso, 162.

65 second draft . . . : the same, 153.

65 shit storm: the same, 154.

65 disaster in Hollywood: the same, 158.

65 I'm going to stay here . . . : Mills, 124.

65 came out sentence by sentence: Lennon, *Conversations*, 85.

65 "The Naked and the Dead Go to Japan: Mailer, *Advertisements*, 73.

65 empty as a theme . . . : the same, 72.

66 most autobiographical novel: Manso, 155.

66 Jewish boy blob: Poirier, 22.

66 an immense institution . . . : Mailer, *Barbary Shore*, 58.

66 nymphomaniac . . . : the same, 11.

66 a saucy lady . . . : Manso, 156.

67 We were all trying . . . : Author's interview with Norman Rosten.

67 Malaquais's philosophy . . . : Manso, 158.

67 He's got the biggest whang . . . : Mailer, *Barbary Shore*, 62.

68 grow up again: Gordon, 74.

68 a quality . . . : Lennon, *Conversations*, 85.

68 colonel . . . : Manso, 148.

69 It is one thing . . . : Lennon, *Critical Essays*, 45–46.

70 proxy . . . Gordon, 79.

70 He puts you through . . . : Manso, 158.

70 depressed . . . history: Mailer, *Barbary Shore*, 5–6.

70 attempt [at] an entrance . . . : Mailer, *Advertisements*, 85.

71 this evil-smelling novel . . . : the same, 83.

71 collapsed into a chapter . . . : the same, 73.

71 cause-and-effect relationships: Manso, 130.

4. The Deer Park (1951–1955)

Interviews: John Aldridge, Norman Rosten, William Styron.
Busch, 193–206; Gordon, 87–112; Mailer, *Advertisements*, 85–293; Manso, 161–218; Merrill, 43–66; Mills, 127–40; Solataroff, 46–81; Wenke, 51–68.

72   depressed . . . : Manso, 161–62.
72   You go out and fuck . . . : the same, 161.
72   esoteric . . . freedom and adventure: the same, 162–63.
73   quoted a beautiful line . . . : the same.
73   elemental and primitive: Mills, 129.
73   exotic: Manso, 164.
73   nice and natural . . . mean and insulting: the same, 164–65.
73   challenge: the same, 172.
74   terrified of: the same, 175.
74   I pick on you . . . : the same, 181.
74   practicing: the same, 166.
74   Mrs. Mailer . . . Norman's feelings: the same, 174.
74   intrigue: the same, 169.
74   Susie came walking in . . . : the same, 174.
74   Bea, why don't you just . . . at one time: the same, 170.
75   stunning . . . dark-skinned: the same, 162.
75   knocked cold: Mills, 134.
75   the old fighter: Manso, 172.
75   absolutely delightful . . . : the same, 176.
76   pliable . . . machine: the same, 189.
76   very, *very* good in bed: the same, 190.
76   Adele is fine . . . : the same: 182.
76   There wasn't a movement . . . : the same, 166.
76   Perhaps he respected . . . : Author's interview with Norman Rosten.
77   Jesus . . . did not: the same.
77   I was just knocked out . . . : Author's interview with William Styron.
77   modest level . . . : Hendrick, ix–x.
77   literary network . . . four or five times: Author's interview with William Styron.
77   There was tremendous excitement . . . go around: Hendrick, viii–ix.
78   Here we are . . . : Mac Shane, 122.
78   a convenient point of reckoning . . . : Hendrick, ix.
78   really thought . . . : Garrett, 91.
78   a hell of a fine guy: Hendrick, 186.
78   It knocked me down . . . : the same, 215.
78   Moving about at night . . . : the same, x.
78   You're stronger than me, Norman: Author's interview with William Styron.

79   You damned Jewboys!: Manso, 202.
79   real late . . . awful to watch: the same, 203.
79   Was there ever such a face: Hendrick, ix.
79   physical ruggedness . . . : Garrett, 79.
79   something of the charisma . . . : the same, 106.
79   Just to tell you . . . : Mailer to Jones, March 16, 1955, James Jones Collection,
     Harry Ransom Humanities Research Center, University of Texas at Austin.
79   now seems . . . : Hendrick, x.
80   Every fucking pulse . . . : Mailer to Jones, March 16, 1955, James Jones
     Collection, Harry Ransom Humanities Research Center, University of Texas at
     Austin.
80   You know . . . love you too: Jones to Mailer, May 3, 1955, Hendrick, 219–20.
     During this period, Jones did not use apostrophes in his letters.
80   raise the house . . . : Mailer, *Advertisements*, 86.
80   the only time . . . : the same.
80   disconnected thoughts . . . : the same, 129.
80   mythical hero . . . : the same, 130.
81   Eitel and Elena . . . : the same.
81   working with my hands . . . the same, 86.
81   an overworked writer . . . : the same, 132.
81   It is so complex . . . : the same, 160.
82   The anonymous narrator: Gordon, 93.
82   The narrator is Sam's *alter ego* . . . : Busch, 196.
82   I know what Sam feels . . . : *Advertisements*, 139–40.
82   I mock Sam . . . : the same, 156.
83   energy and belief . . . : the same, 159.
83   merely in avoiding pleasure: the same, 160.
83   an absolutely extraordinary figure . . . : the same, 146.
83   a counter-clockwise twist . . . : the same, 148.
84   intellectually jejune: Author's interview with Irving Howe.
84   the idea of . . . : the same.
84   We were more political . . . his own interests: the same.
85   silliness of the case . . . the way you talk to me: Manso, 184–87.
86   humbly . . . : the same, 190.
86   somewhat broken . . . subsidiary: the same, 206.
86   heavily in hock: the same.
86   why he was angry . . . : the same.
87   pretensions to secret, primitive knowledge: the same, 190.
87   slight falling out: the same, 193.
87   It was their night . . . one hour there: the same.
87   dull . . . : Mills, 146.
88   delivering harsh . . . : the same.

88   brutal: Manso, 194.

88   bopped . . . : the same, 196.

88   You're always worried . . . : the same.

89   very sweet, nice person: the same, 197.

89   the long lonely vistas . . . : the same, 198.

89   Susy is getting . . . "Keep quiet?": the same, 199.

90   natural born writer . . . sloppy: the same.

90   productive . . . canvases: the same, 201.

90   skip all the family crap: the same, 202.

90   in attendance: the same, 204.

90   hostess gown: the same, 205.

90   ruination . . . : the same.

90   high on it: the same, 207.

91   You don't dare, baby: Mills, 151.

91   gang bang . . . : the same, 153.

92   Okay . . . : the same, 154.

92   gentlemen: Mailer, *Advertisements*, 202.

92   The fine America . . . : the same.

92   obscene . . . not publishing his book: Manso, 208.

92   psychic outlaw: Mailer, *Advertisements*, 204.

92   It feels good . . . take on the world: Manso, 213.

92   Those motherfuckers . . . fall on his face: the same, 210.

93   follower and leader: the same, 231.

93   ferment of ideas: the same.

93   ripping up the silk . . . : Mailer, *Advertisements*, 206.

93   I was never sure . . . : Mailer, *The Deer Park*, 23.

93   for Brooklyn . . . : Mailer, *Advertisements*, 207.

95   For you see . . . : Mailer, *The Deer Park*, 318.

96   invents his thoughts . . . : Busch, 204.

96   the secret hero . . . : Solataroff, 54.

97   evil genius: Lennon, *Conversations*, 92.

97   not enough happened. . . two packs a day: Mailer, *Advertisements*, 211.

97   I'm empty . . . : Mailer to Jones, August 25, 1955, James Jones Collection, Harry Ransom Humanities Research Center, University of Texas at Austin.

97   middling success . . . : Mailer, *Advertisements*, 216.

98   works best in opposition . . . : the same, 162.

98   proper book of an outlaw: the same, 217.

5. Advertisements for Myself (1955–1959)

Interviews: Irving Howe, Norman Rosten, William Styron.
Christian; Lennon, *Conversations*, 29–76; Mailer, *Advertisements*, 294–491; Manso, 219–261; Mills, 162–92.

99   not a finished novelist. . . : Quoted in Manso, 218.
99   like an actor . . . : Mailer, *Advertisements*, 245.
99   running scared . . . : Manso, 220.
100   Queer . . . beaten up: the same, 221.
100   private war on . . . : Mailer, *Advertisements*, 245.
100   one of the bitter provinces . . . : the same, 246.
101   adequate journeyman writer . . . : the same, 248, 255, 256.
101   point of polite intellectual rebuttal . . . : the same, 260–61
101   Man is a rebel: the same, 271.
101   adjust to the warpings . . . : the same, 270.
101   Hip is based on . . . : the same, 280.
102   lack of professionalism: Mills, 169.
102   wondered in which form . . . : Mailer, *Advertisements*, 283.
103   mixed feelings . . . disgraced himself: Author's interview with William Styron.
103   sex in it . . . Jim: Undated note from Jones to Mailer on back of calendar page, May 25, 1954, in James Jones Collection, Harry Ransom Humanities Research Center, University of Texas at Austin.
103   though Ive read . . . : Hendrick, 242.
103   literary or personal . . . untruthful ones: the same, 233–34.
104   deep in that crusty . . . Norman: Mailer to Jones, in James Jones Collection, Harry Ransom Humanities Research Center, University of Texas at Austin.
104   I still believe . . . stand it: Hendrick, 243, 246.
104   Throwing away a certain talent . . . couldn't do anything: Mills, 172.
105   street-smart . . . : Manso, 248.
105   class: the same, 239.
105   Somebody told Jim . . . : the same, 275.
105   Jim was very competitive . . . : the same, 203.
105   delayed honeymoon . . . almost laughable: Manso, 232.
106   snobbery that he was sure . . . : the same, 236.
106   burned out: Mailer, *Advertisements*, 295.
106   in a kind of squirmy way . . .: Confidential interview.
107   the Negro people: Mills, 177.
107   a confounded snob . . . : Manso, 233.
107   They thought . . . : Mills, 177.
107   too much woman for you . . . not Fig: Manso, 238.

107   and me and my friends . . . : Mailer to Rosten, 1958; courtesy of Norman Rosten.
108   an unemployed . . . : Mills, 182.
108   You're not a publisher . . . : the same, 181.
108   insulting . . . : Manso, 239.
108   had no use for you . . . : the same, 244.
108   I'll take her outside . . . : Mills, 183.
108   clay to be molded: Manso, 242.
108   impenetrability: the same, 244.
108   usurping his turf: the same.
109   against the enemy: the same, 246.
109   a very strange gal . . . : the same, 240.
109   Is my wife there . . . : the same, 246.
109   loved it . . . crazy: the same, 240.
109   large standard poodle: Mills, 183.
109   holistic medicine . . . menace to your child: Manso, 253.
109   You're chicken . . . : the same, 268.
110   macho folly . . . : the same, 258.
110   on the wrong train: the same, 262.
110   honk . . . hip: Mills, 190.
110   the nature of failure . . . : Manso, 250.
111   brilliant piece: Author's interview with Irving Howe.
111   The psychopath murders . . . : Mailer, *Advertisements*, 309.
111   the Faustian urge . . . : the same, 300.
112   So it is no accident . . . : the same, 301.
112   a touch grim . . . : the same, 143.
112   That cat . . . : the same, 310.
112   collective violence . . . : the same, 316.
113   a gorgeous flower . . . : the same, 323.
113   The notions of Hip . . . : the same, 341.
113   They feel . . . : Lennon, *Conversations*, 43.
113   pretty notion: Mailer, *Advertisements*, 341.
113   wasn't true enough: Lennon, *Conversations*, 51.
114   your quasi-religious philosophical points . . . too much: Hendrick, 260–62.
115   belligerent hassle . . . sword-twirling: the same.
115   parasites . . . back and forth: Mailer to Jones, March 20, 1958, James Jones Collection, Harry Ransom Humanities Research Center, University of Texas at Austin.
115   It was almost the day . . . nail that down: Author's interview with William Styron.
116   A lot of people . . . : the same.
116   oiling every literary lever . . . : Mailer, *Advertisements*, 426.

117   He felt that somewhere . . . : *The Short Fiction of Norman Mailer*, 59.

117   It was a book . . . : Mailer, *Advertisements*, vii.

118   roughly chronological: the same, ix.

118   *Like many another literary fraud* . . . : the same.

118   So the reader . . . : the same, 85.

119   *Mr. Mailer* . . . : the same, 126.

119   Dead man on the floor: the same, 489.

120   Over and over . . . : the same, 455.

120   I was going to beat . . . : the same, 460.

121   I gave you . . . : the same, 463.

121   Consciousness brought into being . . . : the same, 471–73.

122   Toward its death: the same, 478.

122   Travelling through the non-Euclidean present . . . : the same, 479.

122   emotion of Being: the same, 478.

122   Without looking . . . : the same, 477.

123   there were more items . . . : the same, 486.

123   Am I already on the way out?: the same, 490.

6. Deaths for the Ladies, and Other Disasters (1958–1963)

Interviews: Irving Howe, Stanley Karnow, Max Lerner, Norman Rosten, William Styron.
Gordon, 113–128; Mailer, *Existential Errands*, 198–204; Manso, 262–370; Mills, 193–270; Poirier, 71–95; Silverstein, 277–86.

124   most men who understand women . . . : Mailer, *The Presidential Papers*, 131.

124   most secret admiration: the same, 136.

124   enjoyed . . . : the same, 131.

125   grow up a second time: quoted in Poirier, 76.

125   Village stickman: Mailer, *Advertisements*, 456.

125   dirty little Jew: the same, 461.

125   dirty little boy in himself . . . : Gordon, 122.

125   the flat thin muscles . . . : Mailer, *Advertisements*, 447.

125   Sergius . . . : Silverstein, 284.

125   constant, loathsome bickering . . . a direct answer: Manso, 244–45.

126   projections . . . : Gordon, 125.

127   Esther . . . : Manso, 289.

128   Competitive . . . lit-business stuff: the same, 366–67.

128   spoiled: Author's interview with Irving Howe.

128   Norman corrected her . . . : Manso, 288.

129   the shoulder-punching warmth . . . : Mills, 196.

129   aggressive and unpleasant . . . busted up: Manso, 295–96.

129 Normie the Hun . . . : the same, 271.

129 punching each other out: Mills, 197.

129 Norman would always come dressed . . . : Author's interview with Irving Howe.

130 calming and consoling . . . memorable: Author's interview with Irving Howe.

130 We have another daughter . . . more pent up: Manso, 279–80.

131 Rather well . . . recognition: Styron to Jones, December 7, 1959, James Jones Collection, Harry Ransom Humanities Research Center, University of Texas at Austin.

132 We're all shit . . . : Mills, 207.

132 boozing, fighting . . . : Manso, 297.

132 Do things that frighten you: the same, 299.

132 brash initiate: the same, 300.

133 Why do I need . . . : Mills, 210.

133 just right: the same, 211. William Styron attributes Maas's remarks to Richard Goodwin, another Kennedy advisor. Author's interview with William Styron.

133 Mr. Mailer . . . : Mills, 211.

133 box-office actor: Mailer: *The Presidential Papers*, 38.

133 a writer one knows . . . : the same, 44.

134 a man who lived with death . . . : the same.

134 precisely because . . . : the same, 26.

134 It was a hero . . . : the same, 41–42.

135 packaged commodities . . . : the same, 32.

135 forcing a reality . . . : the same, 60.

135 different person: Manso, 311.

136 fucking around a lot: the same, 319.

136 hunching his shoulders . . . : the same, 317.

136 power structure: the same, 312.

136 let fly: the same, 313.

136 fights quickly broken up . . . : Quoted in Mills, 221.

137 You look like . . . : the same, 223.

137 Things like this . . . : the same.

138 relieve her of cancer: Manso, 319.

138 probably the most horrible day: the same.

138 until this whole thing . . . intelligent and reasonable: the same, 320–21.

139 quite a scrape . . . : Mills, 225.

139 a real splash . . . personal reasons: Manso, 322.

139 overcome . . . tragedy: the same, 335.

139 self-dramatizing males . . . knockoffs: the same, 352.

140 calm, subdued . . . revenge: the same, 330.

140 The defenses . . . : the same, 321.

141   After all . . . : the same, 334.

141   a decade's anger . . . : Atlas, 90.

141   felt somehow . . . : Brower, 103.

141   had no central sensibility: Manso, 327.

141   he invents . . . : the same, 323.

141   creation: the same, 333.

142   mending: Mailer, *Existential Errands*, 201.

142   That first unmanageable cell . . . : the same, 274.

143   Everybody wanted to *touch*: Manso, 351.

143   *motiveless* destructive act: Braudy, 82.

143   countless men before him . . . : the same, 90.

144   sensuous-erotic . . . : the same, 91.

144   dread of being responsible . . . : the same, 95.

144   the fantasy structure . . . : Lucid, *Norman Mailer*, 235.

144   peculiarly difficult . . . : the same, 236.

144   I want to show it to you . . . : Manso, 334.

145   I destroyed forever . . . : Brower, 103.

145   marry him . . . : Atlas, 91.

145   true English eccentric: Manso, 338.

145   a tough-guy friend . . . fed?: the same.

146   She was not . . . both parts of his experience: Mills, 238.

146   upper-crust: the same.

146   He lived with other lives . . . ultimate *shiksa*: the same.

146   what [a man] wants . . . : Mailer, *Cannibals and Christians*, 199.

146   like touching ice water . . . *poof*: Manso, 339.

146   He liked Hedda a lot . . . : Author's interview with Norman Rosten.

147   rowdy attraction: Manso, 364.

147   remarkable similarity . . . : Author's interview with Stanley Karnow.

147   no big deal: Manso, 346.

147   the specific density . . . : Quoted in Mills, 237.

147   My Susie . . . : Manso, 345.

148   a streak of craziness . . . : the same.

148   flipped . . . depressing: the same, 362.

148   a galumphing . . . adored him: the same, 346.

149   January 27, 1963 . . . : the same, 364.

149   At least can say . . . : Brower, 98.

149   We managed . . . : Atlas, 92.

149   Mr. Lady Jeanne: Mills, 270.

149   dismantled engine room telegraph . . . : Brower, 102.

150   the greatest hero . . . : Mailer, *The Presidential Papers*, 68.

150   court wit . . . : the same, 1.

150 great actor . . . : Mailer, the same, 236.

150 negroid white: the same, 260.

151 champion of every lonely adolescent . . . : the same, 241–42.

151 Faust: the same, 242.

151 a part . . . : the same, 247.

151 whipped by the oatmeal . . . : the same, 270.

151 demented: Manso, 363.

151 some sort of center . . . : the same, 261.

152 I like this guy: the same, 266.

7. *An American Dream* (1963–1965)

Interviews: Rust Hills, Helen Meyer.
Brower; Lennon, *Conversations*, 100–103, 209–12; Lennon, *Critical Essays*, 136–44; Gordon, 129–71; Lucid, *Norman Mailer*, 145–78; Manso, 351–404; Mills, 261–87; Parker, 181–212; Schwenger, 16–35; Solotaroff, 124–78; Wagenheim.

153 sweetness and character: the same, Manso 397.

153 little short skirt . . . energy and irreverence: the same, 369.

155 strong-willed . . . fast: the same, 372.

155 little Godfrey . . . fancy boyfriends: the same, 373.

155 frailties: the same, 374.

155 tough act . . . : Mills, 271.

156 Beverly? . . . I'm crazy about her: Manso, 374.

156 fucking his brains out . . . isn't really New York: the same, 375.

156 get going again on my novel: the same, 375.

156 slightly embarrassing: Mills, 269.

157 separate the artist . . . : Lucid, *Norman Mailer*, 5.

157 the book of a man . . . abominably written: Quoted in Mills, 265–66; See *Cannibals and Christians*, 104–130.

157 reestablishing his reputation . . . : Mills, 266.

157 has stooped . . . : Styron to Jones, June 6, 1963, James Jones Collection, Harry Ransom Humanities Research Center, University of Texas at Austin.

158 The whole thing . . . : Hendrick, 304.

158 very grudgingly . . . : Lennon, *Conversations*, 49.

158 too small a window . . . : Mailer, *Advertisements*, 426.

158 Hi . . . fight: Mills, 265

158 quite nasty . . . glory and fame: the same, 267.

159 Don't worry . . . disappointed: Manso, 361.

159 Norman and Beverly Mailer: the same, 375.

159 the spotlight: the same, 377.

159 I don't think . . . : the same, 382.
159 fit right in . . . : the same, 377.
160 Beverly's out walking . . . the last few years: the same, 378.
160 supersober . . . assessment of his life: the same, 379.
160 baby . . . the story is ended: the same, 379–80.
160 ace new boyfriend . . . the fuck alone: the same, 281.
161 He was such a charmer . . . : the same, 382.
161 on the grounds of incompatibility: Mills, 270.
162 If you only knew . . . : *Esquire* Collection, Bentley Library, University of Michigan.
162 so splendid . . . oneself: the same.
163 formed the habit . . . : the same, Manso 386.
164 I wanted a man: Lennon, *Conversations*, 101.
165 more elegant . . . : the same, 102.
165 Irish & European . . . : *Esquire* Collection, Bentley Library, University of Michigan.
165 actor . . . void: Mailer, *An American Dream*, 14.
166 psychological study . . . : the same, 15.
166 come to the end . . . : the same.
166 I did not throw . . . : the same, 11.
166 stiff, overburdened . . . : the same, 10. In the book version, Mailer omits "icy-cold."
167 a great bloody sweet German face . . . : the same, 11.
169 Murder offers the promise . . . : the same, 15.
169 itch . . . politics: the same, 23–24.
169 the overpowering, castrating mother: Wagenheim, 48.
169 women have the power: Lennon, *Critical Essays*, 141.
169 Masculinity is not . . . : Mailer, *Cannibals and Christians*, 201.
170 It must be awful . . . : Mailer, *An American Dream*, 32.
170 I tried to make him jealous once . . . : the same, 33. When Mailer revised the first paragraph of the novel for book publication and omitted the sentence about stealing Kennedy's girl, he made it impossible for readers to guess that Deborah is referring to Kennedy in her remarks to Rojack.
170 more corrupt than me: Lennon, *Conversations*, 102.
171 To have your hero . . . : Brower.
171 guy is on pilgrimage . . . : *Esquire* Collection, Bentley Library, University of Michigan.
171 awfully good . . . : the same.
171 The second installment . . . : Mills, 278.
172 I had the sense . . . : Mailer, *An American Dream*, 44.
172 The lamp by her bed . . . : the same. The novel's phrasing of this scene differs slightly from Mailer's manuscript and the *Esquire* version.

173 I put my five toes . . . : the same, 45.
173 I suppose I was . . . : the same. In the book version Mailer omits "suppose."
173 lay back . . . that I knew: the same, 46–47.
174 to gain an inch . . . : the same, 47.
174 creativity is always . . . : Quoted in Schwenger, 27.
174 Rojack is attempting . . . : Gordon, 143.
174 sexually female . . . : Lennon, *Critical Essays*, 143.
174 I had one of those splittings of a second . . . : Mailer, *An American Dream*, 49.
175 particularly difficult . . . : Manso, 393.
175 long hours . . . : Mills, 279.
176 this sense of constant threat . . . : Lucid, *Norman Mailer*, 174–75.
176 a sentimental conception . . . : Lennon, *Conversations*, 209.
177 Rojack needs . . . : Lennon, *Critical Esasys*, 140.
177 tougher than the other ones: Manso, 293.
178 cold, gray eyes . . . : Gordon, 161.
179 Up your ass . . . : Mailer, *An American Dream*, 181.
179 an enlarged awareness . . . : Wagenheim, 68.
179 It was in the cards . . . : Author's interview with Rust Hills.
180 postpartum depression . . . : Manso, 392.
180 slimmed down . . . who's hung?: the same, 393.
181 suppressed doubts . . . : Parker, 193.
182 I finished a novel . . . : Mailer to Trocchi, Alex Trocchi Collection, Washington University Library, St. Louis, Missouri.
182 gymnastic ropes . . . : Mills, 285–86.

8. *The Armies of the Night* (1965–1968)

Adams, 110–113; Begiebing, 89–112, 172–185; Lennon, *Conversations*, 104–75; Manso, 405–63; Mills, 288–331.

185 Hot damn. Vietnam . . . : Mailer, *Cannibals and Christians*, 71.
185 spoke of an ego . . . : the same, 75.
185 Only, listen . . . : the same, 81–82.
186 crowd went crazy . . . : Manso, 407.
186 qualitatively changed the event . . . : Mills, 291.
186 on cloud nine . . . : Manso, 407.
187 makes you better . . . stretch: the same, 383–84.
188 You look just the same . . . carbon copy: the same, 412.
188 striped bass . . . didn't know beans: the same.
188 Here I am . . . in writin': the same, 413.
189 diatribe . . . dishes: the same, 416.
189 colonial mentality . . . temporary: the same, 389.

189   My son . . . with yourself: the same, 417–18.
190   obscene . . . It stays: the same, 418–19.
190   If Norman . . . : Mills, 294.
191   What did we have . . . so transparent: Manso, 450.
191   last of the tonics . . . : Mailer, *Cannibals and Christians*, 89–90.
191   the Chinks . . . : the same.
192   A reserve of memories . . . : Mailer, *Pieces and Pontifications*, 10.
192   roaring, smarting . . . : Mailer, *Cannibals and Christians*, 48.
192   Huckleberry Finn . . . : Mailer, *Why Are We in Vietnam?*, 6.
192   fucked unless . . . : the same, 116.
193   a Texas youth . . . consciousness: the same, 140–41.
193   dream field . . . deep mystery: the same, 182.
193   Goose your frequency: the same, 183.
193   Disc Jockey to America: the same, 224.
193   Which D.J. . . . : the same.
194   trial period . . . ship came into the dock: Manso, 421.
195   without the kids . . . : the same, 476.
195   passionate . . . injured: the same, 422–23.
195   moving from one activity . . . : Mailer, *Pieces and Pontifications*, 32.
195   If you want to know about it . . . : Manso, 417.
196   Incest is always insane . . . : Mailer, *The Deer Park: A Play*, 174.
196   He's going to kill me . . . bad contusion: Manso, 427.
197   You know why you need me? . . . : the same, 415.
197   Wait a minute . . . private parts: Mills, 295.
197   Beverly, I'm going to . . . : the same.
197   If we keep arguing . . . cool off: Manso, 415.
197   Don't hit him . . . : the same, 423.
197   pretty blatant . . . totally enamored: the same, 440.
198   absolute courtesy: the same, 420.
198   cut away all dramatic . . . : Mailer, *The Deer Park: A Play*, 11–12.
198   I think I got back . . . : Lennon, *Conversations*, 161.
199   pugnacious . . . : Adams, 112.
199   piece of material . . . : Lennon, *Conversations*, 142.
199   hogs the closeups: Katherine Dieckmann, "Ads for the Self," *Village Voice*, January 17, 1989, 66.
199   a growling, grunting . . . : Kael, "Celebrities Make Spectacles of Themselves," *The New Yorker*, January 20, 1968, 90.
200   In the first 45 minutes . . . : the same, 141.
200   to talk themselves . . . promised disaster: Mailer, *Armies*, 154.
200   this great bravura . . . : Lennon, *Conversations*, 143.
200   intellectual machines: the same, 164.

201   modesty . . . : Mailer, *Armies*, 93.
202   I feel . . . embattled: the same, 456.
202   righteous old toot: the same, 20.
203   cut . . . : Lennon, *Conversations*, 159.
203   a cross between . . . : the same, 161.
203   a lot of money around: Manso, 476.
204   writing against great resistance . . . : Mailer, *Pieces and Pontifications*, 152.
206   Evil: Manso, 463.
206   Let's go downstairs . . . killed by Norman: the same, 469.
207   packing a piece . . . : Mailer, *Maidstone*, 240.
207   shorter and fatter . . . grin: Beauman, 52.
208   magic and power . . . : Toback, 22.
208   the bounce and snap . . . : Beauman, 56.
208   I hit you . . . : Manso, 481.
208   Mailer's mafia-style walk . . . : the same, 29.
209   struck at the softest part . . . : the same.
209   I'm a catalyst . . . : Beauman, 74.
211   the real protagonist of this filming: the same, 106.
211   attacked out of all the plots . . . : the same, 179.
211   anticipating the formation . . . : the same, 178–79.

9. King of the Hill (1968–1972)

Interviews: Irving Howe, Sandra Kraskin, Elizabeth Reis, Richard Weinberg.
Manso, *Mailer*, 490–531; Manso, *Running Against the Machine*; Mills, 332–386;
Naipaul; Pilati, Solotaroff, 242–60; Weber; Woodley.

212   I knew . . . : Author's interview with Richard Weinberg.
212   Brahmin types . . . fucked over: Manso, *Mailer*, 472.
       I've seen so much of myself . . . : Norman Mailer to James Dickey, October 27,
       1969, Washington University Libraries, St. Louis, Missouri.
213   It was possible . . . : Mailer, *Miami*, 49.
214   He had lived . . . : the same, 188.
214   It seemed to him . . . : the same, 185.
215   rope trip . . . : Manso, 495–96.
215   It was his first prize . . . : Mills, 336.
215   I just heard . . . really got into it: Manso, 489.
216   making a scenario . . . Who's that: the same.
216   In front of his parents . . . Norman Mailer is: the same, 495.
216   irreligiously about Norman . . . : the same, 496.
216   imperious . . . receiving people: the same, 495.
216   Self-critical . . . horrow show: the same, 497.

217   big, broad . . . insider: Author's interview with Elizabeth Reis.
218   What struck me . . . his publicity: Author's interview with Sandra Kraskin.
218   Provincetown . . . the actor in him: the same.
219   chauvinist . . . never offensive: the same.
219   He was so against . . . convenient for him: the same.
219   It was quite a trip . . . : Author's interview with Elizabeth Reis.
219   That was Mailer being folksy . . . For this: the same.
220   funny . . . orgasms: Author's interview with Sandra Kraskin.
220   literally trying . . . shit that: the same.
221   tinkering . . . : Manso, *Running Against the Machine*, 303.
221   turn this big excessive city . . . : 304.
221   Mailer, the wild-eyed Jewish . . . : the same.
222   You guys got me running . . . : the same, 306.
223   all the way: the same, 24.
223   I think I'm serious . . . : Woodley, 72.
223   This was not the Mailer . . . : Manso, *Running Against the Machine*, 109.
223   I served up last . . . : Flaherty, 122.
224   like a candidate . . . : Mills, 342.
224   It's a bit like . . . : the same.
224   a tacky bunch . . . : Manso, *Running Aginst the Machine*, 298.
224   his worst self . . . : Manso, *Mailer*, 505.
224   If you have certain ideas . . . foreseen: Manso, *Running Against the Machine*,
      68.
224   Alienation is the disease . . . ground: the same, 127.
225   Politics is property . . . : the same, 128.
225   theoretically attractive . . . purgatory: the same.
225   OK . . . : the same, 278.
225   dramatized a fundamental issue . . . : the same, 133–34.
225   I hope the Lord . . . : the same, 158.
225   Why doesn't your man . . . : Flaherty, 144.
225   You are always writing . . . : Naipaul, 171.
226   Homebred Harold Macmillan: Flaherty, 144.
226   the left hand pawing . . . : the same, 20.
226   abrupt, swifty, pithy . . . in town: Naipaul, 171, 175.
226   You are asking . . . approve of it: the same, 176.
226   Quintessence of animal energy . . . : Manso, *Running Against the Machine*,
      126–27.
226   Right hand in his pocket: the same, 275.
227   I'm tired . . . : the same, 259.
227   There's too much . . . : the same, 256.
227   One doesn't work . . . : the same, 139–40.
228   If someone . . . : Flaherty, 65.

228 hanger-on . . . : Manso, *Mailer*, 502.
228 You'll talk . . . : Flaherty, 209.
229 the booth sounded . . . : the same, 211.
229 as nutty as we are: the same.
229 rocking to and fro . . . : the same.
229 Square with surly . . . : Manso, *Running Against the Machine*, 312.
229 good . . . shill them: Flaherty, 162.
230 She was screaming . . . : Manso, *Mailer*, 506.
230 They'd played . . . : Manso, 507.
230 fucking . . . grow old alone: the same, 513.
230 I told her . . . doesn't matter: the same, 512.
231 central . . . idealized them: the same, 513.
231 one of the great . . . : the same.
232 Yes, real Americans . . . : Mailer, *Of a Fire on the Moon*, 13.
232 Now it was as if . . . : the same, 21.
232 words, like pills . . . : the same, 25.
232 passive bodies . . . accelerating opposites: the same, 47.
233 exceptional future . . . : the same, 48.
233 technology and the absence of emotion . . . : the same, 108.
233 an exact study . . . : the same, 164.
233 some very large chances have been taken: the same, 187.
233 Who was to say . . . : the same, 315.
234 clammy to the touch: the same, 363.
234 aisles of quiet fear: the same, 365.
234 Quoted in it was his profession . . . : the same, 458.
234 It is a technical fact . . . : Solotaroff, 250.
234 so large a home: Mailer, *The Prisoner of Sex*, 9.
234 shopping, cooking, and cleaning . . . : the same, 10.
235 much cleaner work . . . : Solotaroff, 253.
235 hero-creator: Poirier, 105.
235 alternated duty days . . . : Mailer, *The Prisoner of Sex*, 10.
235 a true American love story . . . : Mills, 357.
235 a rather sweet, tenuous voice: Manso, 531.
236 he knew at last . . . : Mailer, *The Prisoner of Sex*, 12.
236 You might try reading . . . : the same, 19.
236 Your views on women . . . : the same, 21.
236 *An American Dream* is . . . : the same, 27.
236 a few of the women . . . : the same, 39.
236 female sexuality . . . our author: Millet, 11–12.
236 As he settles . . . : the same, 330.
237 land of Millett . . . : Mailer, *The Prisoner of Sex*, 93.
237 based on a set of values . . . : Millet, 329.

237   in and out of this question . . . : Lennon, *Conversations*, 347.

237   dangerous . . . femaleness: Adams, *Will the Real Norman Mailer Please Stand Up?*, 216–19.

238   caught . . . technological chain of being: Mailer, *Pieces and Pontifications*, 49–50.

239   half boss-man . . . : Lennon, *Critical Essays*, 104.

239   wearing a floozy . . . : Manso, 521.

239   carnival barker: Greer, 214.

239   ardent feminist phase . . . : Author's interview with Sandra Kraskin.

239   three pretty solid women . . . : Manso, 522.

240   as if he were a little boy: Mills, 371.

240   I liked him better . . . : the same, 372.

240   locked into the body . . . : Quoted in Greer, 92.

240   For his mind . . . : the same.

241   One senses . . . : the same.

241   The concept of the worshiped feminine . . . : the same.

241   like a wounded child . . . : Quoted in Mills, 366.

241   There has been . . . : Quoted in Mailer, *Pieces and Pontifications*, 71.

242   something blow in his brain: the same, 57.

242   tender and caressing . . . : the same, 58–59.

242   Are you all really . . . : the same, 68.

242   Extraordinary arrogance . . . : the same, 69–70.

242   in the nuts: the same, 70.

242   did not simply . . . : the same, 72.

243   Why don't you . . . : the same, 68.

243   easily hospitable . . . : Adams, *Will the Real Norman Mailer Please Stand Up?*, 237.

243   I found that bewildering . . . : the same, 225.

244   a certain big novel . . . : Mailer, *Existential Errands*, ix–x.

244   America's greatest ego . . . : the same, 4.

244   So Clay punched . . . : the same, 16.

245   He was so bad . . . : the same, 59.

10. *Marilyn* (1972–1973)

Interviews: Norman Rosten.
Adams, *Will the Real Norman Mailer Please Stand Up?*, 216–43; Bosworth; Lennon, *Conversations*, 193–227; Manso, 532–59; Mills, 386–410.

246   This is no good . . . to think: Manso, 526; Mills, 381.

246   Learned fast . . . come up with this: Manso, 526–28.

247   obscene . . . bring out the best: Mailer, *Pieces and Pontifications*, 148.

247   scared . . . broke it on?: Manso, 529.

247 Be happy . . . think of your father: the same, 531–32.
248 There was a real sadness . . . dream was destroyed: the same, 25.
248 Upstairs . . . sitting there: the same, 531.
249 Is that broad stacked! . . . : Mills, 387–88.
249 developed torso . . . rude surprise: Adams, *Will the Real Norman Mailer Please Stand Up?*, 224–26.
249 nearer to them . . . : the same, 231.
250 The radical movement . . . : the same.
250 Get their names: Bosworth, 6.
250 democratic secret police . . . : the same.
250 I blew it . . . : Mills, 391–92.
250 a fool of himself . . . : Manso, 533–34.
251 Must size up the opposition: Mills, 390.
251 this little old woman . . . : Manso, 534.
251 I think it's all wonderful . . . : Mills, 392.
252 what struck Norman . . . : Manso, 537.
252 completed the first 65,000 . . . : the same.
253 modest depth: Mailer, *Marilyn*, 364.
253 pick my brain: Manso, 539.
253 it was hard . . . clashed with Arthur's: Author's interview with Norman Rosten.
253 One writer . . . : Manso, 539.
253 nasty letters . . . : Mailer to Rosten, December 1, 1959; courtesy of Norman Rosten.
254 the movie star . . . : Mailer, *Existential Errands*, 135.
254 magnified mirror of ourselves: Mailer, *Marilyn*, 18.
255 secret ambition . . . the best in her: the same, 23.
255 Set a thief . . . : the same, 23–24.
255 strange woman . . . : the same, 24.
255 prove a recurrent wound . . . : the same, 22.
255 Has Mailer created . . . : Lennon, *Critical Essays*, 75.
256 You're always running into . . . : Rollyson, *Marilyn Monroe: A Life of the Actress*, 206.
256 close fit of a role: Mailer, *Marilyn*, 27.
256 first focus of her life . . . : the same, 71.
257 an actor can only squander . . . : the same, 151.
257 simpler in their surface . . . : Mailer, *Existential Errands*, 116.
257 a character . . . : Mailer, *Marilyn*, 163–64.
257 as lovely and vulnerable . . . : the same, 268.
257 historical eminence . . . : the same, 325.
258 Never does she look . . . : the same, 302.
258 She is triumphant and crushed . . . : the same, 304.
258 No force from outside . . . : the same, 334.

259   I've got to say no . . . : Quoted in Mills, 403.

11. *The Executioner's Song* (1974–1979)

Interviews: John Aldridge, Jere Herzenberg, Sandra Kraskin.
Brenner; Lennon, *Conversations*, 228–70; Mailer, *Pieces and Pontifications*, 58–107;
Manso, 562–608; Medwick; Mills, 411–32.

262   bitterness . . . at once: Mailer, *Pieces and Pontifications*, 91.
263   Anybody who knows anything . . . you need a shit: the same, 92–94.
263   sexual vanity . . . not good enough: the same, 97–98.
264   If there were charms . . . : Mailer, *The Fight*, 22.
264   Like a snake . . . : the same, 20.
265   Men or women . . . : the same, 38.
266   dark as Africa . . . : Mailer, the same, 91.
266   singularly cool: the same, 92.
268   Say, Bundini . . . : the same, 170–71.
269   Then a big projectile . . . : the same, 208.
270   You have heard . . . : the same, 177.
271   In Africa . . . : Quoted in Mills, 413.
271   too rich: Manso, 562.
271   Could I crash? . . . : Mills, 414.
271   I walked in . . . : Quoted in Mills, 414.
272   I was loved . . . : Manso, 563.
272   We stood . . . did that: Medwick, 280.
272   the fuss: Manso, 566.
272   charming, funny and witty . . . : Quoted in Mills, 416.
272   He was giving me . . . : Manso, 567.
272   a thick silver ring . . . : Medwick, 280.
273   I wanted him . . . : Manso, 567.
273   read them all at once . . . : Medwick, 280.
273   I think Carol . . . : Manso, 563.
273   Give me six months: Mills, 416.
273   I knew he had at least . . . : Manso, 568,
273   starved: the same, 569.
274   an attractive disparate group . . . don't do anything else: Goodman, 49.
274   Me, I knew . . . : Manso, 569.
274   no conditions . . . : the same, 570.
274   Suppose in five years . . . : the same.
275   really agile . . . : the same, 571.
275   She was easy . . . : the same, 572.
275   Once we were going out . . . : the same, 574.

275 very low-cut . . . I'm Barbara Norris: the same, 575.
276 they all thought . . . : the same, 573.
276 I gather . . . : the same, 574.
277 everything he thinks . . . : the same, 575.
277 glitter . . . moving and doing: the same, 600.
277 mellow . . . sheer entertainment: the same.
277 Before, Norman . . . : the same, 603.
278 carry . . . maverick: Mills, 26.
278 they will become bored . . . : the same, 27.
278 Genius may depend . . . : Mailer, *Genius and Lust*, 86.
279 Man's sense of awe . . . : the same, 93–94.
279 That self-acquired Brooklyn culture . . . : the same, 369.
279 burning dark eyes . . . : the same, 182.
279 false ego . . . : the same.
279 emotional as blood: the same, 183.
279 a faithful and tortured young writer . . . : the same.
280 What characterizes narcissism . . . : the same, 185.
280 in those seven years . . . : the same, 191.
280 He was excited . . . : Mailer, "In Search of Carter," 20.
281 a powerful God . . . : the same, 77.
281 Mailer did too much of the talking: the same, 20.
281 another variety of spaceman . . . : the same, 80.
281 Ancient Mariner Compulsion . . . : McDonald, 37.
281 opening a valve: Lennon, *Conversations*, 232.
282 embodied many of the themes . . . : the same, 263.
282 I know you . . . another time: Mailer, *The Executioner's Song*, 73.
282 you can control people with your mind: the same, 366.
282 an actor . . . : the same, 941.
282 Texas accent: the same, 34.
282 GI . . . : the same, 368.
283 You can . . . : Lennon, *Conversations*, 267.
283 Look, I've got this girl . . . : Manso, 580.
283 You're right . . . : the same.
283 beneath him: the same, 581.
283 I spent the first six months . . . : Lennon, *Conversations*, 267.
284 some ironic framework: the same, 251.
284 would probably violate the material . . . : Mills, 427.
284 move through everybody's head . . . the novel: Mailer, *Pieces and Pontifications*, 178.
284 10,000 habits . . . : Lennon, *Conversations*, 245.
284 strong and simple: Mills, 427.
284 little essay . . . ex-wives: Davis, 9.

284   ridiculous . . . : Lennon, *Conversations*, 251.

285   like a sponge: Manso, 584.

285   two detectives on the fat side: Lennon, *Conversations*, 268.

285   passion for verification: the same.

285   She's lying . . . : the same.

285   Gary started hitting . . . : Mailer, *The Executioner's Song*, 31.

286   what probably did occur . . . : the same.

286   voice . . . : Manso, 581–82.

286   Before I got started . . . : Davis, 9.

286   more interesting . . . : Lennon, *Conversations*, 234.

286   very little invention: the same, 244.

286   focus upon the main character . . . : the same, 260.

287   I've sort of used up my audience . . . : Lennon, *Conversations*, 266.

287   tremendously fed up with personality: Mills, 427.

287   too much for me . . . : Davis, 9.

287   They're going to say . . . : Lennon, the same, 253.

287   Another major American protagonist . . . : Davis, 8–9.

288   I need money . . . : Author's interview with Jere Herzenberg.

288   So we tried it . . . : the same.

288   Okay, this chapter . . . : the same.

288   meticulous on this book . . . : the same.

288   I created what he wanted . . . : the same.

288   There wasn't a day . . . : the same.

289   And Gary said . . . : the same.

289   the white plains of Utah: the same.

289   He was a doll . . . clicked: the same.

289   Occasionally . . . Nothing: the same.

290   You have to understand . . . too young: the same.

290   I think it's time . . . : Mailer, *The Executioner's Song*, 21.

290   The first silence came in: the same, 25.

291   Before leaving work . . . : the same, 136.

292   Gary walked around the corner . . . : the same, 226–27.

293   I was always capable . . . conditioning: Lodge, 27.

293   the very subject . . . : Didion, 26.

293   Why'd you do it . . . : Mailer, *The Executioner's Song*, 292.

294   Schiller performs the role . . . : Lodge, 28.

294   Do you remember . . . : Mailer, *The Executioner's Song*, 850.

294   he was qualified . . . : the same, 808.

294   the story is as accurate . . . : the same, 1051.

295   Sometimes you sound . . . : the same, 849.

295   Barry tended to shape his questions . . . : the same, 837.

295   the author of a true-life novel . . . : Johnson, 4.

295   the text is mined . . . : the same, 3.
295   Oh, Gary . . . : Mailer, *The Executioner's Song*, 318.

12. Ancient Evenings (1979–1982)

Interviews: Herzenberg, Styron.
Abel; Atlas; Bailey; Brenner; Kakutani; Lennon, *Conversations*, 271–329; Farber; Mailer, *Pieces and Pontifications*, 103–90; Manso, 597–673; Medwick; Mills, 13–37, 432–34; Munson; Schumacher; Sheffield; Utter; Vespa; Weber.

297   Listen . . . black eye: Smilgis, 24–26.
298   The number of things . . . : Manso, 511–12.
299   tuned into him: Mailer, *Pieces and Pontifications*, 127.
299   I won't let . . . tramples them: Smilgis, 26.
299   Dominate sex: Mailer, *Pieces and Pontifications*, 114–15.
299   riproaring sex . . . nice Nelly: the same, 104.
299   wholesome farm-boy: Rebecca West to Anthony West, September 3, 1962, Rebeca West Collection, University of Tulsa, Tulsa, Oklahoma.
299   Well, I think . . . : Mailer, *Pieces and Pontifications*, 104.
299   more passionate: the same, 128.
300   At long last . . . astonishing book: Quoted in Manso, 606–607.
300   imaginary memoir: Lennon, *Conversations*, 271.
300   I was never satisfied . . . : the same, 129.
300   out of respect . . . now: the same, 277.
301   When I sat . . . : Mailer, *Of Women and Their Elegance*, 131–32.
301   I confess . . . : Mailer, *Pieces and Pontifications*, 130.
302   IN A MERRY MARRIAGE-GO-ROUND . . . formal type of ritual: *People*, November 3, 1980, 43.
302   I was fascinated . . . perform: Buck, 492.
303   dreaded doing it . . . : the same, 492-93.
304   I'm a good American boy . . . : Quoted in Herbert Mitgang, "Book Ends." *The New York Times Book Review*, December 7, 1980.
304   intense . . . correspondence: Abbott, x.
305   devastating nature of civilized violence: the same, 191.
305   There is a paradox . . . : the same, xiii.
305   psychological experimentation . . . chained to my bed: the same, 45–46.
307   new writer . . . get out: the same, xviii.
307   in combat: the same, 30.
307   At thirty-seven . . . : the same, 15.
307   No one . . . : the same, 26.
307   I'm tenuous . . . : the same, 50.
307   My vision of life . . . : the same, 195.
307   the most unjust . . . : the same, 129.

307   find my life again . . . : the same, 197.
307   Abbott looks to understand the world . . . : the same, xvi.
307   I am much more impressed . . . : the same, xvii.
307   I have never accepted . . . : the same, 18.
308   I keep waiting . . . : the same, 16.
308   niggers: Manso, 622.
308   hints of weakness and vulnerability: the same, 623.
308   extremely angry . . . temper: Farber, B4.
308   One gets . . . probably one of the most fascinating: the same.
309   extremely violent temper . . . nothing like that: the same.
310   stormed in . . . Abbott was going through: Passaro, 66–67.
310   You wrote the book . . . : Manso, 625.
310   He was very sweet . . . totally taken: the same, 625–26.
311   Gilmoresque stories: the same.
311   cobra eyes . . . : the same, 628.
311   How could we . . . : Quoted in Abel, 67.
311   romantic fiction . . . : Bailey, 122.
311   I'm gonna blow . . . : Manso, 631.
312   I don't take orders . . . *too aggressive*: the same, 631–32.
312   how the customers . . . kill me: the same, 631–32.
312   Adan died so fast . . . : Christon.
312   reached around . . . terrific blow: Rabinowitz.
312   pool going from . . . : Manso, 632.
313   never carried a weapon . . . : the same, 642.
313   awesome . . . : Quoted in Abel, 64.
313   claims that he endured . . . : Vespa, 67.
313   extremely subdued: Farber, 26.
313   make a separation . . . : Manso, 634.
313   bullshit . . . : the same, 636.
314   fictionalized: Montgomery.
314   killed a decent guy: Manso, 640.
314   fated . . . events: the same, 639–40.
314   Norman has to follow . . . : the same, 649.
314   expression on Norman's face . . . : the same, 642.
315   the worst New York press gang bang . . . fascist state: Quoted in Mills, 16.
315   If you want my blood . . . atonement of a criminal: the same.
315   I'm willing to gamble . . . No more questions: the same, 17–18.
315   You are full of shit . . . : the same,18.
316   Instead of starting off . . . : Manso, 644.
316   My God . . . by himself: the same.
316   What the hell . . . : Mills, 35.
317   Is essentially a false literature . . . : Sheffield, 13.

317   young and pretty . . . wasn't a fighter: the same, 13–14.
318   thought Abbott . . . wanted him to be: the same.
318   If I had passed away . . . : Quoted in Mills, 23.
319   piece of journalism: the same.
319   *Nihil humanum* . . . : the same.
319   barbaric . . . my life: the same, 24.
319   so *good* . . . : Manso, 653.
319   it literally began . . . : the same, 665.
319   The 50 pages Walter saw . . . : the same.
320   absolutely no need for my book: the same.
320   Sooner or later . . . : Weber, 96.
320   I'd read a chapter . . . : Brenner, 37.
320   all-encompassing novel . . . different occupations: Schumacher, 14.
320   consciousness that's so different . . . : Lennon, *Conversations*, 296.
322   the problem of identity . . . : Wenke, 218.
322   exploring power relationships . . . : Lennon, *Conversations*, 331.
322   tactile, sensitive, visceral people: the same, 303.
322   It's a world of dominance . . . : Weber, 104.
323   In Egypt . . . : Lennon, *Conversations*, 301.
323   the long slow current . . . : Mailer, *Ancient Evenings*, 312.

13. *Tough Guys Don't Dance* (1983–1987)

Interviews: Norman Rosten; Lawrence Shaw; William Styron.
Abrams; Ansen; Bloom; Boyum; Brenner; Canby; Chambers; Clemons; Clendenin; Cockburn; Davis; DeMott; Epstein; Fiedler; Fuller; Gehr; Giddons; Goodman; Gray; Jaehne; Kael; Koenig; Lennon, *Conversations*; Mano; McDowell; Margaronis and Pochoda; Medwick; Merkin; Mitgang; Prescott; Reuter; Richman; Rosenbaum; Rovit; Robertson; Schumacher; Schneir; Settle; Smith; Stade; Weber; Wilentz; Wolcott.

324   cultivate my own garden . . . art as war: Lennon, *Conversations*, 295–96.
325   homosexuals want to become . . . : Gray, 82–93.
325   a very self-conscious generation . . . : Lennon, *Conversations*, 374.
325   Look . . . : Brenner, 30.
326   A Pharaoh complex: the same.
326   If any of us . . . odd man out: the same, 33.
326   some fairly serious threats: the same, 31.
326   youthful arrogance . . . : the same.
326   It takes a toll . . . : the same.
326   great wisdom as a writer . . . : Gray, 84.
327   a small-town politician . . . : Brenner, 33.
327   great success as a father . . . : Gray, 83.

338 We may be . . . beyond our comprehension: the same, 401–402.

338 There is something audacious . . . : "Norman Mailer Elected President of PEN," *Publisher's Weekly*, August 17, 1984, 15.

339 are in radical conflict . . . : Reuter.

339 Is there a connection . . . interesting form of it: the same.

340 I'm bored with myself: Abrams, 21.

340 There's not much point . . . panic: Rovit, 213–14.

340 Someone is in danger . . . : the same, 214.

340 the largest gathering . . . how to do it: McDowell, "Mailer Earns Praise for PEN Efforts."

341 literary slugfest . . . the same.

341 We want . . . : Wilentz, 22.

341 Norman almost . . . the critics: McDowell, "Mailer Earns Praise for PEN efforts."

341 high official . . . betrayed its charter: Mitgang.

341 at the feet of . . . listening to him: the same.

342 inappropriate: Goodman, A1.

342 supports governments . . . : Goodman, C11.

342 bullying guards . . . : Margaronis and Pochoda, 117.

342 the letter . . . : McDowell, "Shultz Issue Dominates PEN Congress Sessions."

342 There are Nobel Prize winners . . . : Goodman, C11.

342 I don't feel comfortable . . . : McDowell, "Shultz Issue Dominates PEN Congress Sessions."

342 lined with a battery of TV cameras . . . : Reuter, "Shultz Sparks Dispute at Start of International Pen Congress," 18.

342 out of place in their own home . . . read the letter: Margaronis and Pochoda, 116.

343 enough of a figurehead . . . world scale: "The Writer's Imagination and the Imagination of the State: Two Views", *The New York Review of Books*, February 13, 1986, 23.

343 The evils of the state . . . complex individual: the same.

343 division d'opinion . . . state occasion: Margaronis and Pochoda, 116–17.

343 silly bad manners . . . : Goodman, A1.

343 a representative . . . : Reuter, "Shultz Sparks Dispute at Start of International PEN Congress," 18.

344 puritanical leftists: Margaronis and Pochoda, 116.

344 as another shining example . . . : Reuter, "Shultz Sparks Dispute at Start of International PEN Congress," 18

344 adroit and even disarming: the same.

344 touched on . . . : Keonig, 41.

344 America is proud to have you . . . espouse: Goodman, C11.

344 an imaginative order of his own: Koenig, 41.

344   where writers can speak . . . : Goodman, C11
344   creativity forged in the crucible . . . : Koenig, 41.
344   baffled by the disturbance: Margaronis and Pochoda, 117.
344   old comrades: Reuter, "Shultz Sparks Dispute at Start of International PEN Congress," 18.
344   I didn't invite . . . : Margaronis and Pochoda, 117.
344   The letter . . . : McDowell, "Shultz Issue Dominates PEN Congress Sessions."
344   do something about: Reuter, "Shultz Sparks Dispute at Start of International PEN Conference," 18.
344   sabotage this evening: the same.
344   literary bureaucrat . . . : McDowell, "Shultz Issue Dominates PEN Congress Sessions."
345   sparring . . . down my neck: Koenig, 41.
345   with the beginning of a twinkle . . . right: the same.
345   private and individual . . . lie to it: "The Writer's Imagination and the Imagination of the State: Two Views," *The New York Review of Books*, February 13, 1986, 24–25.
345   boisterous but terrifically genial: Koenig, 44.
345   tremendous achievement . . . grandstanding: the same.
345   we women . . . : Schneir, 82.
346   If they will not give . . . : the same.
364   The men . . . : McDowell, "Women at PEN Caucus Demand a Greater Role."
346   had he been . . . : Schneir, 82.
346   how this looks . . . to the world: McDowell, "Women At PEN Caucus Demand a Greater Role."
346   the entire front section . . . : Schneir, 82.
346   There were six months . . . : McDowell, "PEN Congress Ends with a Protest," 11.
346   as the only writer . . . : Schneir, 83.
346   decision-making roles: McDowell, "Women at PEN Caucus Demand a Greater Role."
347   There was a time . . . : the same.
347   We invited . . . : McDowell, "PEN Congress Ends with a Protest," 11.
347   You can leave . . . : Koenig, 47.
347   upset . . . : McDowell, "PEN Congress Ends with a Protest." 11.
347   great mistake . . . out of it: Goodman, "Norman Mailer Offers a PEN Postmortem."
348   at first . . . indignant women: Goodman, "At PEN, a Feeling of Community."
348   Norman Mailer . . . I fear: Cockburn, 103.
348   flirtation with pomp and circumstance . . . : Margaronis and Pochoda, 117–18.
349   aging male beauties . . . any longer: Lennon, *Conversations*, 358.

349 Did you ever worry . . . really filthy joke: Author's interview with Lawrence Shaw.

350 picking up four-letter words . . . about a penny: Author's interview with Norman Rosten.

350 like to play . . . : Chambers.

350 If I had put a tape . . . : Author's interview with Lawrence Shaw.

351 certain psychic impulses . . . well earned: Rosten, 22.

351 lots of . . . You're cowards: the same, 24–26.

351 the emphasis more on . . . any two Normans: the same, 27.

352 Don't you know . . . little fucker: the same, 35–36.

352 thirty thousand Shakespeareans . . . : Smith, 34.

353 mad farce: the same.

353 executive: Jaehne, 14.

353 practical nature . . . the money: the same, 16.

353 the Michelin man: the same.

354 One's living free . . . 40 years: the same, 14, 16.

354 years ago . . . : Robertson.

354 style of people's relationships: Jaehne, 14.

354 out of category . . . anything at all: the same.

354 a maddening mixture . . . possibly be: the same, 17.

354 I think Norman hates women . . . : the same, 15.

355 I like women . . . to a woman: the same.

355 Stop that: the same.

355 You're supposed . . . : Merkin, 49.

355 benign director: Jaehne, 15.

355 policeman . . . get it: the same, 16.

355 Debra, I'm not trying to see you . . . : Smith, 37.

355 a cross between . . . Provincetown: "People," *Time*, December 1, 1986, 58.

356 expansive . . . : Smith, 33.

356 We finished . . . : the same, 37.

356 derisive laughter . . . shouldn't direct: Ansen, 76.

356 narration in a film . . . : Smith, 34.

357 An easy film . . . : Canby, C14.

357 Mailer isn't enough . . . : Kael, 106.

357 it's difficult to distinguish . . . : Boyum, 250.

357 *Tough Guys* manages . . . : Gehr, 66.

357 Somehow the movie . . . : Rosenbaum, 115.

14. *Harlot's Ghost* (1987–   )

Interviews: Norman Rosten.
Collins; Mailer, *Pieces and Pontifications*; Mallory; Trebey

358	concerned as much . . . : Mailer, *Pieces and Pontifications*, 159.
358	There are no answers . . . : the same.
359	What a crazy country . . . : the same, 204.
359	facts are wiped out . . . : the same, 160.
360	No vein . . . : the same, 161.
360	No one would be certain . . . : the same, 162.
360	It is novelistically exciting . . . : the same, 164.
360	Where is the foot of identity . . . : the same, 165.
360	mammoth of shuffled identities: the same, 166.
361	the objective correlative: Mailer, "Harlot's Ghost," 84.
361	*glommed* . . . lips: the same, 80.
361	To put one's heels . . . : the same, 86.
362	amid an orgasm of strobe . . . Wolfe's feelings: Trebey, 22.
363	Listen, hon . . . in one's life: Collins, C17.
363	A pretty poor show . . . : the same.
364	I'm not tall . . . : Mallory, 83.
364	I once made love . . . : the same, 80.
364	never got together . . . prayer answered: the same, 148.
364	the nest . . . : Author's interview with Norman Rosten.
365	paradoxes of a great artist . . . : Mailer, *Pieces and Pontifications*, 87.
365	You never write . . . : Author's interview with Norman Rosten.
365	I didn't start . . . serving the meal: Mailer, *Pieces and Pontifications*, 150.

BIBLIOGRAPHY

Abel, Lionel. "Murder and the Intellectuals." *Commentary*, November 1981, 64–68.

Abbott, Jack Henry. *In the Belly of the Beast: Letters from Prison* (1981). New York: Vintage Books, 1982.

Abrams, Gary. "For Mailer, a 'Tough' Job: Pounds for His Thoughts." *Los Angeles Times*, September 23, 1984, 1, 21.

Adams, Laura. *Existential Battles: The Growth of Norman Mailer*. Athens, Ohio: Ohio University Press, 1976.

_____ (ed.). *Will the Real Norman Mailer Please Stand Up?* Port Washington, N.Y.: Kennikat Press, 1974.

Ansen, David. "The Naked, Blond, Baffled and Dead." *Newsweek*, September 21, 1987, 76.

Atlas, James. "Life with Mailer." *The New York Times Magazine*, September 9, 1979, 53–55, 86–92, 98, 102–104.

_____. "The Literary Life of Crime." *The New Republic*, September 9, 1981, 21–23.

Bailey, Carl. "Eye on Publishing." *Wilson Library Bulletin*, October 1981, 121–122.

Beauman, Sally. "Norman Mailer, Movie Maker." *New York*, 1968, 50–56.

Begiebing, Robert J. *Acts of Regeneration: Allegory and Archetype in the Works of Norman Mailer*. Columbia: University of Missouri Press, 1980.

Bellow, Saul. *Dangling Man* (1944). New York: Signet Books, 1965.

Bloom, Harold. "Norman in Egypt." *The New York Review of Books*, April 28, 1983, 3–4, 6.

Bosworth, Patricia. "Fifth Estate at the Four Seasons." *The Saturday Review*, March 1973, 5–7.

Boyum, Joy Gould. "Tough Guys Don't Dance." *Glamour*, November 1987, 249.

Braudy, Leo (ed.). *Norman Mailer: A Collection of Critical Essays*. Englewood Cliffs, N.J.: Prentice Hall, 1972.

Brenner, Marie. "Mailer Goes Egyptian." *New York*, March 28, 1983, 28–38.

Brower, Brock. "Always the Challenger." *Life*, September 24, 1965, 94–117.

Buck, Joan Julie. "Dreaming America." *Vogue*, November 1981, 441–442, 492–493.

Bufithis, Philip H. *Norman Mailer*. New York: Frederick Ungar, 1978.

Busch, Frederick. " 'Whale at Shaggy Dog': Melville and 'The Man Who Studied Yoga.' " *Modern Fiction Studies*, 19 (Summer 1973), 193–206.

Canby, Vincent. "Film: Norman's Mailer's Tough Guys Don't Dance." *The New York Times*, September 18, 1987, C14–15.

Chambers, Andrea. "Crime and Puzzlement: The Real Life Mystery Behind Norman Mailer's New Thriller." *People*, September 10, 1984.

Clemons, Walter. "Mailer in Egypt." *Vanity Fair*, May 1983, 61–64.

Clendenin, Dudley. "Mailer Takes the Stand for Writer in Drug Case." *The New York Times*, March 24, 1983, 14.

Cockburn, Alexander. "Foot-in-Mouth Disease." *The Nation*, February 1, 1986, 103.

Collins, Glenn. "Norman Mailer Complains About Mention in 'Tru.' " *The New York Times*, December 21, 1989, C17.

Davis, Kenneth. "Norman Mailer." *Publishers Weekly*, October 9, 1979, 8–9.

Davis, Robert Gorham. "Excess Without End." *The New Leader*, May 16, 1983, 14–16.

De Mott, Benjamin. "Norman Mailer's Egyptian Novel." *The New York Times Book Review*, April 10, 1983, 1, 34–36.

Didion, Joan. "I want to go ahead and do it." *The New York Times Book Review*, October 7, 1979, 1, 26–27.

Epstein, Joseph. "Mailer Hits Bottom." *Commentary*, July 1983, 62–68.

Farber, M. A. "Killing Clouds Ex-Convict Writer's New Life." *The New York Times*, July 26, 1981, 1, 26.

————. "Freedom for Convict-Author: Complex and Conflicting Tale." *The New York Times*, August 17, 1981, A1, B4.

Fiedler, Leslie. "Going for the Long Ball." *Psychology Today*, June 1983, 16–17.

Flaherty, Joe. *Managing Mailer*. New York: Coward-McCann, 1969.

Fuller, Edmund. "Mailer in Egypt: Neck-Deep in Nile Mud." *Wall Street Journal*, April 23, 1983, 30.

Garrett, George. *James Jones*. New York: Harcourt Brace Jovanovich, 1984.

Gehr, Richard. "Tough Guys Don't Dance." *Video*, May 1988, 66.

Giddens, Gary. "Ra, Ka, Bah Humbug." *The Nation*, June 25, 1983, 803–804.

Goodman, Mark. "Before He's Naked or Dead, Norman Mailer Goes for Broke: The Biggest Novel of All." *People*, November 10, 1975, 47–50.

Goodman, Walter. "Shultz Faces Critics in Speech Opening 48th PEN Assembly." *The New York Times*, A1, C11.

————. "At PEN, a Feeling of Community." *The New York Times*, January 20, 1986, 25.

————. "Norman Mailer Offers a PEN Post-mortem." *The New York Times*, January 27, 1986, 24.

Gordimer, Nadine. "The Writer's Imagination and the Imagination of the State." *The New York Review of Books*, February 13, 1986, 24–25.

Gordon, Andrew. *An American Dreamer: A Psychoanalytic Study of the Fiction of Norman Mailer*. London: Associated University Presses, 1980.

Greer, Germaine. "My Mailer Problem." *Esquire*, September 1971, 90–93, 214–218.

Gutman, Stanley T. *Mankind in Barbary: The Individual and Society in the Novels of Norman Mailer*. Hanover, N.H.: University Press of New England, 1975.

Hendrick, George (ed.). *To Reach Eternity: The Letters of James Jones*. Foreword by William Styron. New York: Random House, 1989.

Jaehne, Karen. "Mailer's Minuet." *Film Comment*, July–August 1987, 11–17.

Johnson, Diane. "Death for Sale." *The New York Review of Books*, December 6, 1979, 3–4, 6.

Kakutani, Michiko. "The Strange Case of the Writer and the Criminal." *The New York Times Book Review*, September 20, 1982, 1, 36–37.

_____. "Mailer and Vidal at PEN Celebration." *The New York Times*, November 13, 1985, C15.

Kael, Pauline. "Temporary Madnesses: Forster, Mailer, Hepburn." *The New Yorker*, 103–108.

Koenig, Rhoda. "Give Me Your Obelisk." *New York*, April 25, 1983, 71–72.

Leeds, Barry H. *The Structured Vision of Norman Mailer*. New York: New York University Press, 1969.

Lennon, J. Michael (ed.). *Conversations with Norman Mailer*. Jackson: University Press of Mississippi, 1988.

_____. *Critical Essays on Norman Mailer*. Boston: G. K. Hall, 1986.

Lindner, Robert. *The Fifty Minute Hour* (1955). New York: Bantam, 1956.

_____. *Prescription for Rebellion* (1952). New York: Grove Press, 1962.

_____. *Must You Conform?* New York: Holt, Rinehart and Winston, 1955.

Lodge, David. "From a view to a death." *Times Literary Supplement*, January 11, 1980, 27–28.

Lucid, Robert F. *Norman Mailer: The Man and His Work*. Boston: Little, Brown, 1971.

_____. *The Long Patrol: 25 Years of Writing from the Work of Norman Mailer*. New York: World, 1971.

Lynn, Kenneth. "One-Round Writer?" *Commentary*, March 1983, 84–86, 88.

McDonald, Susan S. "The Journalistic Profile: Full-Face." *The National Review*, January 7, 1977, 37–38.

McDowell, Edwin. "Little, Brown Rejects New Norman Mailer Novel." *The New York Times*, October 6, 1983, 32.

_____. "Mailer Earns Praise for PEN Efforts." *The New York Times*, December 23, 1985, 12.

_____. "Shultz Issue Dominates PEN Congress Sessions." *The New York Times*, January 14, 1986, 12.

_____. "Women at PEN Caucus Demand a Greater Role." *The New York Times*, January 17, 1986, 26.

_____. "PEN Congress End with a Protest." *The New York Times*, January 18, 1986, 11.

MacShane, Frank. *Into Eternity: The Life of James Jones*. Boston: Houghton, Mifflin, 1985.

Mailer, Norman. *Advertisements for Myself* (1959). New York: Berkeley Windhover Books, 1976.

————. *An American Dream* (1964). New York: Dell, 1966.

————. *Ancient Evenings*. Boston: Little, Brown, 1983.

————. *The Armies of the Night*. New York: Signet, 1968.

————. *Barbary Shore* (1951). New York: Grosset & Dunlap, 1963.

————. *Cannibals and Christians*. New York: Dial, 1966.

————. "Cosmic Ventures: A meditation on God at war." *Esquire*, December 1989, 156–158.

————. "A Country, Not a Scenario." *Parade*, August, 19, 1984, 4–9.

————. *The Deer Park* (1955). New York: Berkeley, 1967.

————. *The Deer Park: A Play*. New York: Dial, 1967.

————. *The Executioner's Song*. Boston: Little, Brown, 1979.

————. *Existential Errands*. Boston: Little, Brown, 1972.

————. *The Fight*. Boston: Little, Brown, 1975.

————. "A Folly Repeated: On Conviction and Creative Martyrdom, as Reflected by the Salmon Rushdie Controversy." *Writer's Digest*, July 1989, 78–79, 80.

————. "Harlot's Ghost." *Esquire*, July 1988, 80–90.

————. *Genius and Lust: A Journey Through the Major Writings of Henry Miller*. New York: Grove Press, 1976.

————. "Jackie, the Prisoner of Celebrity." *Esquire*, December 1983, 185–189.

————. *Maidstone: A Mystery*. New York: Signet, 1971.

————. *The Naked and the Dead* (1948). New York: Signet, n.d.

————. *Marilyn* (1972). New York: Warner Books, 1973.

————. *Of a Fire on the Moon*. Boston: Little, Brown, 1970.

————. *Of Women and Their Elegance*. New York: Simon & Schuster, 1980.

————. *Pieces and Pontifications*. Boston: Little, Brown, 1982.

————. "The Poor American in London." *Esquire*, October 1983, 49–62.

————. *The Presidential Papers*. New York: Putnam, 1963.

————. *The Prisoner of Sex*. Boston: Little, Brown, 1971.

————. "The Search for Carter." *The New York Times Magazine*, September 26, 1976, 19–21, 69–92.

————. *The Short Fiction of Norman Mailer*. New York: Pinnacle Books, 1981.

————. *St. George and the Godfather*. New York: Signet, 1972.

————. *Tough Guys Don't Dance*. New York: Random House, 1984.

————. *A Transit to Narcissus*. New York: Howard Fertig, 1978.

————. "Until Dead." *Parade*, February 8, 1981, 6–11.

————. *Why Are We in Vietnam?* (1967) New York: Berkeley, 1968.

————. "The Writer's Imagination and the Imagination of the State." *The New York Review of Books*, February 13, 1986, 23–24.

Mallory, Carole. "Norman Mailer: The Power of Sex." *M*, February 1990, 79–83, 146–148.

Mano, D. Keith. "The Naked and the Mummified." *National Review*, October 14, 1983, 1293.

Manso, Peter. *Mailer: His Life and Times*. New York: Simon & Schuster, 1985.

————. (ed.). *Running Against the Machine: The Mailer–Breslin Campaign*. New York: Doubleday, 1969.

Margaronis, Maria, and Elizabeth Pochoda. "Bad Manners and Bad Faith." *The Nation*, February 1, 1986, 116–119.

Medwick, Cathleen. "Mailer and Mailer." *Vogue*, May 1983, 274, 277, 280, 343.

————. "Style Is Character: An Interview with Norman Mailer." *Vogue*, May 1983, 279, 343.

Merrill, Robert. *Norman Mailer*. Boston: Twayne, 1978.

Merkin, Daphne. "His Brilliant (New) Career?" *American Film*, October 1987, 42–49.

Millett, Kate. *Sexual Politics*. New York: Doubleday, 1970.

Mills, Hilary. *Mailer: A Biography*. New York: Empire Books, 1982.

Mitgang, Herbert. "PEN Invitation to Shultz Criticized." *The New York Times*, January 10, 1986, section 3:24.

Montgomery, Paul L. "Abbott Rejects Account of Him as Violent Man." *The New York Times*, January 19, 1982, section 2:3.

Munson, Naomi. "The Literary Life of Crime." *The New Republic*, September 9, 1981, 18–21.

Naipaul, V. S. *The Overcrowded Barracoon*. New York: Knopf, 1972.

Parker, Hershel. *Flawed Texts and Verbal Icons: Literary Authority in American Fiction*. Evanston: Northwestern University Press, 1984.

Passaro, Vince. "The Highbrow Days and Downtown Nights of Erroll McDonald." *Esquire*, January 1991, 64–68.

Pilati, Joe. "Mailer for Mayor: On the Steps of City Hall." *Commonweal*, May 16, 1969, 255–256.

Podhoretz, Norman. Introduction to *Barbary Shore*. New York: Grosset & Dunlap, 1963.

Poirier, Richard. *Norman Mailer*. New York: Viking, 1972.

Prescott, Peter. "Tales from Beyond the Tomb." *Newsweek*, April 18, 1983, 82.

Reuter, Madalynne. "1000 Writers to Meet in New York at PEN International Congress." *Publishers Weekly*, February 8, 1985, 23.

————. "Shultz Sparks Dispute at Start of International PEN Congress." *Publishers Weekly*, January 24, 1986, 18.

Richman, Alan. "No Longer Such a Tough Guy, Norman Mailer Frets Over His Shaky Career as a Filmmaker." *People*, October 5, 1987, 40–42.

Robertson, Nan. "Mailer Will Star with His Movies." *The New York Times*, January 19, 1984, 17.

Rollyson, Carl. *Marilyn Monroe: A Life of the Actress*. Ann Arbor, Mi: UMI Research Press, 1986.

Rosenbaum, Ron. "The Trouble with Tough Guys." *Mademoiselle*, November 1987, 112, 115, 284.

Rosten, Norman. *Neighborhood Tales*. New York: Braziller, 1986.

Rovit, Earl. "The Ropewalker." *The Nation*, September 15, 1984, 213–215.

Schneir, Miriam. "The Prisoner of Sexism." *Ms.*, April 1986, 82–83.

Schumacher, Michael. "Modern Evenings: An Interview with Norman Mailer." *Writer's Digest*, October 1983, 30–34.

Schwenger, Peter. *Phallic Critiques: Masculinity and Twentieth-Century Literature.* London: Routledge & Kegan Paul, 1984.

Settle, Mary Lee. "Ancient Evenings." *Los Angeles Times*, April 24, 1983, 1, 4.

Sheffield, Paul Ray. "Slitting Open the Belly of the Beast." *The Threepenny Review*, Winter 1990, 13–15.

Silverstein, Howard. "Norman Mailer: The Family Romance and Oedipal Fantasy." *American Imago*, 34 (Fall 1977), 277–286.

Simon, John. "Waltz of the Toreadors." *New York*, December 2, 1985, 33.

Smilgis, Martha. "Once Norman's Conquest, The Fourth Mrs. Mailer Fights Her Final Marital Battle." *People*, February 26, 1979, 24–26.

Smith, Dinita. "Tough Guys Make Movie." *New York*, January 12, 1987, 32–37.

Sokolov, Raymond A. "Flying High with Mailer." *Newsweek*, December 9, 1968, 83–88.

Solotaroff, Robert. *Down Mailer's Way.* Urbana: University of Illinois Press, 1974.

Stade, George. "A Chthonic Novel." *The New Republic*, May 2, 1983, 32–34, 36.

Stark, John. "*Barbary Shore*: The Basis of Mailer's Best Work." *Modern Fiction Studies*, 17, Autumn 1971, 403–408.

Suess, Raymond Karl. "Tom Sawyer, Horatio Alger and Sammy Glick: A Biography of Young Mailer." St. Louis University: Ph.D dissertation, 1974.

Toback, James. "At Play in the Fields of the Bored." *Esquire*, December 1968, 151–155, 22–36.

Utter, Glen H. "Literature, Politics, and Violence: The Case of Norman Mailer." *Lamar Journal of the Humanities*, Spring 1984, 27–37.

Vespa, Mary. "A Lifelong Con Springs Himself with a Book," *People*, 62, 67.

Wagenheim, Allan J. "Square's Progress: *An American Dream*." *Critique*, 10, 1967, 45–68.

Weber, Bruce. "Mailer's Flight to Ancient Egypt." *Harper's Bazaar*, May 1983, 96, 104, 160–161.

Wenke, Joseph. *Mailer's America.* Hanover, N.H.: University Press of New England, 1987.

Wilentz, Amy. "A Rampancy of Writers." *Time*, January 13, 1986, 22.

Wolcott, James. "Enter the Mummy." *Harper's*, May 1983, 81–83.

Woodley, Richard. "A Literary Ticket for the 51st State." *Life*, May 30, 1969, 71–73.

INDEX